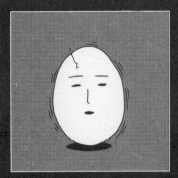

O N E

From now on, monsters of various designs are sure to show up, so I'm excited!

—ONE

Manga creator ONE began *One-Punch Man* as a webcomic, which quickly went viral, garnering over 10 million hits. In addition to *One-Punch Man*, ONE writes and draws the series *Mob Psycho 100* and *Makai no Ossan*.

TWO YEARS AGO
Put on some pants!
Wow! This is funny!

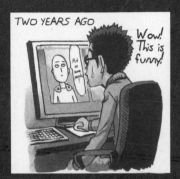

Y U S U K E M U R A T A

I first encountered the original *One-Punch Man* on Twitter. I got to know the author there and then made a direct appeal to draw it. It was a very modern way to do things!

—Yusuke Murata

A highly decorated and skilled artist best known for his work on *Eyeshield 21*, Yusuke Murata won the 122nd Hop Step Award (1995) for *Partner* and placed second in the 51st Akatsuka Award (1998) for *Samui Hanashi*.

ONE-PUNCH MAN | 02

ONE + YUSUKE MURATA

★ THE STORIES, CHARACTERS AND INCIDENTS MENTIONED IN THIS PUBLICATION ARE ENTIRELY FICTIONAL.

ONE-PUNCH MAN

02

STORY BY
ONE

ART BY
YUSUKE
MURATA

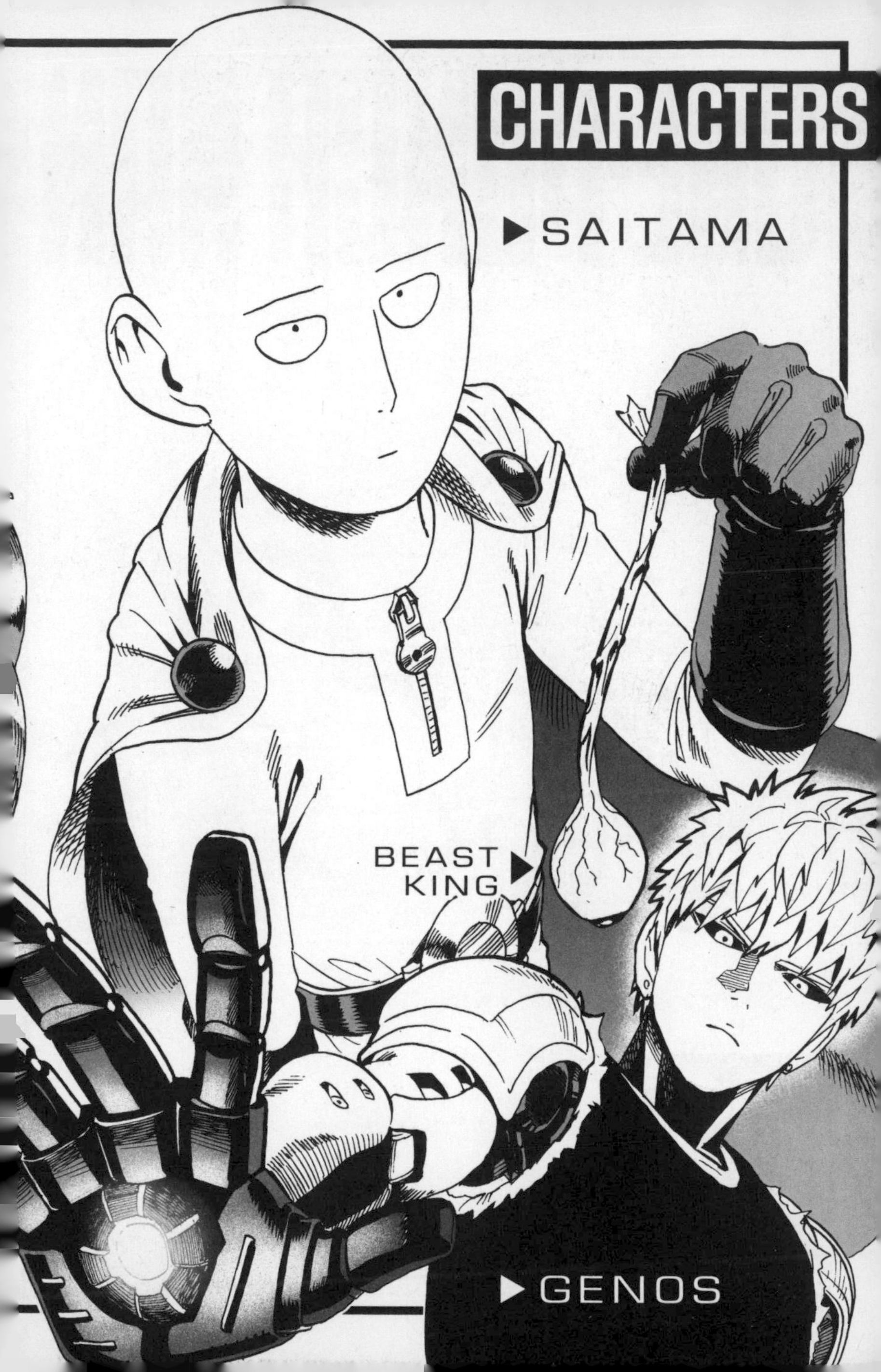
CHARACTERS
SAITAMA
BEAST KING
GENOS

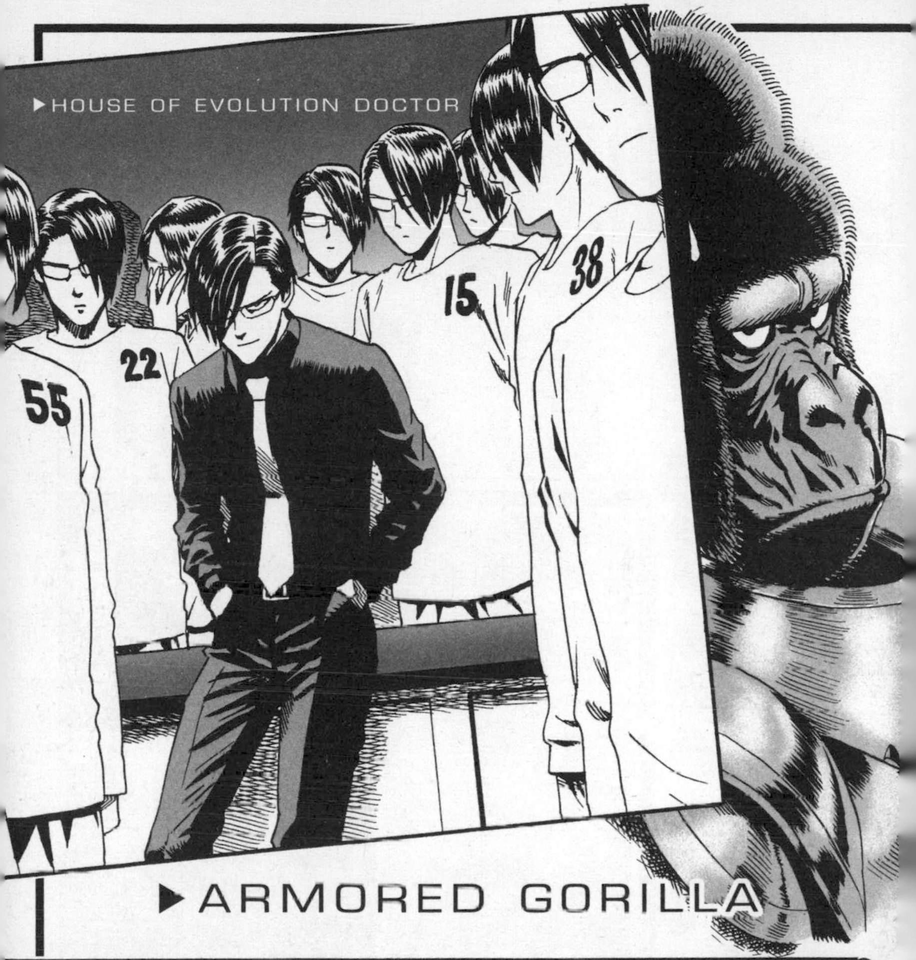
▶HOUSE OF EVOLUTION DOCTOR
▶ARMORED GORILLA

STORY

A single man arose to face the evil threatening humankind.

His name was Saitama. He became a hero for fun. Three years of special training made him lose all his hair, but he gained invincible power. He achieved such strength that he can defeat any opponent, however strong, with one punch.

Unable to make use of his full strength, he is unsatisfied as a hero, but a cyborg named Genos asks to become his pupil! Then the House of Evolution takes an interest in Saitama's power and sends monstrous assassins after him...

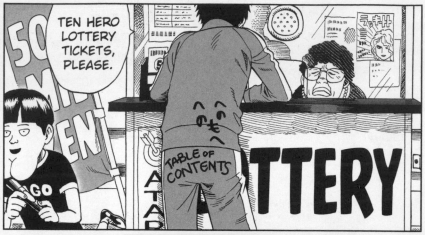

TEN HERO LOTTERY TICKETS, PLEASE.
GO
TABLE OF CONTENTS
TTERY

CONTENTS

ONE-PUNCH MAN VOLUME TWO

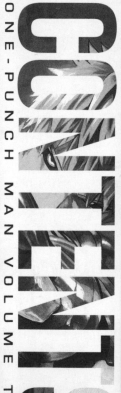

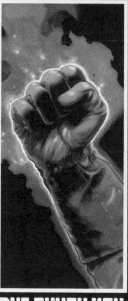

ONE-PUNCH MAN

ONE + YUSUKE MURATA

My name is Saitama. I am a hero. My hobby is heroic exploits. I got too strong. And that makes me sad. I can defeat any enemy with one blow. I lost my hair. And I lost all feeling. I want to feel the rush of battle. I would like to meet an incredibly strong enemy. And I would like to defeat it with one blow. That's because I am One-Punch Man.

02

THE SECRET TO STRENGTH

PUNCH 9: HOUSE OF EVOLUTION

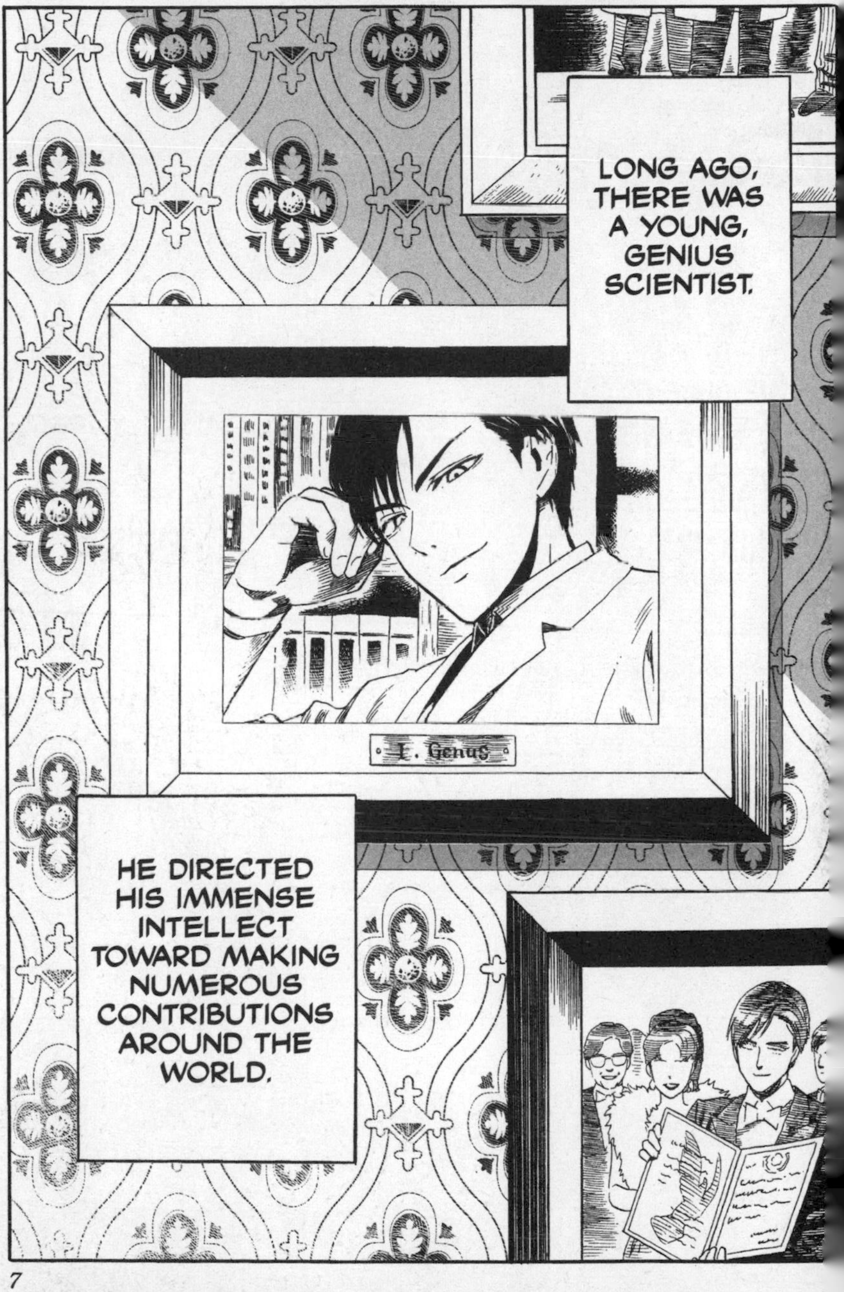
LONG AGO, THERE WAS A YOUNG, GENIUS SCIENTIST.
I. Genus
HE DIRECTED HIS IMMENSE INTELLECT TOWARD MAKING NUMEROUS CONTRIBUTIONS AROUND THE WORLD.

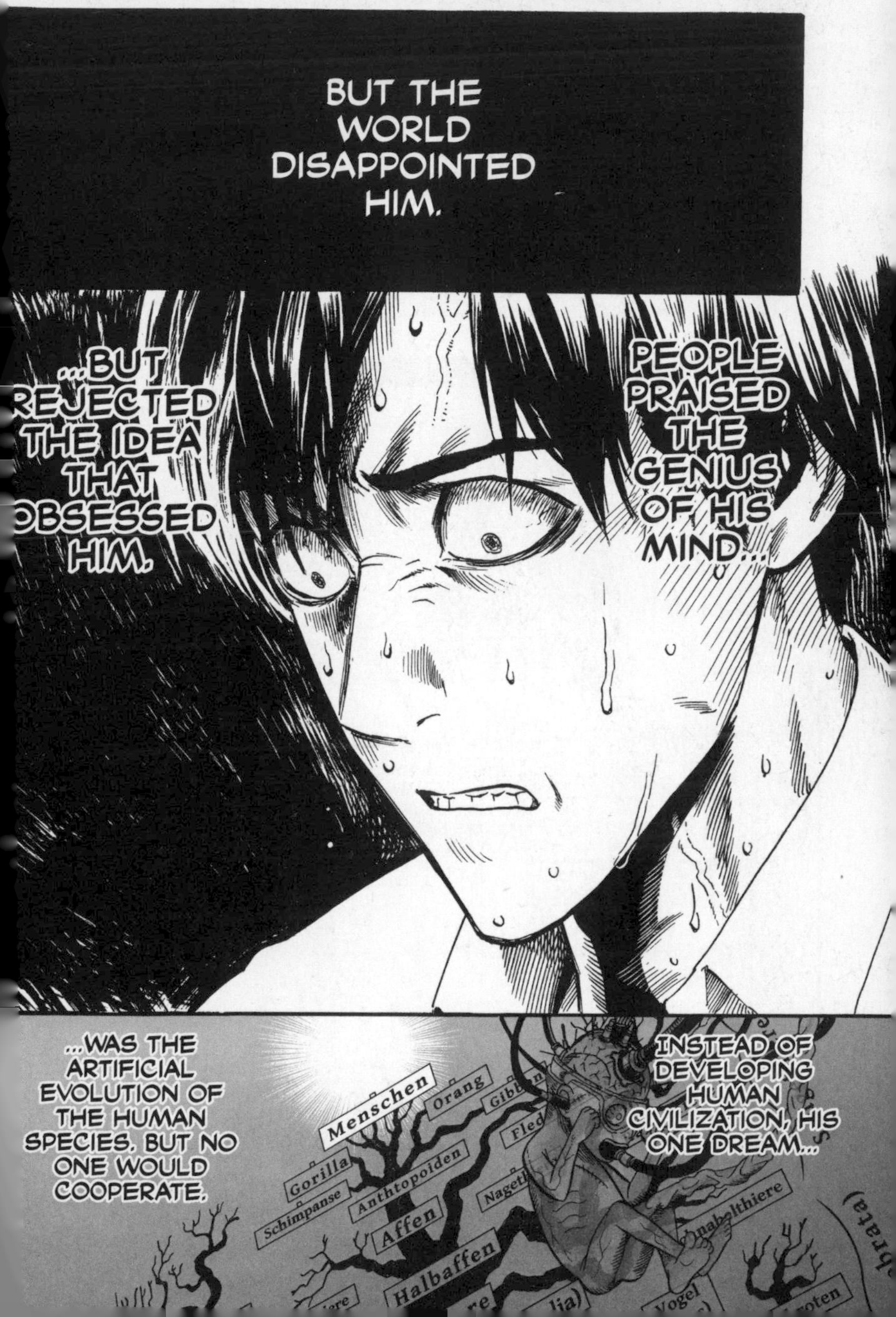
BUT THE WORLD DISAPPOINTED HIM.
PEOPLE PRAISED THE GENIUS OF HIS MIND...
...BUT REJECTED THE IDEA THAT OBSESSED HIM.
INSTEAD OF DEVELOPING HUMAN CIVILIZATION, HIS ONE DREAM...
...WAS THE ARTIFICIAL EVOLUTION OF THE HUMAN SPECIES. BUT NO ONE WOULD COOPERATE.
Menschen
Orang
Gorilla
Schimpanse
Anthtopoiden
Affen
Halbaffen

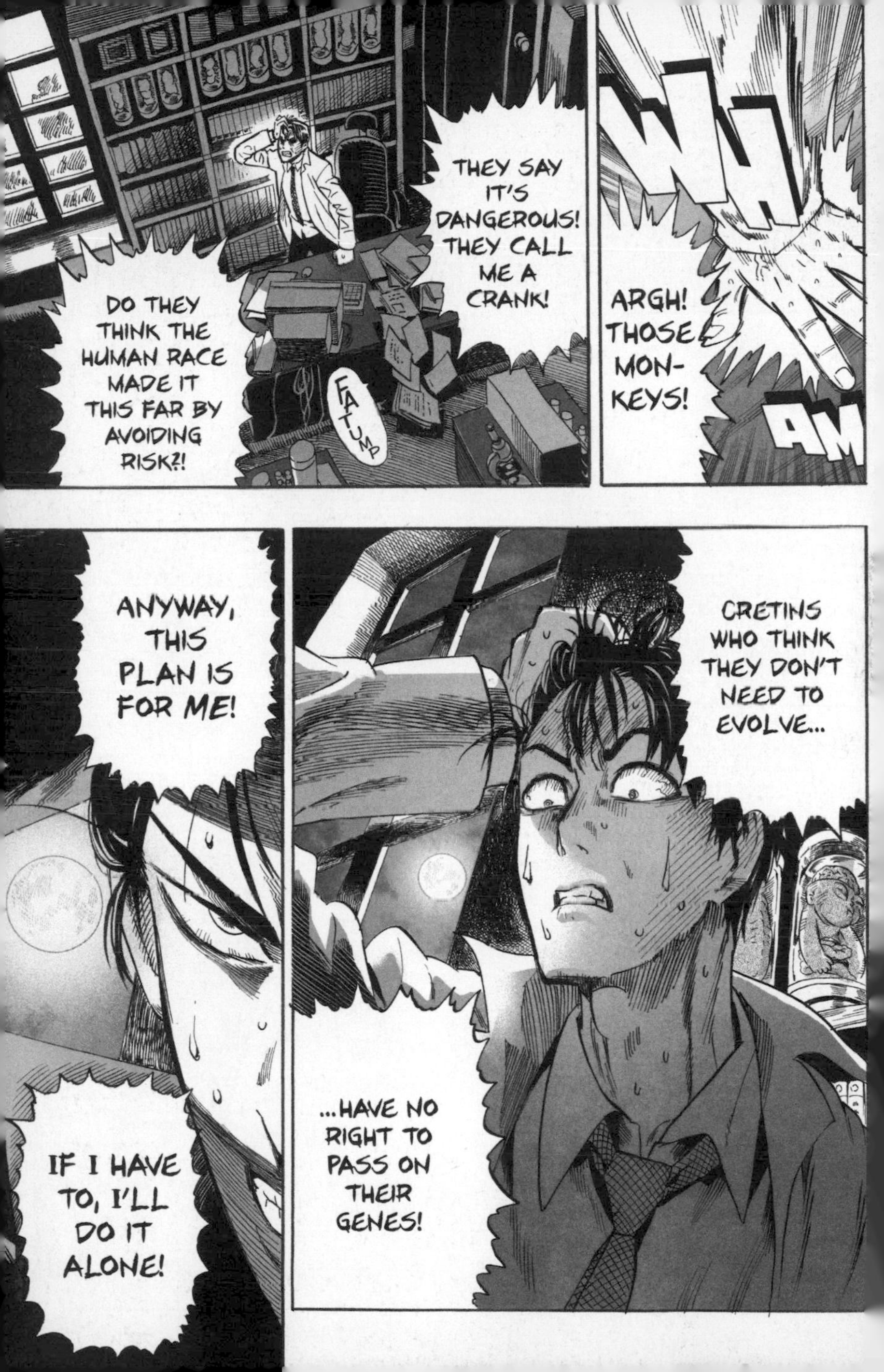
WHA
AM
ARGH! THOSE MONKEYS!
THEY SAY IT'S DANGEROUS! THEY CALL ME A CRANK!
DO THEY THINK THE HUMAN RACE MADE IT THIS FAR BY AVOIDING RISK?!
FATUMP
CRETINS WHO THINK THEY DON'T NEED TO EVOLVE...
...HAVE NO RIGHT TO PASS ON THEIR GENES!
ANYWAY, THIS PLAN IS FOR ME!
IF I HAVE TO, I'LL DO IT ALONE!

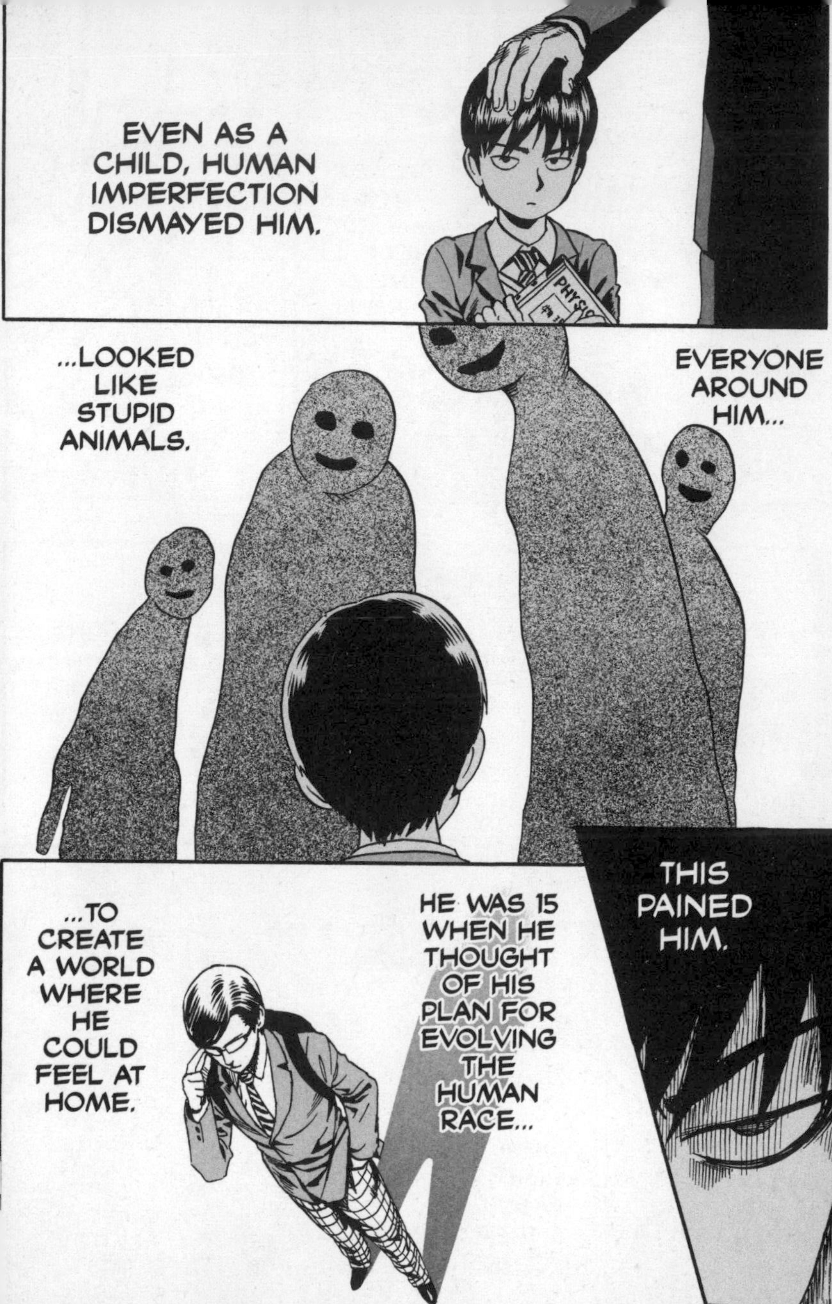
EVEN AS A CHILD, HUMAN IMPERFECTION DISMAYED HIM.
EVERYONE AROUND HIM...
...LOOKED LIKE STUPID ANIMALS.
THIS PAINED HIM.
HE WAS 15 WHEN HE THOUGHT OF HIS PLAN FOR EVOLVING THE HUMAN RACE...
...TO CREATE A WORLD WHERE HE COULD FEEL AT HOME.

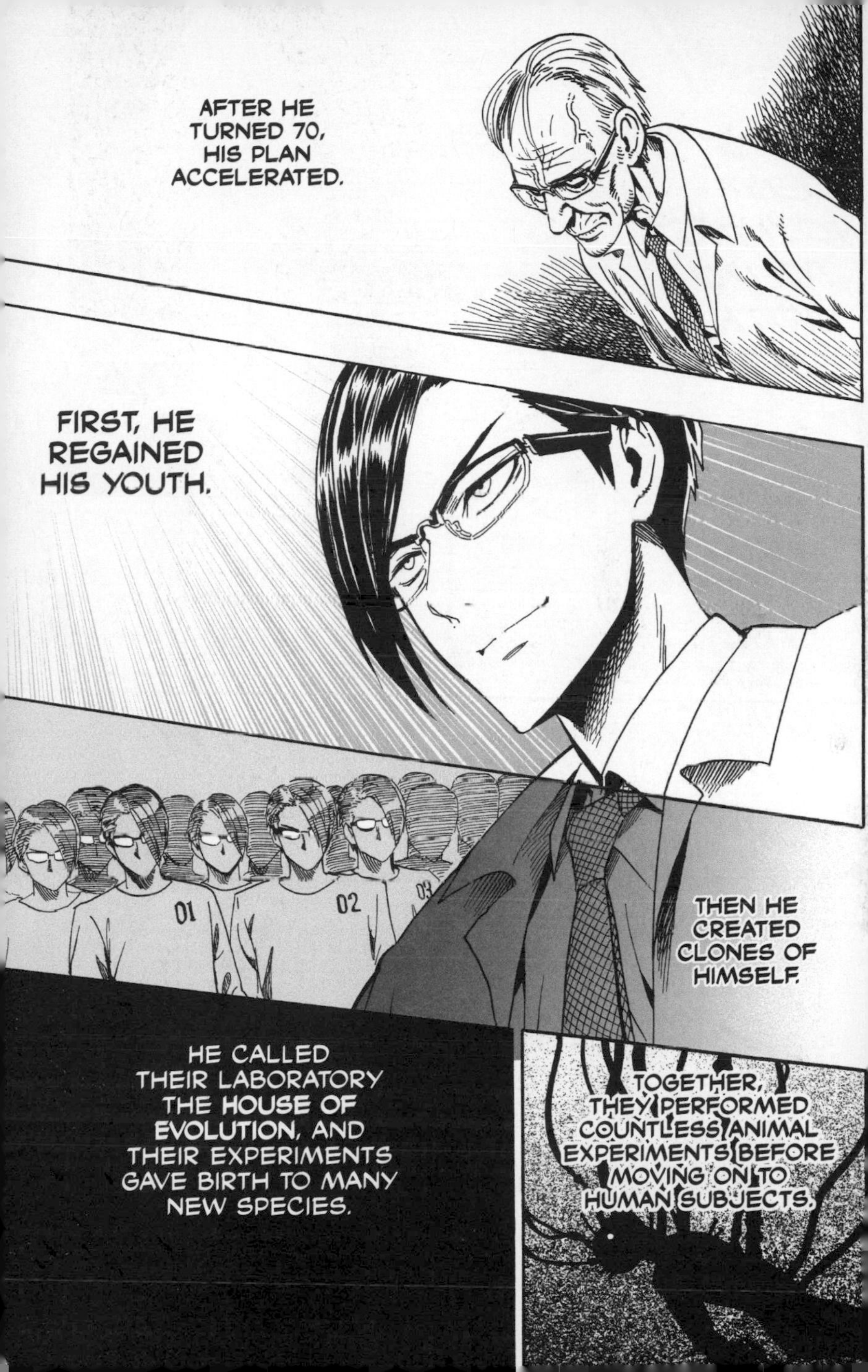
AFTER HE TURNED 70, HIS PLAN ACCELERATED.
FIRST, HE REGAINED HIS YOUTH.
THEN HE CREATED CLONES OF HIMSELF.
01
02
TOGETHER, THEY PERFORMED COUNTLESS ANIMAL EXPERIMENTS BEFORE MOVING ON TO HUMAN SUBJECTS.
HE CALLED THEIR LABORATORY THE HOUSE OF EVOLUTION, AND THEIR EXPERIMENTS GAVE BIRTH TO MANY NEW SPECIES.

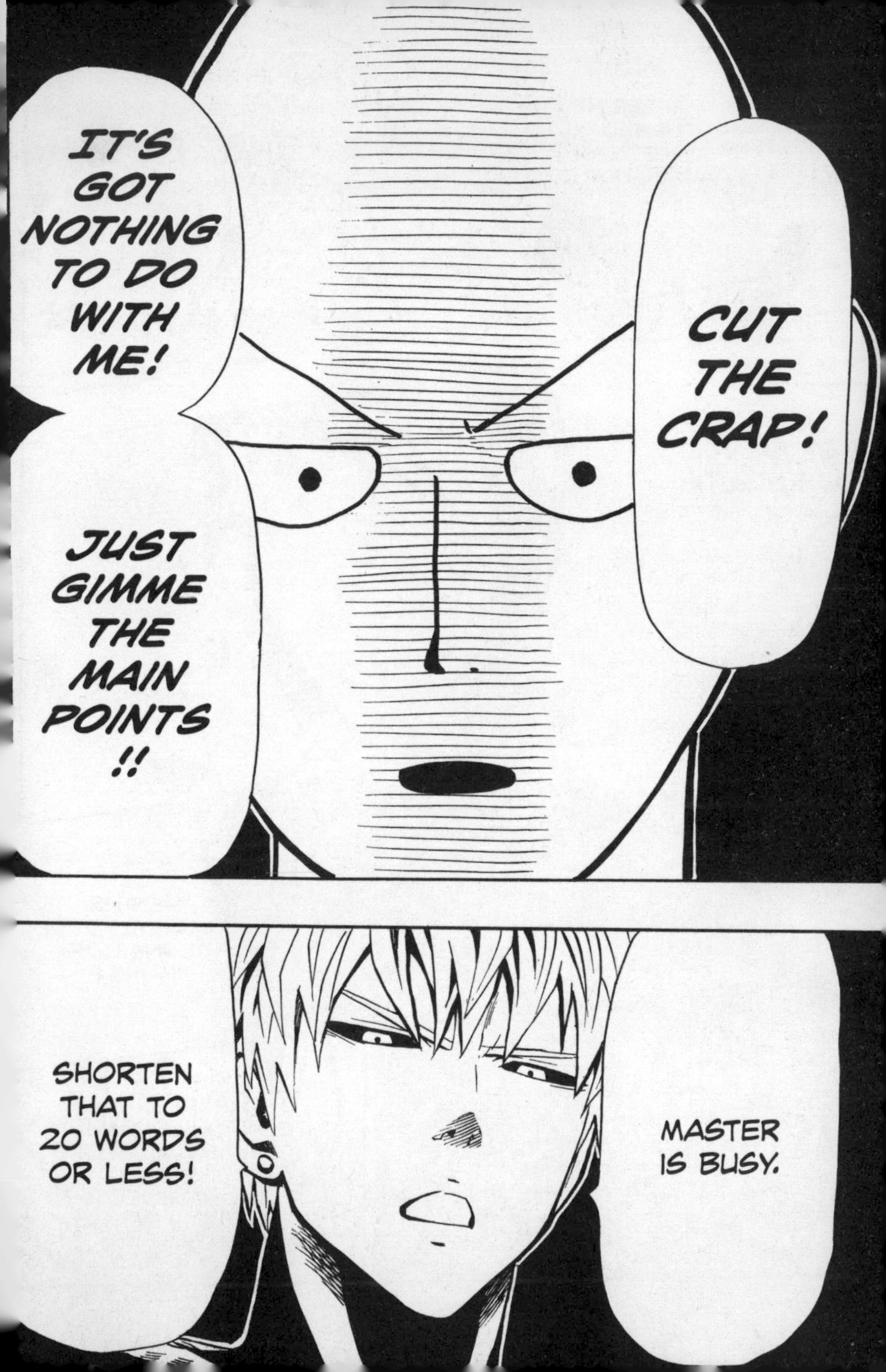
CUT THE CRAP!
IT'S GOT NOTHING TO DO WITH ME!
JUST GIMME THE MAIN POINTS!!
MASTER IS BUSY.
SHORTEN THAT TO 20 WORDS OR LESS!

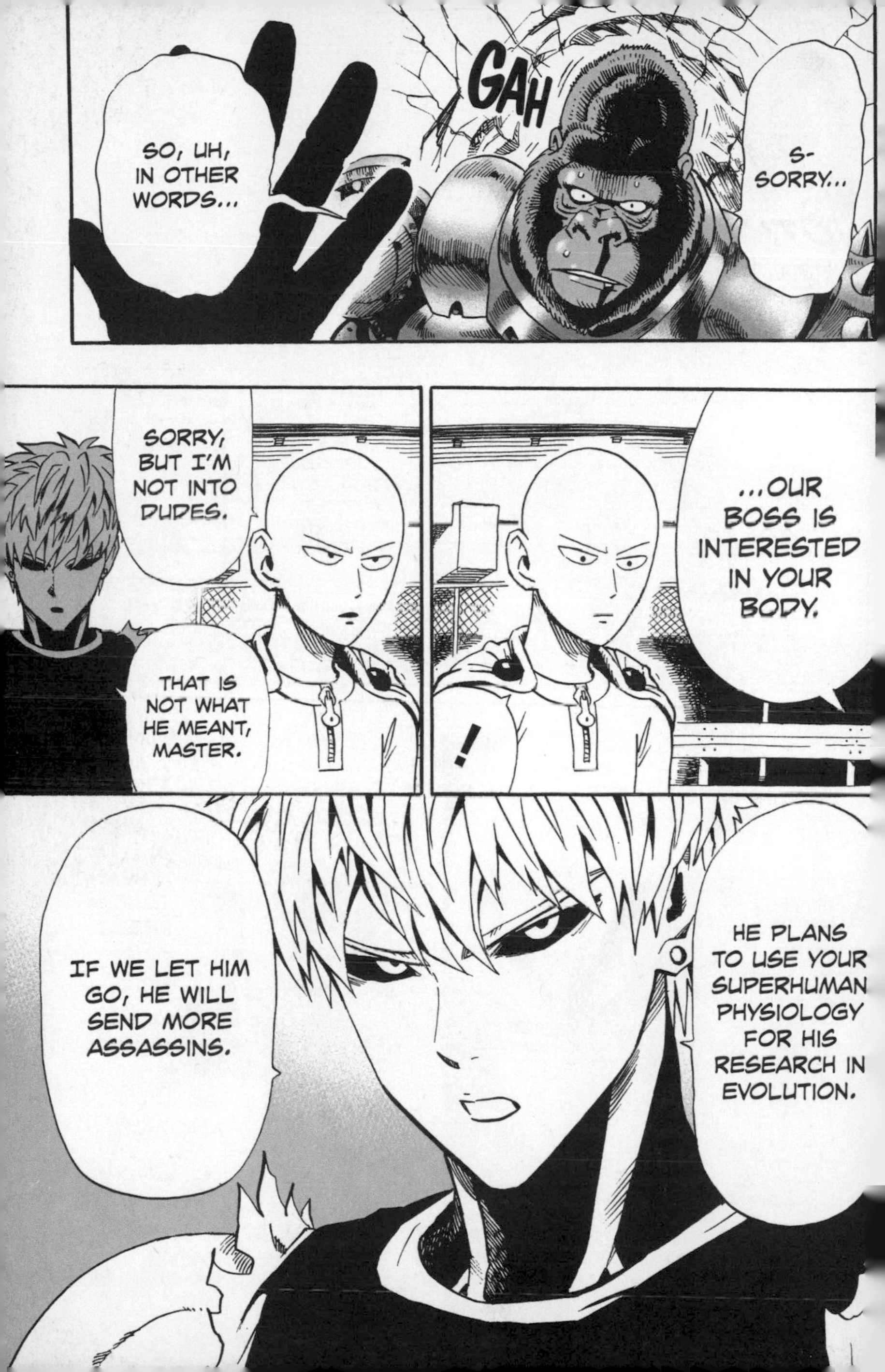
S-SORRY...
GAH
SO, UH, IN OTHER WORDS...
...OUR BOSS IS INTERESTED IN YOUR BODY.
!
SORRY, BUT I'M NOT INTO DUDES.
THAT IS NOT WHAT HE MEANT, MASTER.
HE PLANS TO USE YOUR SUPERHUMAN PHYSIOLOGY FOR HIS RESEARCH IN EVOLUTION.
IF WE LET HIM GO, HE WILL SEND MORE ASSASSINS.

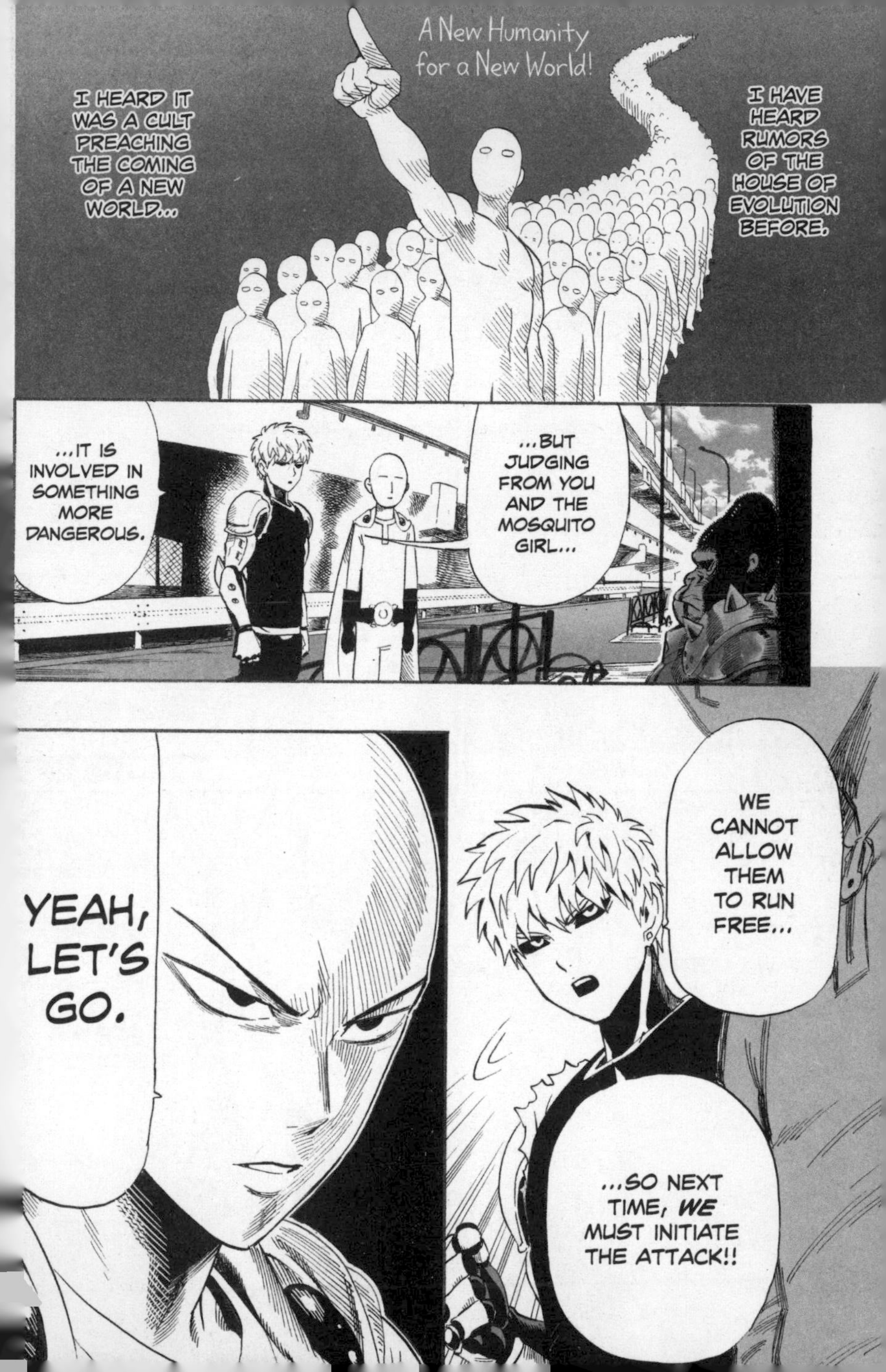

I HAVE HEARD RUMORS OF THE HOUSE OF EVOLUTION BEFORE.
A New Humanity for a New World!
I HEARD IT WAS A CULT PREACHING THE COMING OF A NEW WORLD...
...BUT JUDGING FROM YOU AND THE MOSQUITO GIRL...
...IT IS INVOLVED IN SOMETHING MORE DANGEROUS.
WE CANNOT ALLOW THEM TO RUN FREE...
...SO NEXT TIME, ***WE*** MUST INITIATE THE ATTACK!!
YEAH, LET'S GO.

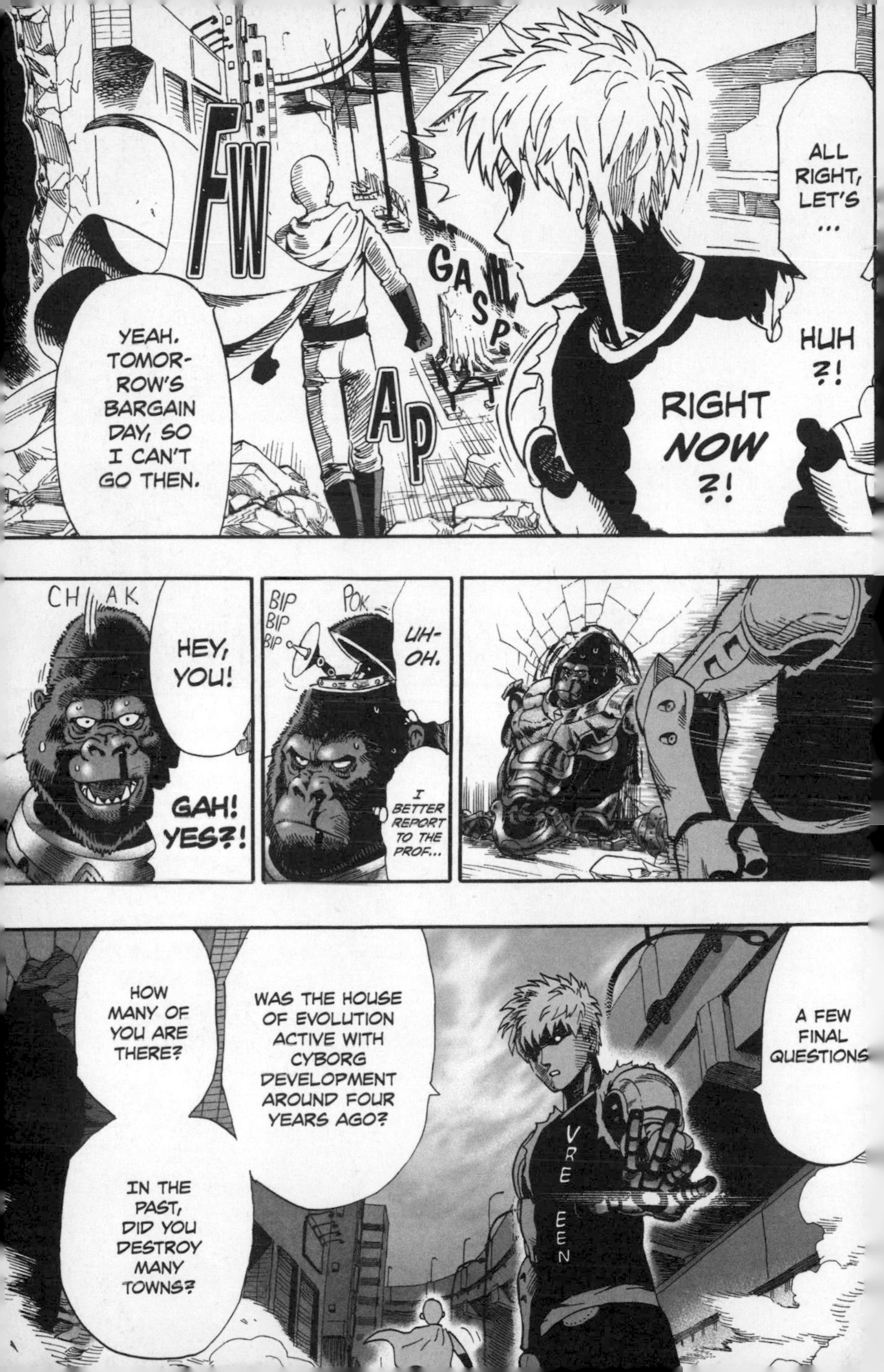
ALL RIGHT, LET'S ...
HUH ?!
RIGHT NOW ?!
GASP
FW
AP
YEAH. TOMORROW'S BARGAIN DAY, SO I CAN'T GO THEN.
POK
BIP BIP BIP
UH-OH.
I BETTER REPORT TO THE PROF...
CH AK
HEY, YOU!
GAH! YES?!
A FEW FINAL QUESTIONS
VRE EEN
WAS THE HOUSE OF EVOLUTION ACTIVE WITH CYBORG DEVELOPMENT AROUND FOUR YEARS AGO?
HOW MANY OF YOU ARE THERE?
IN THE PAST, DID YOU DESTROY MANY TOWNS?

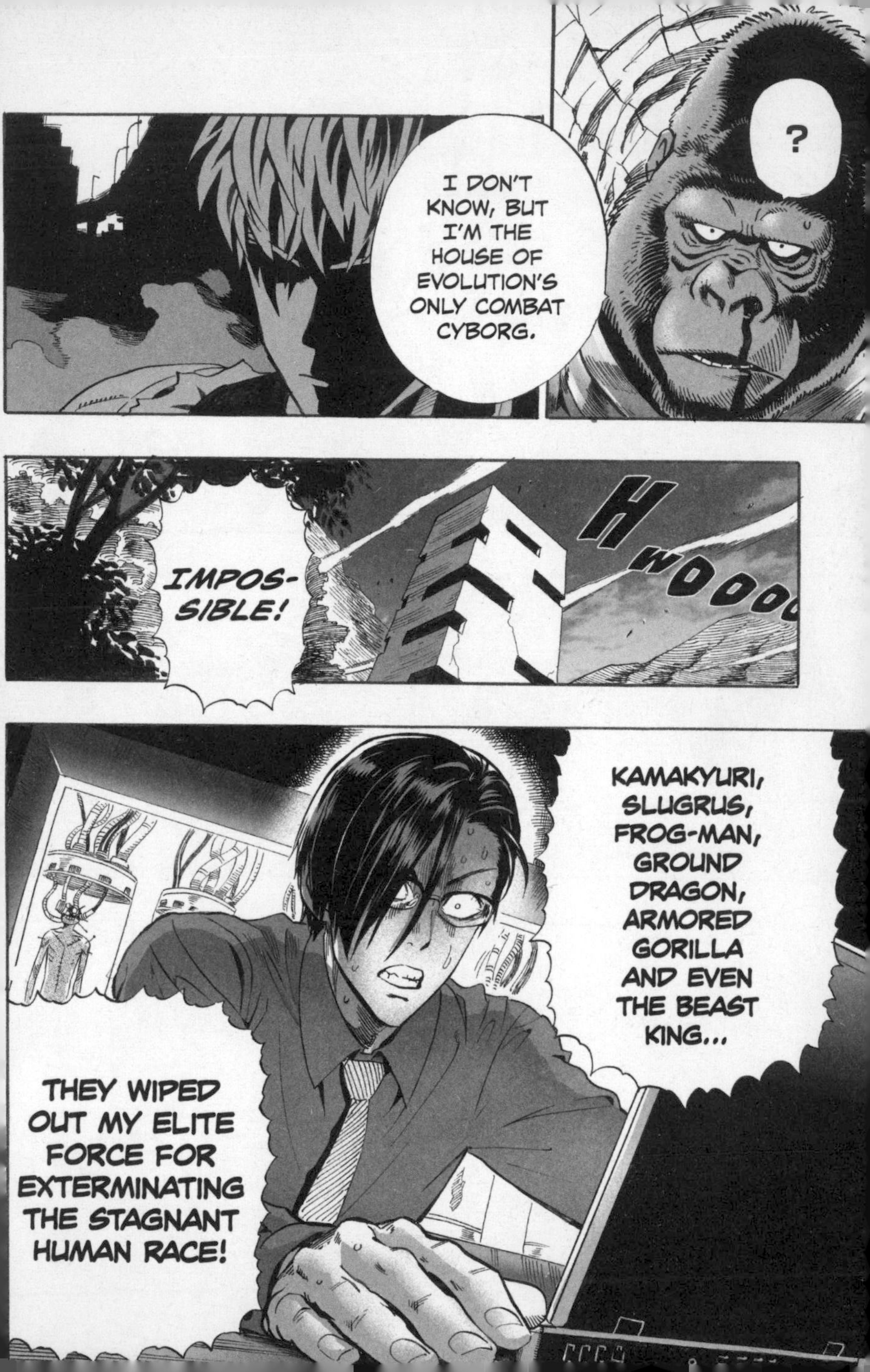
?
I DON'T KNOW, BUT I'M THE HOUSE OF EVOLUTION'S ONLY COMBAT CYBORG.
HWOOOO
IMPOS-SIBLE!
KAMAKYURI, SLUGRUS, FROG-MAN, GROUND DRAGON, ARMORED GORILLA AND EVEN THE BEAST KING...
THEY WIPED OUT MY ELITE FORCE FOR EXTERMINATING THE STAGNANT HUMAN RACE!

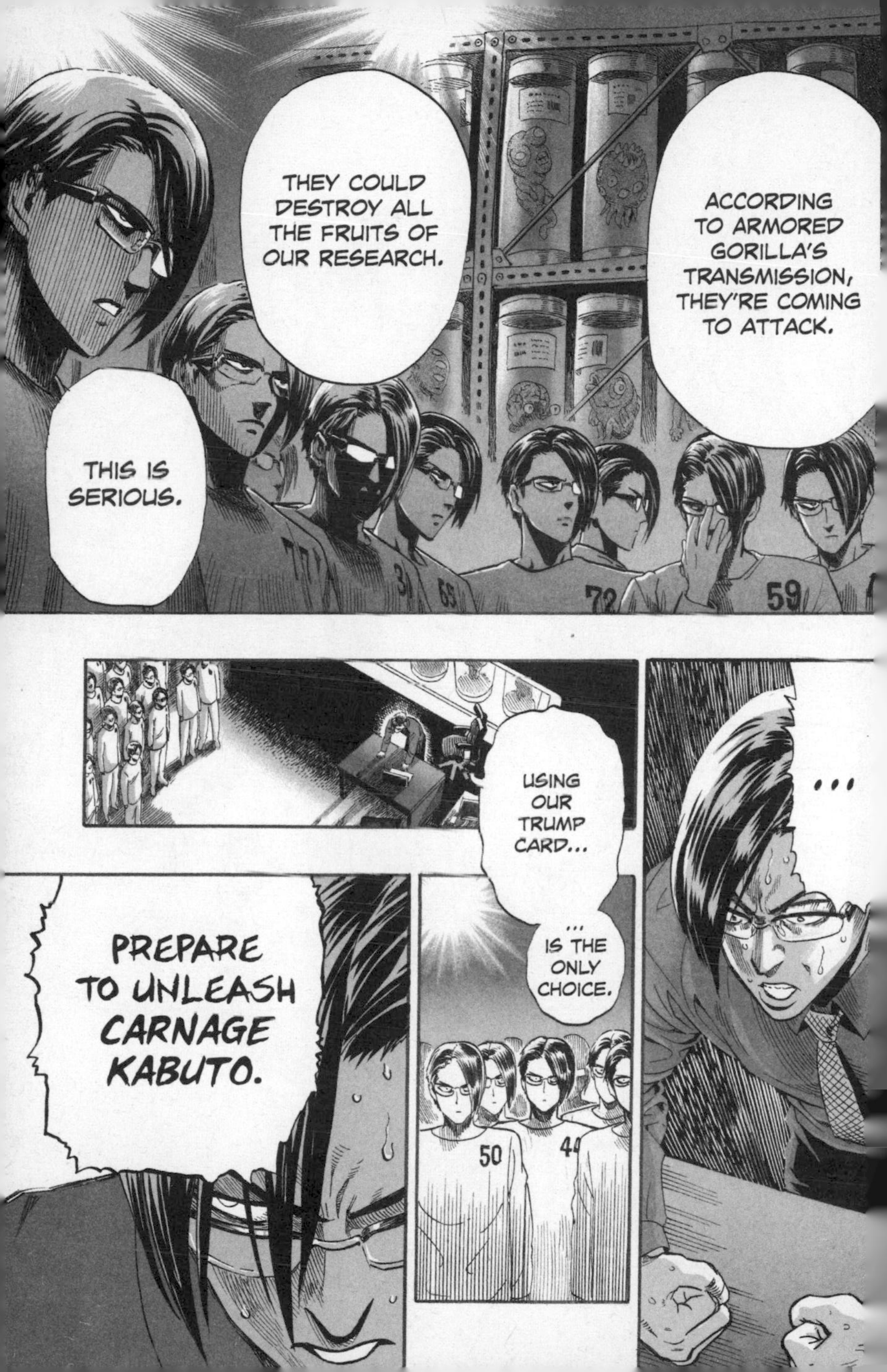
ACCORDING TO ARMORED GORILLA'S TRANSMISSION, THEY'RE COMING TO ATTACK.
THEY COULD DESTROY ALL THE FRUITS OF OUR RESEARCH.
THIS IS SERIOUS.
...
USING OUR TRUMP CARD...
... IS THE ONLY CHOICE.
PREPARE TO UNLEASH CARNAGE KABUTO.

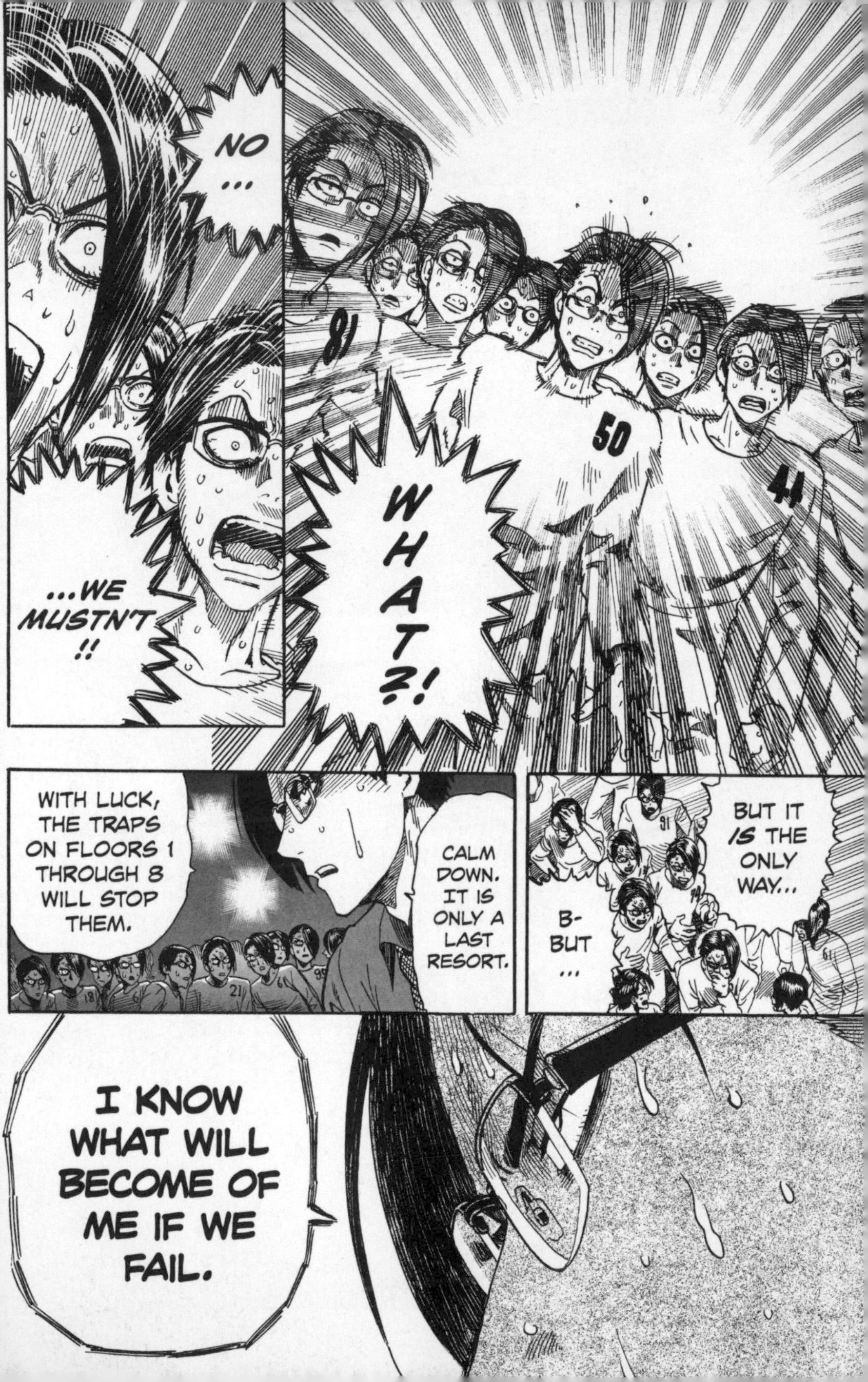
WHAT?!
NO ...
...WE MUSTN'T !!
BUT IT *IS* THE ONLY WAY...
B-BUT ...
CALM DOWN. IT IS ONLY A LAST RESORT.
WITH LUCK, THE TRAPS ON FLOORS 1 THROUGH 8 WILL STOP THEM.
I KNOW WHAT WILL BECOME OF ME IF WE FAIL.

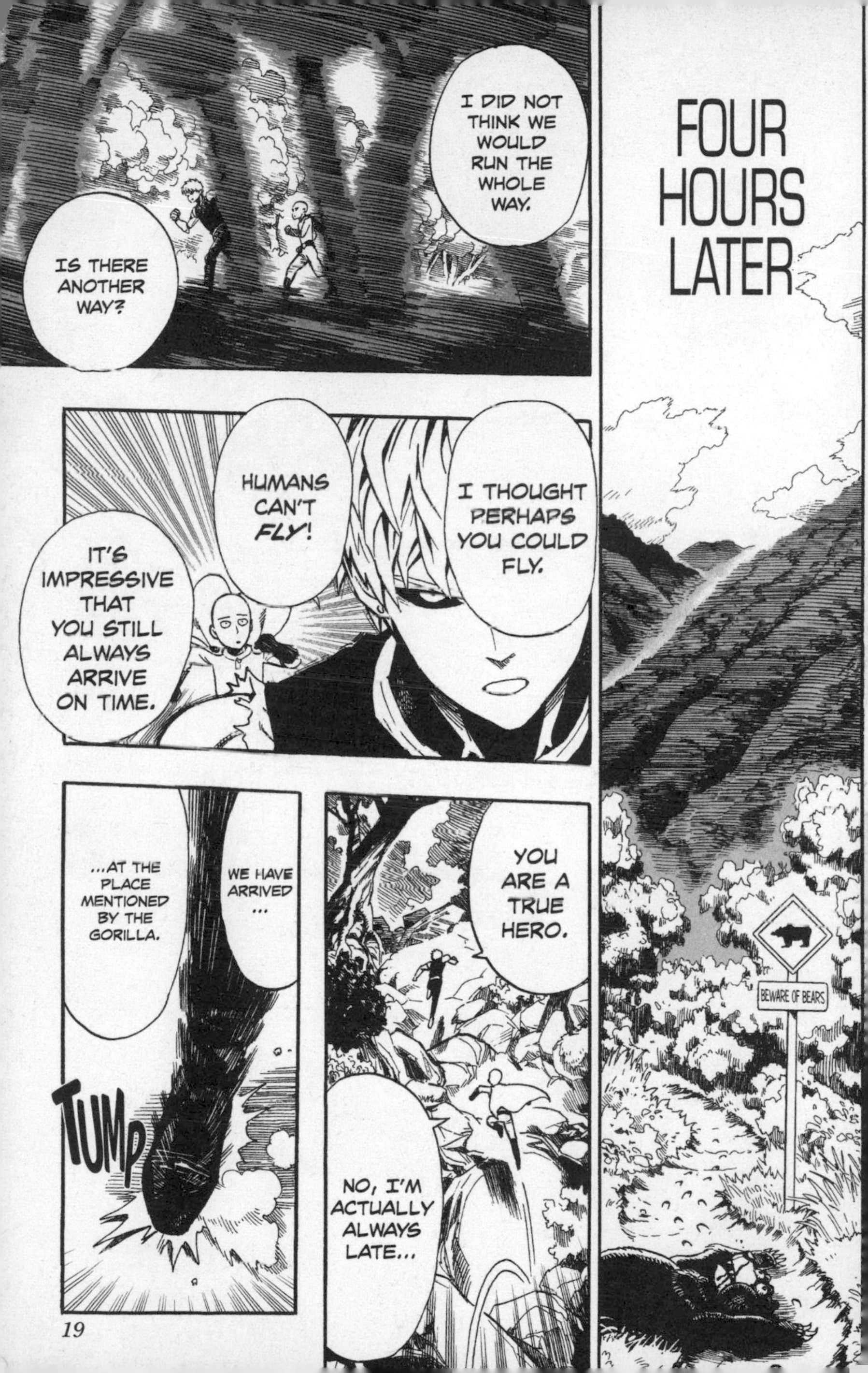
FOUR HOURS LATER
BEWARE OF BEARS
I DID NOT THINK WE WOULD RUN THE WHOLE WAY.
IS THERE ANOTHER WAY?
I THOUGHT PERHAPS YOU COULD FLY.
HUMANS CAN'T *FLY*!
IT'S IMPRESSIVE THAT YOU STILL ALWAYS ARRIVE ON TIME.
YOU ARE A TRUE HERO.
NO, I'M ACTUALLY ALWAYS LATE...
WE HAVE ARRIVED ...
...AT THE PLACE MENTIONED BY THE GORILLA.
TUMP

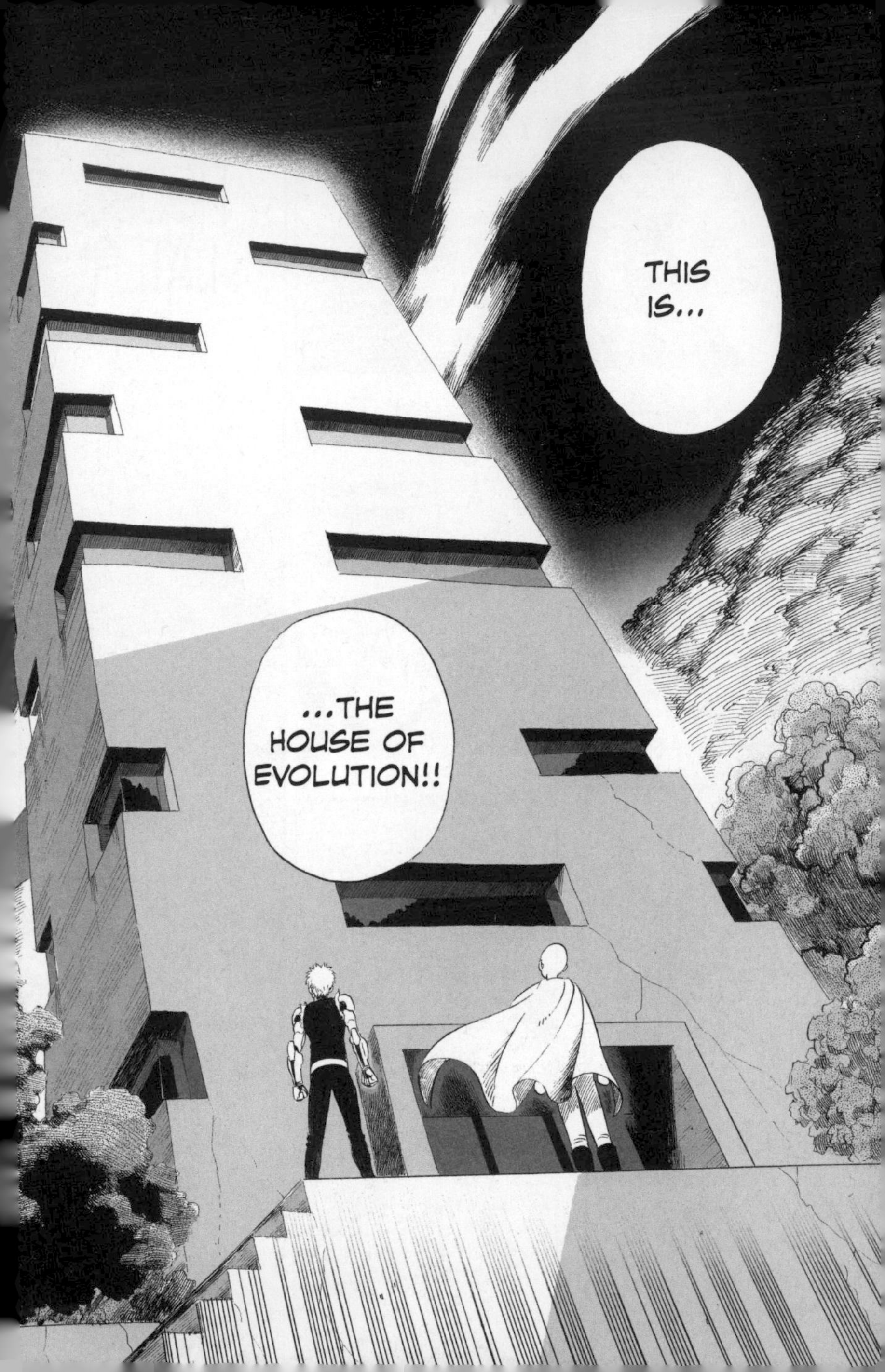
THIS IS...
...THE HOUSE OF EVOLUTION!!

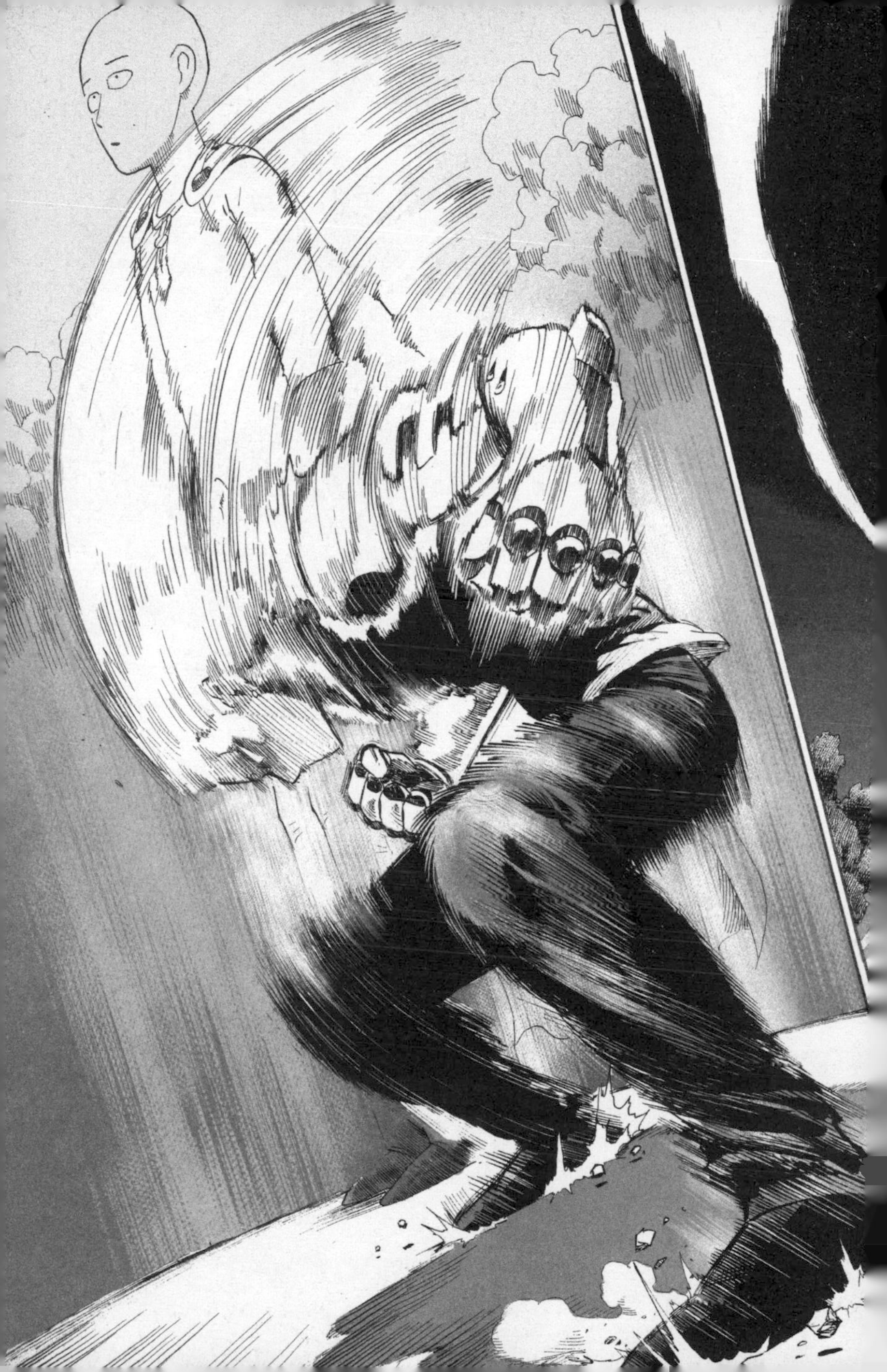

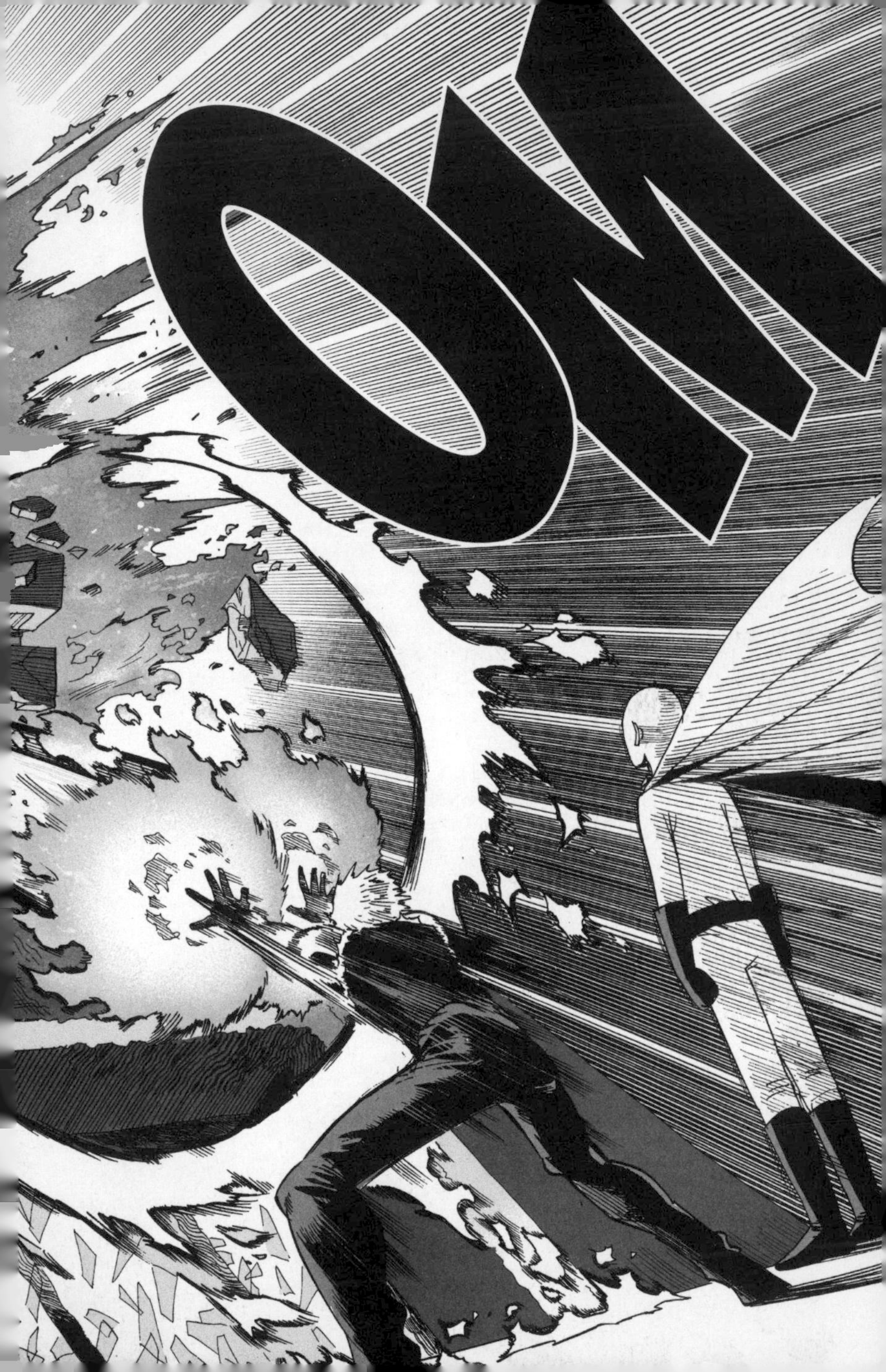
OM

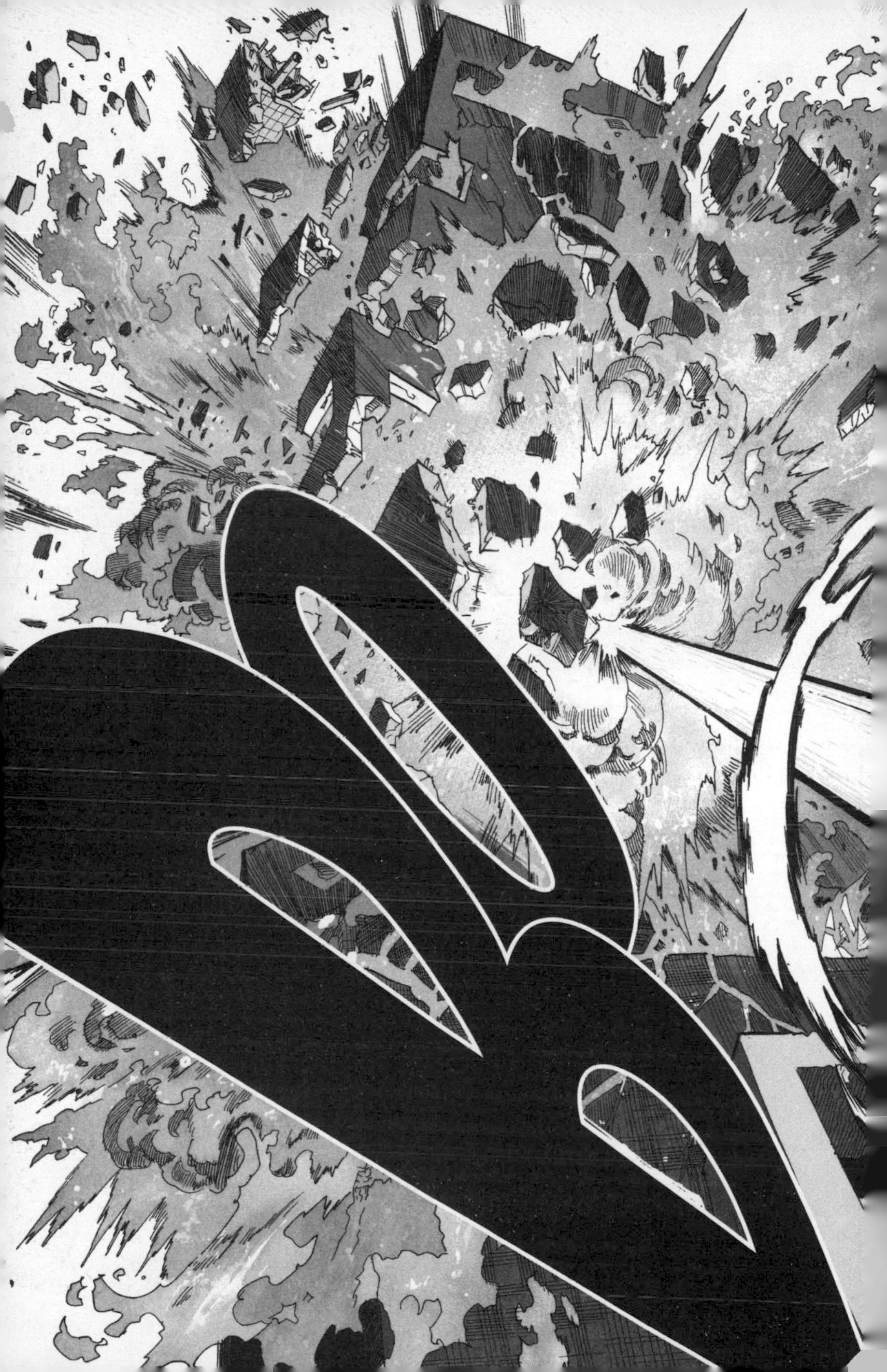

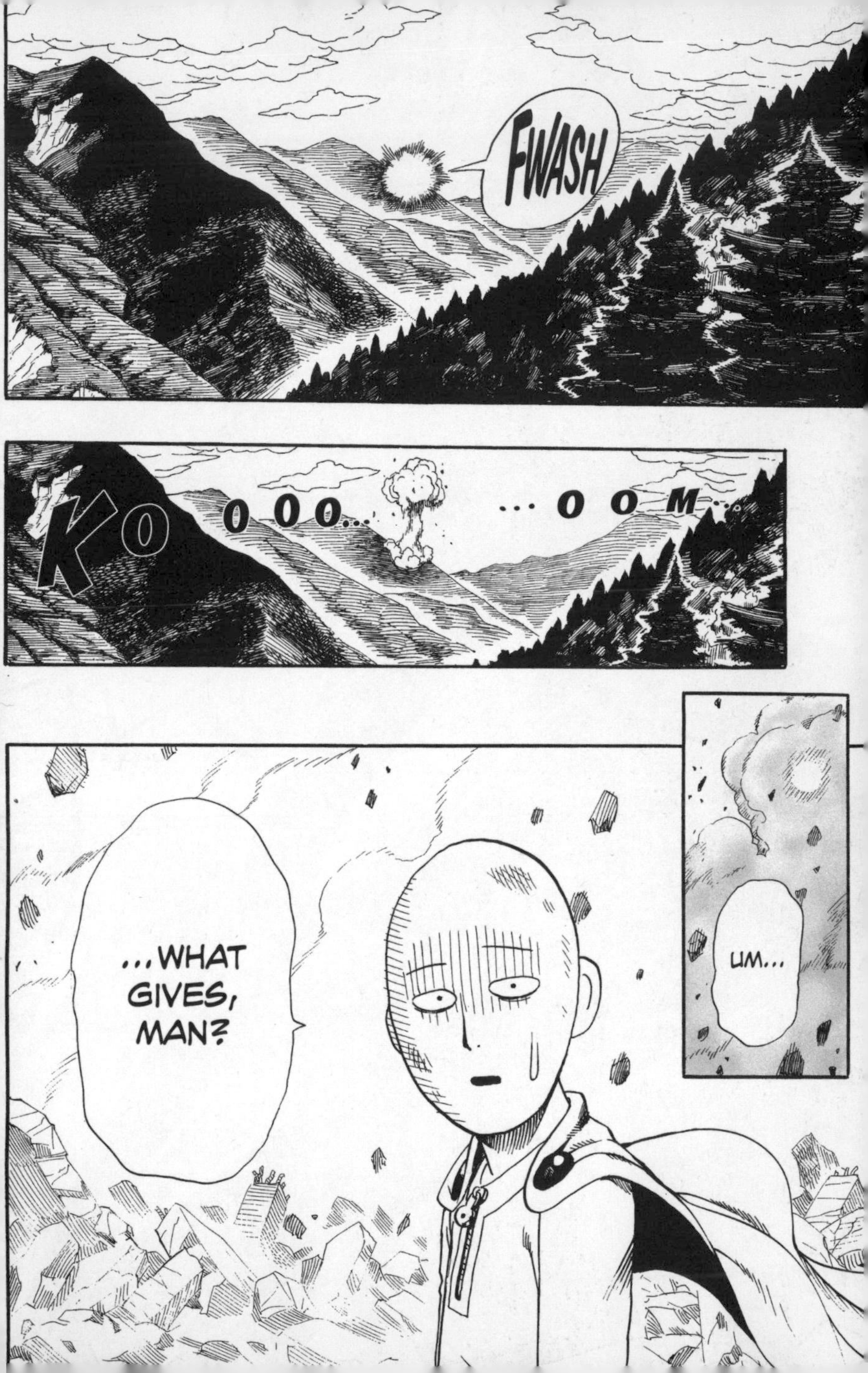
FWASH
KOOOO... ...OOM...
UM...
...WHAT GIVES, MAN?

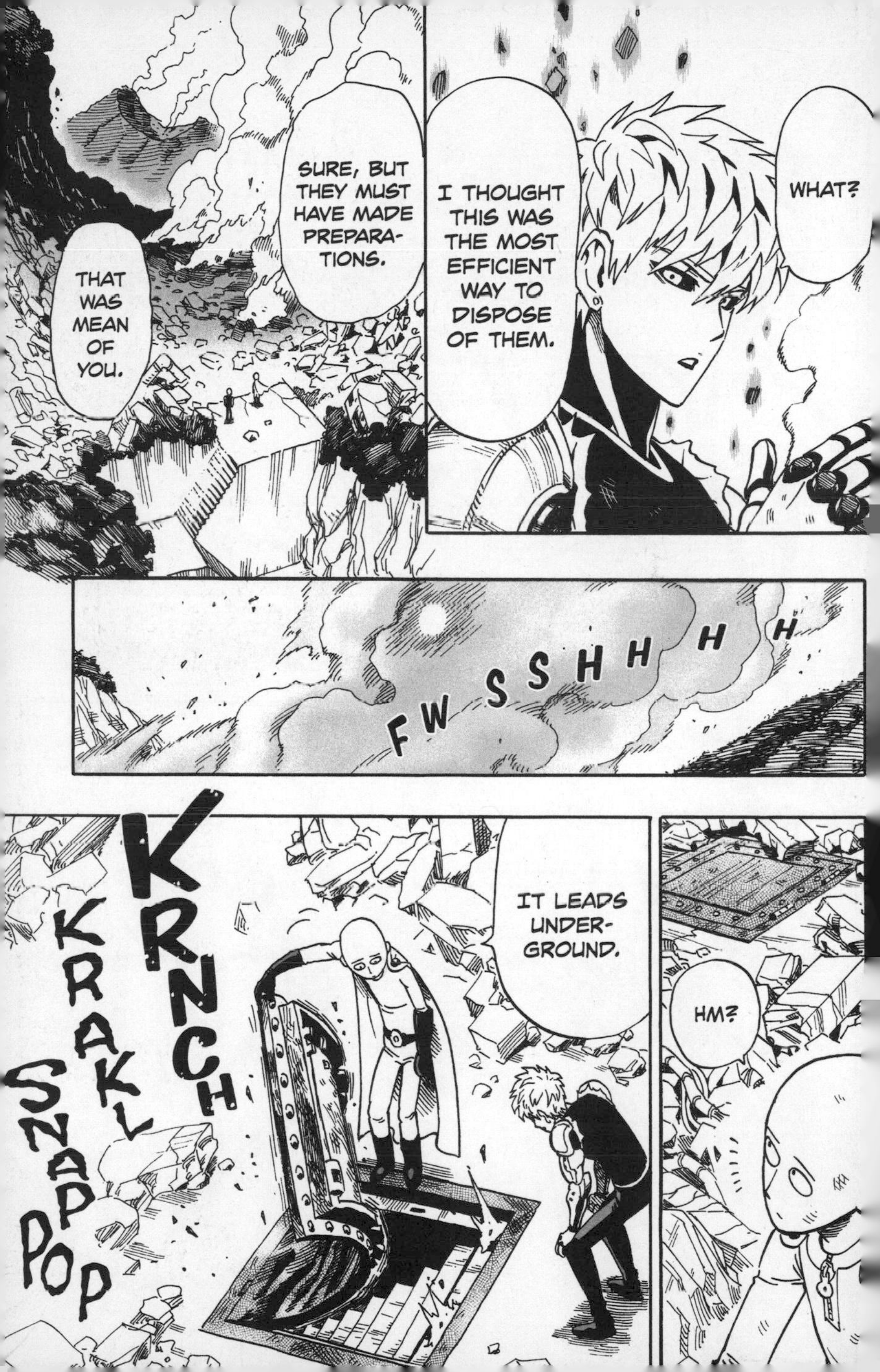
WHAT?
I THOUGHT THIS WAS THE MOST EFFICIENT WAY TO DISPOSE OF THEM.
SURE, BUT THEY MUST HAVE MADE PREPARATIONS.
THAT WAS MEAN OF YOU.
FWSSHHHH
HM?
IT LEADS UNDERGROUND.
KRNCH
KRAKL
SNAP
POP

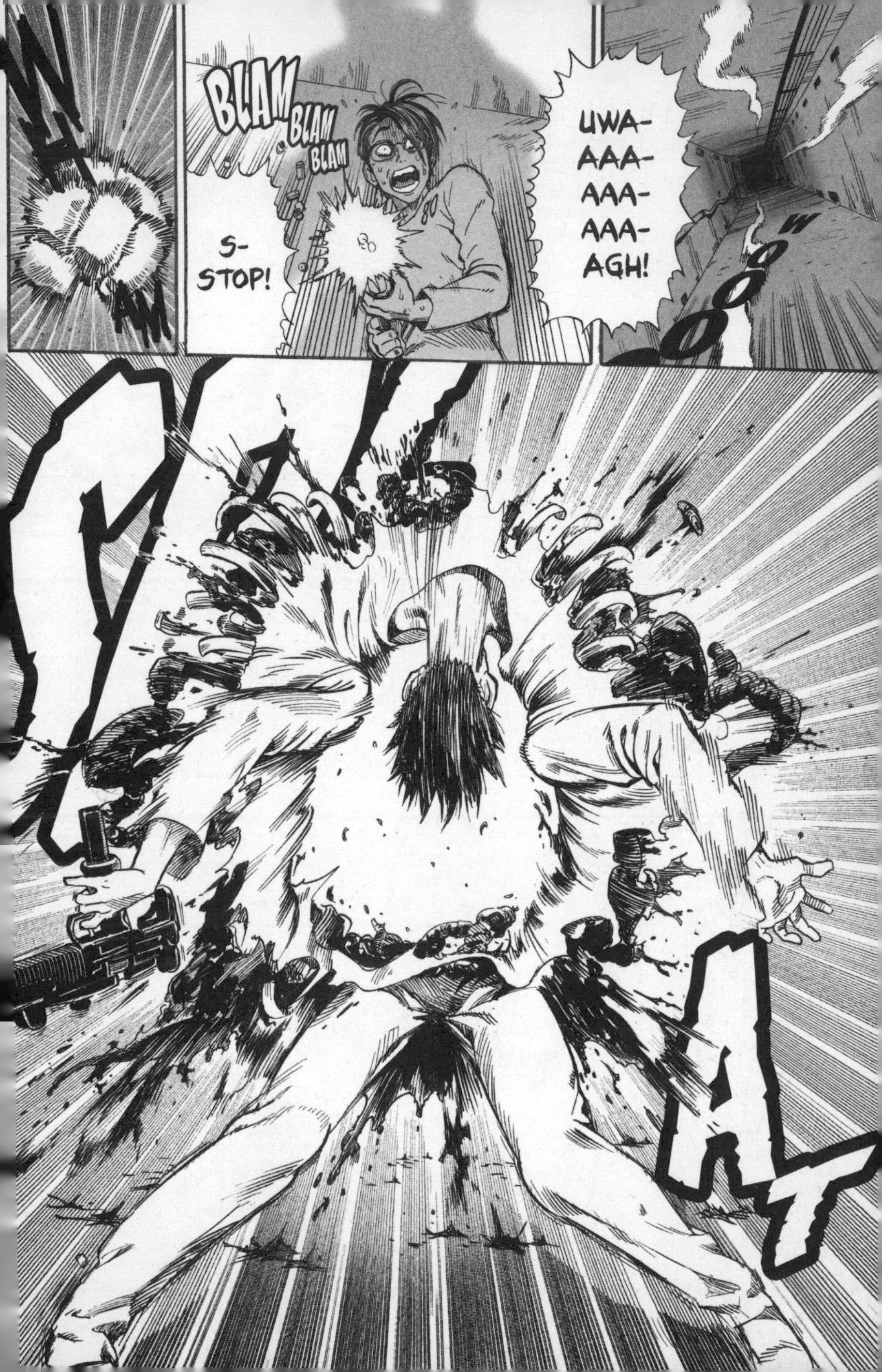
UWA-AAA-AAA-AAA-AGH!
BLAM BLAM BLAM
S-STOP!

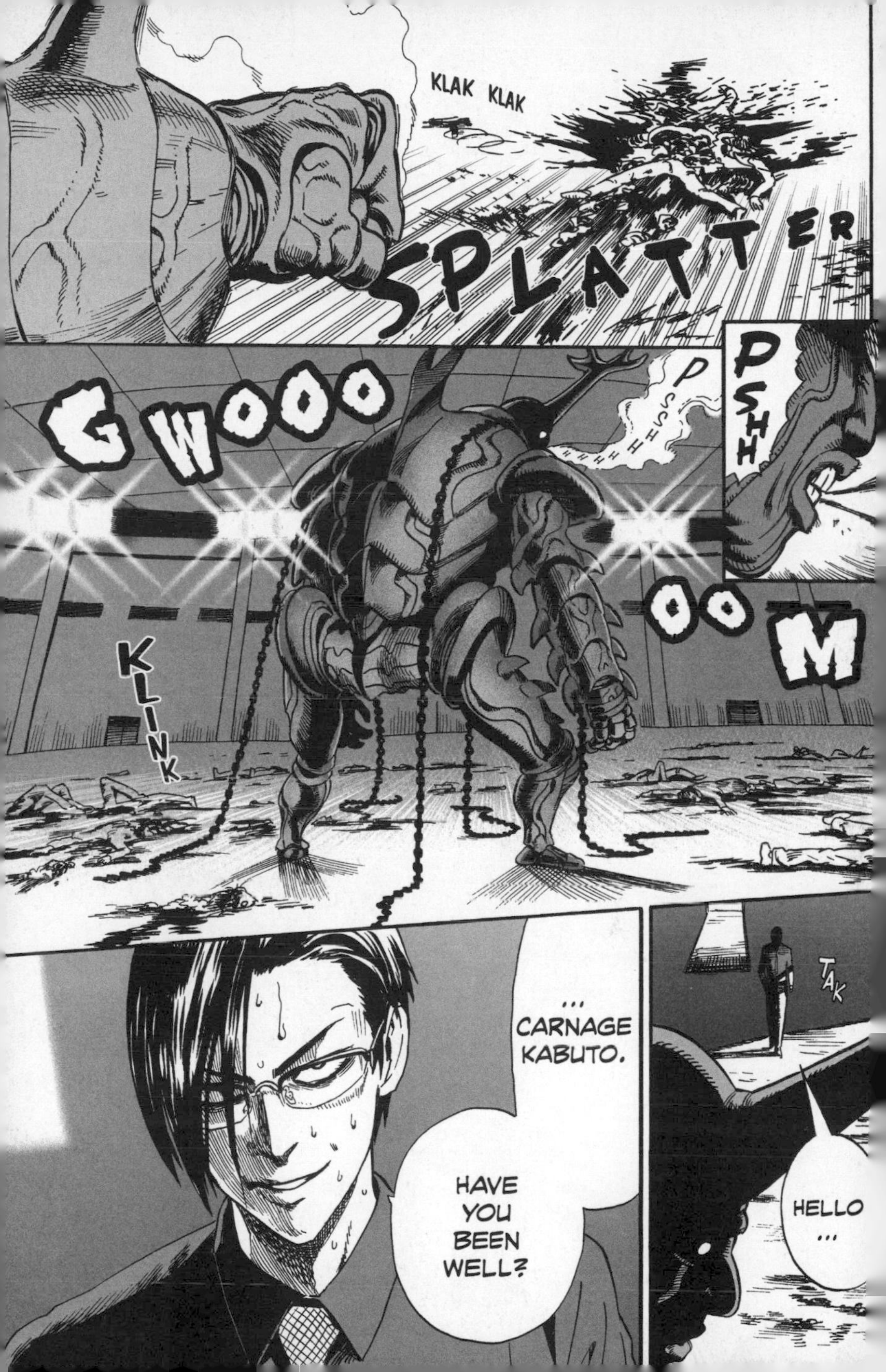
KLAK KLAK
SPLATTER
PSHH
PSSHH
GWOOO
OOM
KLINK
TAK
HELLO ...
... CARNAGE KABUTO.
HAVE YOU BEEN WELL?

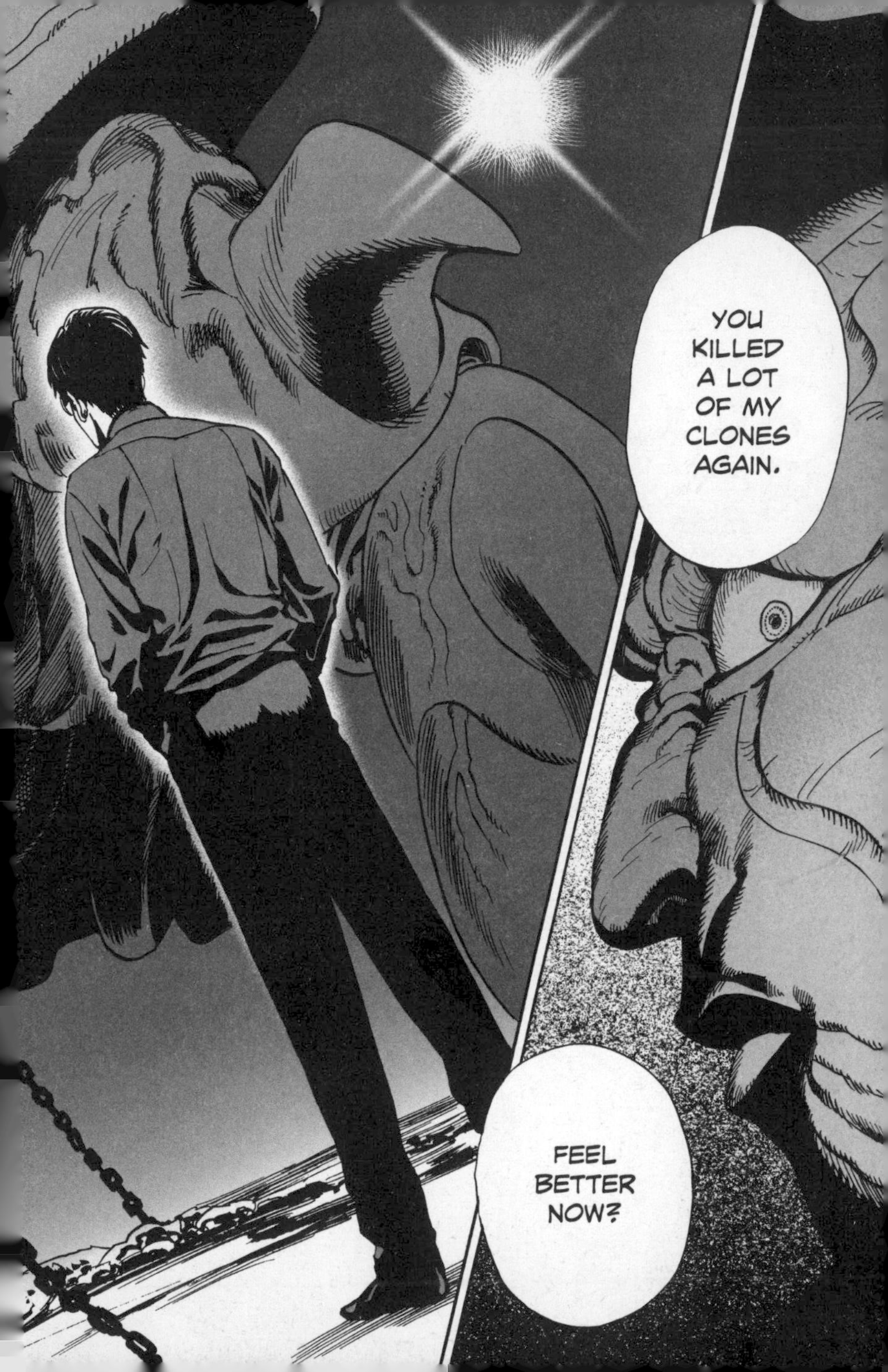
YOU KILLED A LOT OF MY CLONES AGAIN.
FEEL BETTER NOW?

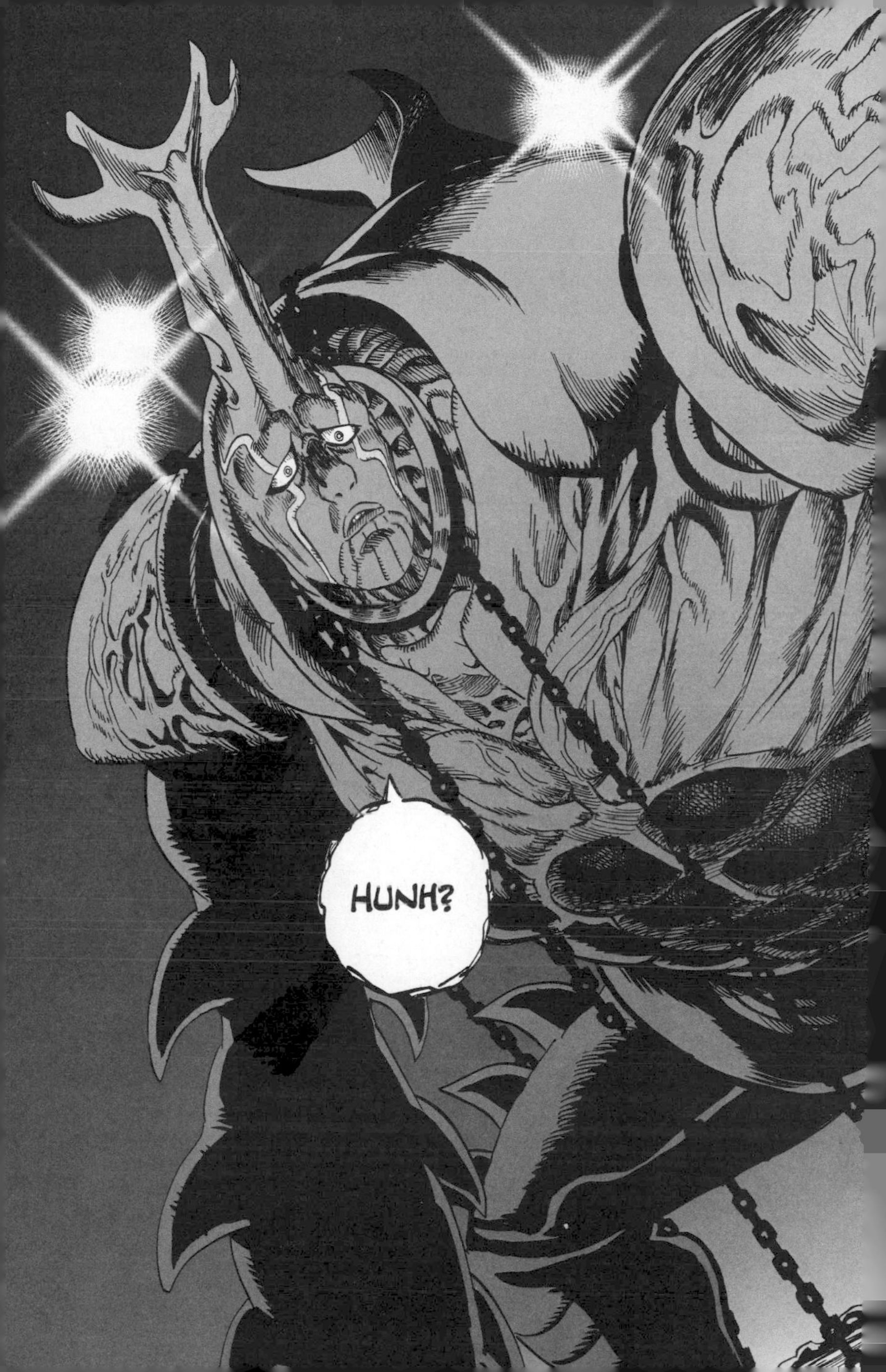
HUNH?

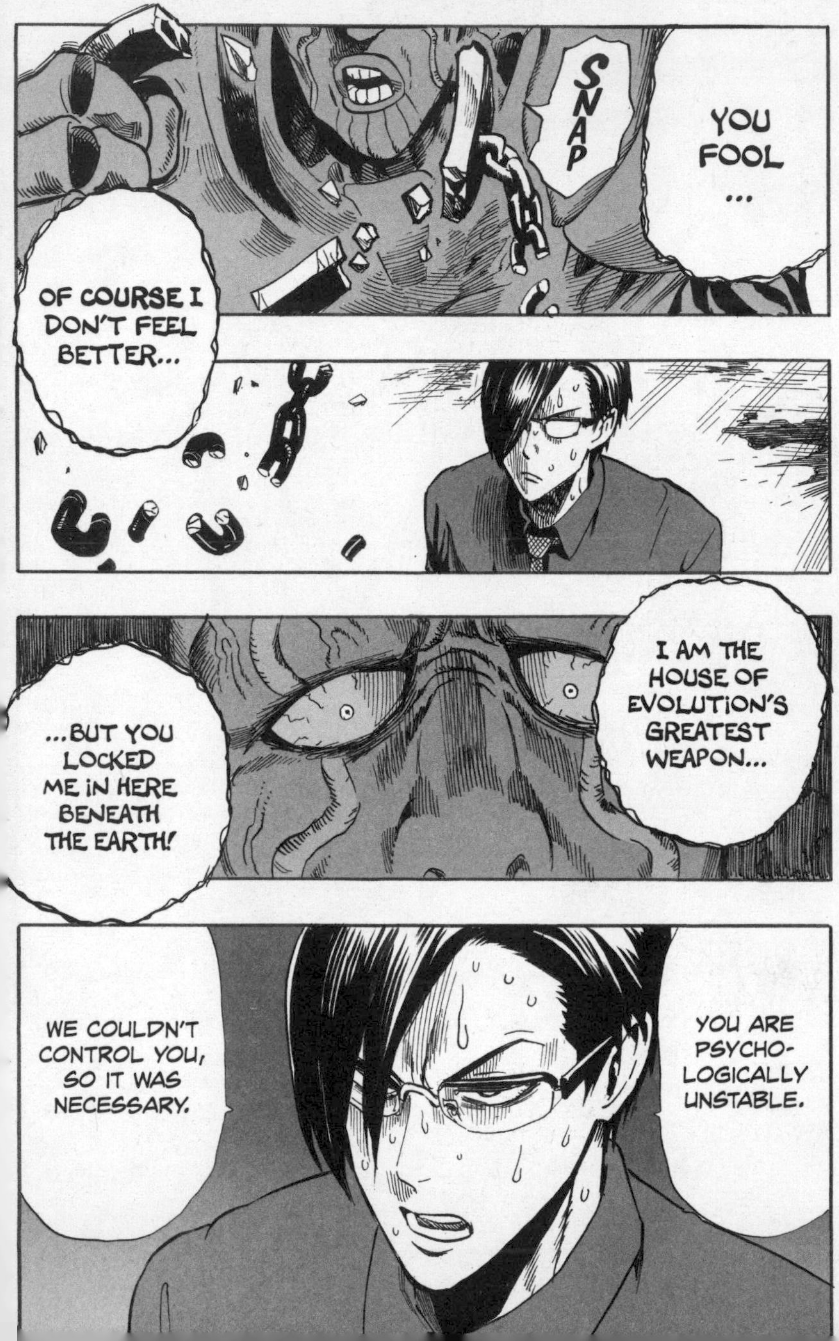
YOU FOOL ...
SNAP
OF COURSE I DON'T FEEL BETTER...
I AM THE HOUSE OF EVOLUTION'S GREATEST WEAPON...
...BUT YOU LOCKED ME IN HERE BENEATH THE EARTH!
YOU ARE PSYCHO-LOGICALLY UNSTABLE.
WE COULDN'T CONTROL YOU, SO IT WAS NECESSARY.

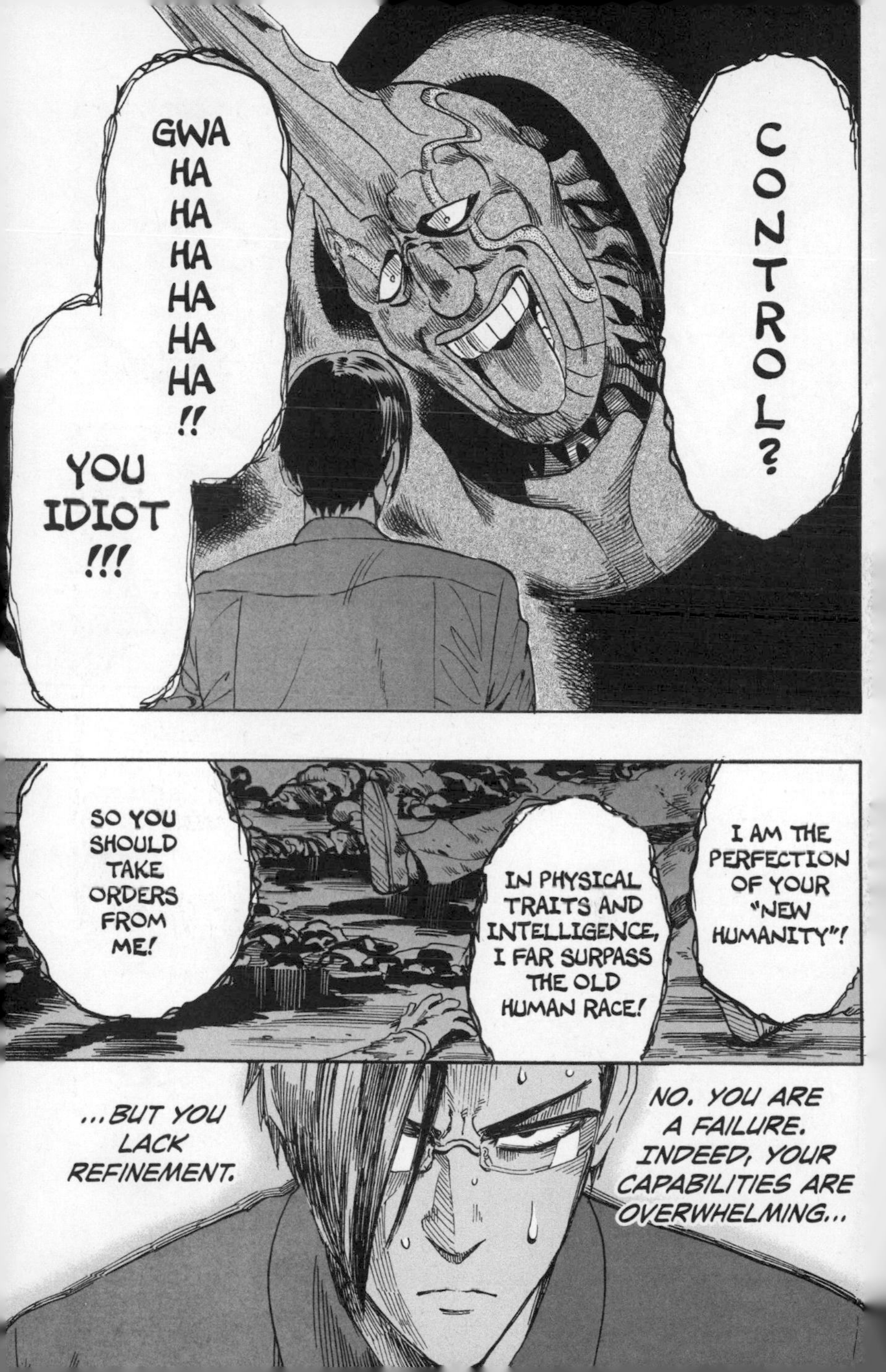
CONTROL?
GWAHAHAHAHAHAHAHAHA!!
YOU IDIOT!!!
I AM THE PERFECTION OF YOUR "NEW HUMANITY"!
IN PHYSICAL TRAITS AND INTELLIGENCE, I FAR SURPASS THE OLD HUMAN RACE!
SO YOU SHOULD TAKE ORDERS FROM ME!
NO. YOU ARE A FAILURE. INDEED, YOUR CAPABILITIES ARE OVERWHELMING...
...BUT YOU LACK REFINEMENT.

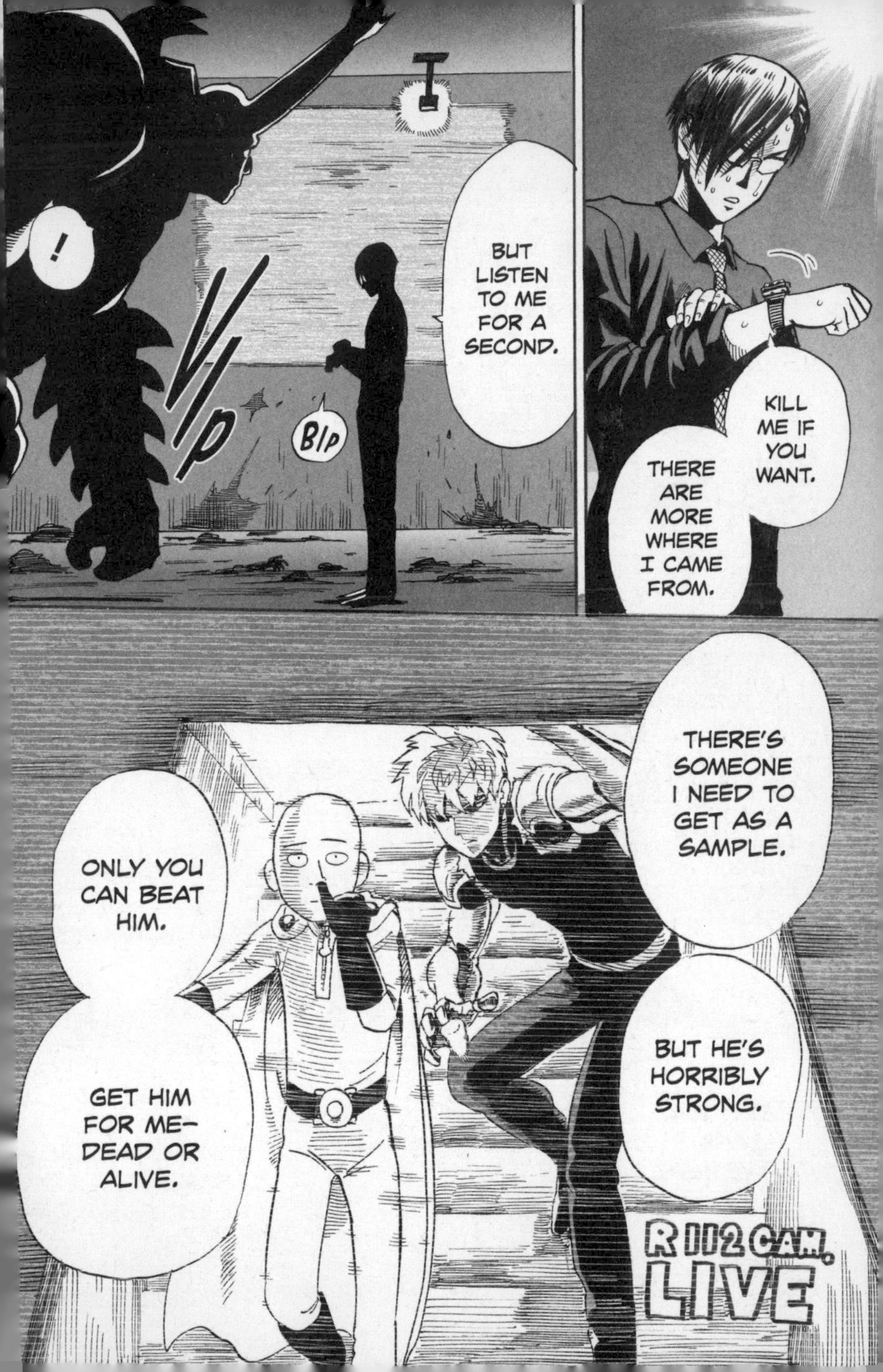
KILL ME IF YOU WANT.
THERE ARE MORE WHERE I CAME FROM.
BUT LISTEN TO ME FOR A SECOND.
BIP
!
THERE'S SOMEONE I NEED TO GET AS A SAMPLE.
BUT HE'S HORRIBLY STRONG.
ONLY YOU CAN BEAT HIM.
GET HIM FOR ME—DEAD OR ALIVE.
R 112 CAM. LIVE

PUNCH 10: MODERN ART

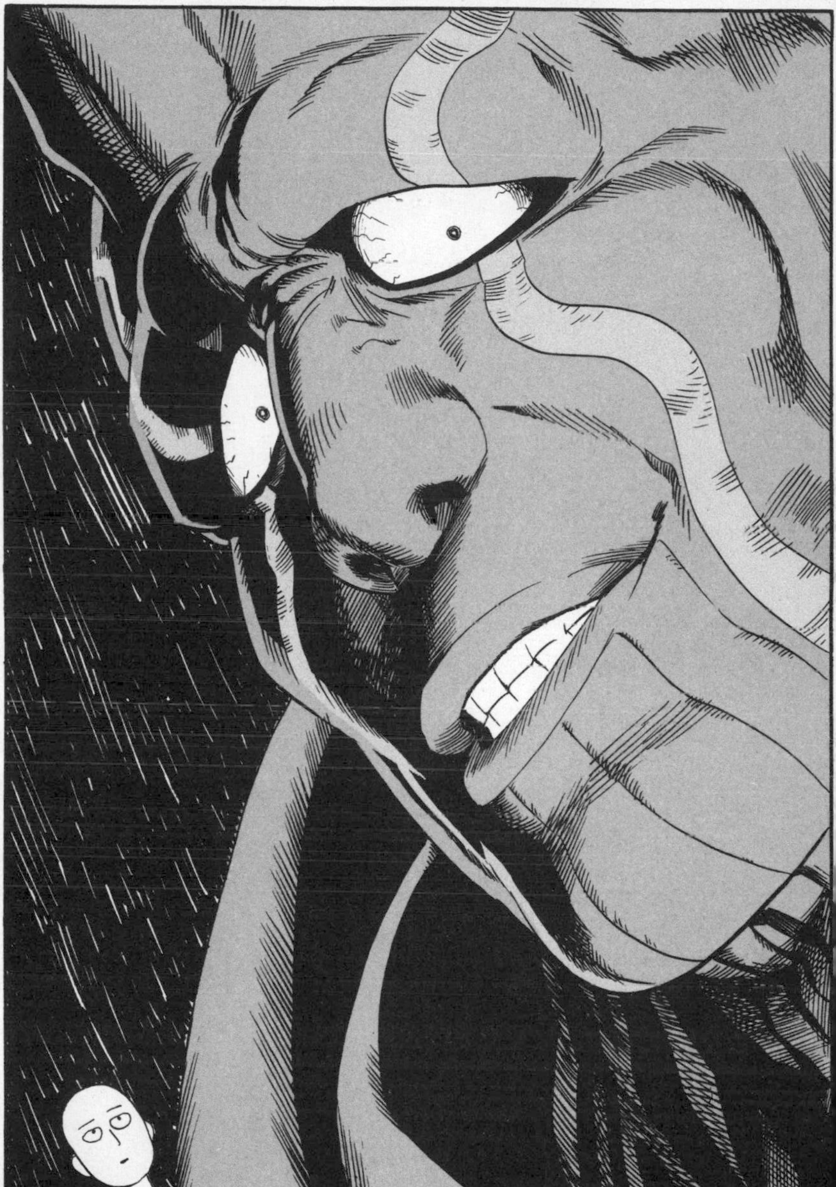

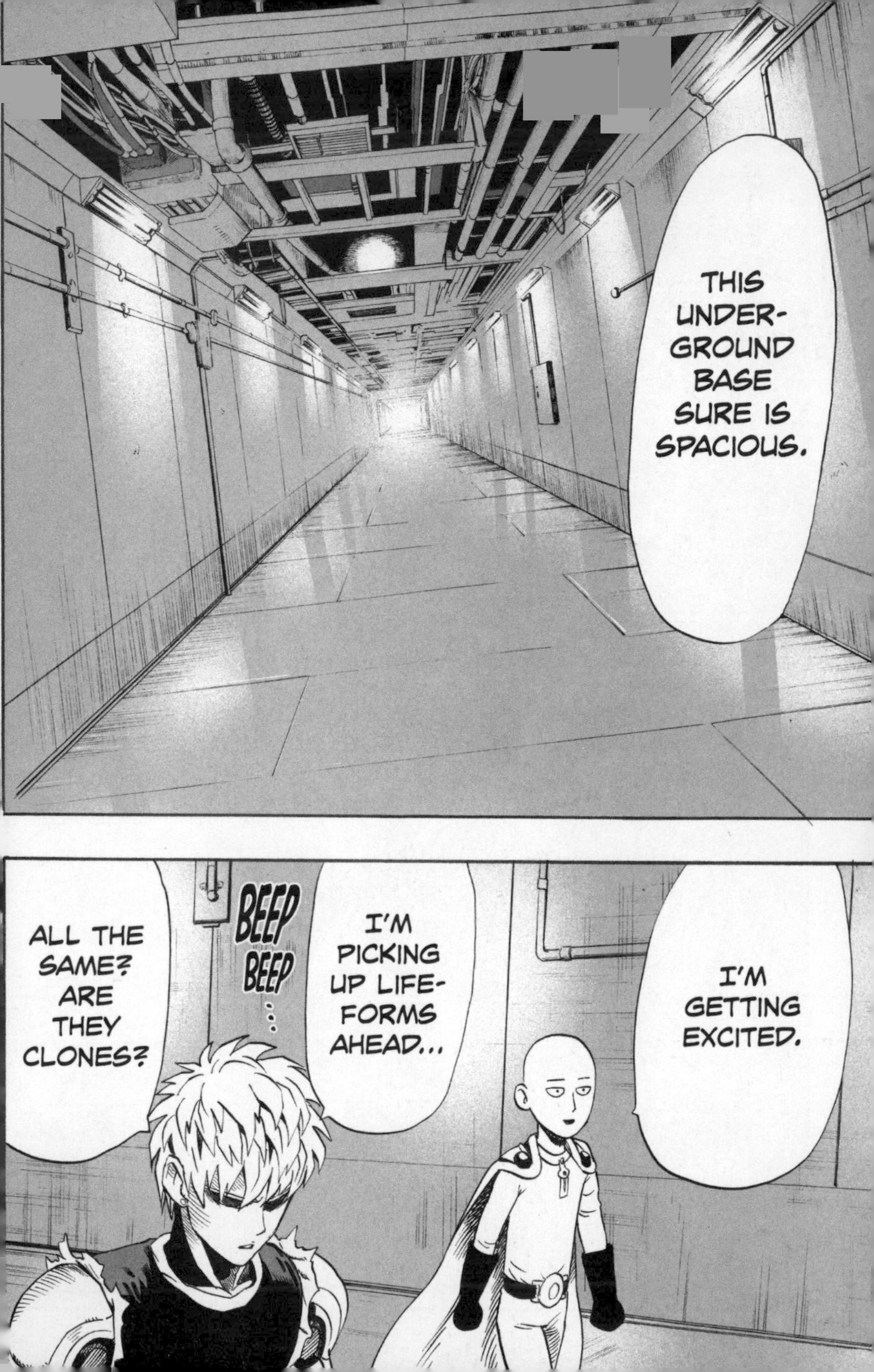
THIS UNDER-GROUND BASE SURE IS SPACIOUS.
I'M GETTING EXCITED.
I'M PICKING UP LIFE-FORMS AHEAD...
BEEP BEEP...
ALL THE SAME? ARE THEY CLONES?

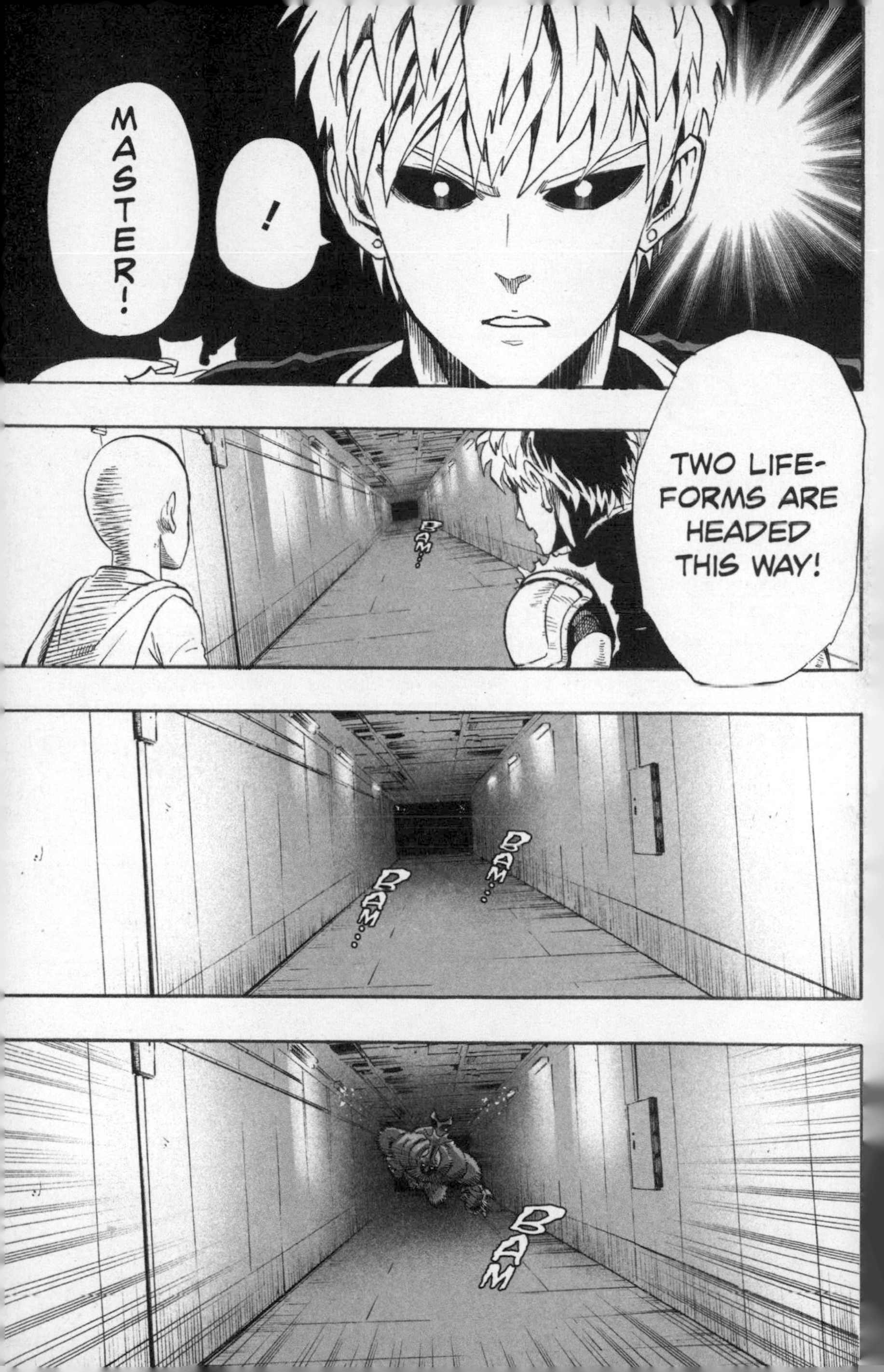
!
MASTER!
TWO LIFE-FORMS ARE HEADED THIS WAY!
BAM...
BAM...
BAM...
BAM BAM

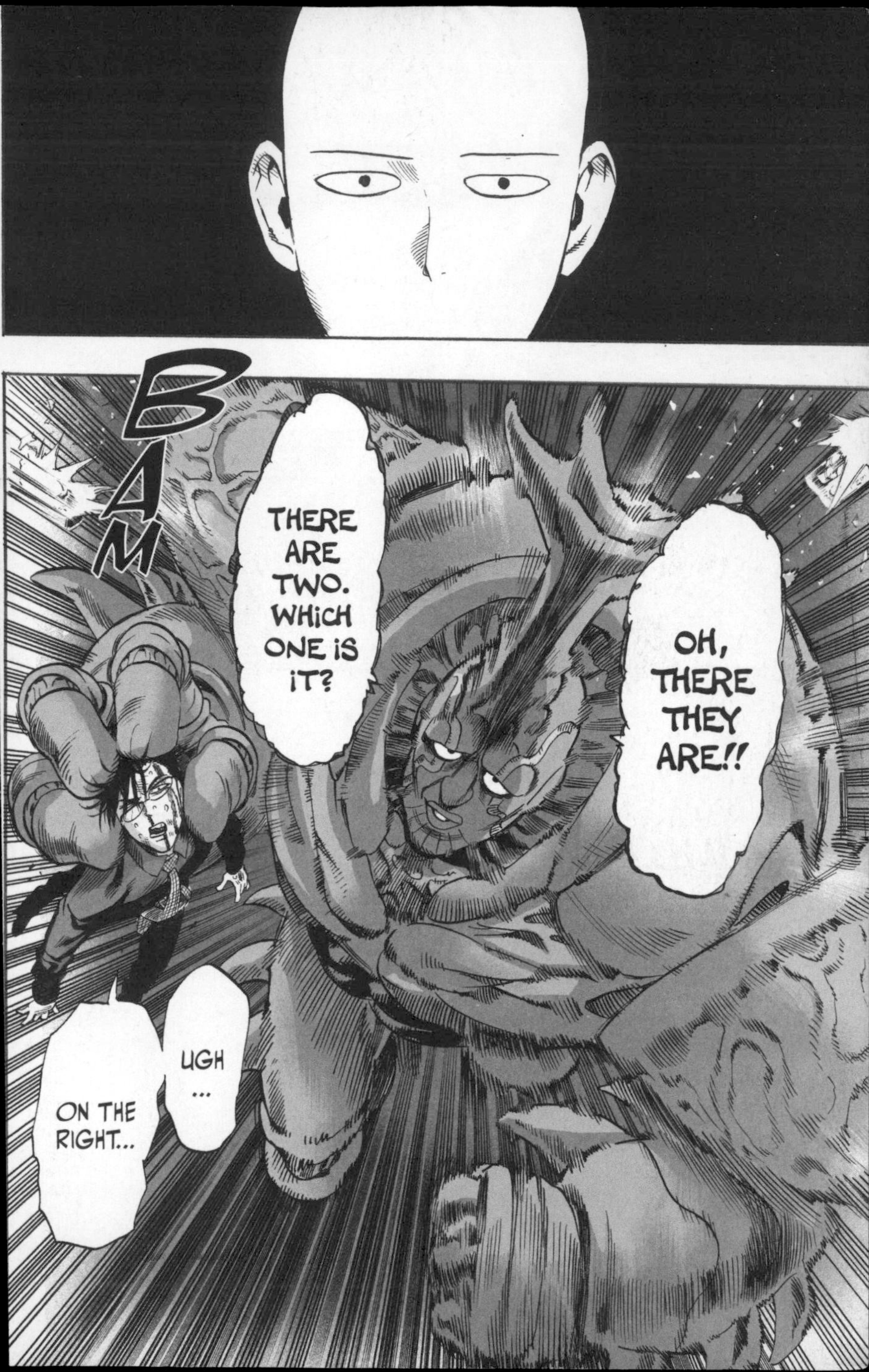
BAM
OH, THERE THEY ARE!!
THERE ARE TWO. WHICH ONE IS IT?
UGH ...
ON THE RIGHT...

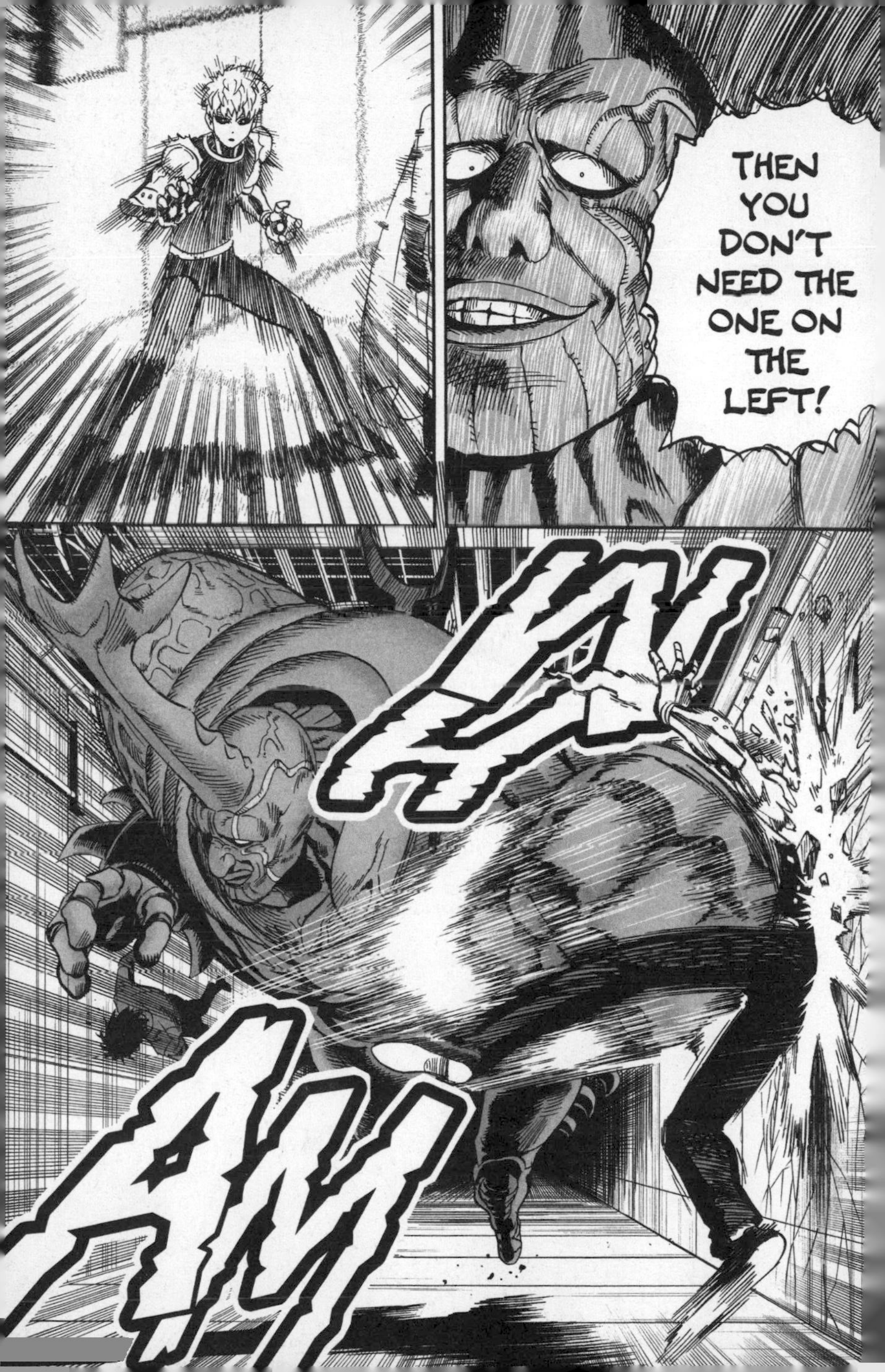
THEN YOU DON'T NEED THE ONE ON THE LEFT!
WHAM

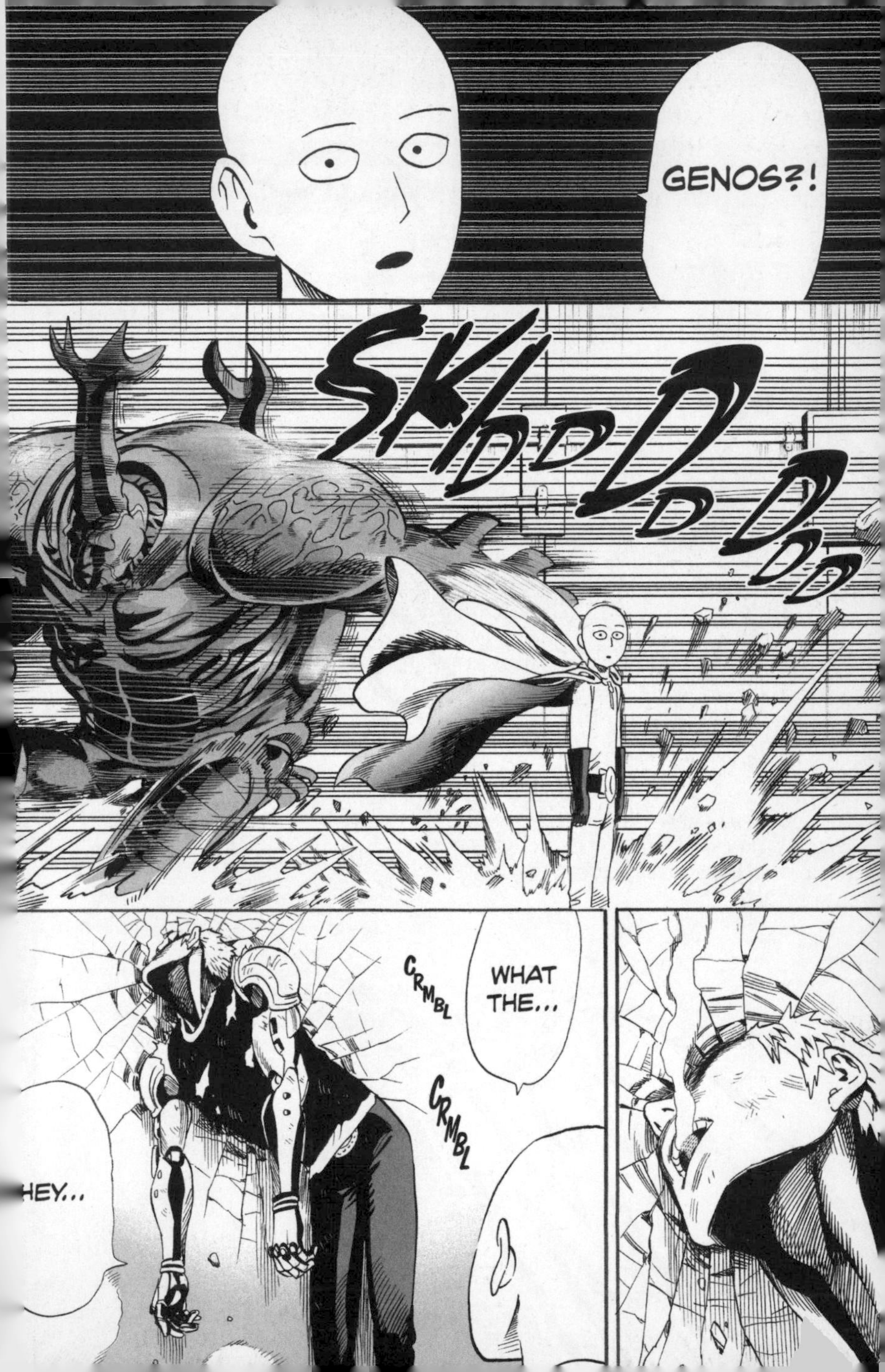
GENOS?!
SKDDDDDDDDD
WHAT THE...
CRMBL
CRMBL
HEY...

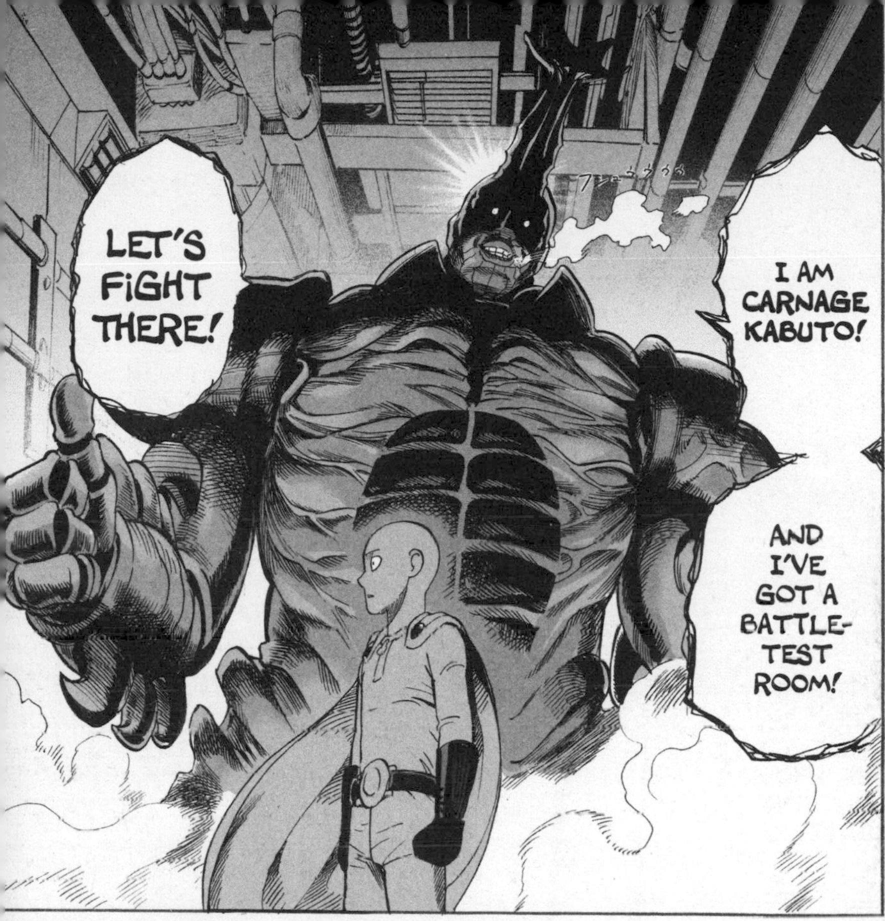
I AM CARNAGE KABUTO!
AND I'VE GOT A BATTLE-TEST ROOM!
LET'S FIGHT THERE!

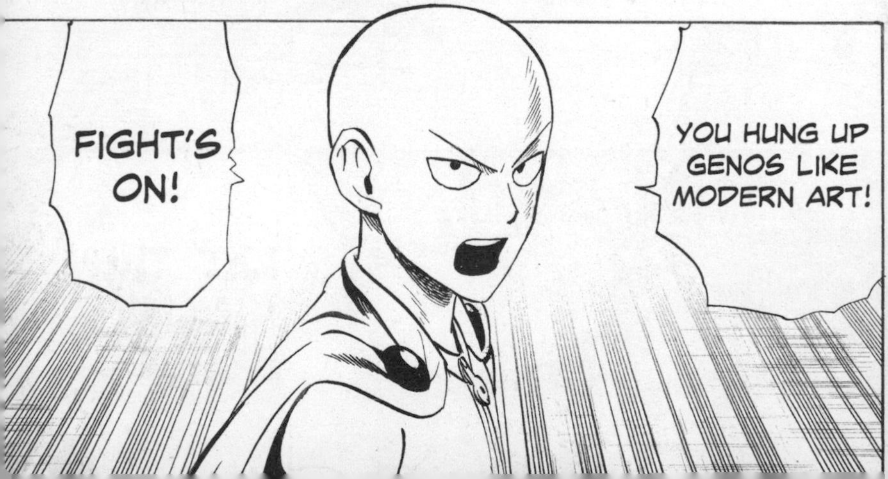
YOU HUNG UP GENOS LIKE MODERN ART!
FIGHT'S ON!

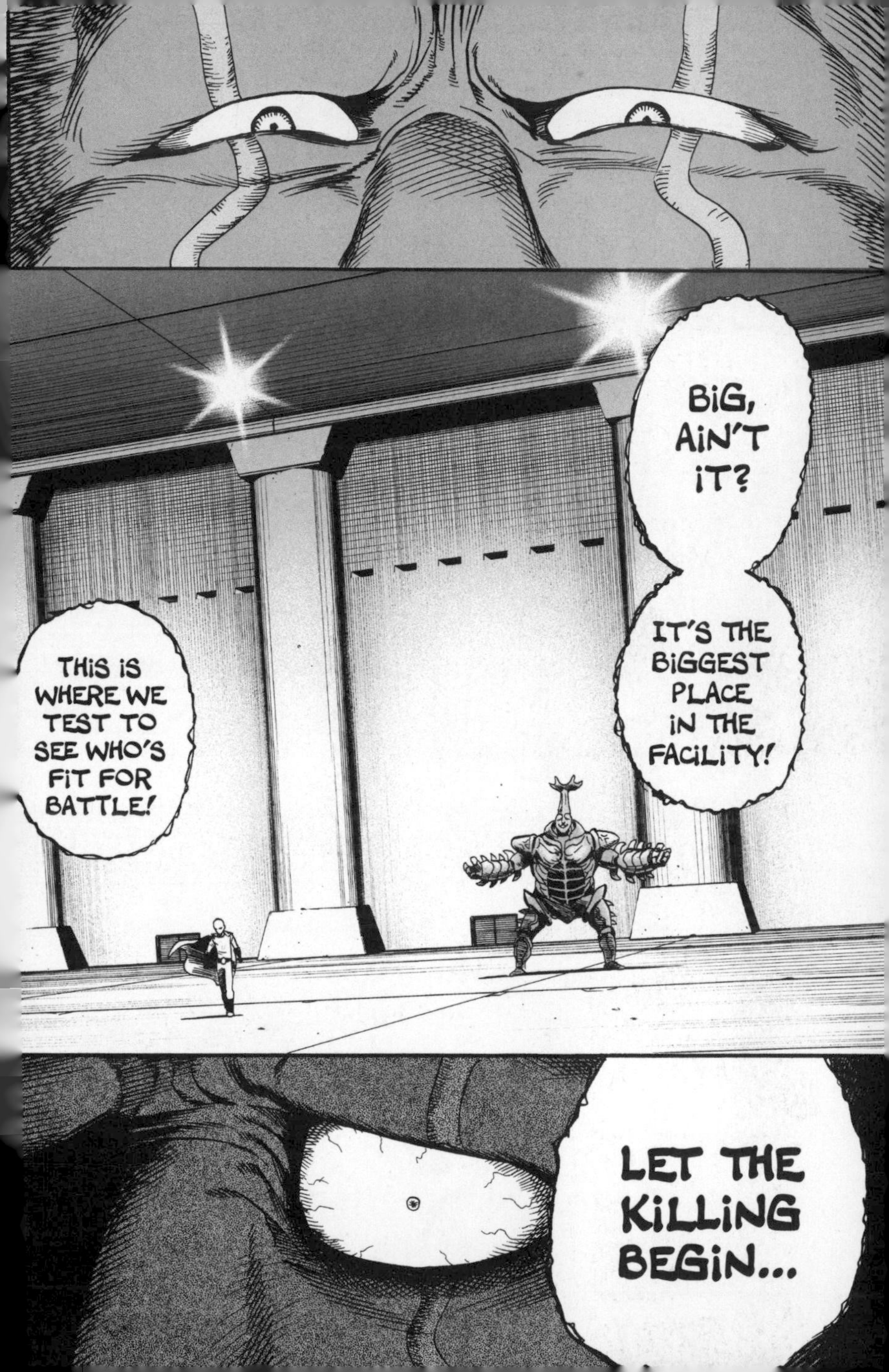
BIG, AIN'T IT?
IT'S THE BIGGEST PLACE IN THE FACILITY!
THIS IS WHERE WE TEST TO SEE WHO'S FIT FOR BATTLE!
LET THE KILLING BEGIN...

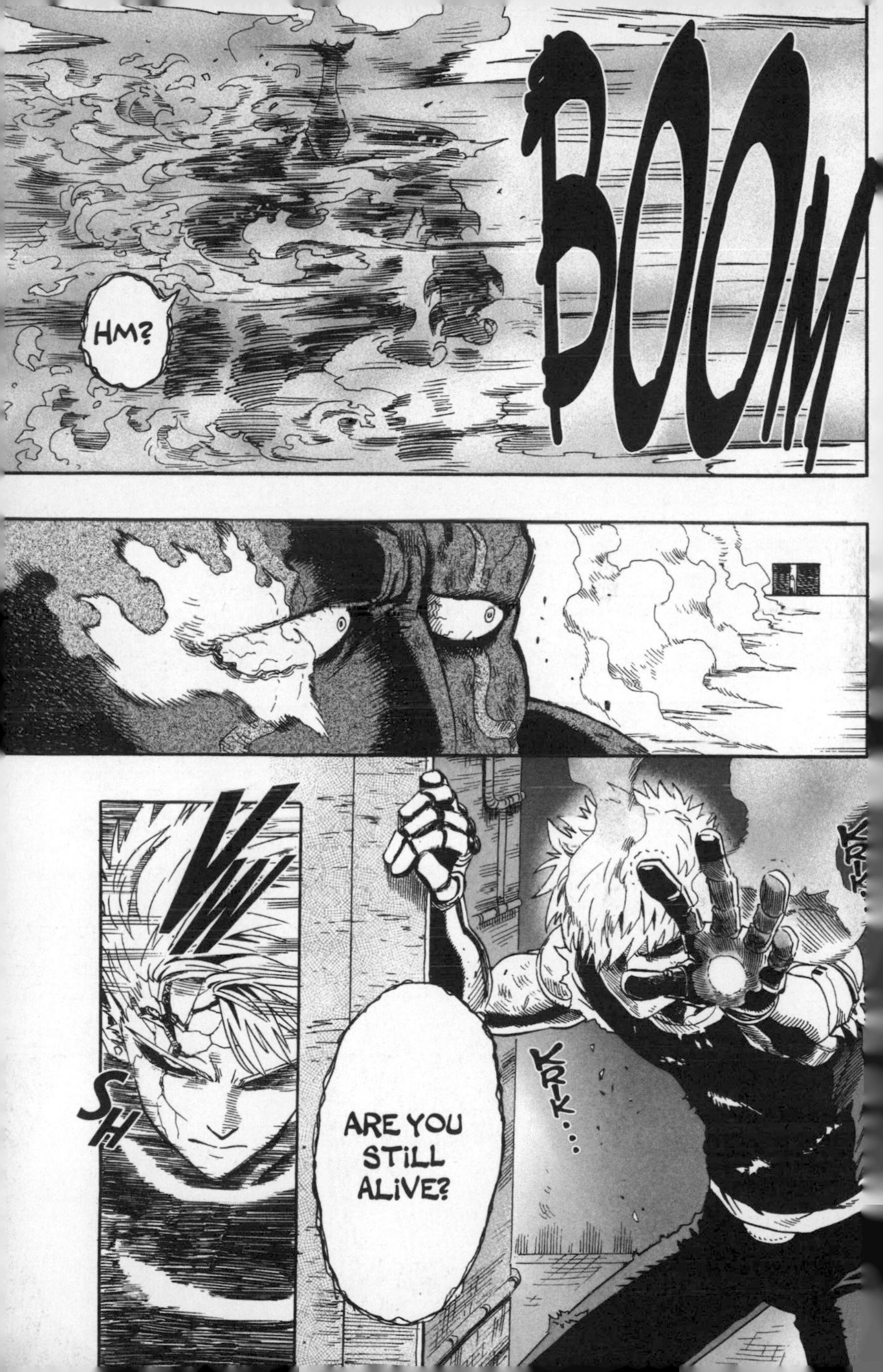
BOOM
HM?
KRIK...
KRIK...
ARE YOU STILL ALIVE?
VM
SH

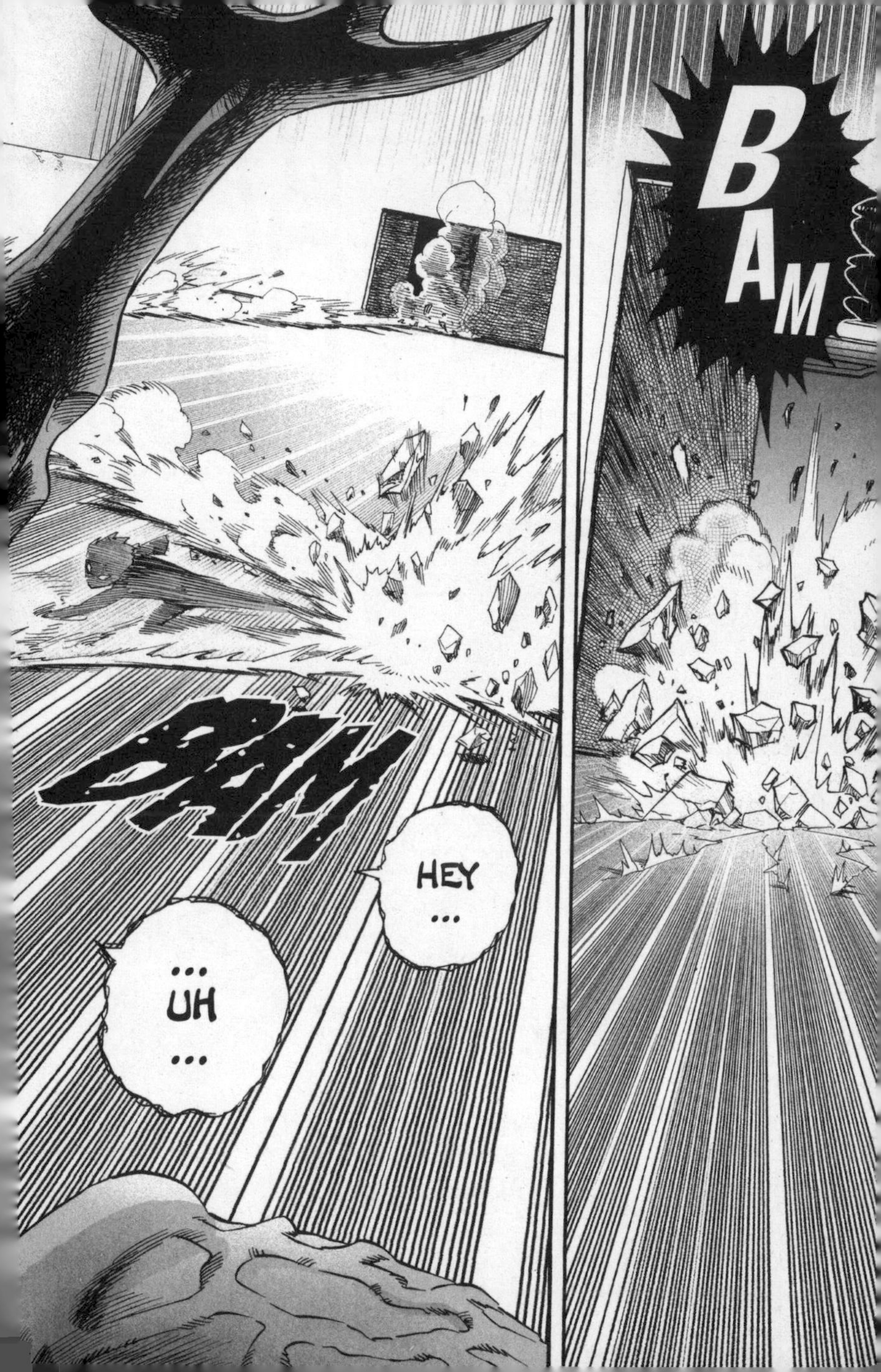
BAM
BAM
HEY ...
... UH ...

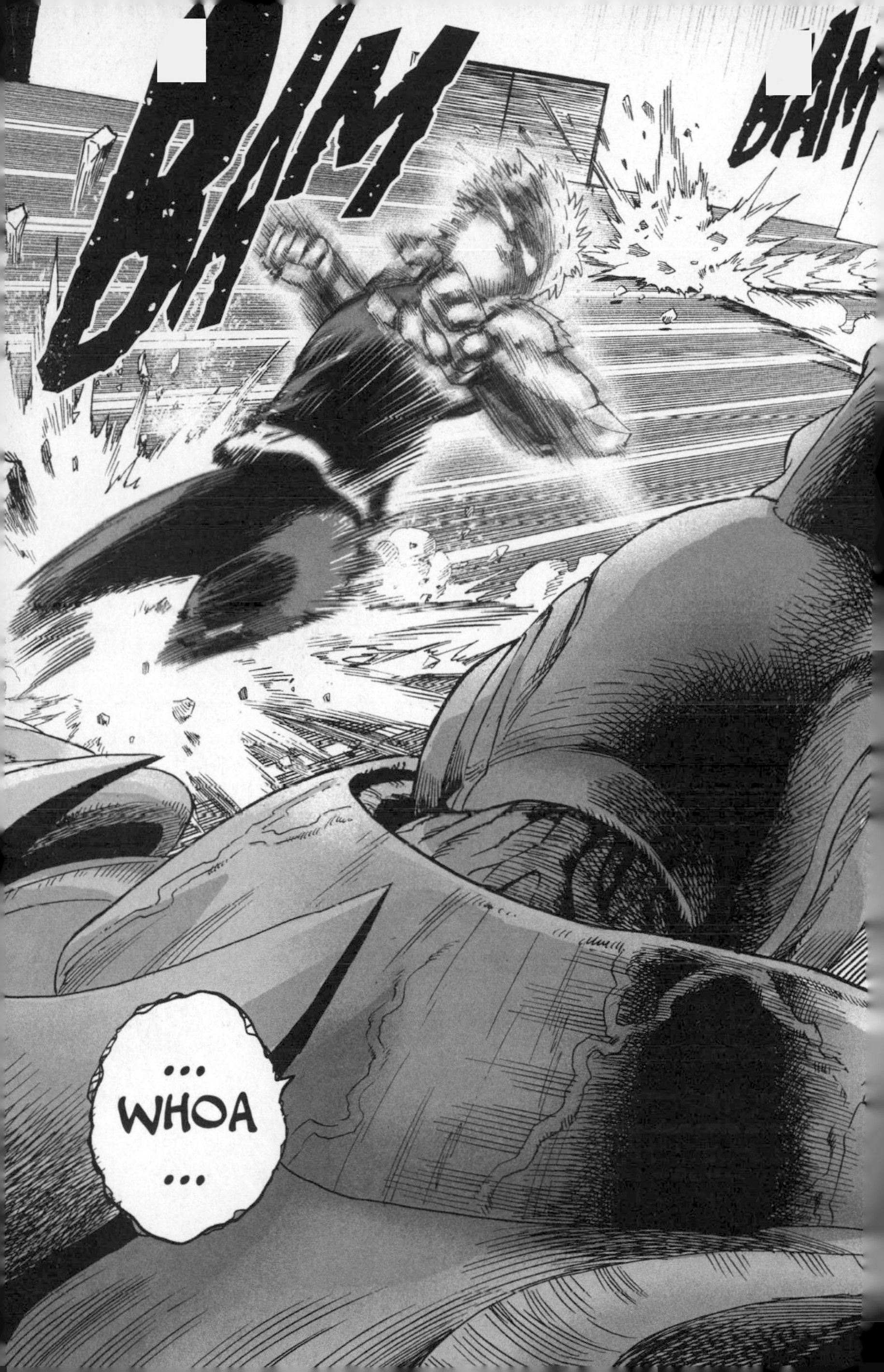
BAM
BAM
... WHOA ...

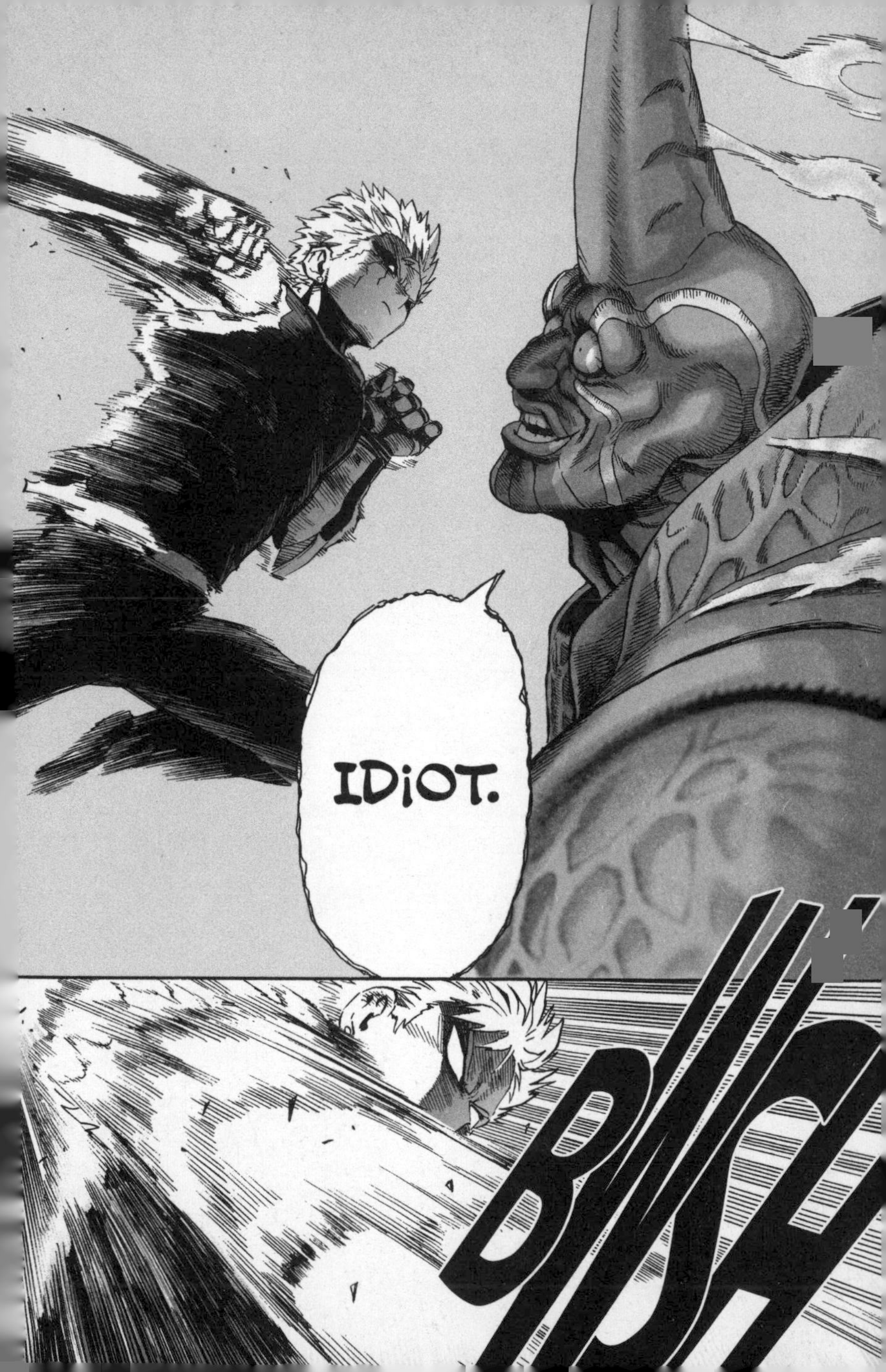
IDiOT.
BISH

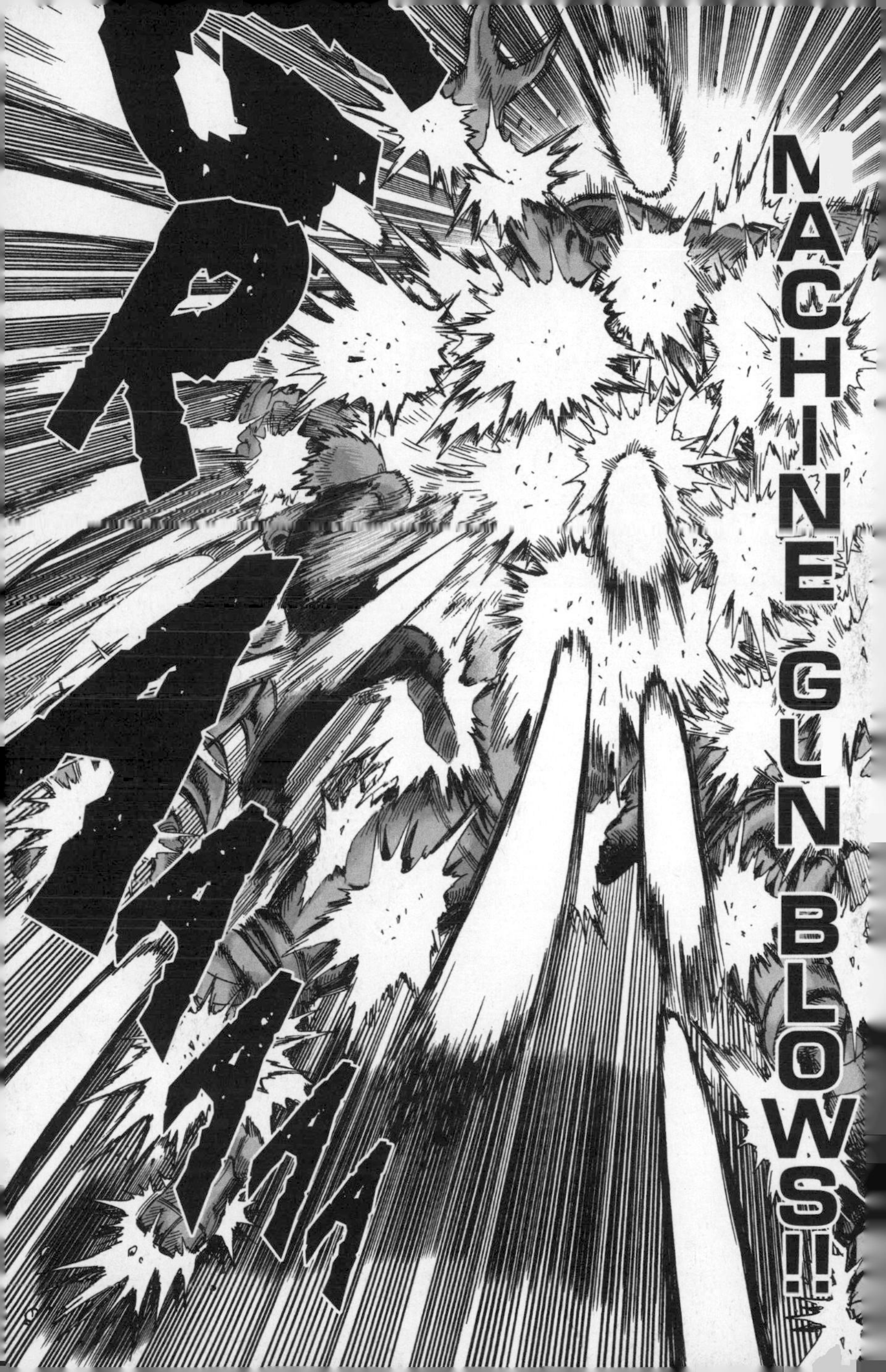
MACHINE GUN BLOWS!!

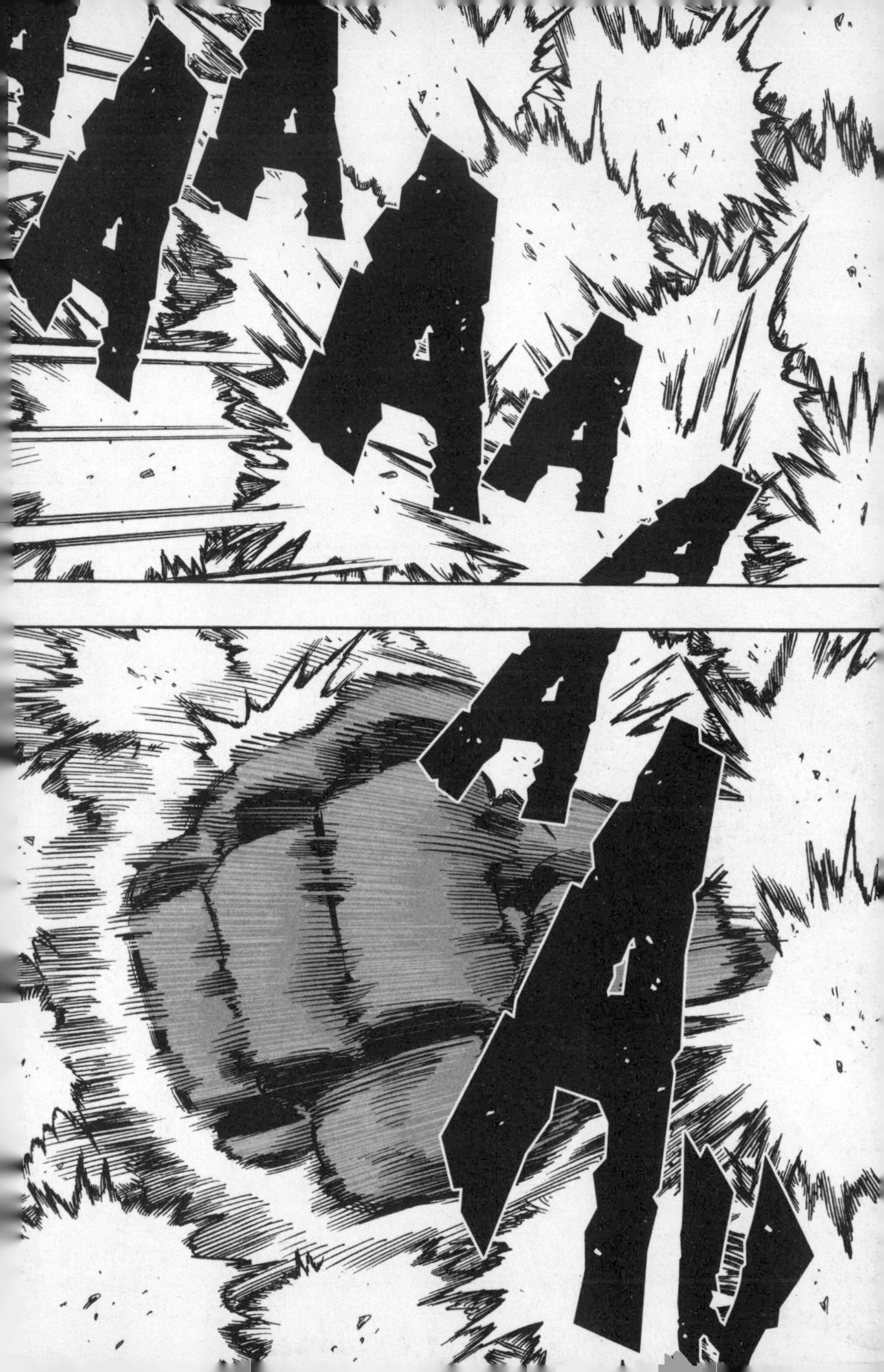
AAAAAAAA!!

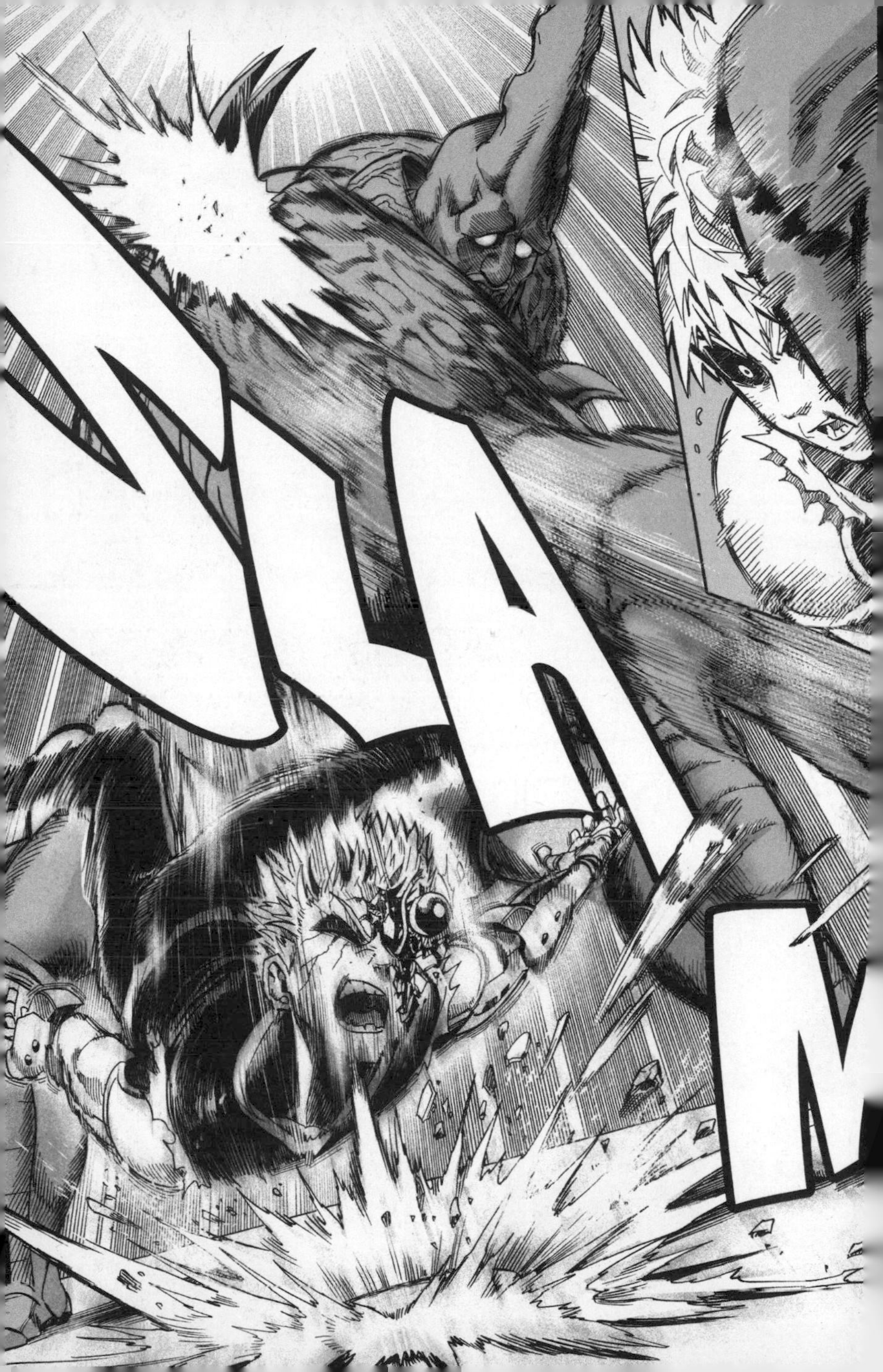

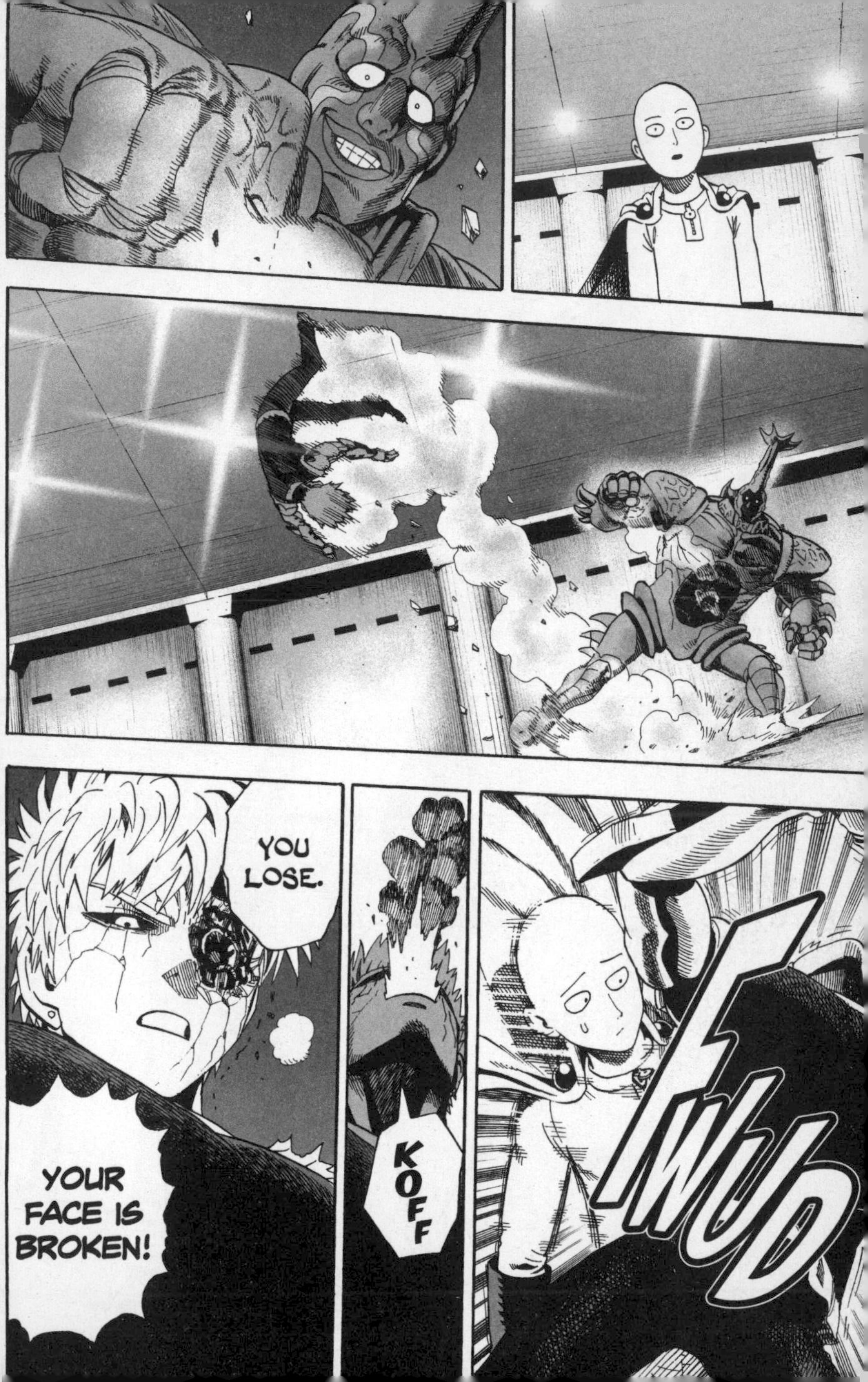
THUD
KOFF
YOU LOSE.
YOUR FACE IS BROKEN!

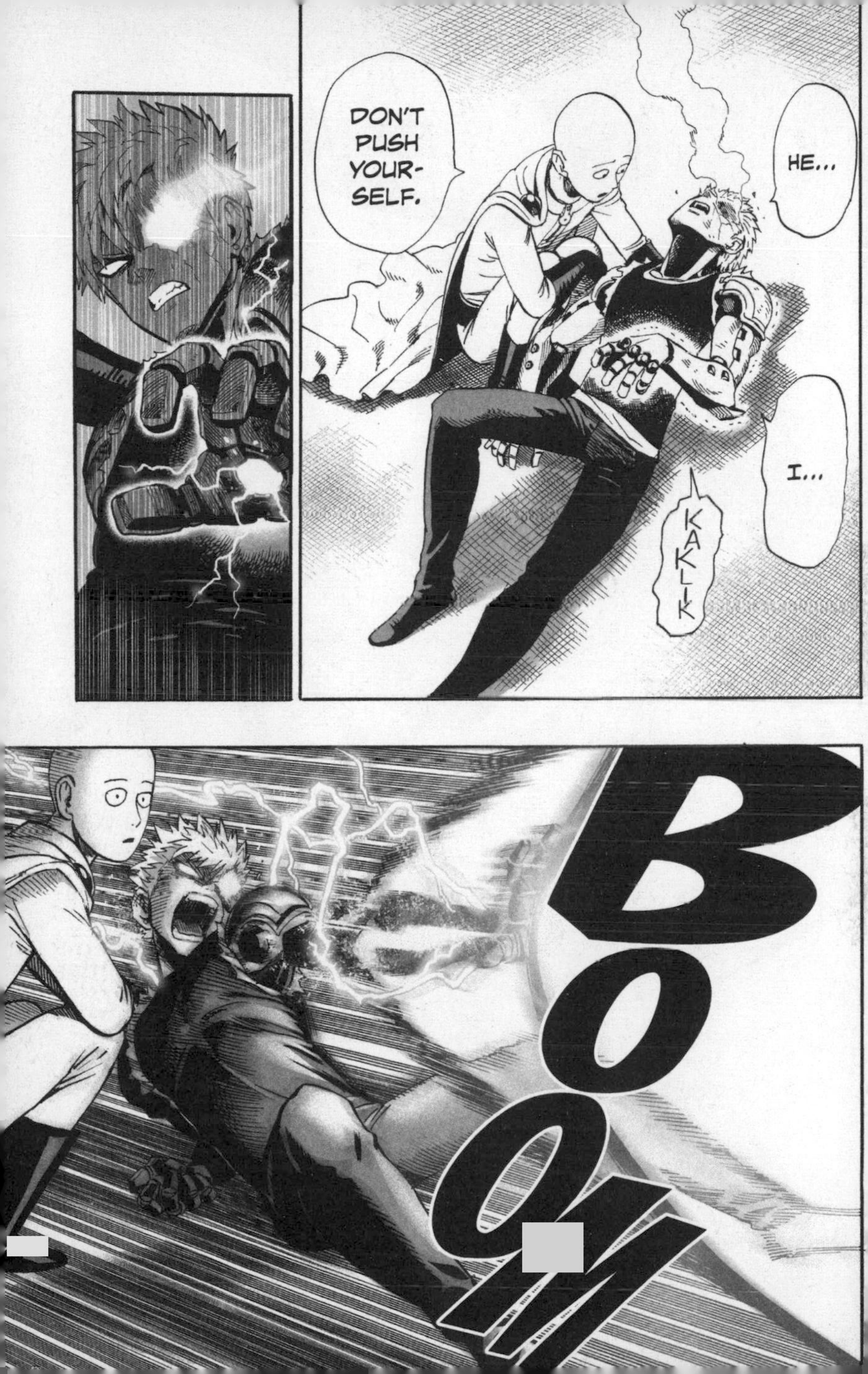
HE...
I...
KAKLIK
DON'T PUSH YOUR-SELF.
BOOM

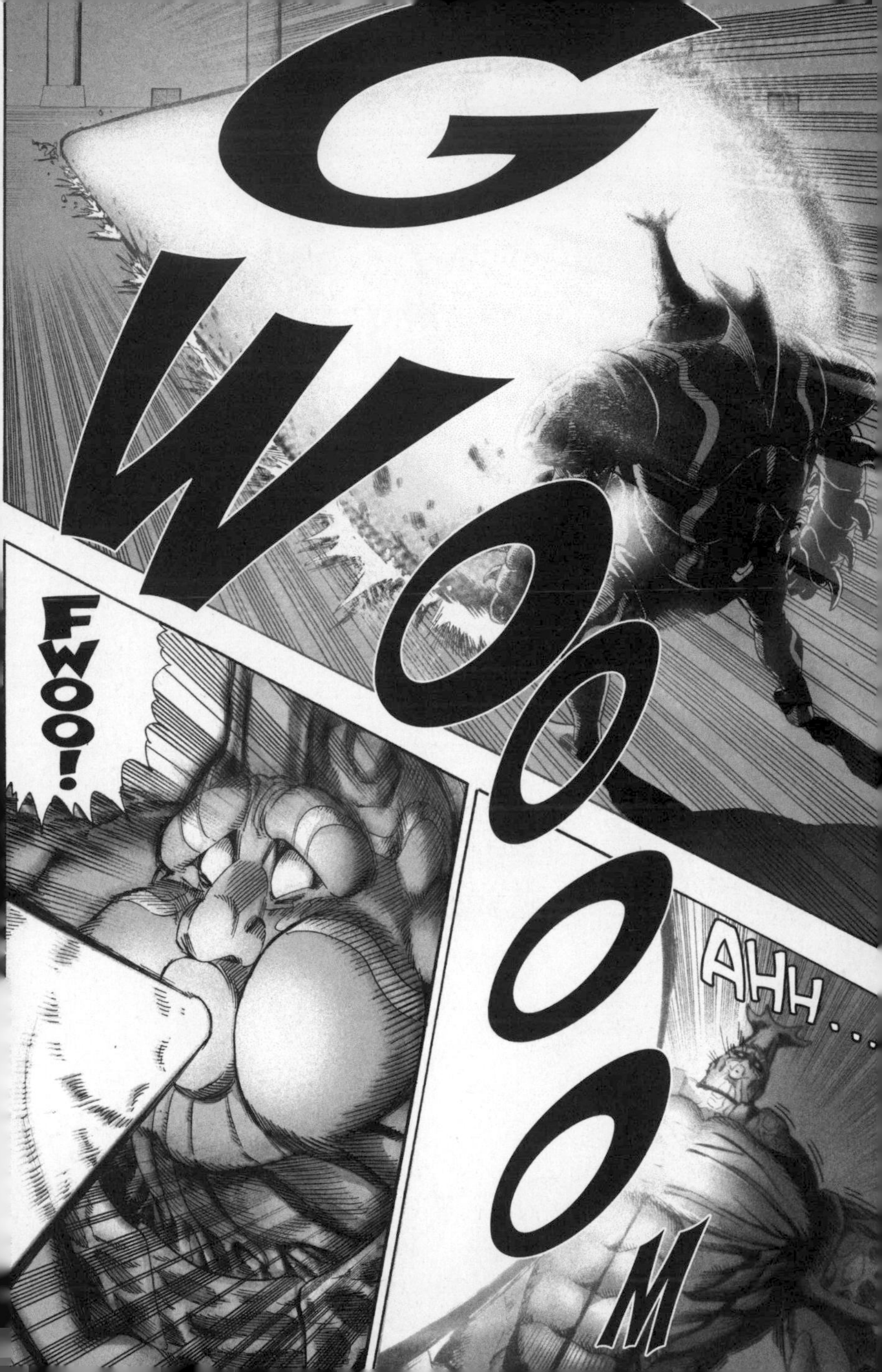
GWOOOOOOM
FWOO!!
AHH...

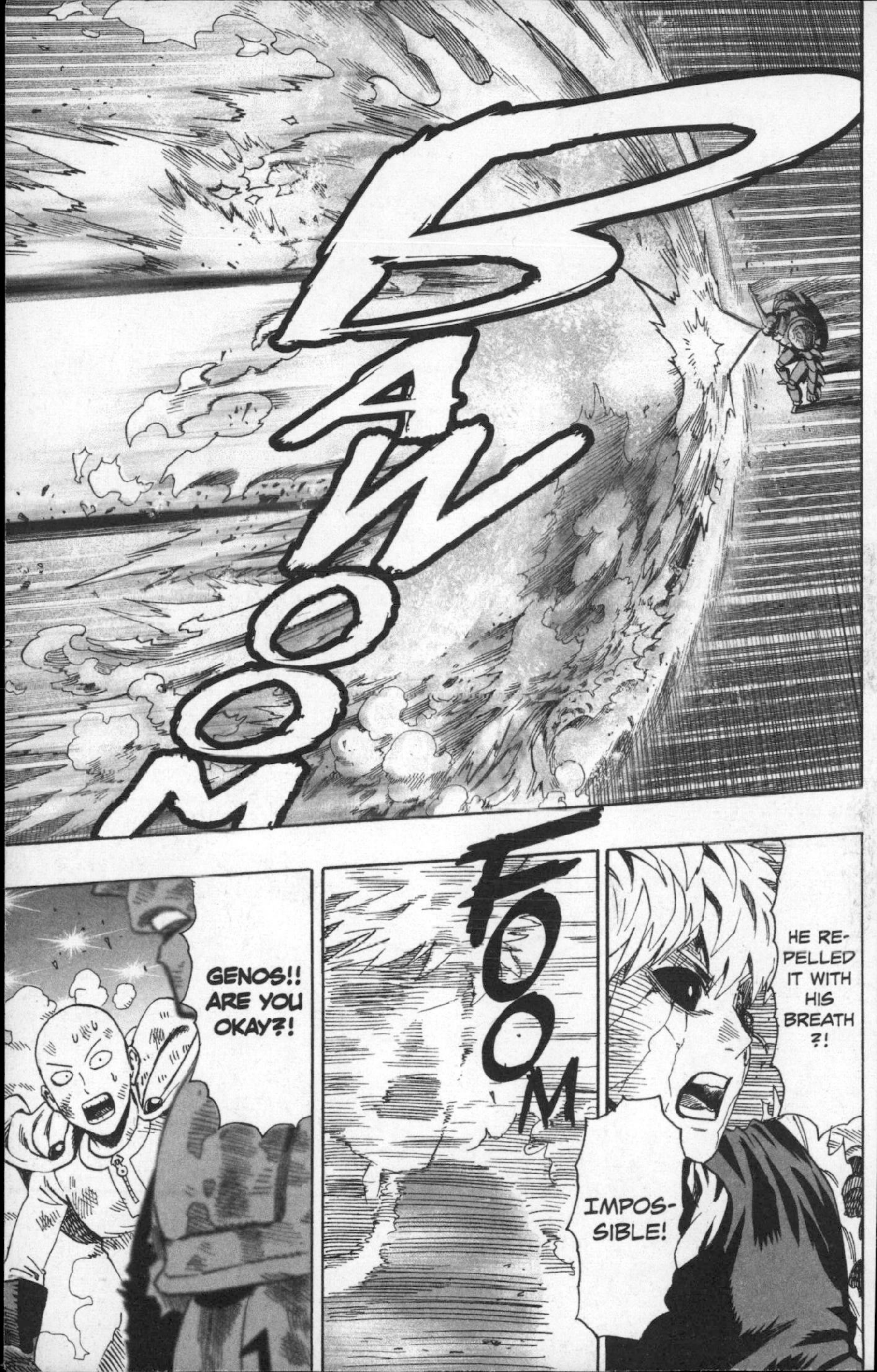
BAWOOM
FOOOM
HE RE-PELLED IT WITH HIS BREATH?!
IMPOS-SIBLE!
GENOS!! ARE YOU OKAY?!

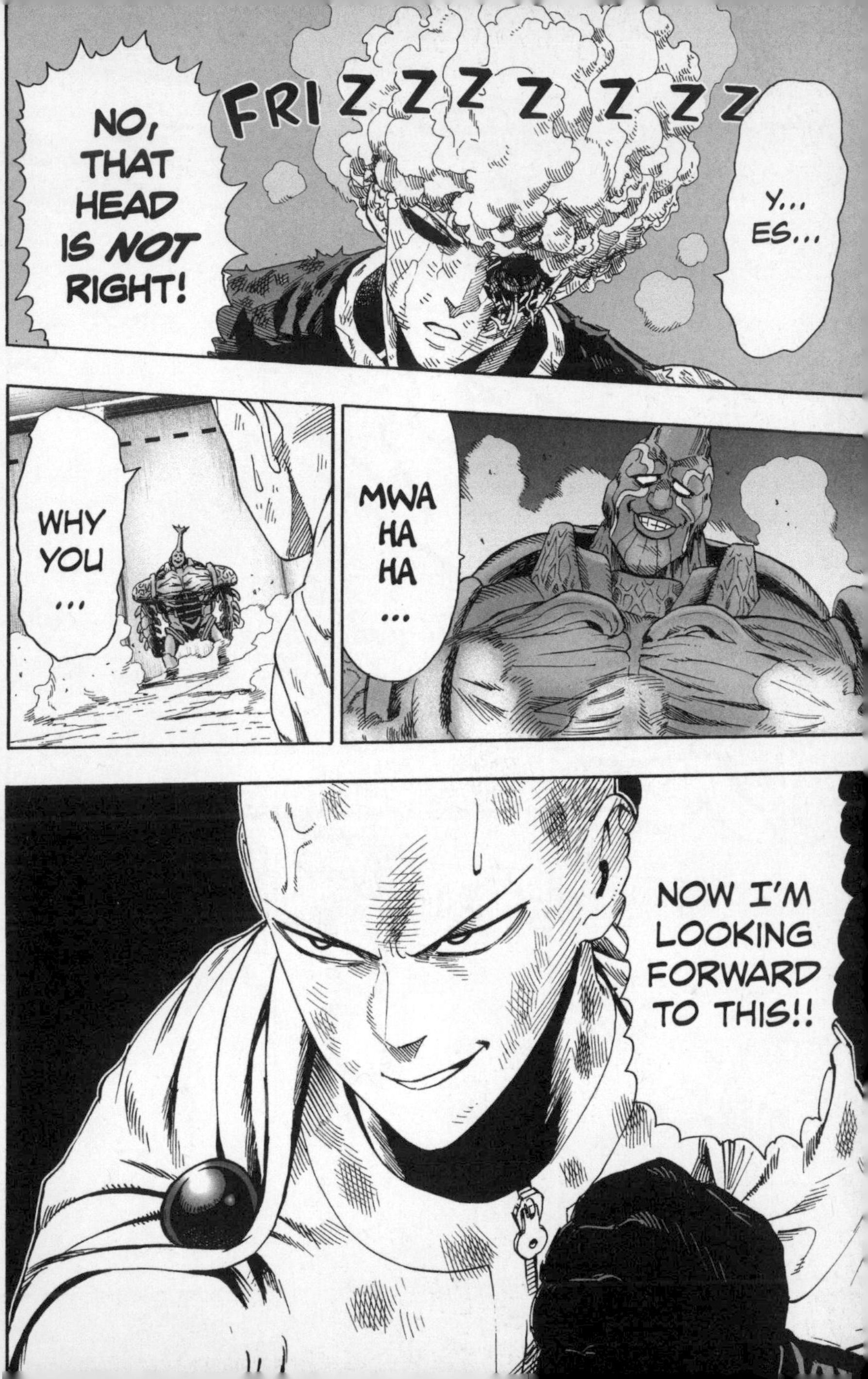
FRI Z Z Z Z Z Z Z
Y... ES...
NO, THAT HEAD IS *NOT* RIGHT!
MWA HA HA ...
WHY YOU ...
NOW I'M LOOKING FORWARD TO THIS!!

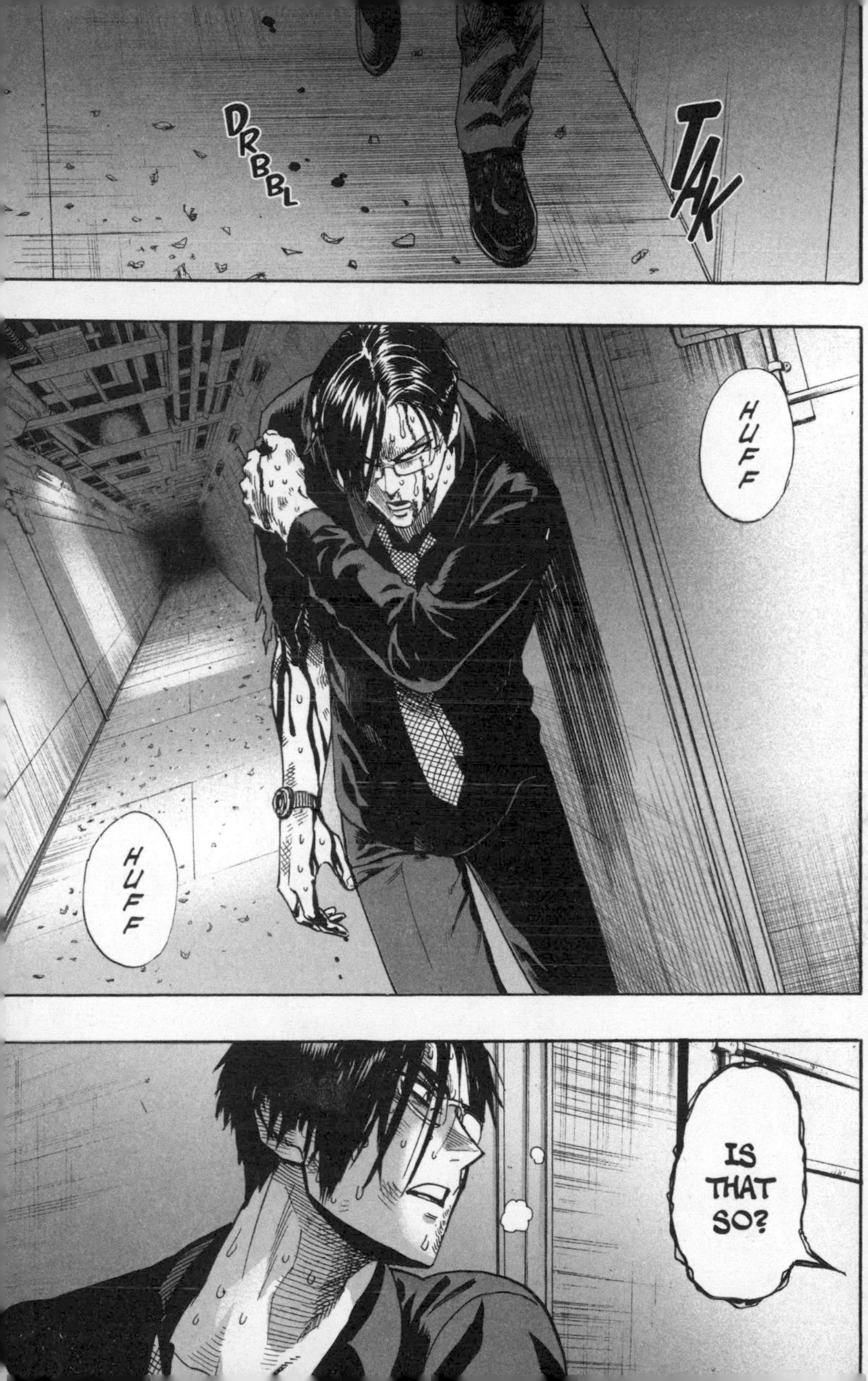
TAK
DRBBL
HUFF
HUFF
IS THAT SO?

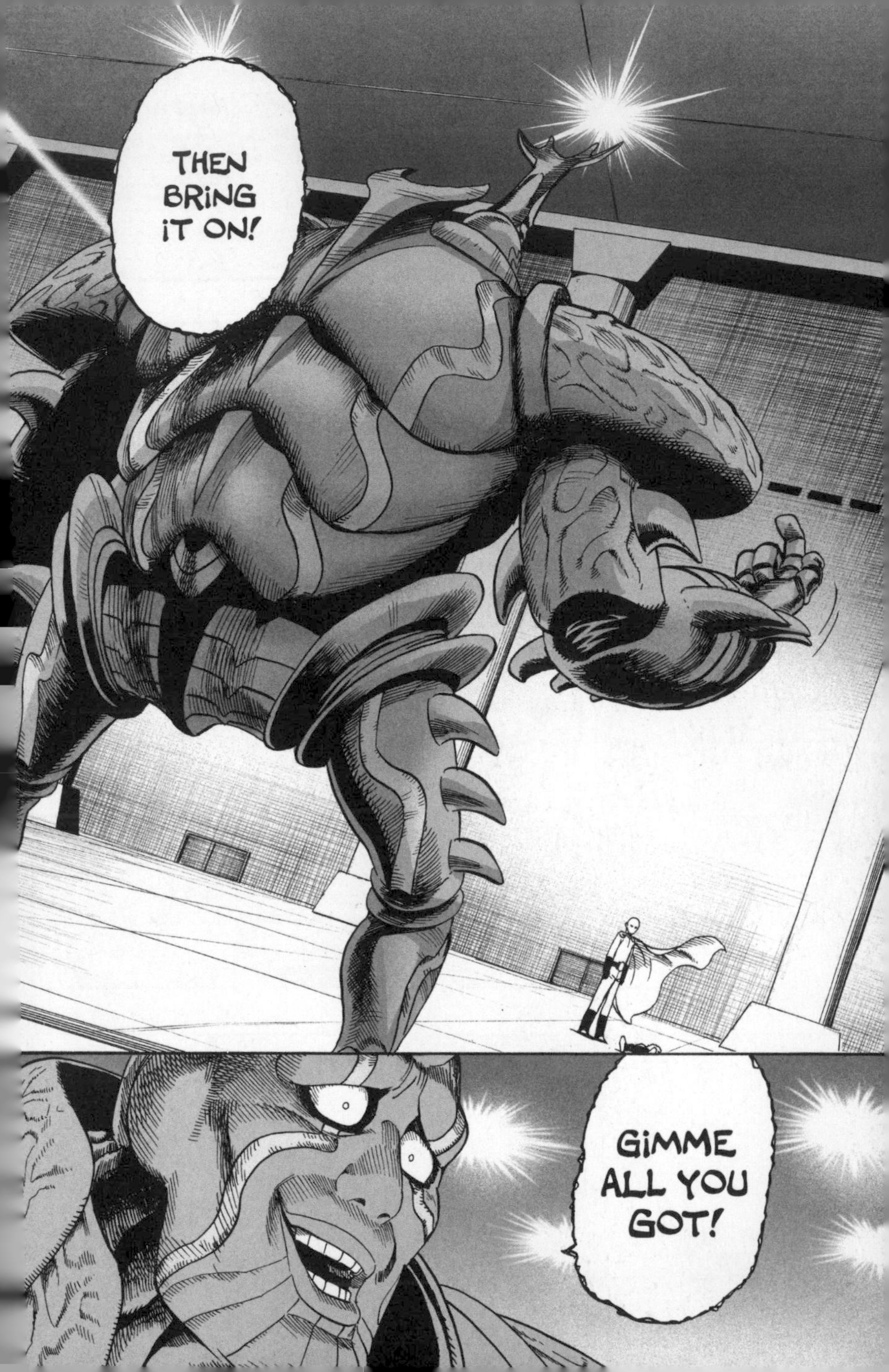
THEN BRING IT ON!
GIMME ALL YOU GOT!

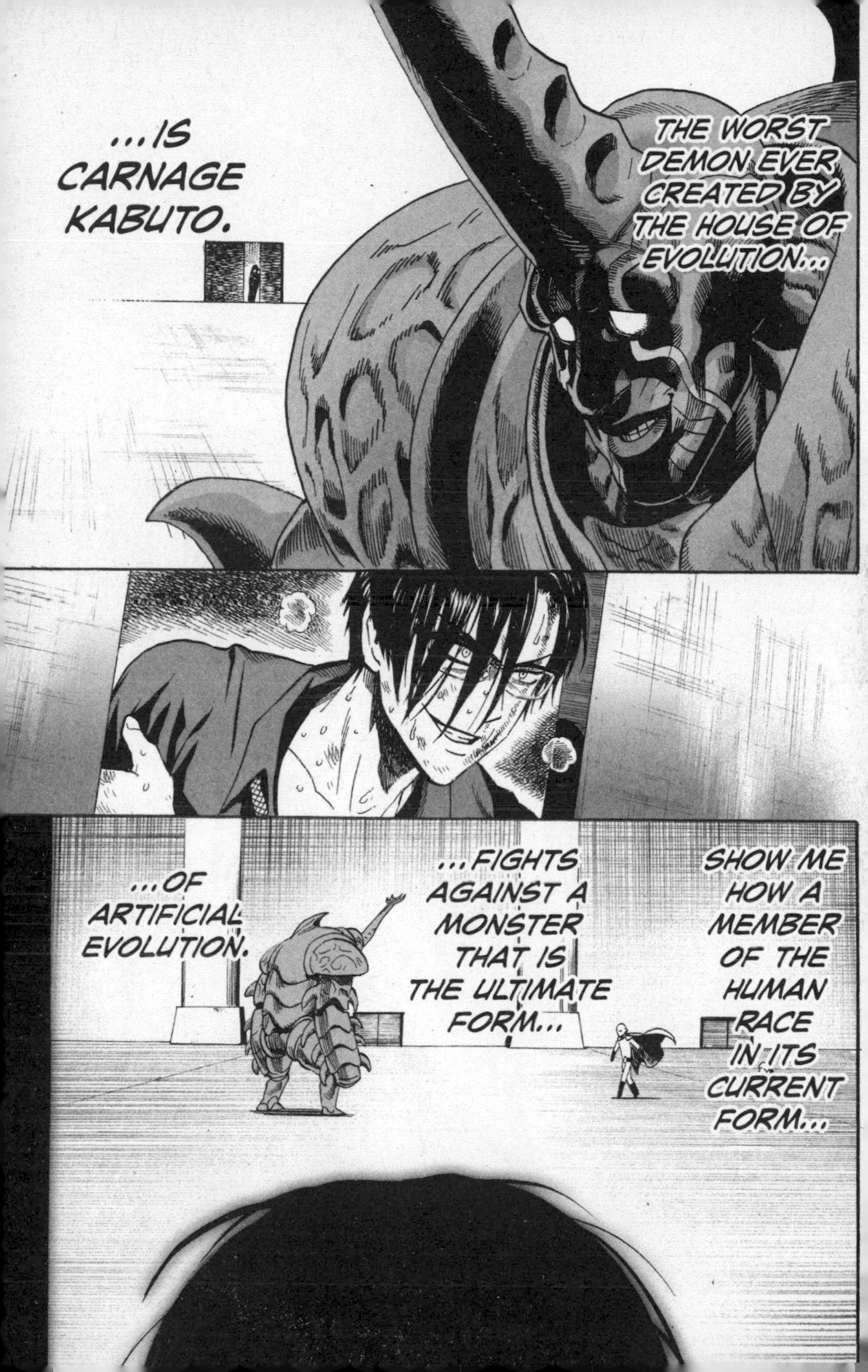
THE WORST DEMON EVER CREATED BY THE HOUSE OF EVOLUTION...
...IS CARNAGE KABUTO.
SHOW ME HOW A MEMBER OF THE HUMAN RACE IN ITS CURRENT FORM...
...FIGHTS AGAINST A MONSTER THAT IS THE ULTIMATE FORM...
...OF ARTIFICIAL EVOLUTION.

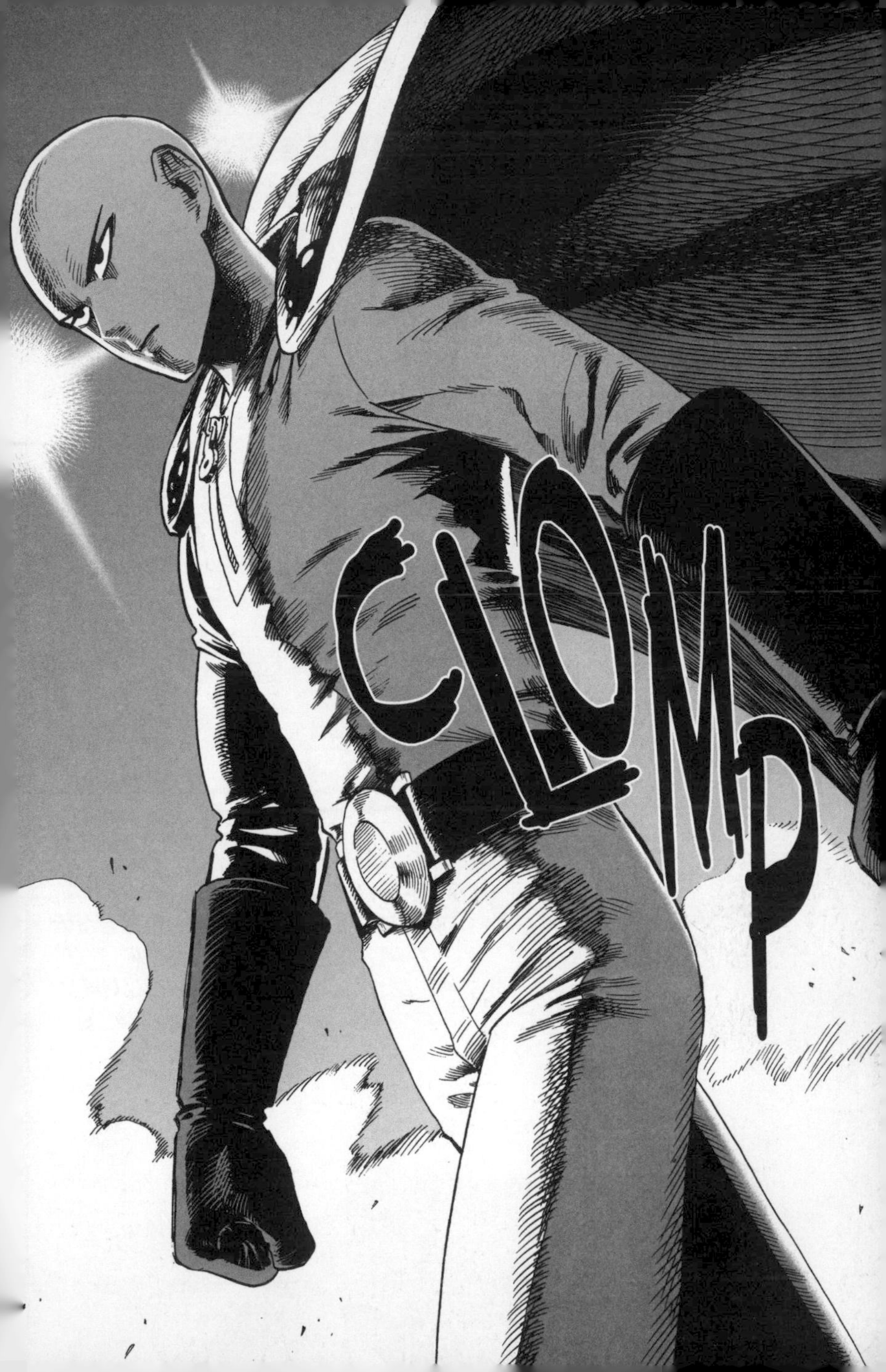
CLOMP

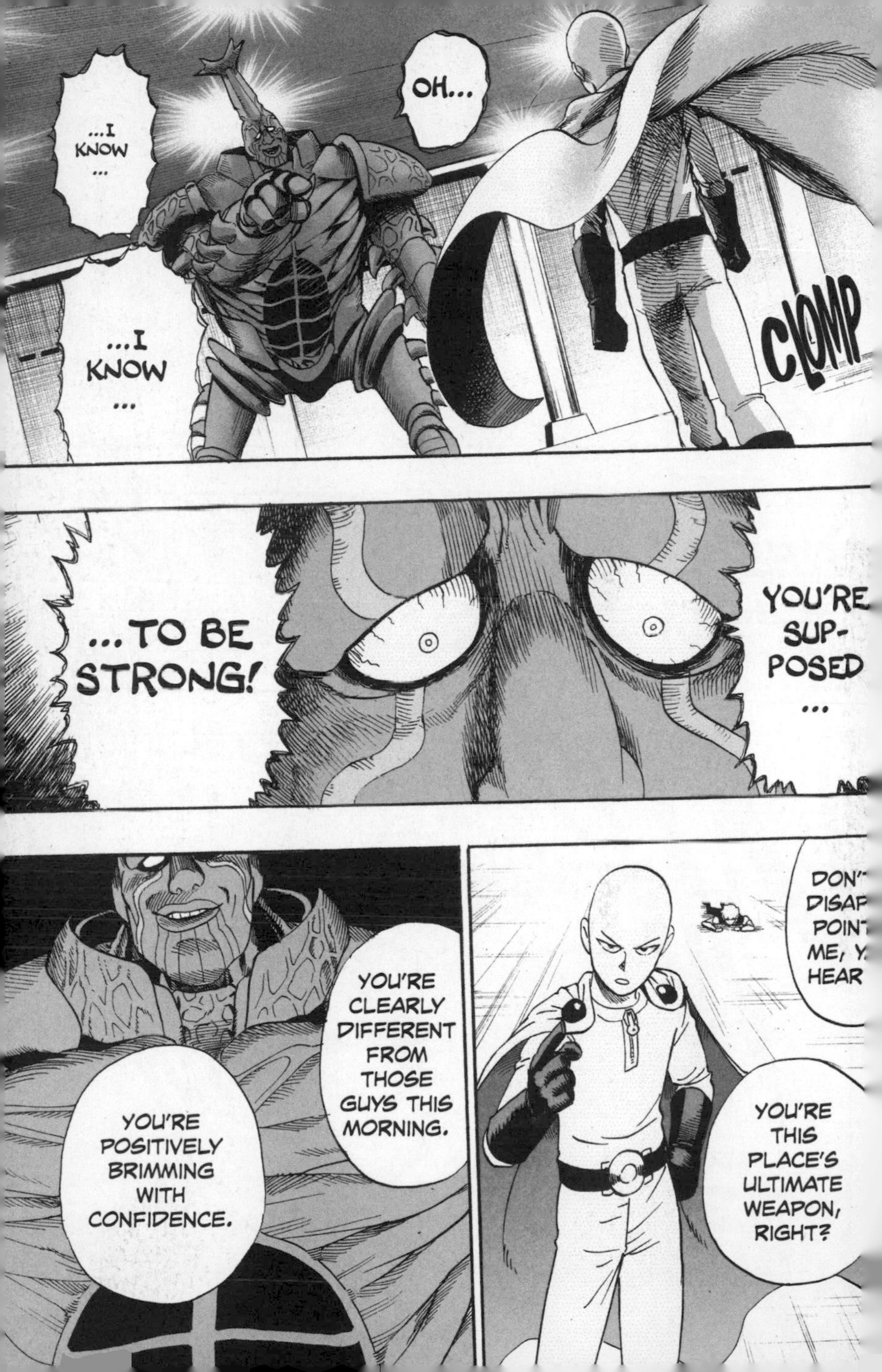
OH...
CLOMP
...I KNOW...
...I KNOW...
YOU'RE SUP-POSED...
...TO BE STRONG!
DON'T DISAP POINT ME, Y HEAR
YOU'RE THIS PLACE'S ULTIMATE WEAPON, RIGHT?
YOU'RE CLEARLY DIFFERENT FROM THOSE GUYS THIS MORNING.
YOU'RE POSITIVELY BRIMMING WITH CONFIDENCE.

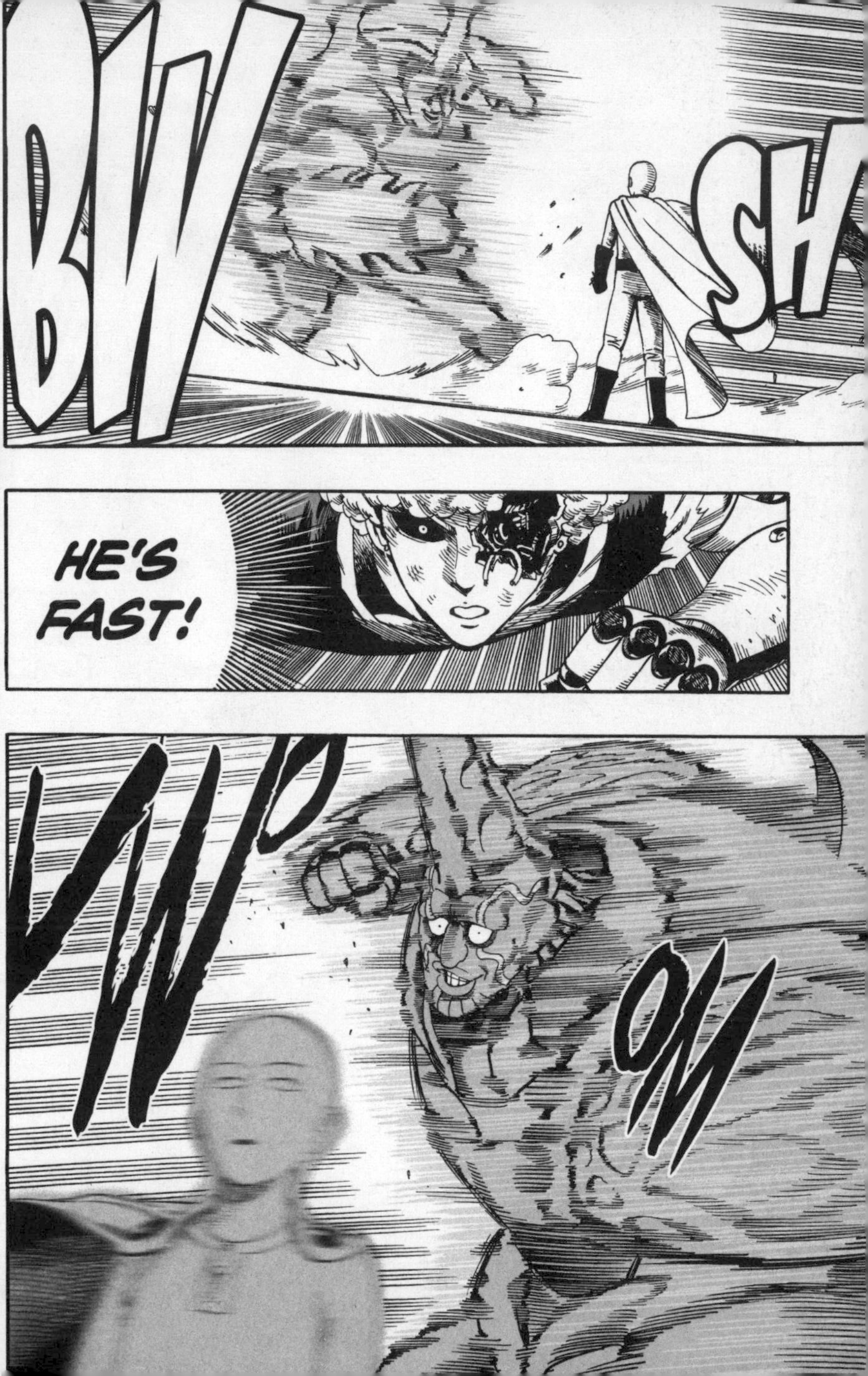
SH
BW
HE'S FAST!

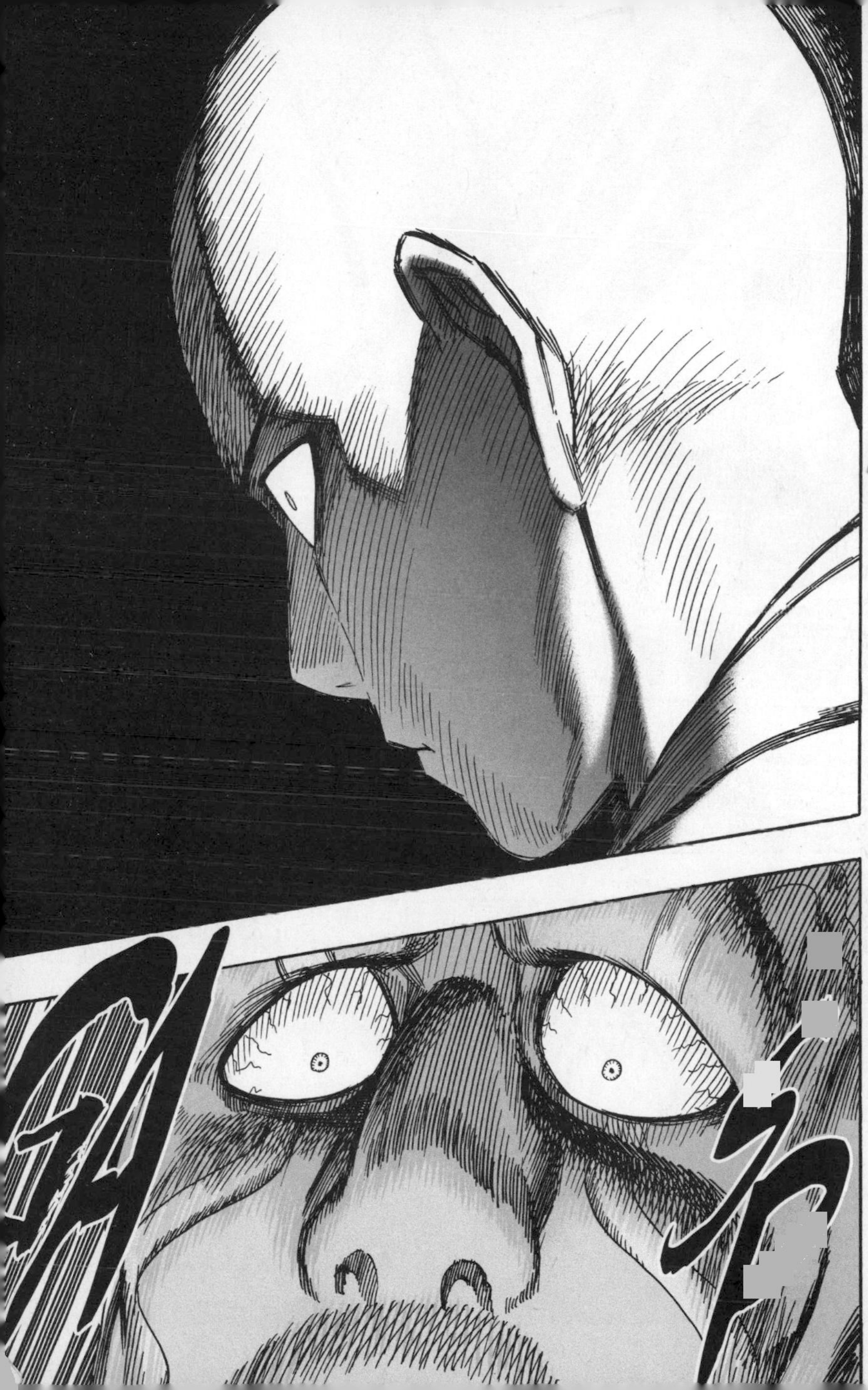

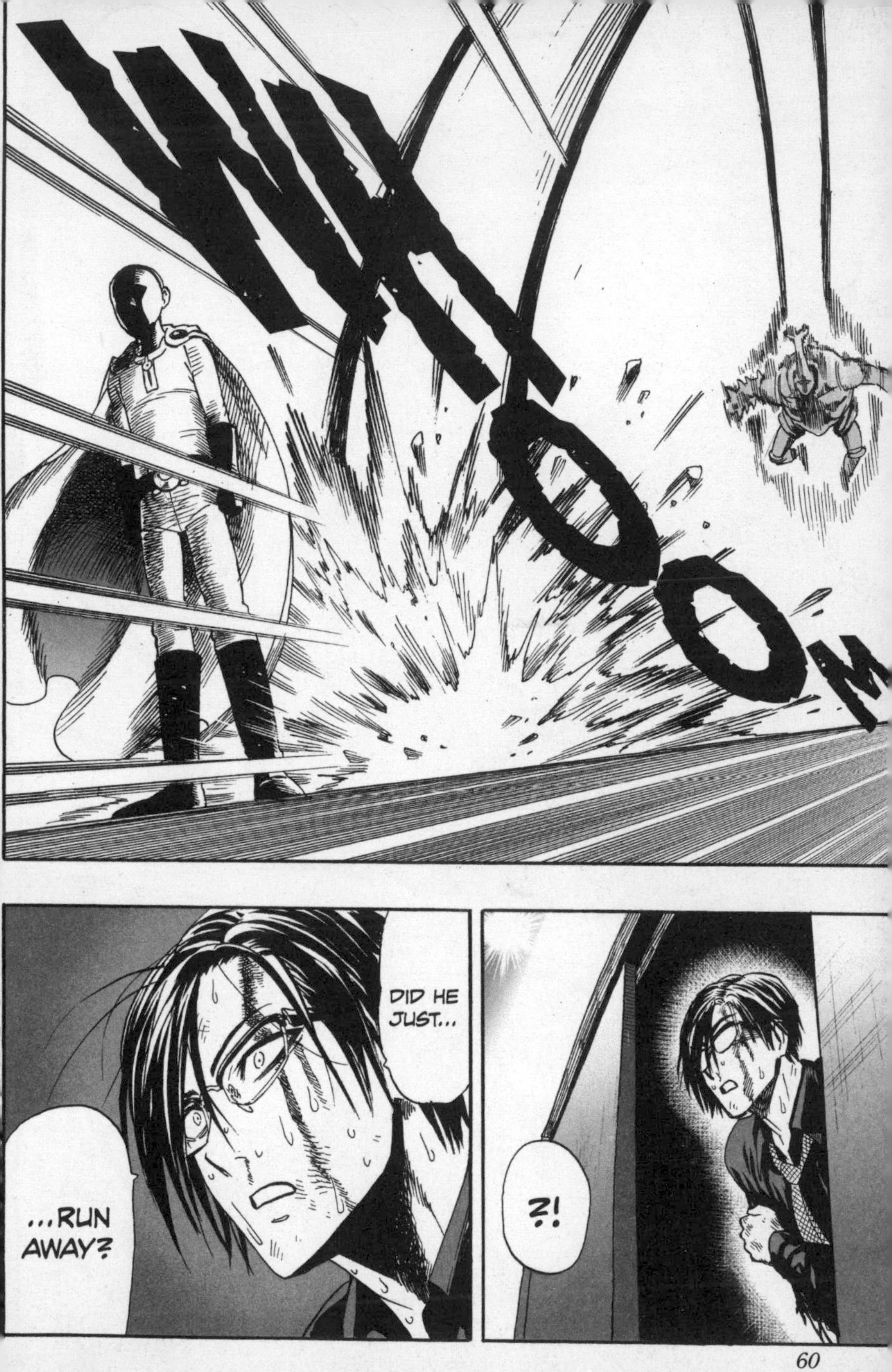
WHOOOM
?!
DID HE JUST...
...RUN AWAY?

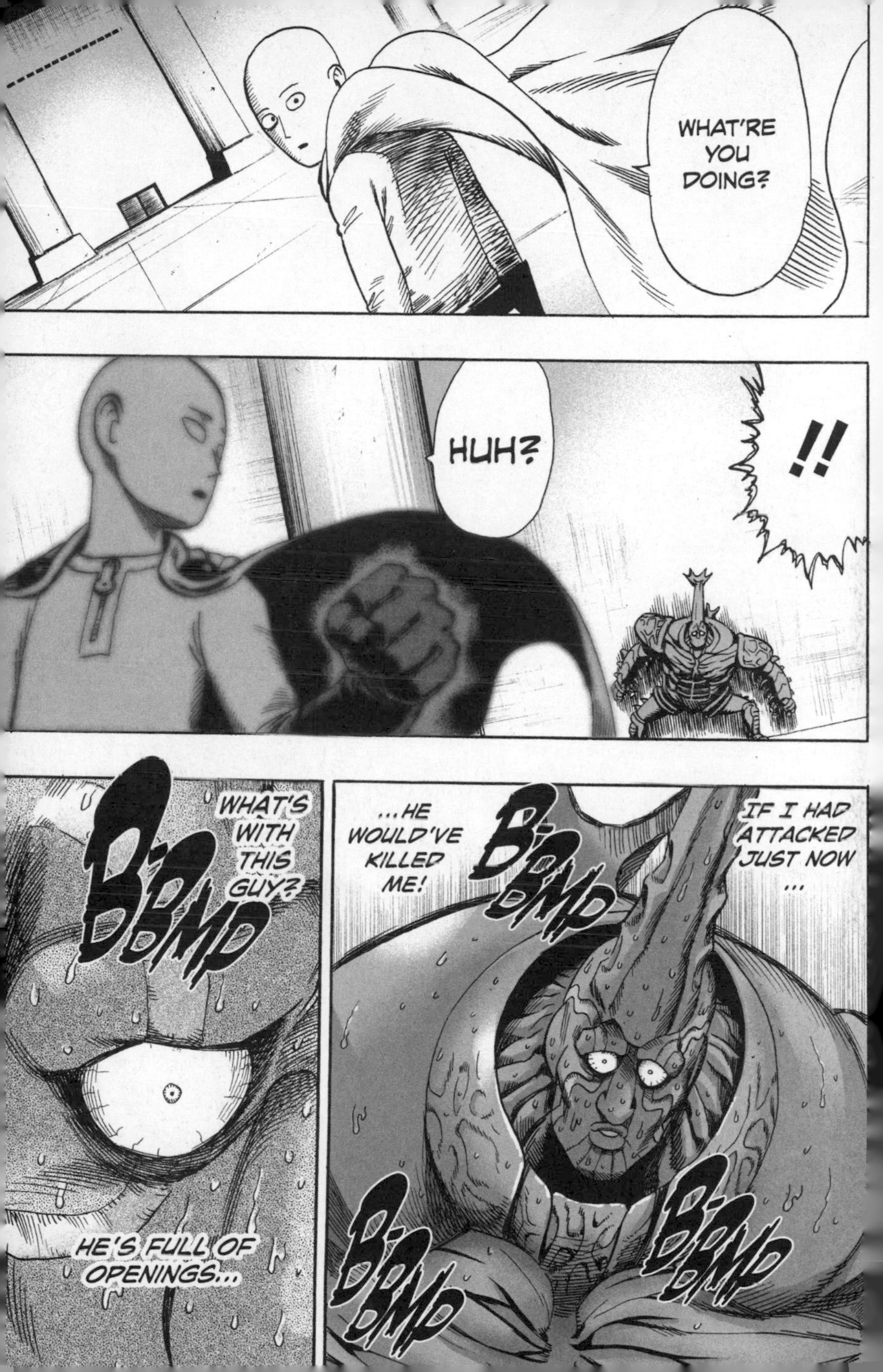
WHAT'RE YOU DOING?
!!
HUH?
IF I HAD ATTACKED JUST NOW ...
B-BMP
...HE WOULD'VE KILLED ME!
B-BMP
B-BMP
WHAT'S WITH THIS GUY?
B-BMP
HE'S FULL OF OPENINGS...

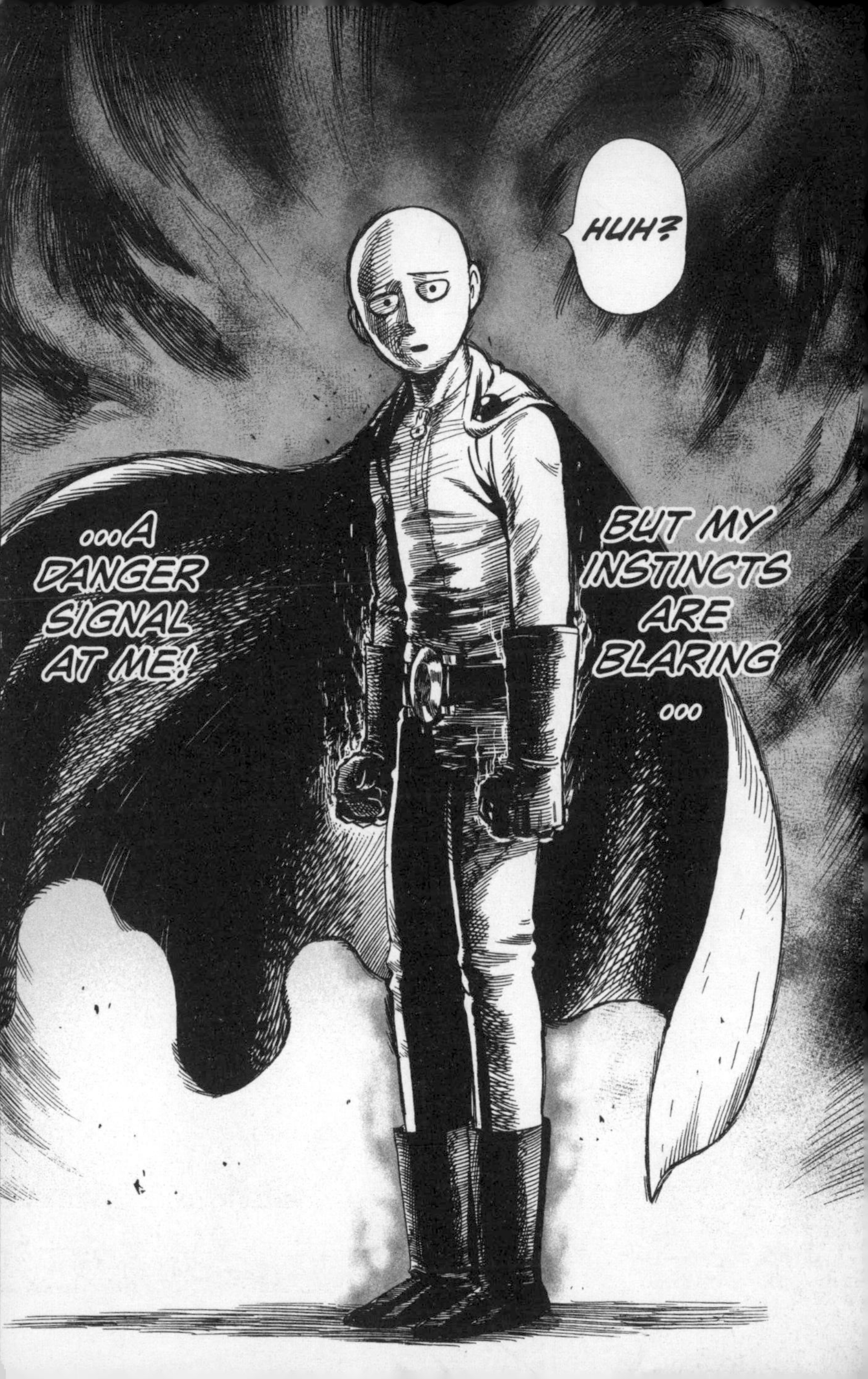
HUH?
BUT MY INSTINCTS ARE BLARING...
...A DANGER SIGNAL AT ME!

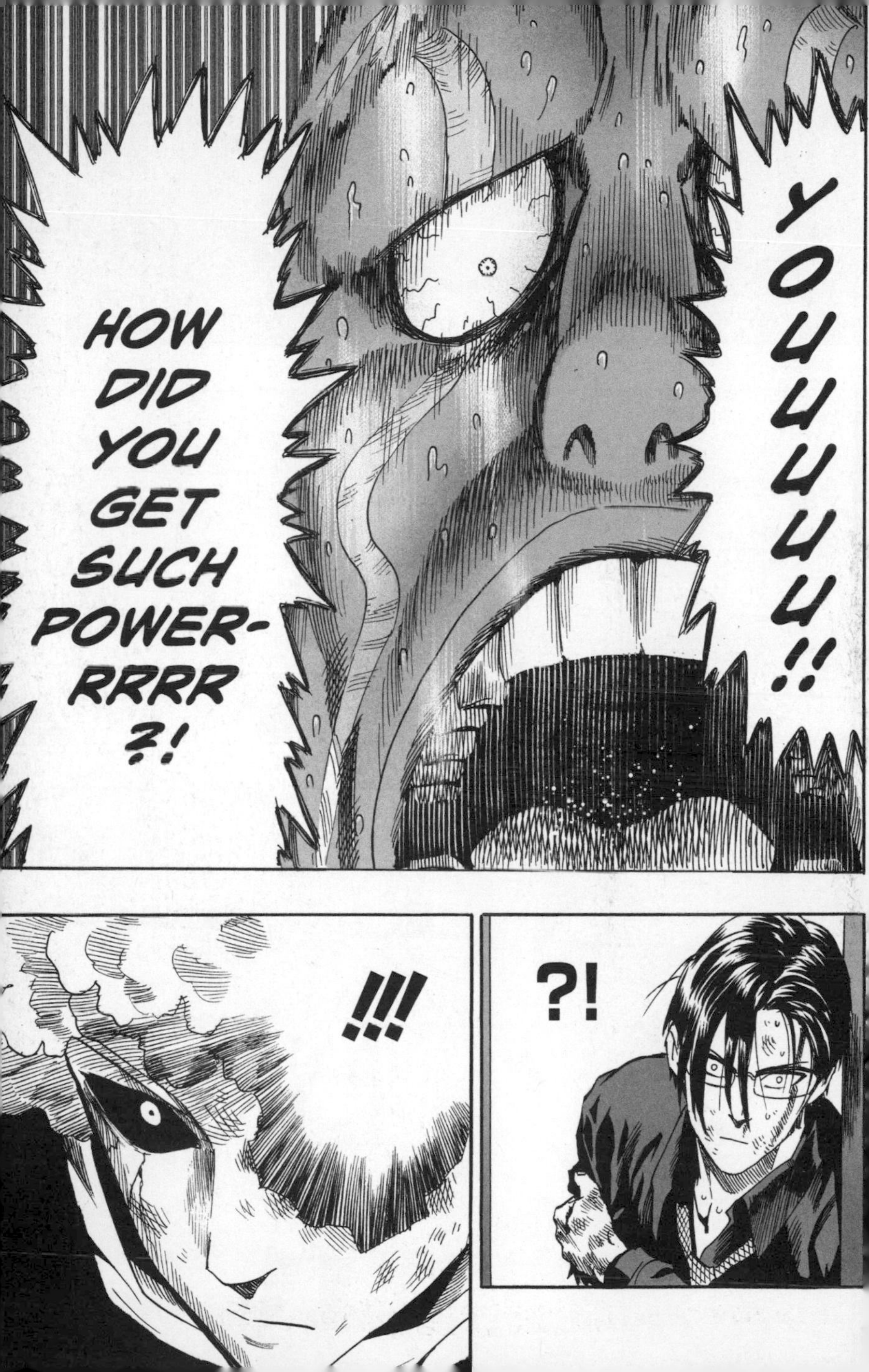
YOUUUUU!!
HOW DID YOU GET SUCH POWER-RRRR ?!
?!
!!!

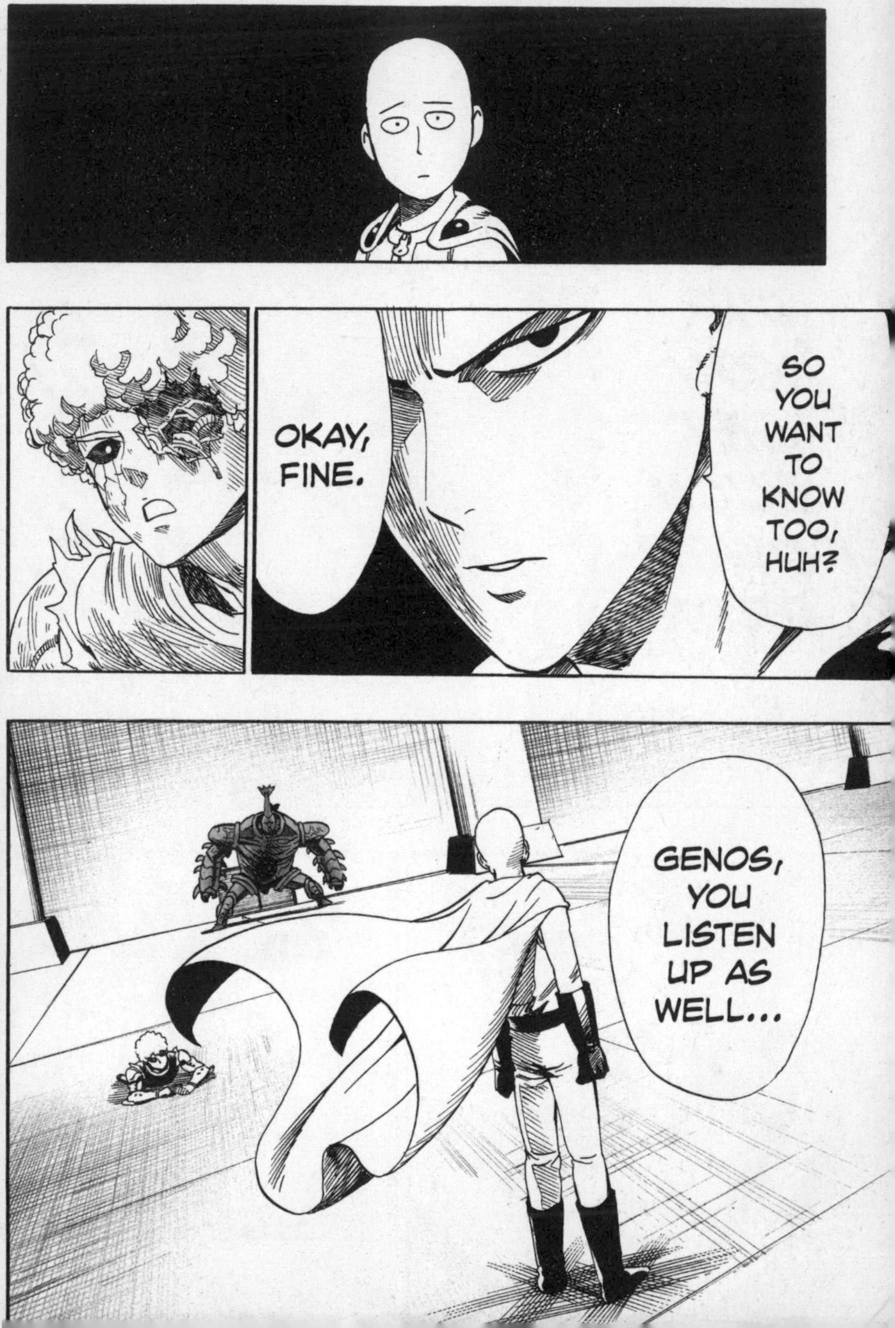
SO YOU WANT TO KNOW TOO, HUH?
OKAY, FINE.
GENOS, YOU LISTEN UP AS WELL...

PUNCH 11: THE SECRET TO STRENGTH

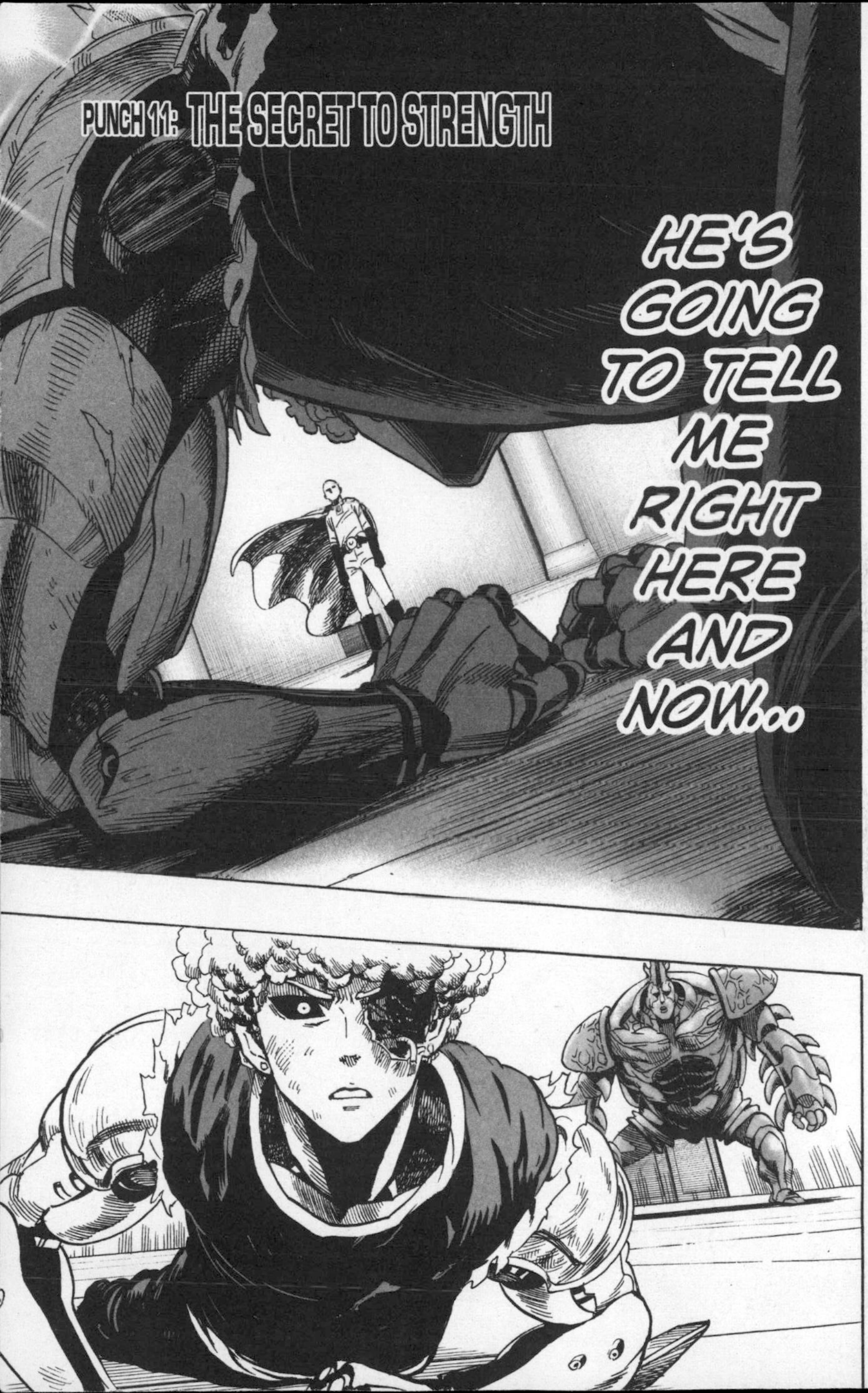
HE'S GOING TO TELL ME RIGHT HERE AND NOW...

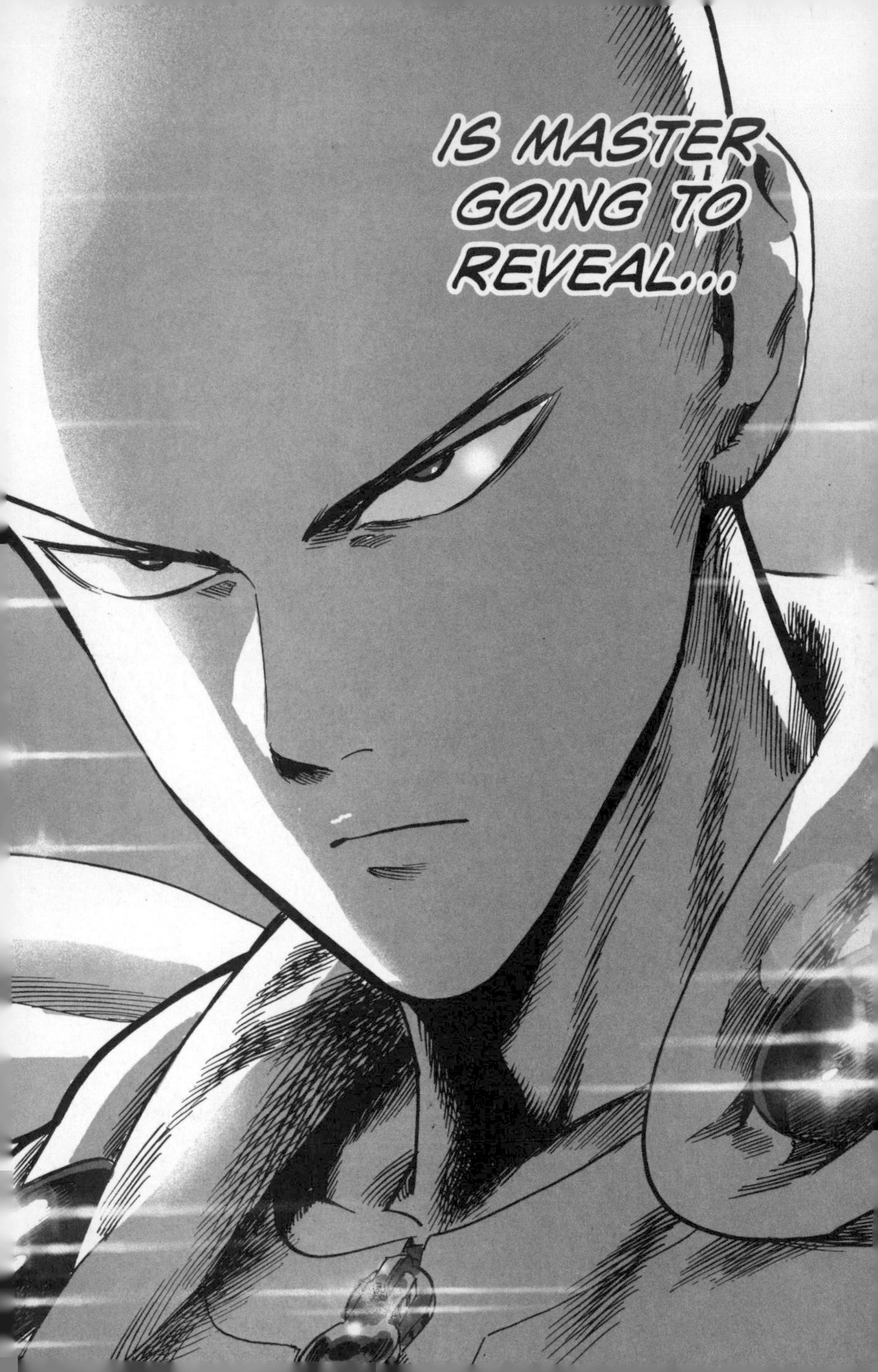
IS MASTER GOING TO REVEAL...

PUNCH 11: THE SECRET TO STRENGTH

...THE SECRET TO HIS STRENGTH?

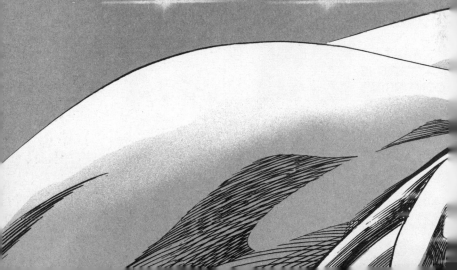

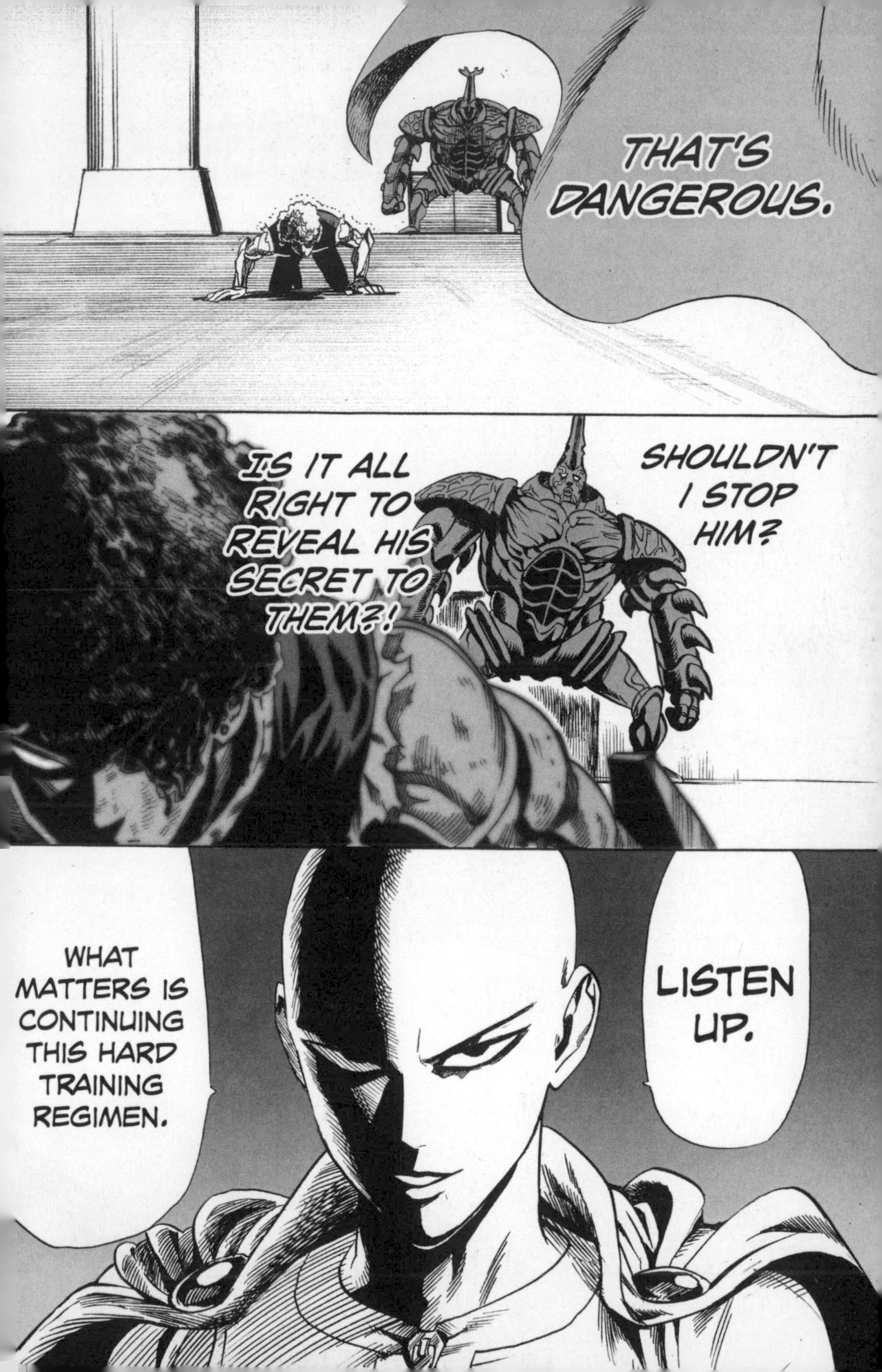
THAT'S DANGEROUS.
SHOULDN'T I STOP HIM?
IS IT ALL RIGHT TO REVEAL HIS SECRET TO THEM?!
LISTEN UP.
WHAT MATTERS IS CONTINUING THIS HARD TRAINING REGIMEN.

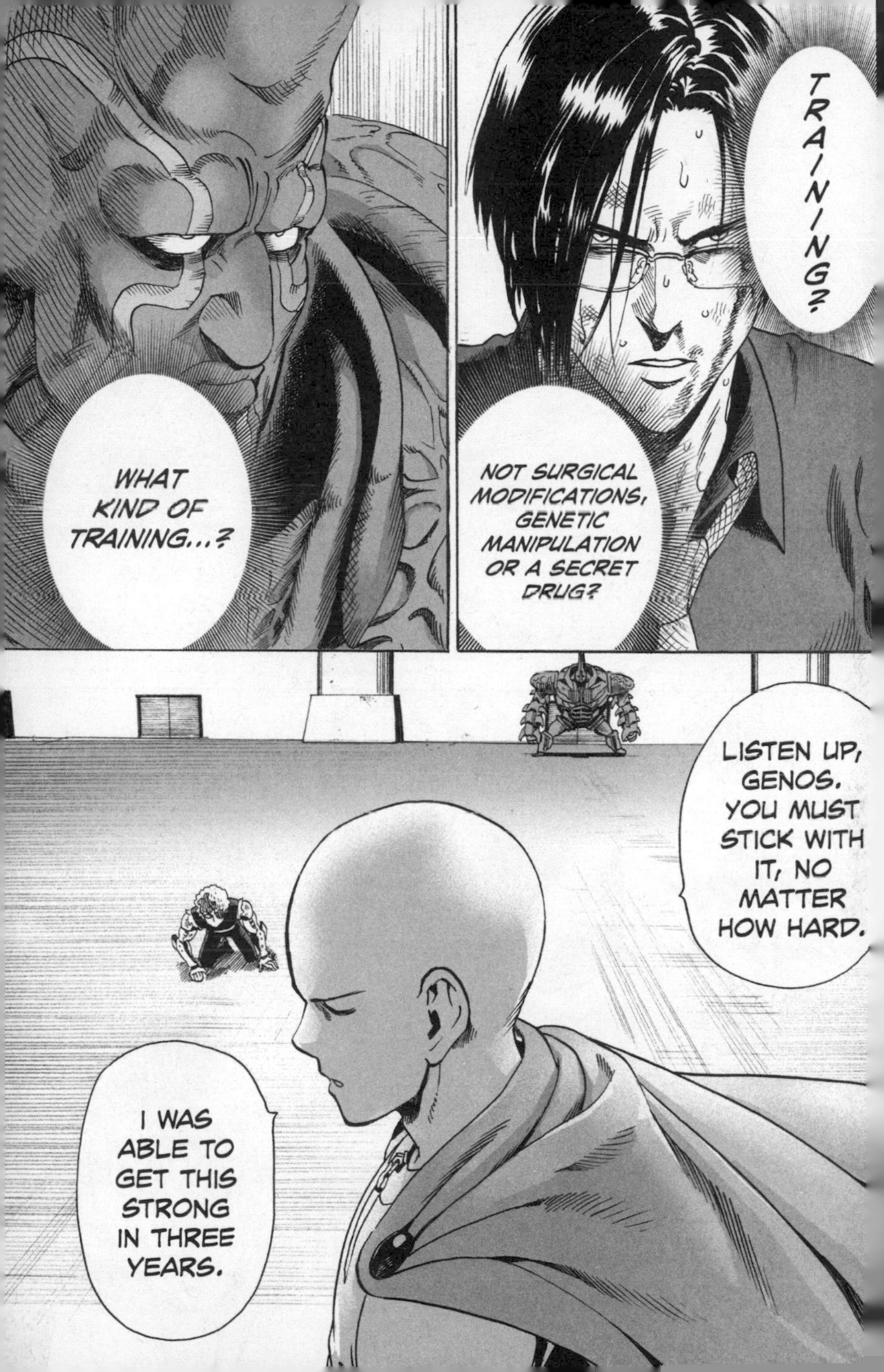
TRAINING?
NOT SURGICAL MODIFICATIONS, GENETIC MANIPULATION OR A SECRET DRUG?
WHAT KIND OF TRAINING...?
LISTEN UP, GENOS. YOU MUST STICK WITH IT, NO MATTER HOW HARD.
I WAS ABLE TO GET THIS STRONG IN THREE YEARS.

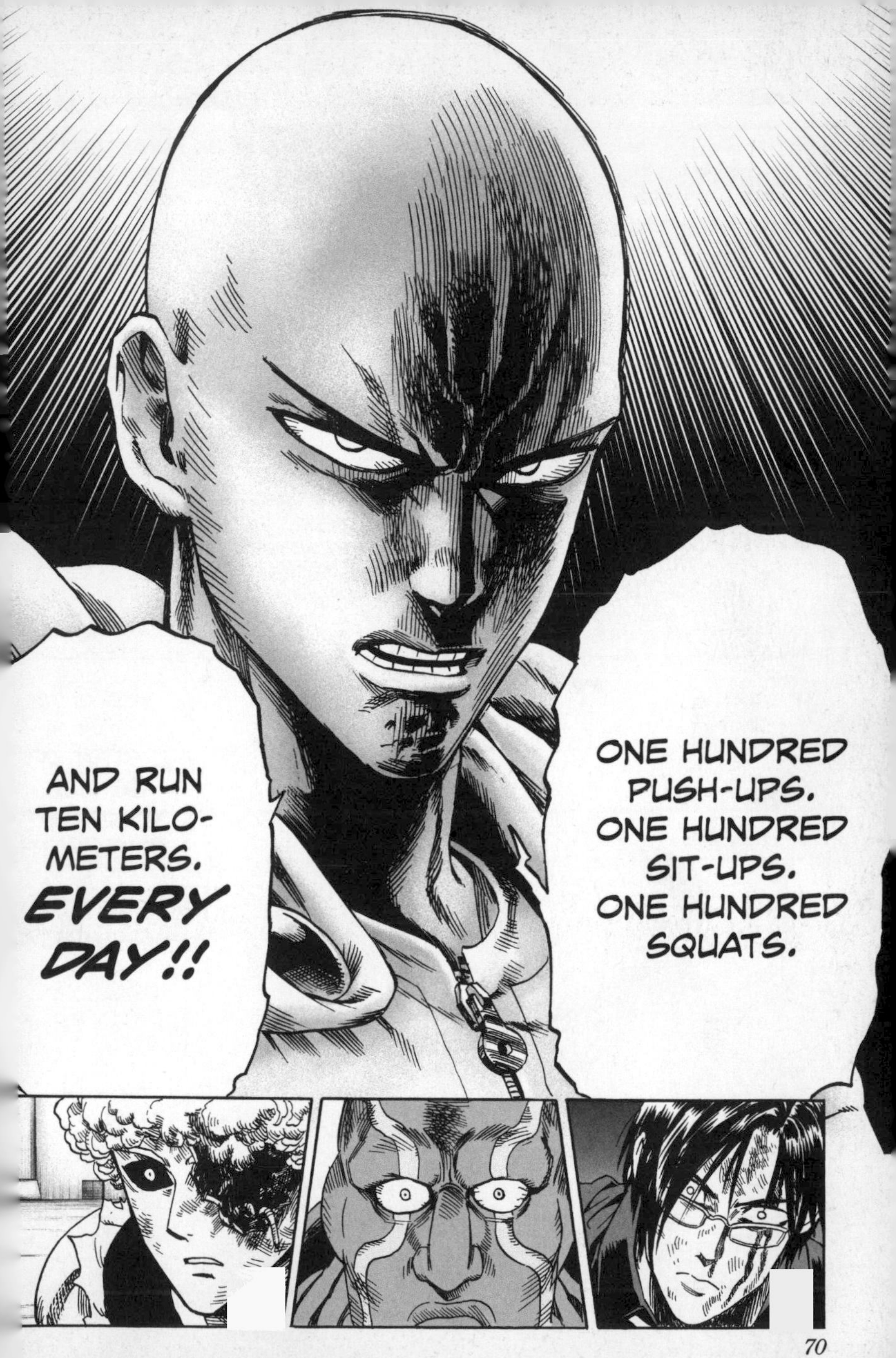
ONE HUNDRED PUSH-UPS. ONE HUNDRED SIT-UPS. ONE HUNDRED SQUATS.
AND RUN TEN KILO-METERS. *EVERY DAY!!*

READ THIS WAY

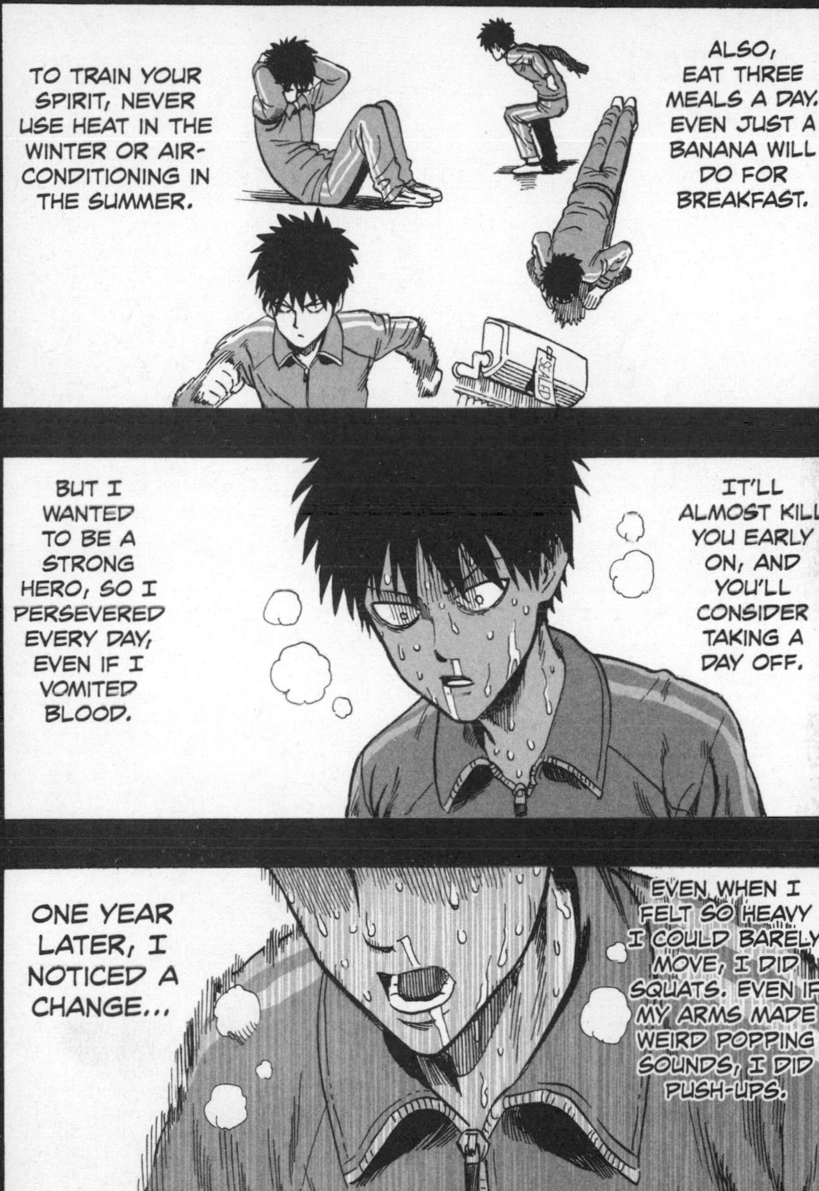

ALSO, EAT THREE MEALS A DAY. EVEN JUST A BANANA WILL DO FOR BREAKFAST.
TO TRAIN YOUR SPIRIT, NEVER USE HEAT IN THE WINTER OR AIR-CONDITIONING IN THE SUMMER.
SEALED
IT'LL ALMOST KILL YOU EARLY ON, AND YOU'LL CONSIDER TAKING A DAY OFF.
BUT I WANTED TO BE A STRONG HERO, SO I PERSEVERED EVERY DAY, EVEN IF I VOMITED BLOOD.
EVEN WHEN I FELT SO HEAVY I COULD BARELY MOVE, I DID SQUATS. EVEN IF MY ARMS MADE WEIRD POPPING SOUNDS, I DID PUSH-UPS.
ONE YEAR LATER, I NOTICED A CHANGE...

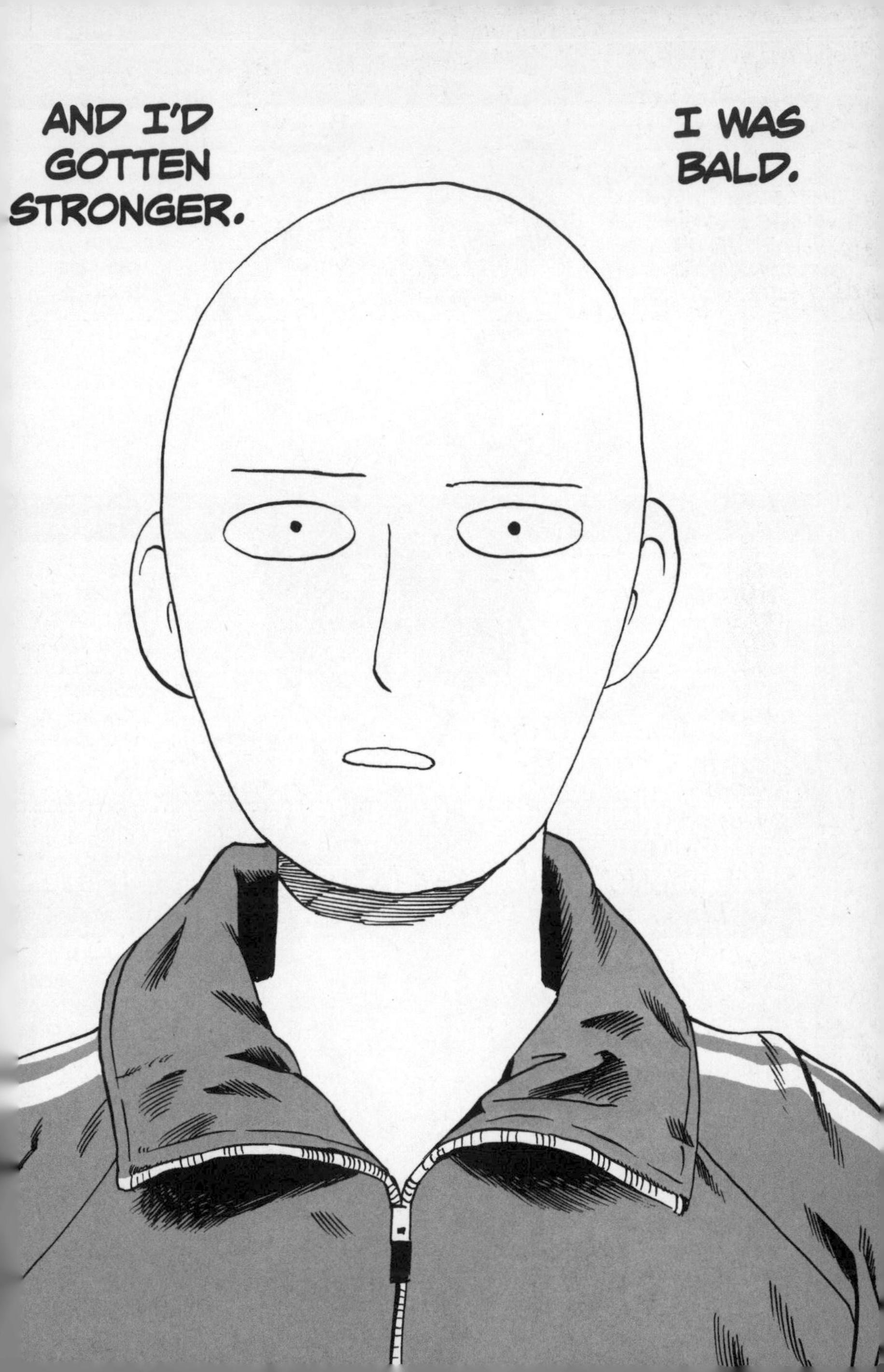
I WAS BALD.
AND I'D GOTTEN STRONGER.

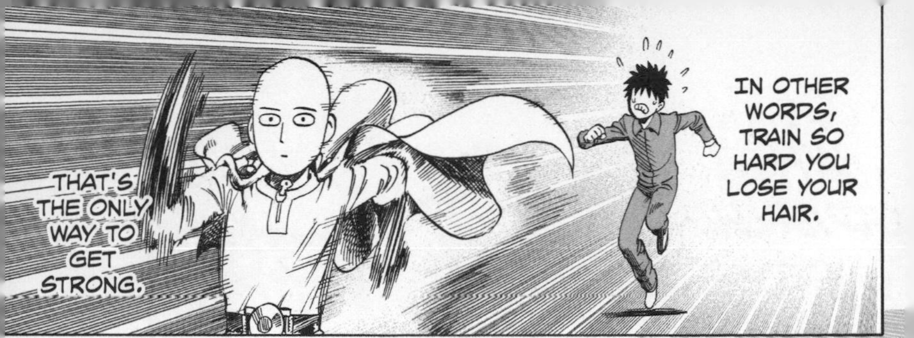
IN OTHER WORDS, TRAIN SO HARD YOU LOSE YOUR HAIR.
THAT'S THE ONLY WAY TO GET STRONG.
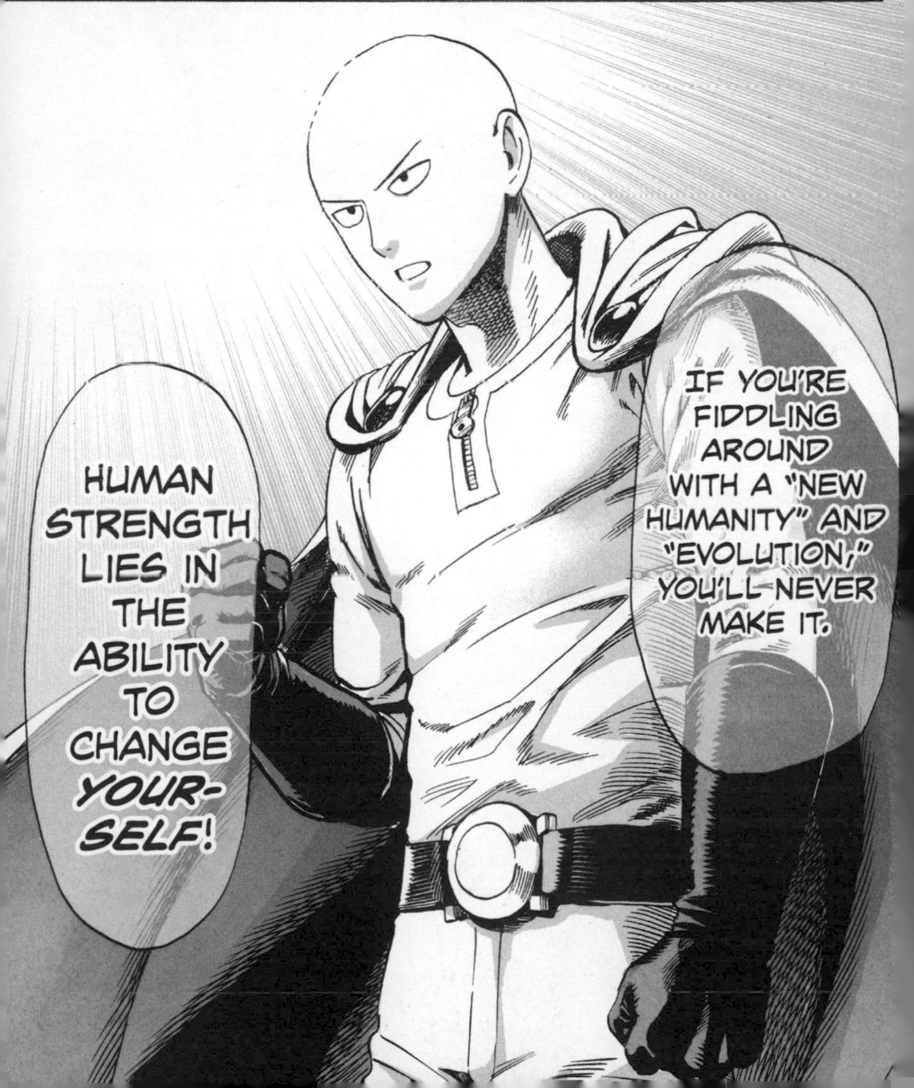
IF YOU'RE FIDDLING AROUND WITH A "NEW HUMANITY" AND "EVOLUTION," YOU'LL NEVER MAKE IT.
HUMAN STRENGTH LIES IN THE ABILITY TO CHANGE *YOURSELF*!

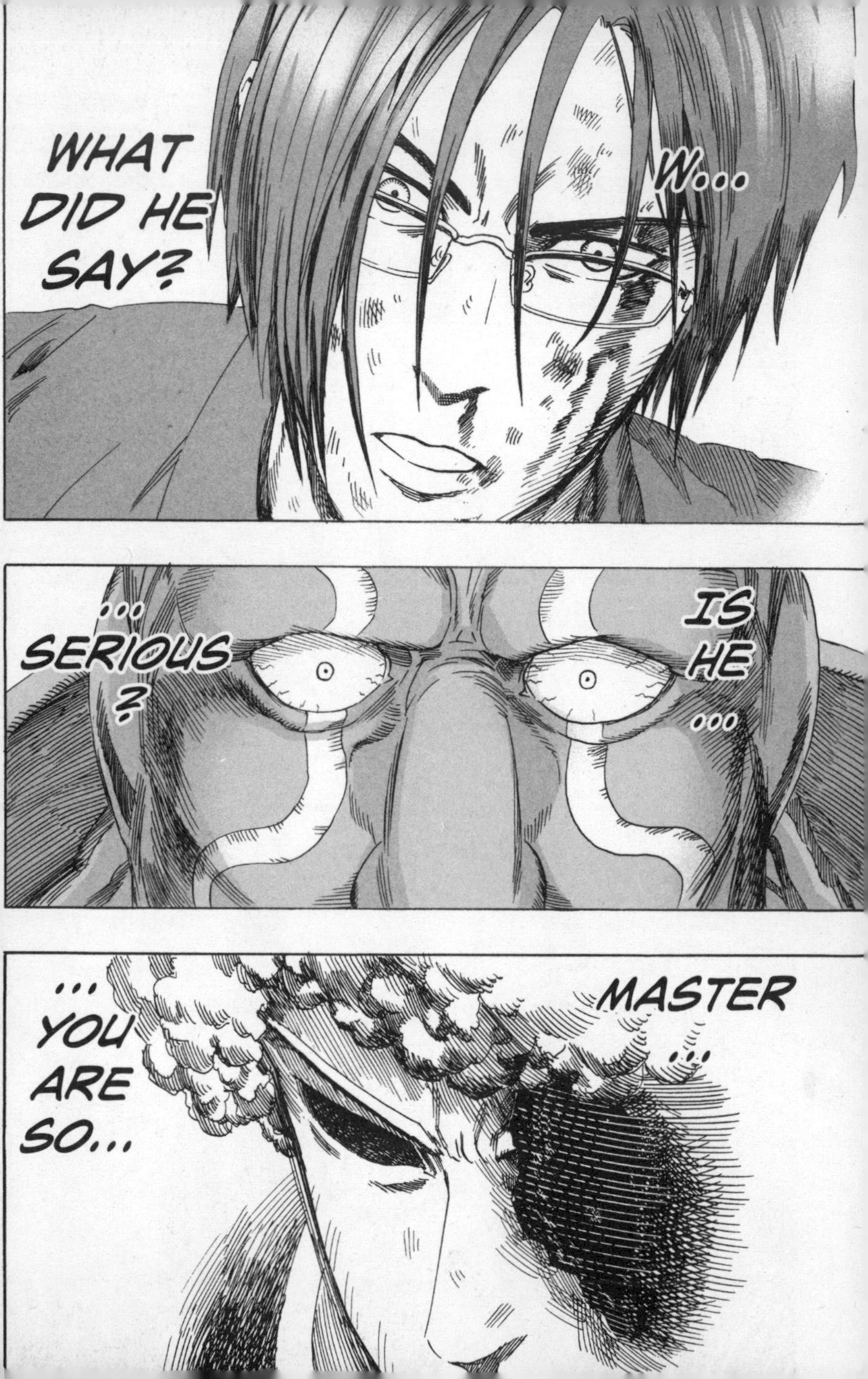
W...
WHAT DID HE SAY?
IS HE...
...SERIOUS?
MASTER...
...YOU ARE SO...

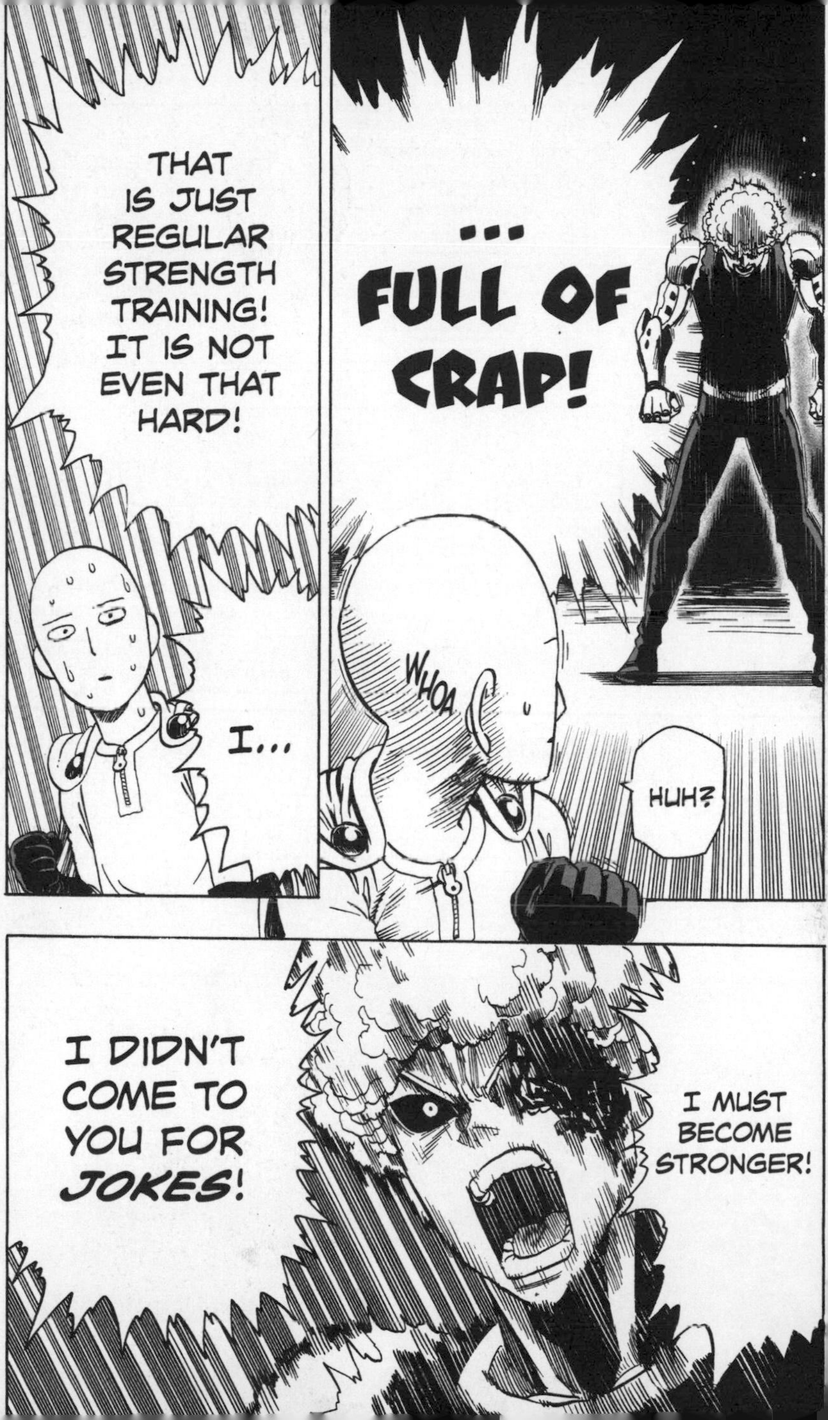
THAT IS JUST REGULAR STRENGTH TRAINING! IT IS NOT EVEN THAT HARD!
I...
...FULL OF CRAP!
WHOA
HUH?
I DIDN'T COME TO YOU FOR *JOKES*!
I MUST BECOME STRONGER!

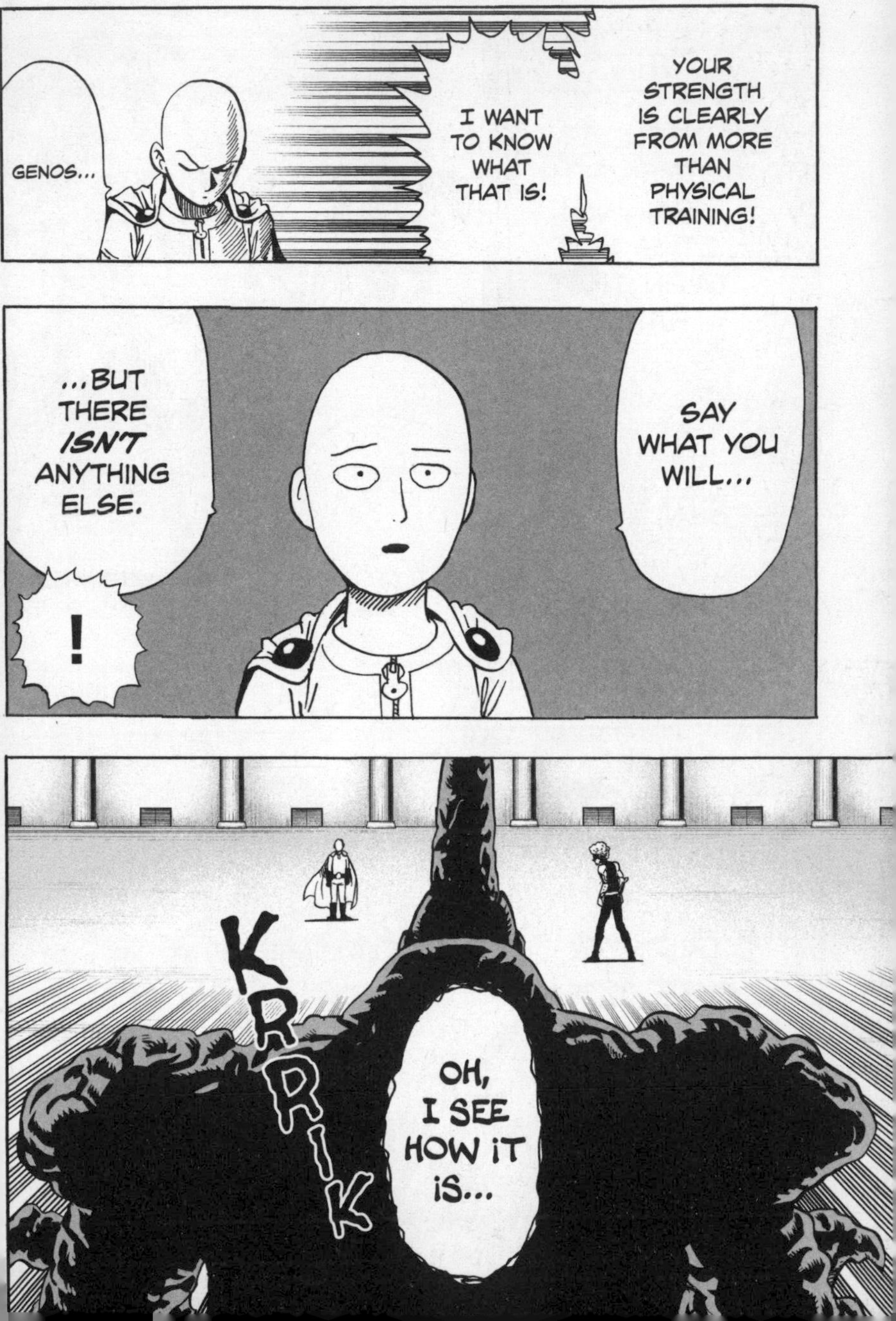
YOUR STRENGTH IS CLEARLY FROM MORE THAN PHYSICAL TRAINING!
I WANT TO KNOW WHAT THAT IS!
GENOS...
SAY WHAT YOU WILL...
...BUT THERE *ISN'T* ANYTHING ELSE.
!
OH, I SEE HOW IT IS...
KRRIK

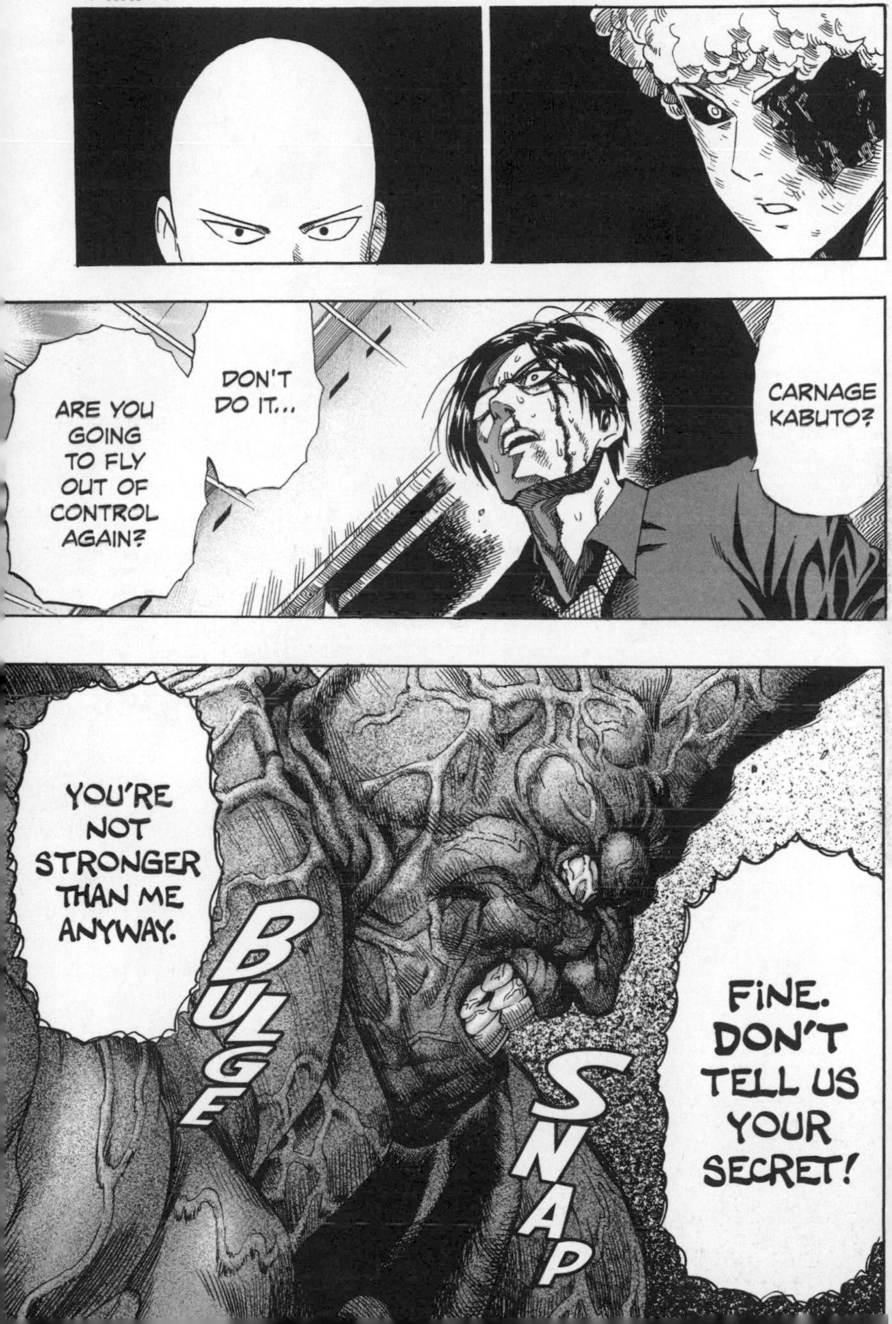
READ THIS WAY
CARNAGE KABUTO?
DON'T DO IT...
ARE YOU GOING TO FLY OUT OF CONTROL AGAIN?
FINE. DON'T TELL US YOUR SECRET!
SNAP
BULGE
YOU'RE NOT STRONGER THAN ME ANYWAY.

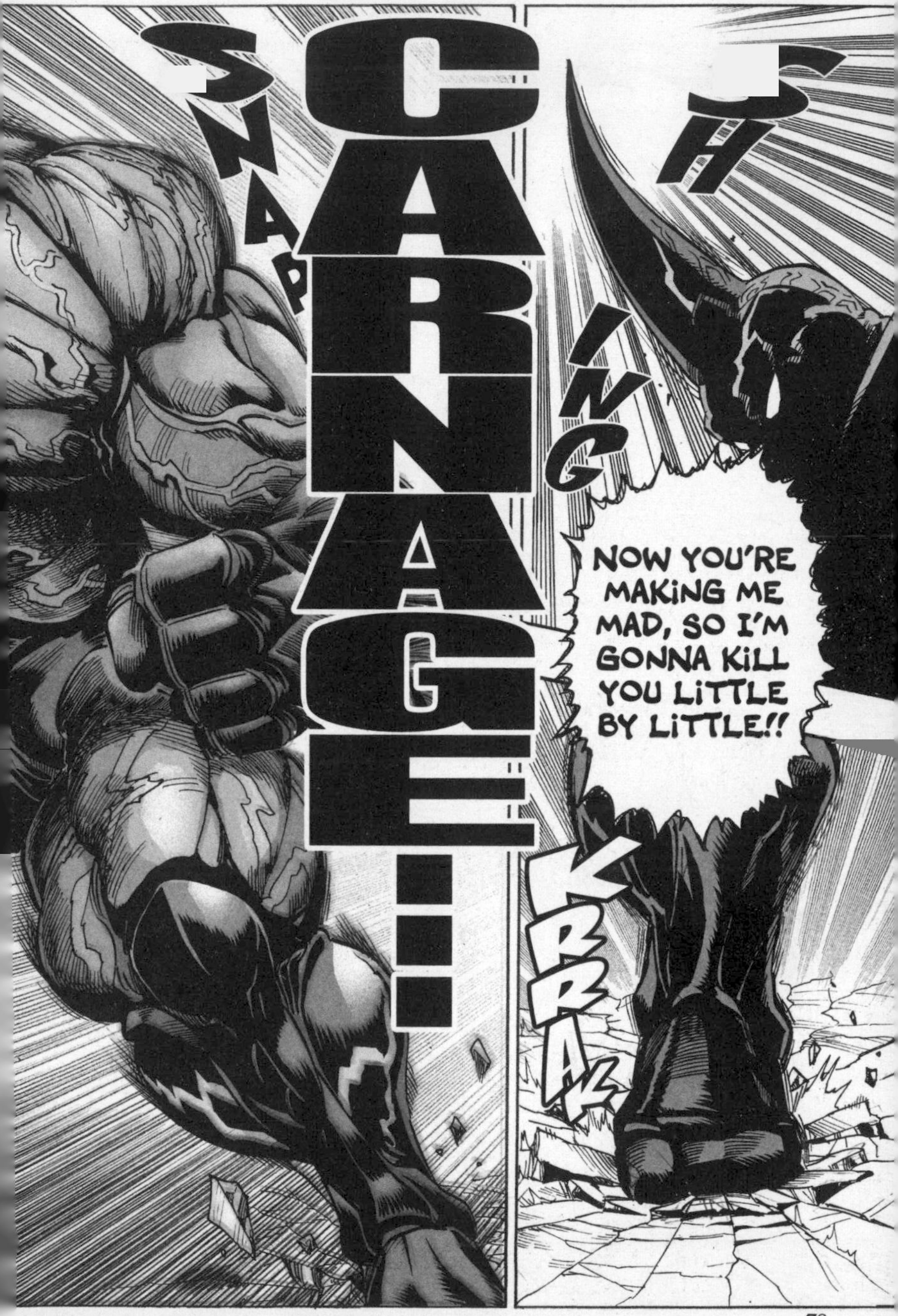
SHING
NOW YOU'RE MAKING ME MAD, SO I'M GONNA KILL YOU LITTLE BY LITTLE!!
KRRAK
SNAP
CARNAGE!!!

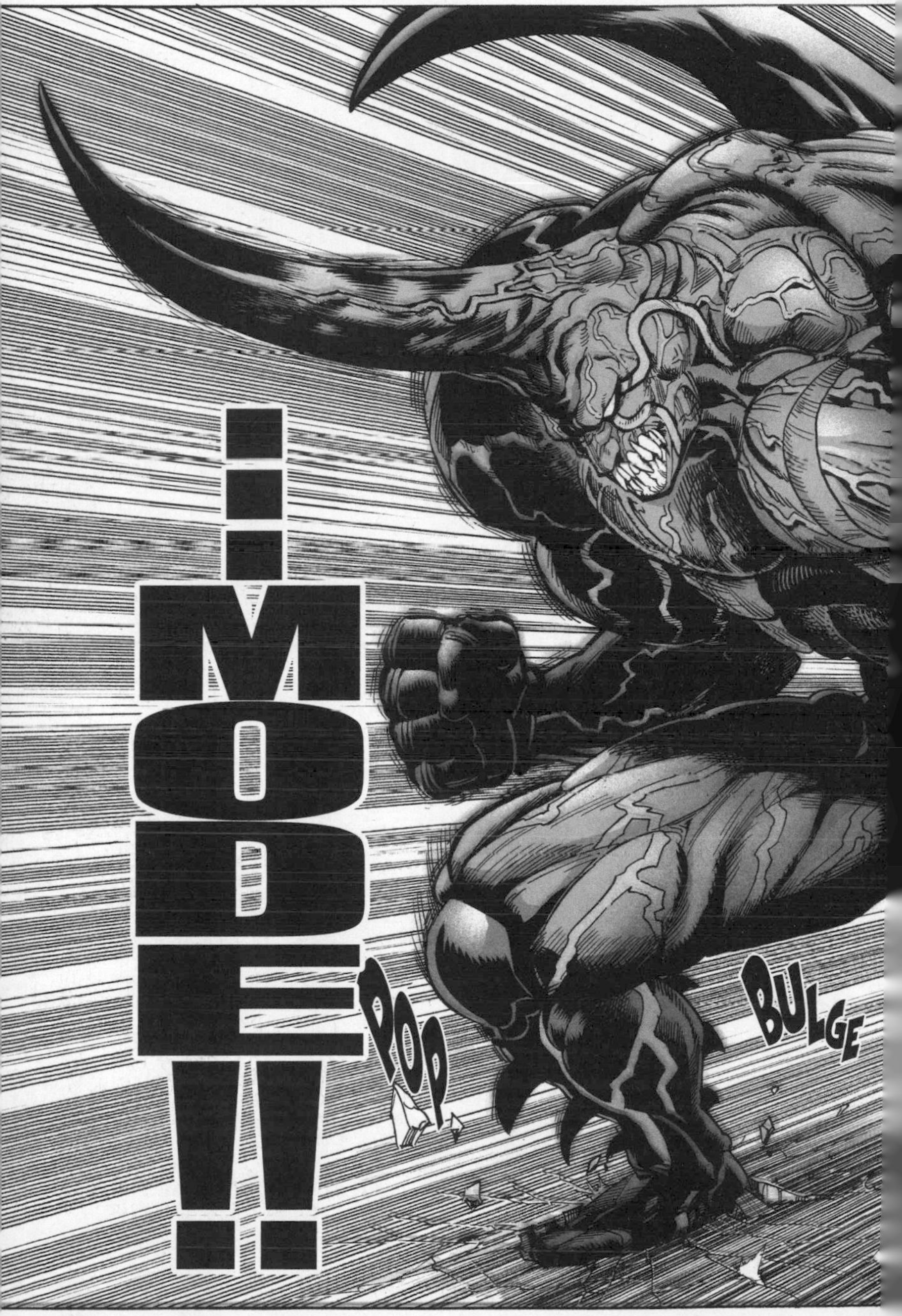

MODE!!
POP
BULGE

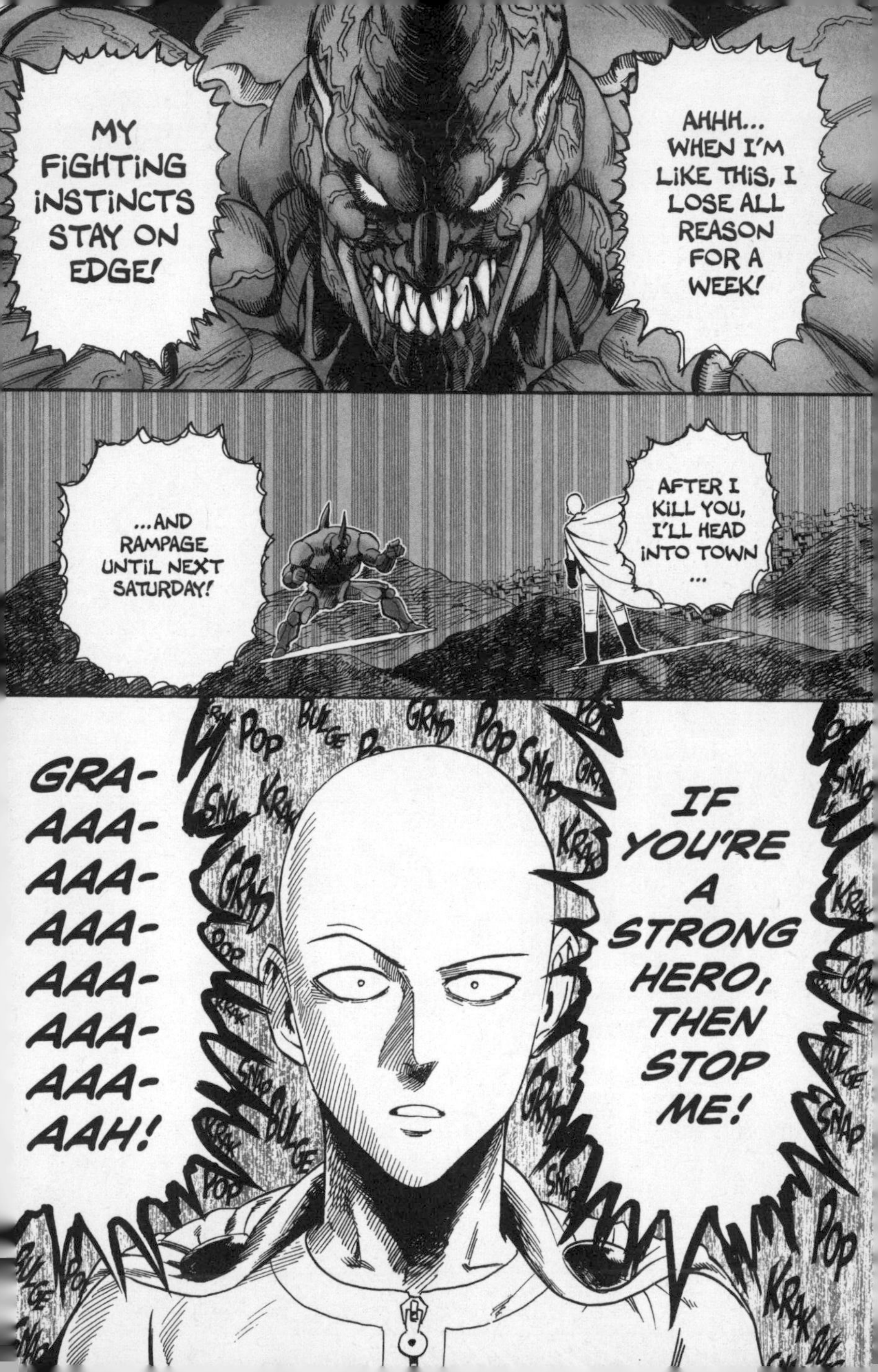
AHHH... WHEN I'M LIKE THIS, I LOSE ALL REASON FOR A WEEK!
MY FIGHTING INSTINCTS STAY ON EDGE!
AFTER I KILL YOU, I'LL HEAD INTO TOWN ...
...AND RAMPAGE UNTIL NEXT SATURDAY!
IF YOU'RE A STRONG HERO, THEN STOP ME!
GRA-AAA-AAA-AAA-AAA-AAA-AAA-AAH!

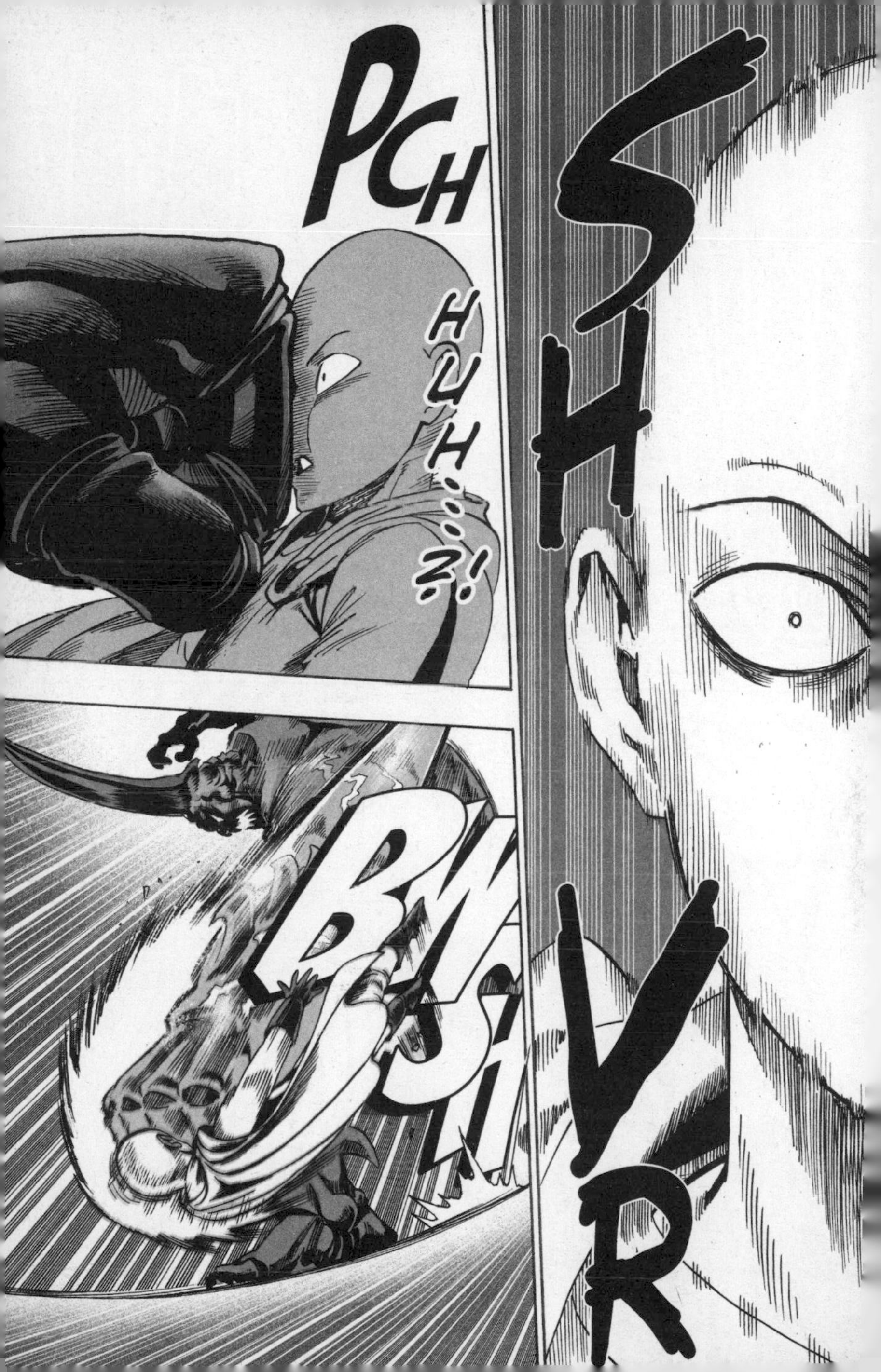
SHVR
PCH
HUH...?!

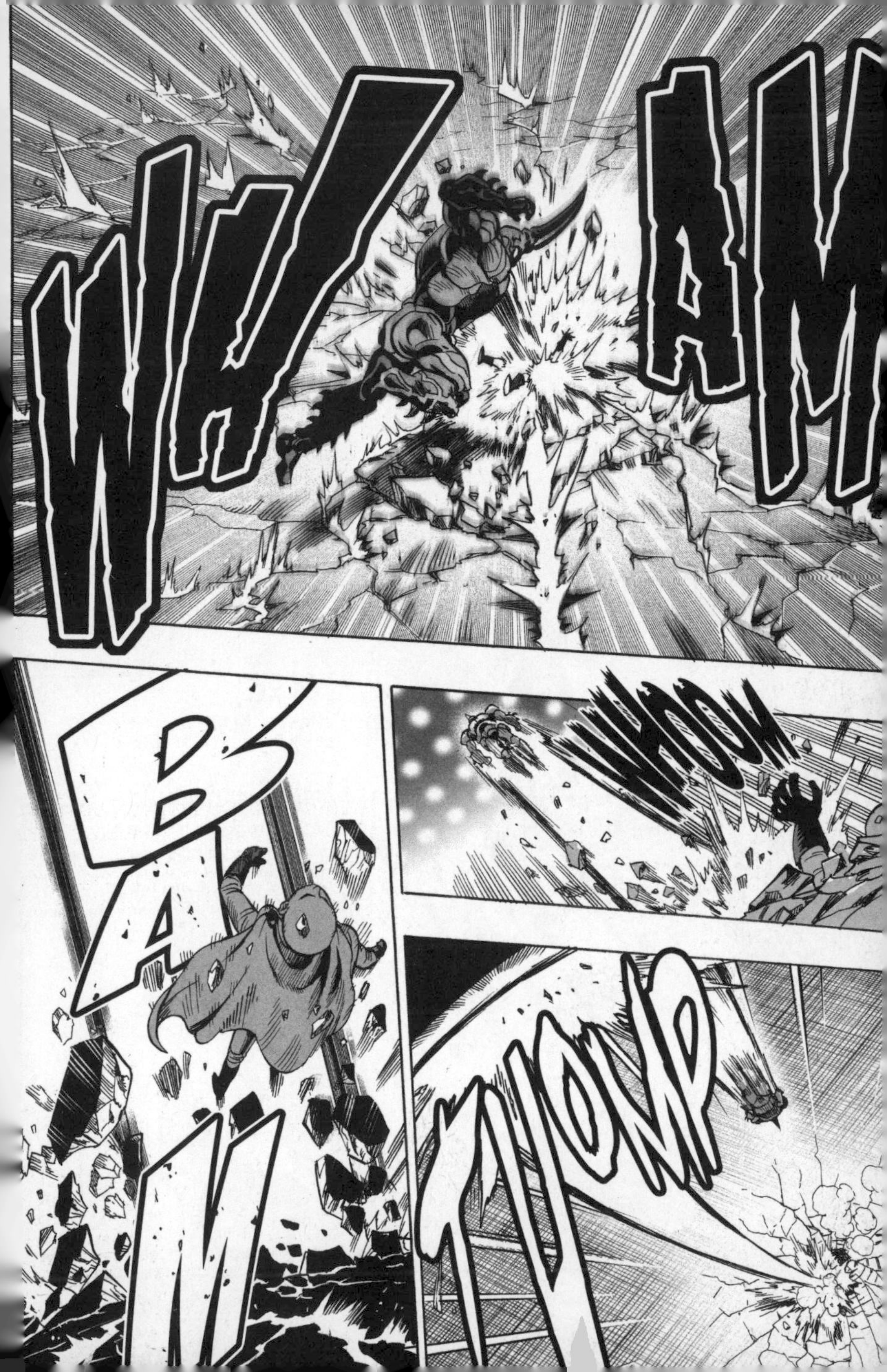
WHAM
WHOOM
WHOMP
BAM

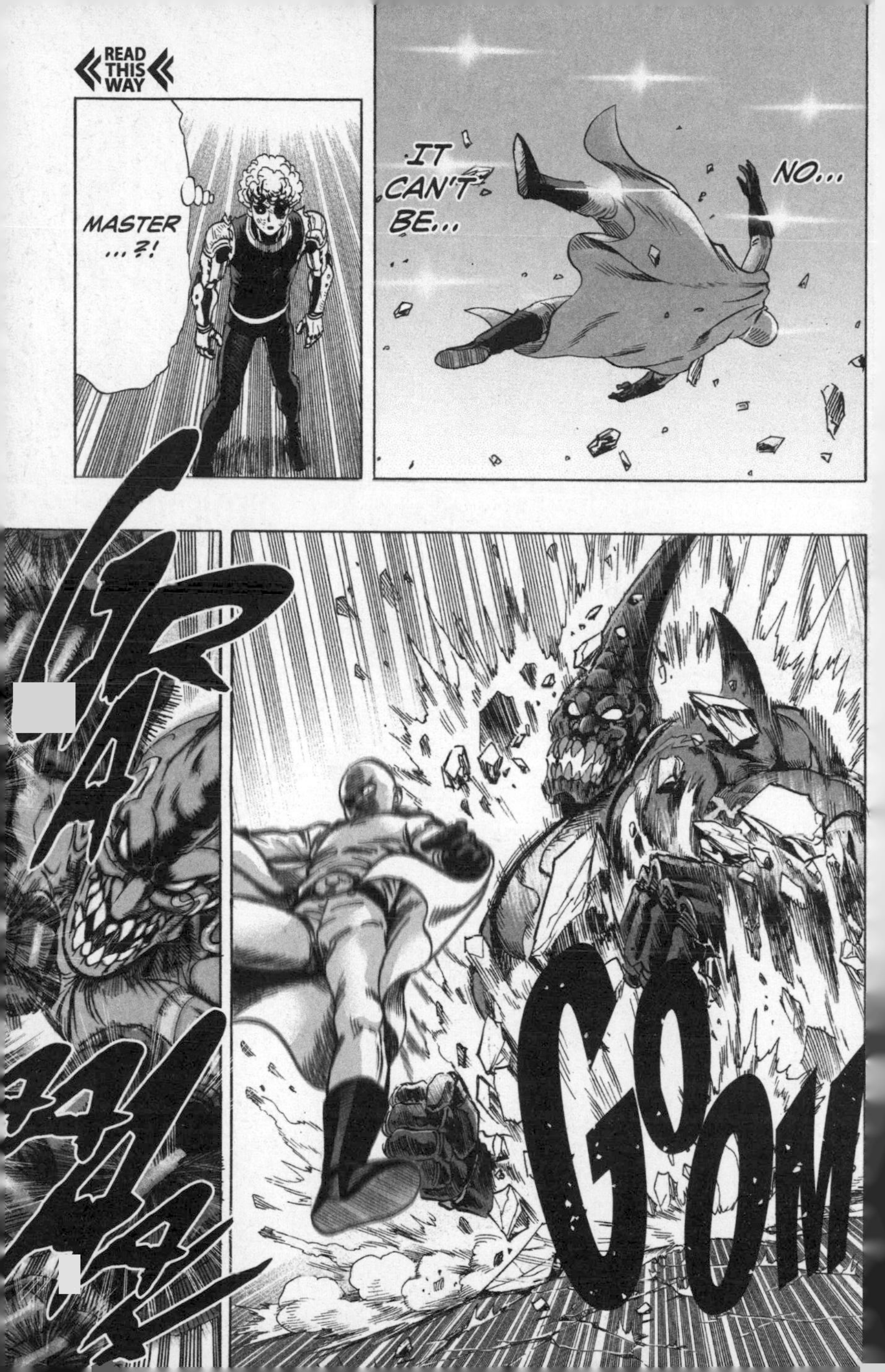
READ THIS WAY
NO...
IT CAN'T BE...
MASTER ...?!
GOOM

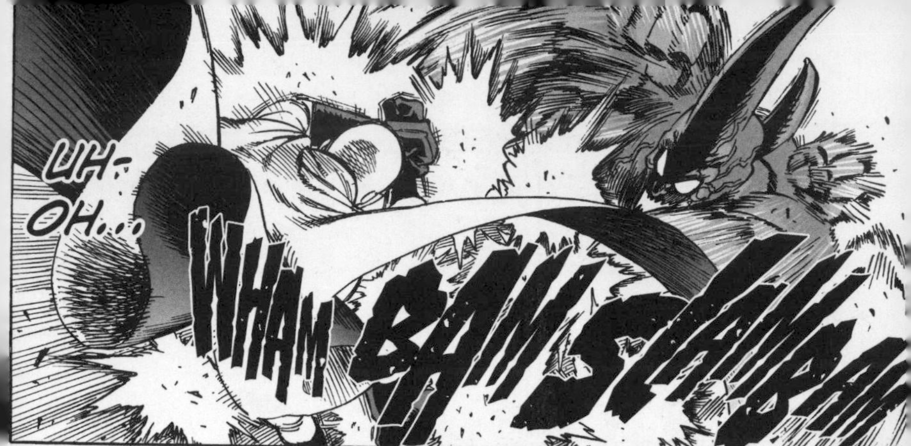
BAMSMABAM
WHAM
UH-OH...
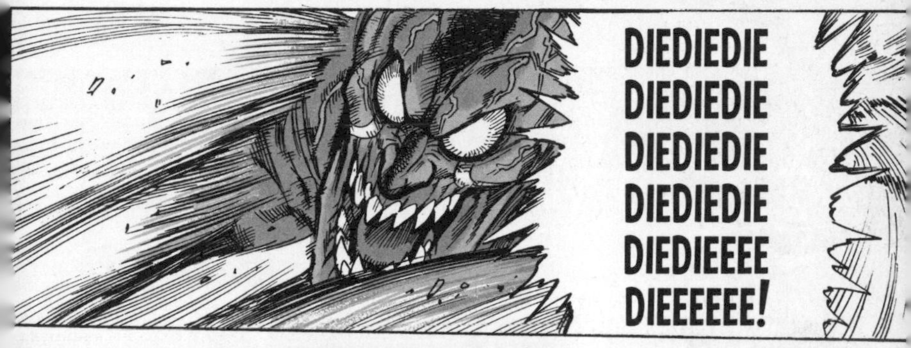
DIEDIEDIE DIEDIEDIE DIEDIEDIE DIEDIEDIE DIEDIEEEE DIEEEEEE!
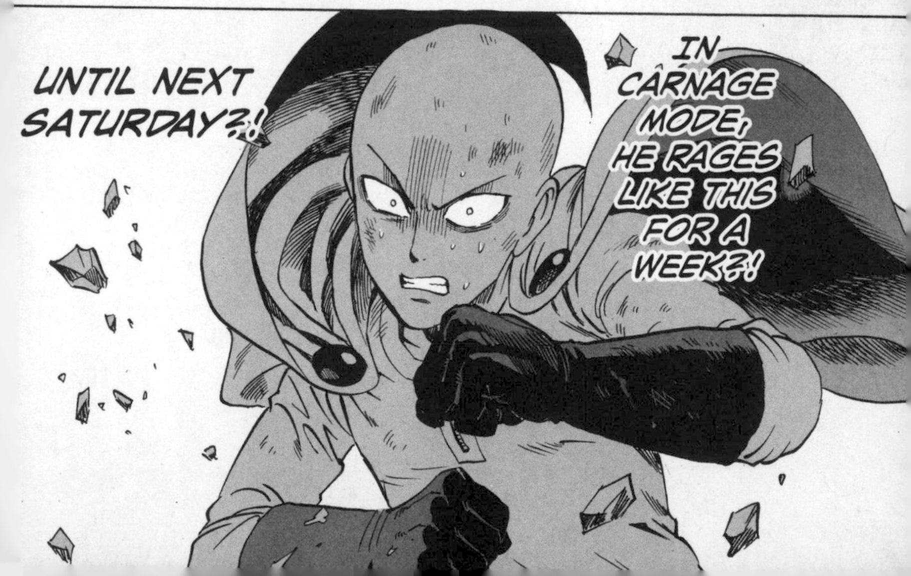
IN CARNAGE MODE, HE RAGES LIKE THIS FOR A WEEK?!
UNTIL NEXT SATURDAY?!

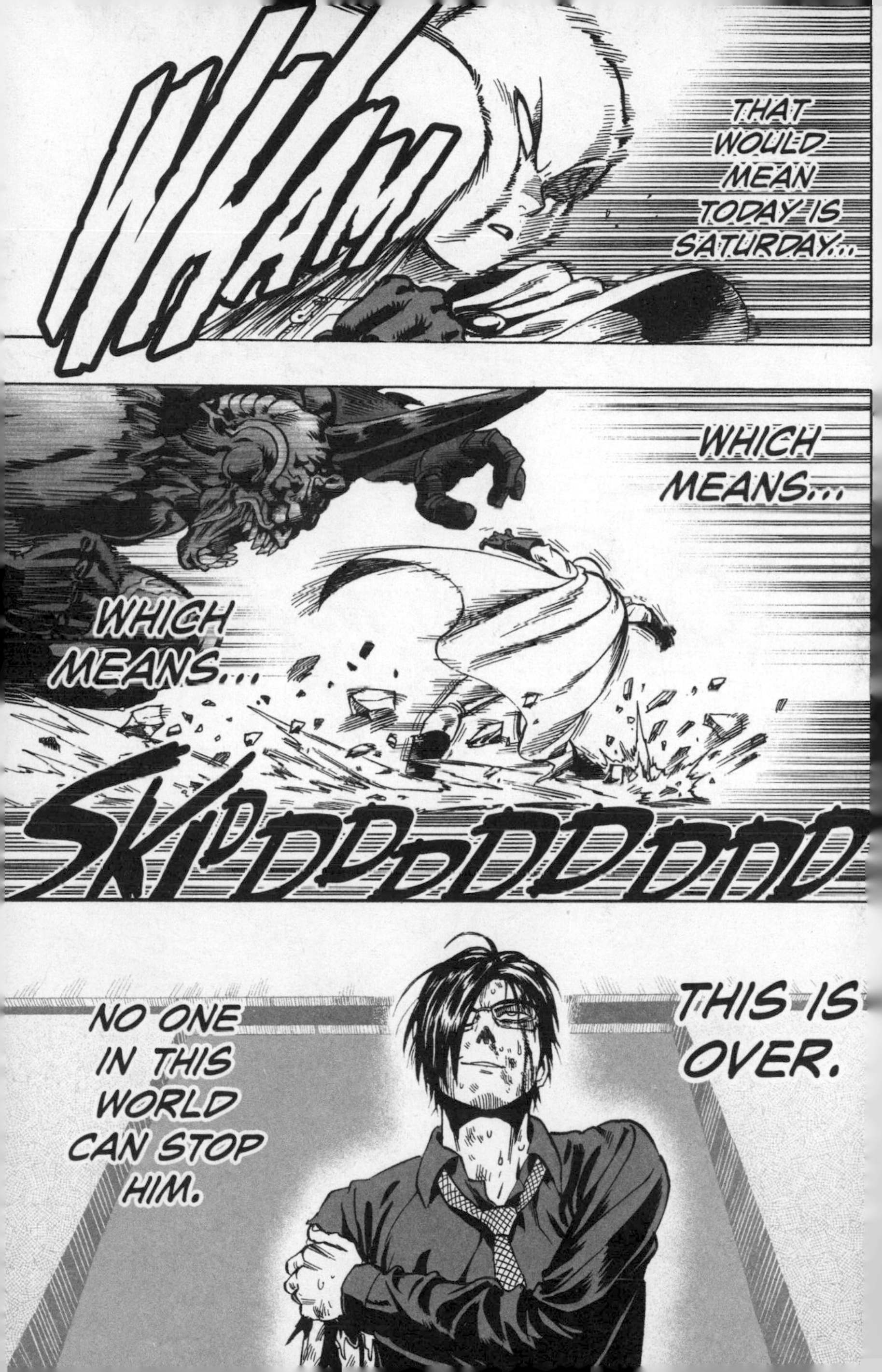
WHAM
THAT WOULD MEAN TODAY IS SATURDAY...
WHICH MEANS...
WHICH MEANS...
SKIDDDDDDDDD
THIS IS OVER.
NO ONE IN THIS WORLD CAN STOP HIM.

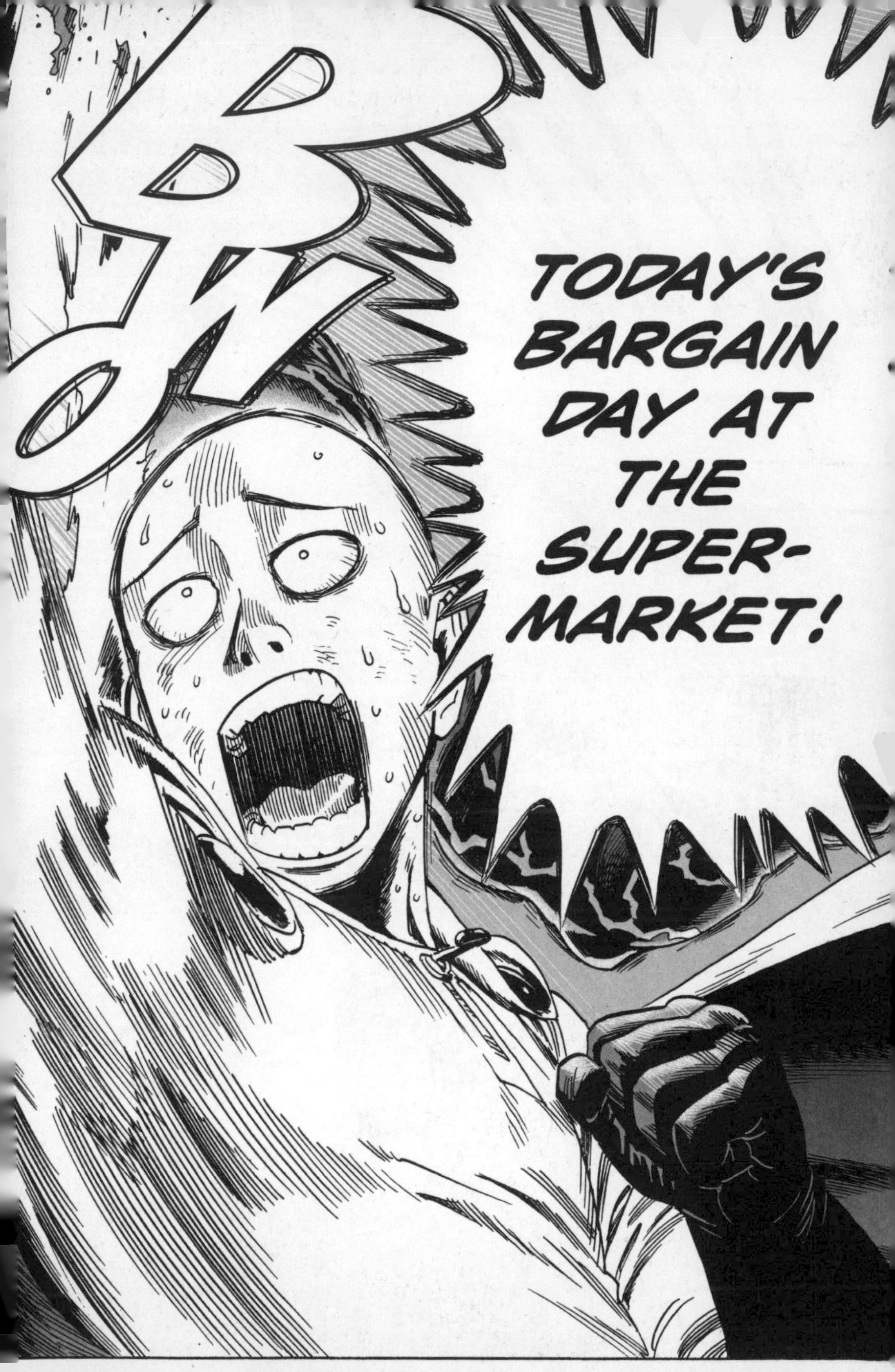
TODAY'S BARGAIN DAY AT THE SUPER-MARKET!

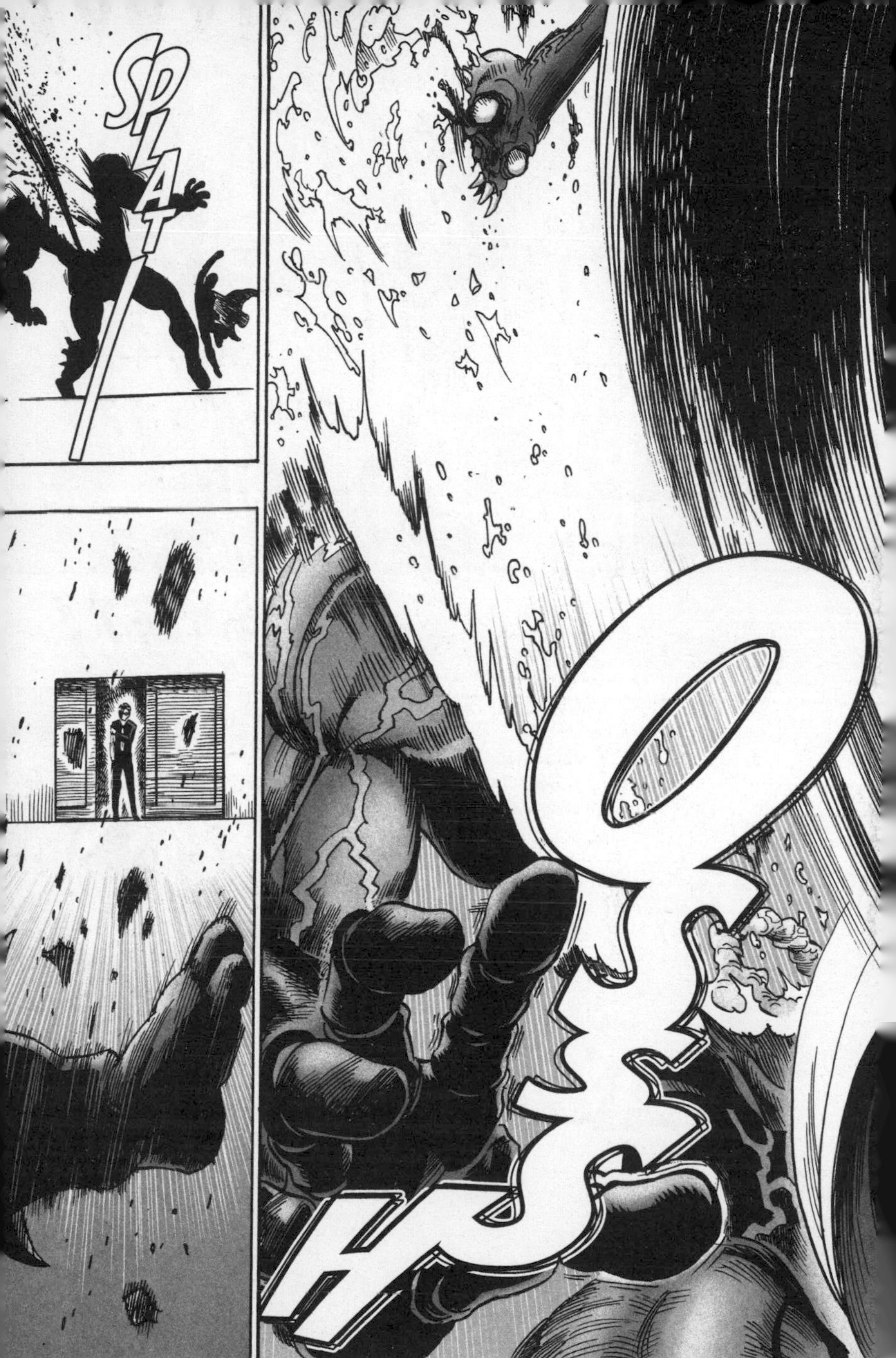
SPLAT

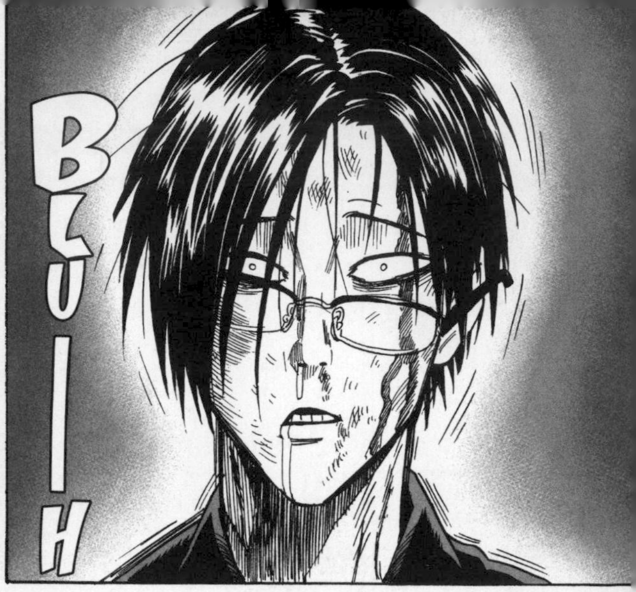
BLUIIH
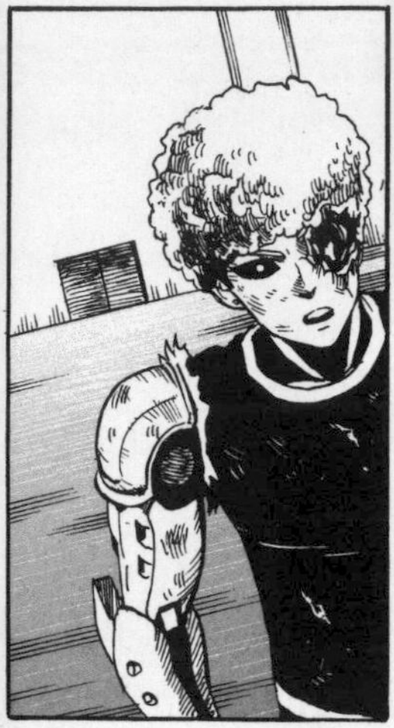
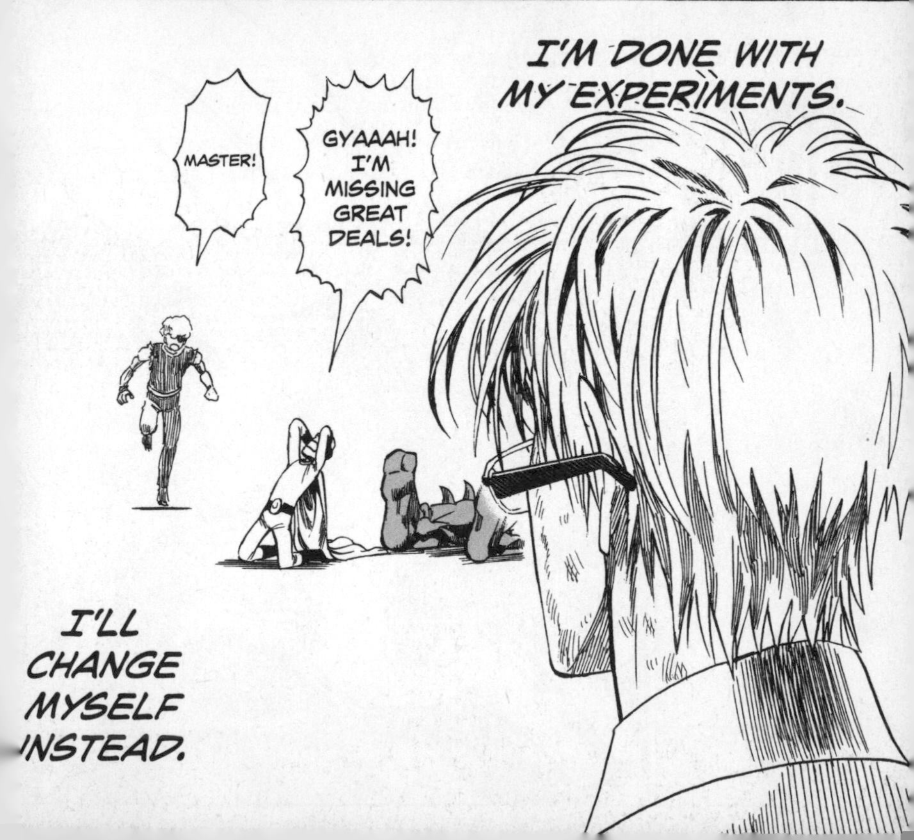
I'M DONE WITH MY EXPERIMENTS.
GYAAAH! I'M MISSING GREAT DEALS!
MASTER!
I'LL CHANGE MYSELF INSTEAD.

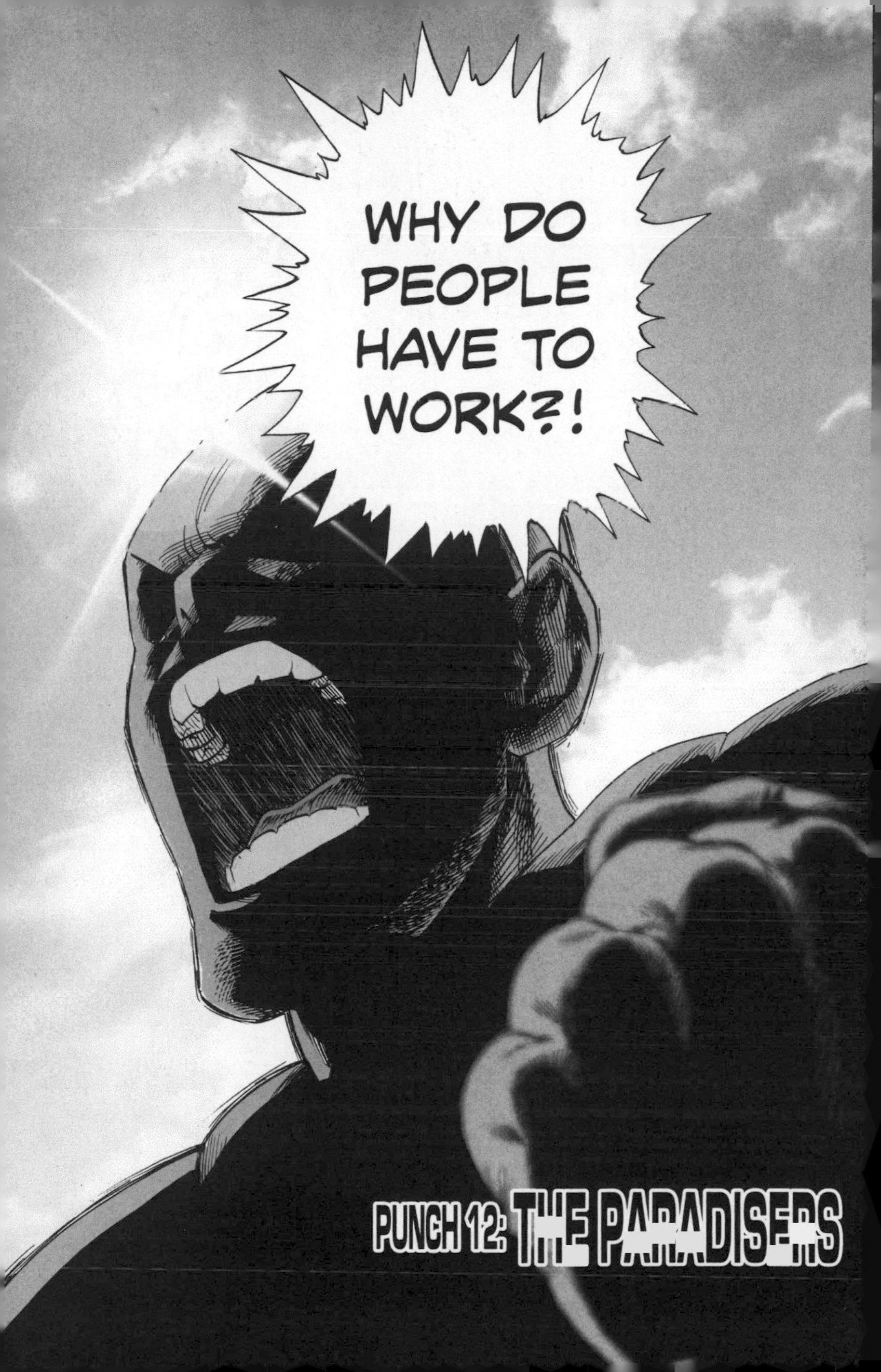
WHY DO PEOPLE HAVE TO WORK?!

PUNCH 12: THE PARADISERS

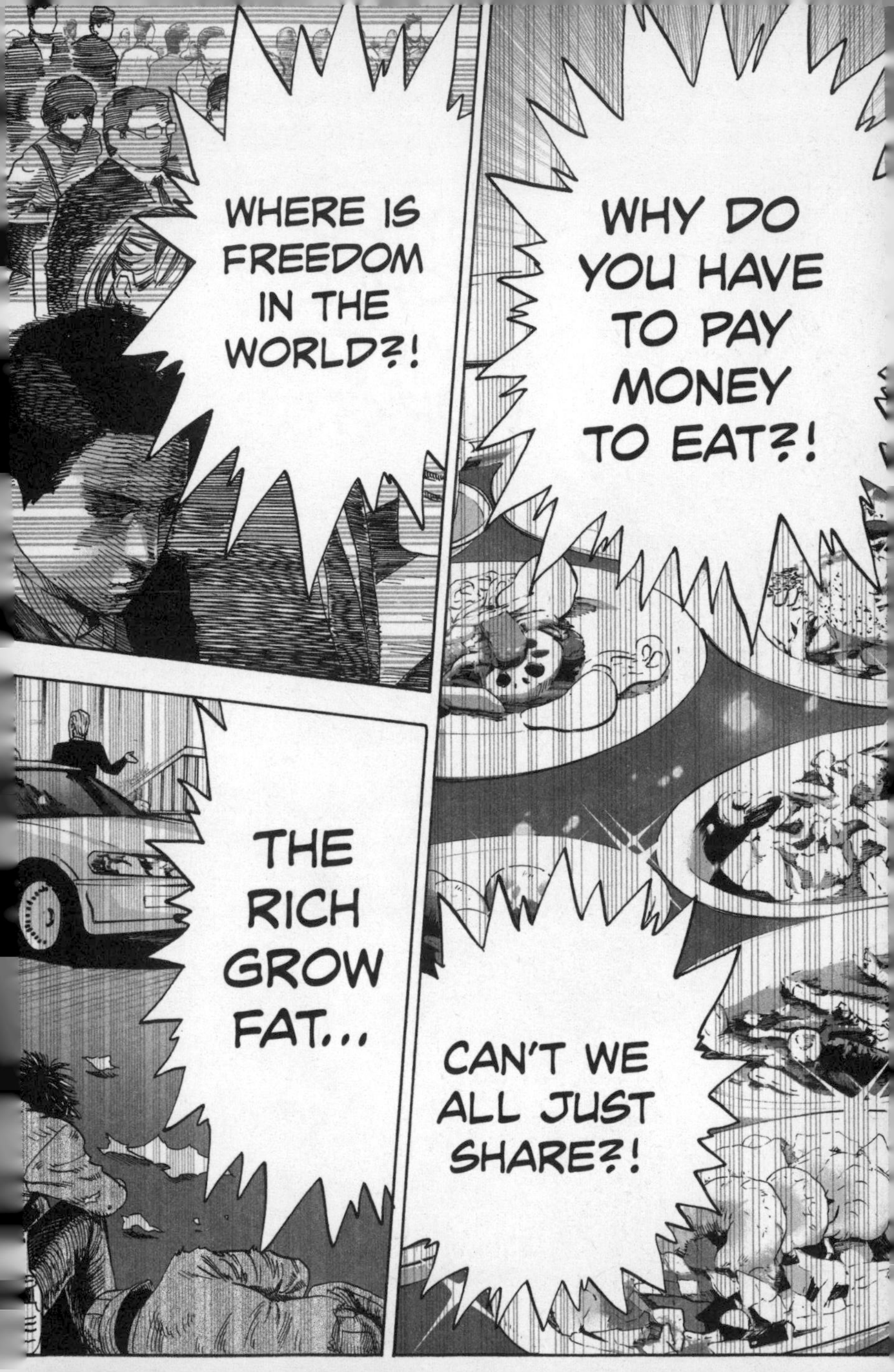
WHY DO YOU HAVE TO PAY MONEY TO EAT?!
CAN'T WE ALL JUST SHARE?!
WHERE IS FREEDOM IN THE WORLD?!
THE RICH GROW FAT...

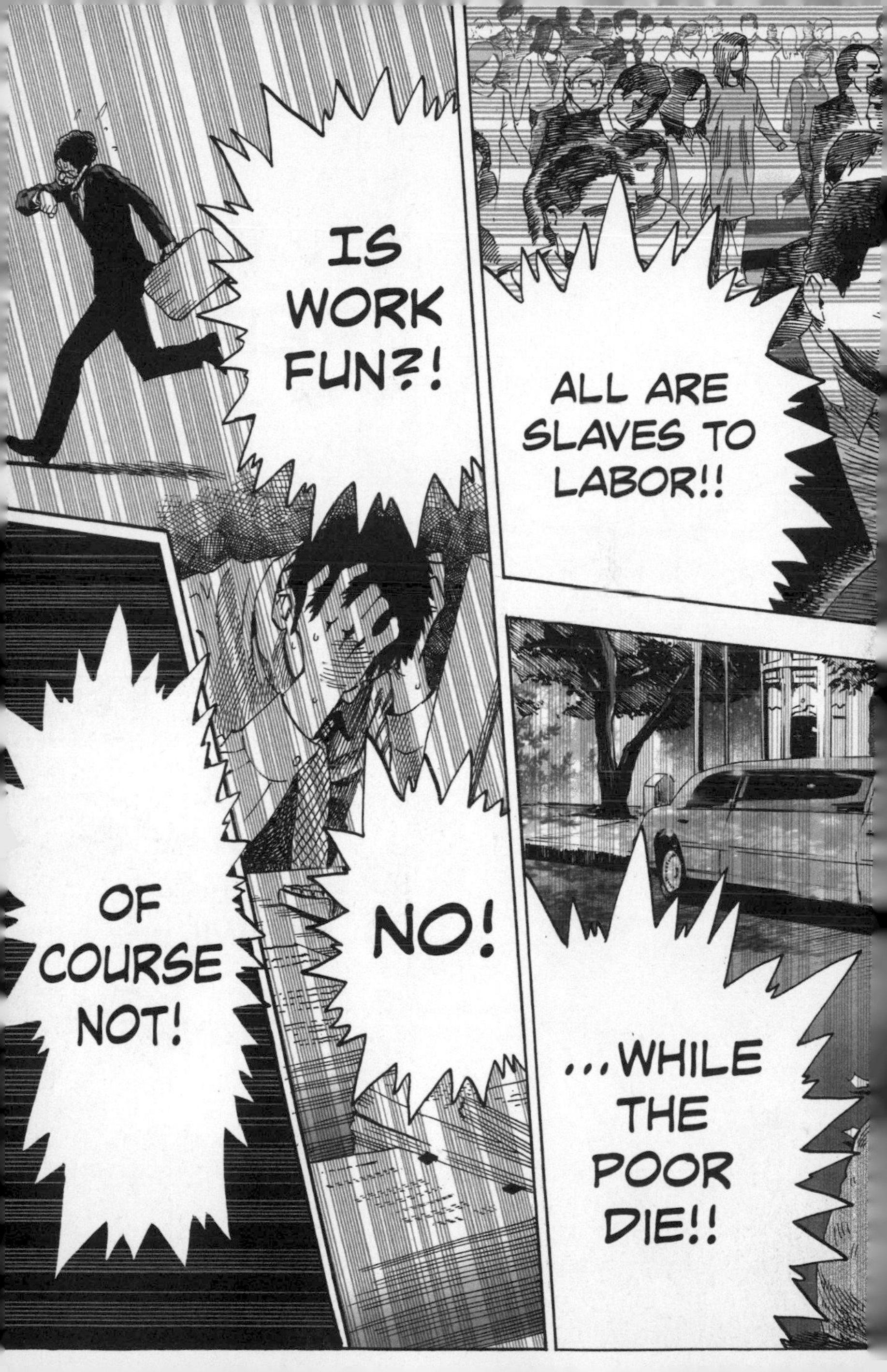
IS WORK FUN?!
NO!
OF COURSE NOT!
ALL ARE SLAVES TO LABOR!!
...WHILE THE POOR DIE!!

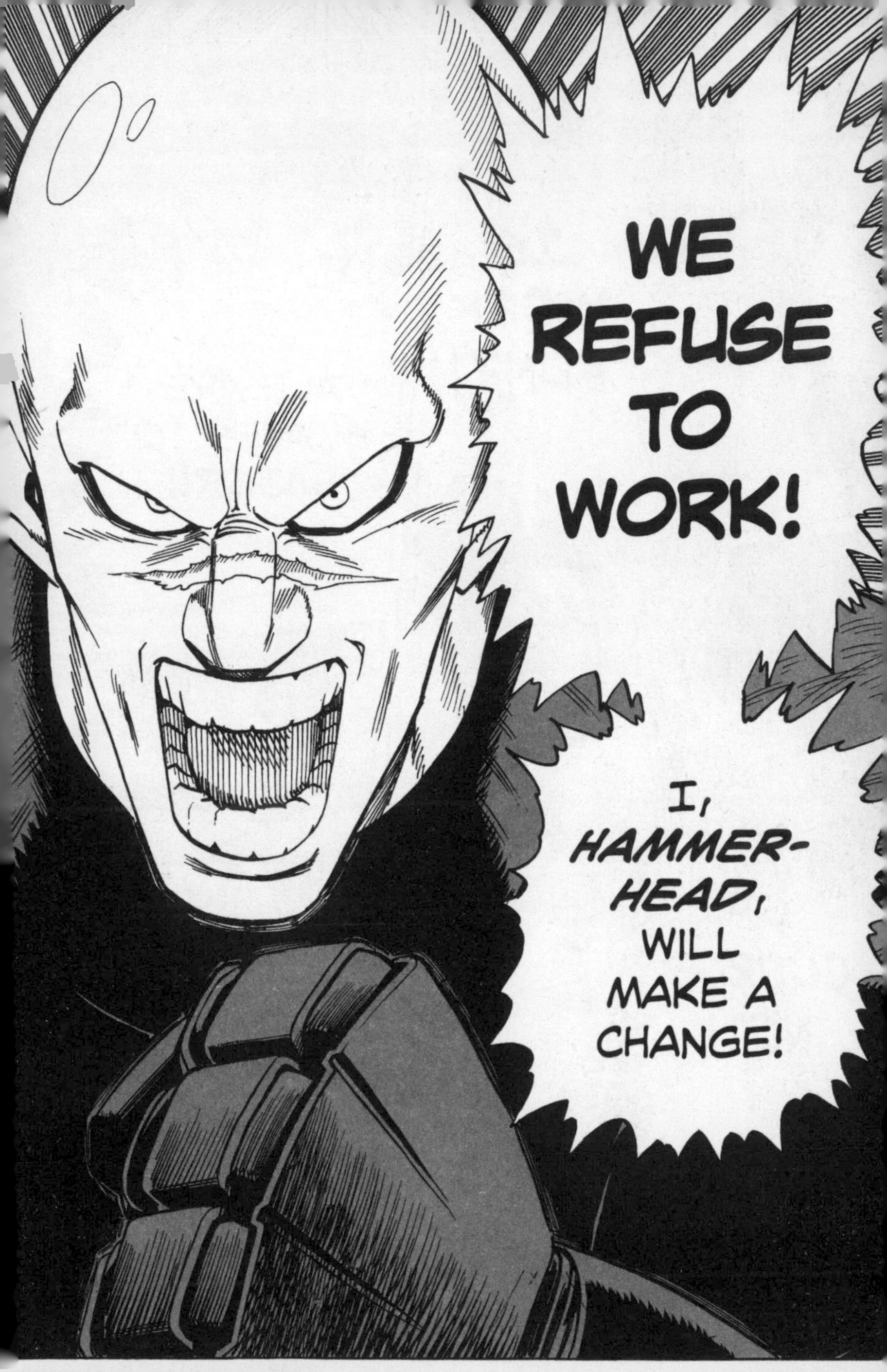
WE REFUSE TO WORK!
I, HAMMER-HEAD, WILL MAKE A CHANGE!

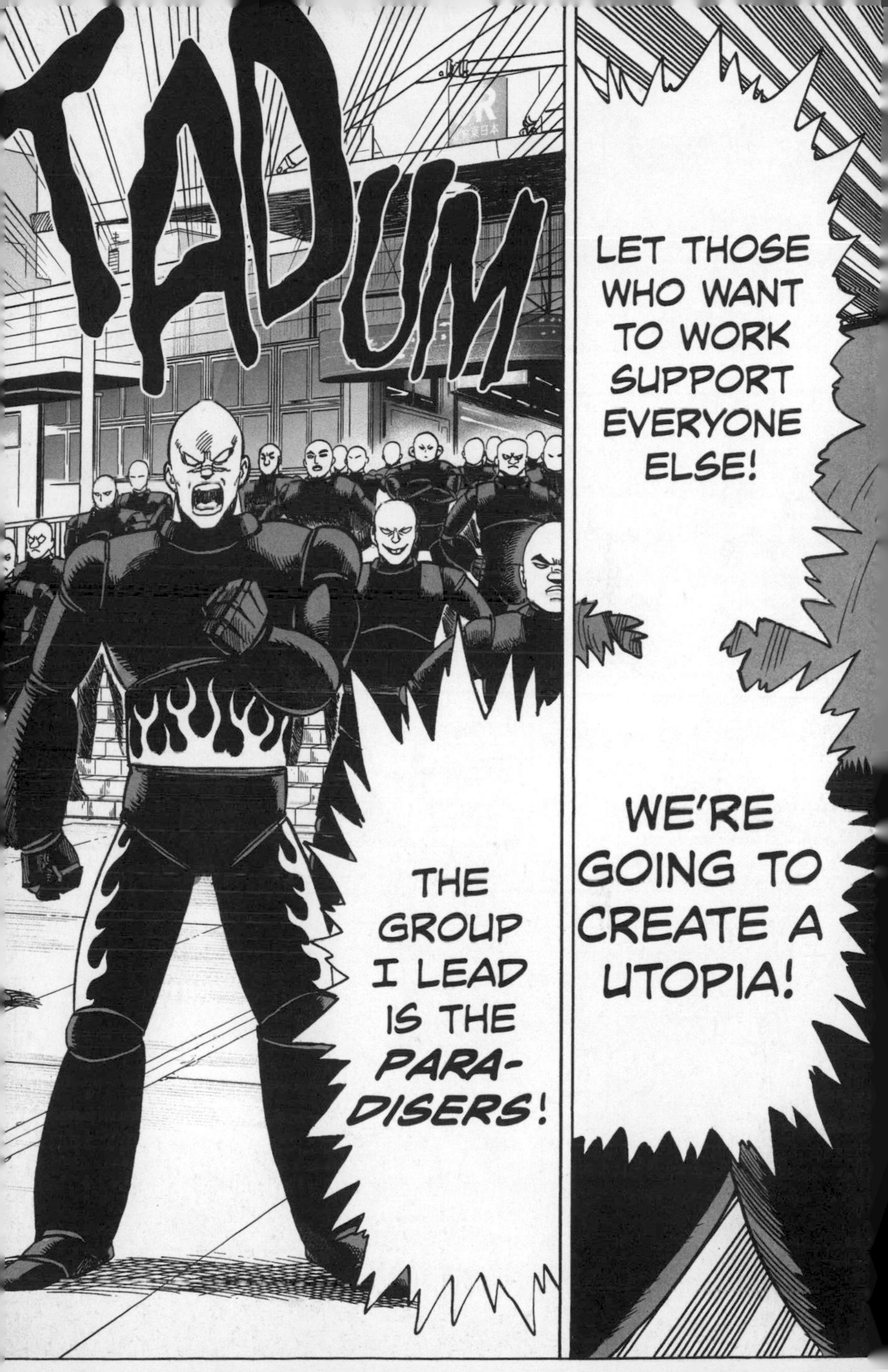
LET THOSE WHO WANT TO WORK SUPPORT EVERYONE ELSE!
WE'RE GOING TO CREATE A UTOPIA!
TADUM
THE GROUP I LEAD IS THE *PARADISERS*!

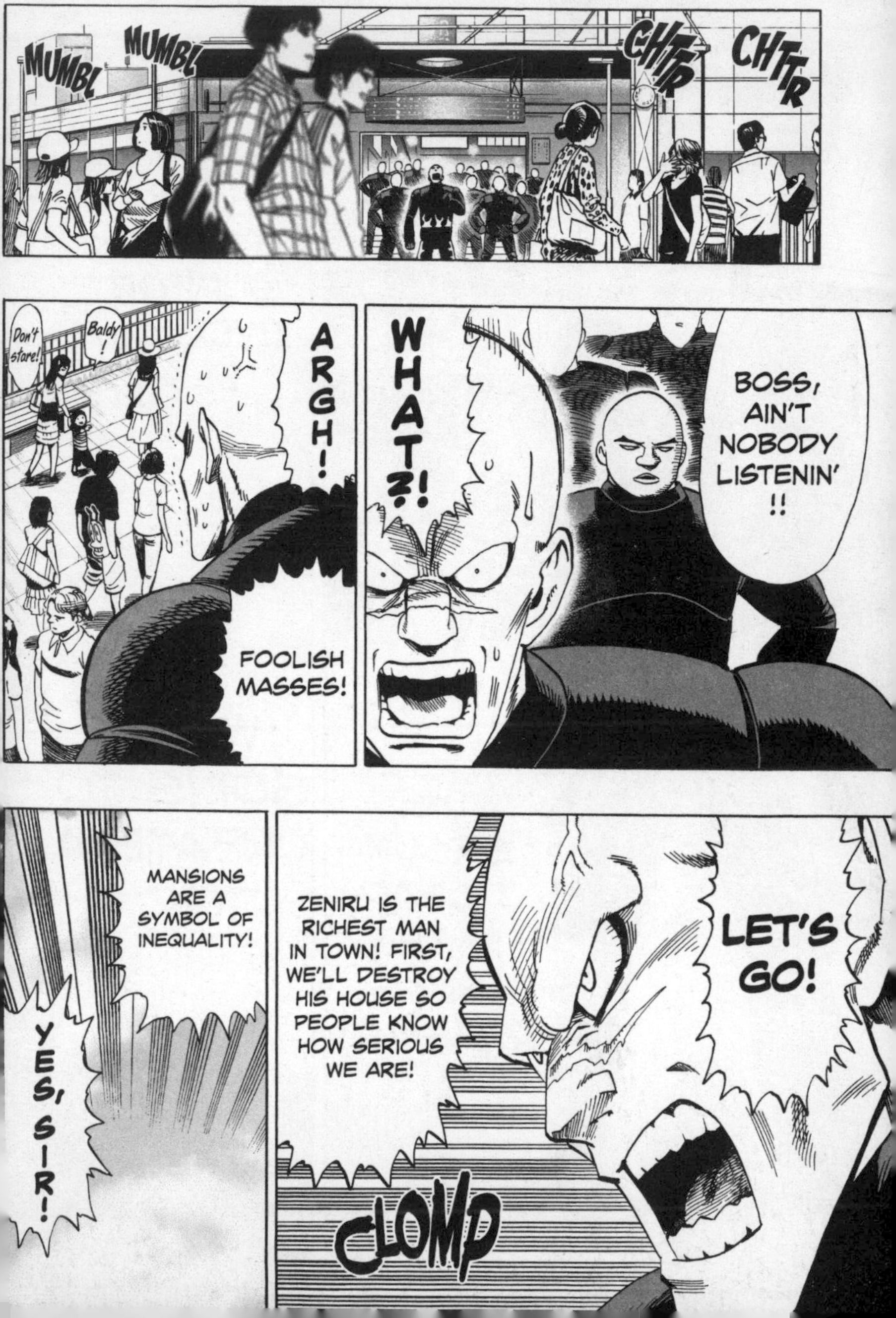
CHTTR
CHTTR
MUMBL
MUMBL
BOSS, AIN'T NOBODY LISTENIN' !!
WHAT?!
ARGH!
FOOLISH MASSES!
Baldy!
Don't stare!
LET'S GO!
ZENIRU IS THE RICHEST MAN IN TOWN! FIRST, WE'LL DESTROY HIS HOUSE SO PEOPLE KNOW HOW SERIOUS WE ARE!
CLOMP
MANSIONS ARE A SYMBOL OF INEQUALITY!
YES, SIR!

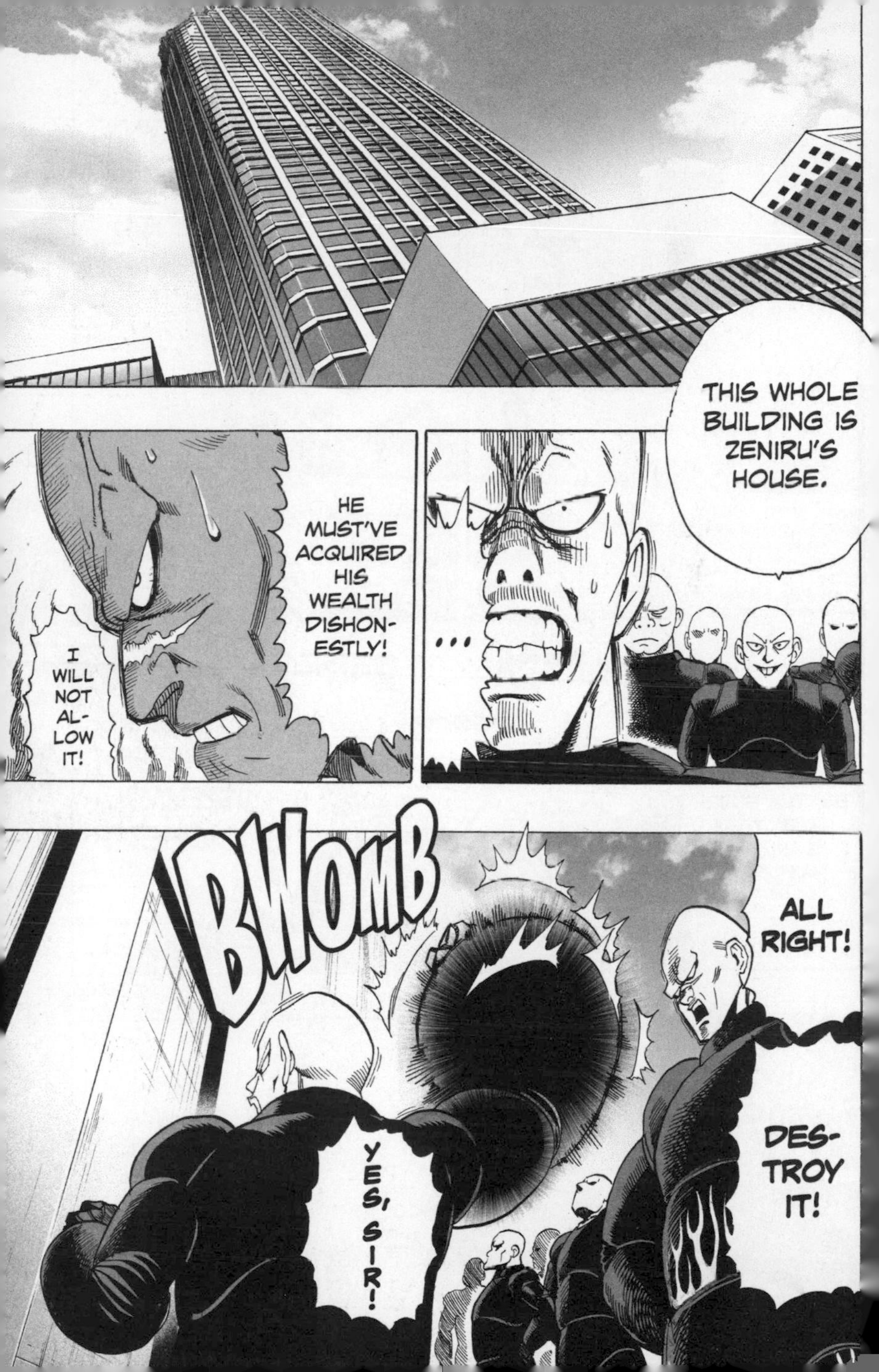
THIS WHOLE BUILDING IS ZENIRU'S HOUSE.
...
HE MUST'VE ACQUIRED HIS WEALTH DISHON-ESTLY!
I WILL NOT AL-LOW IT!
BWOMB
ALL RIGHT!
DES-TROY IT!
YES, SIR!

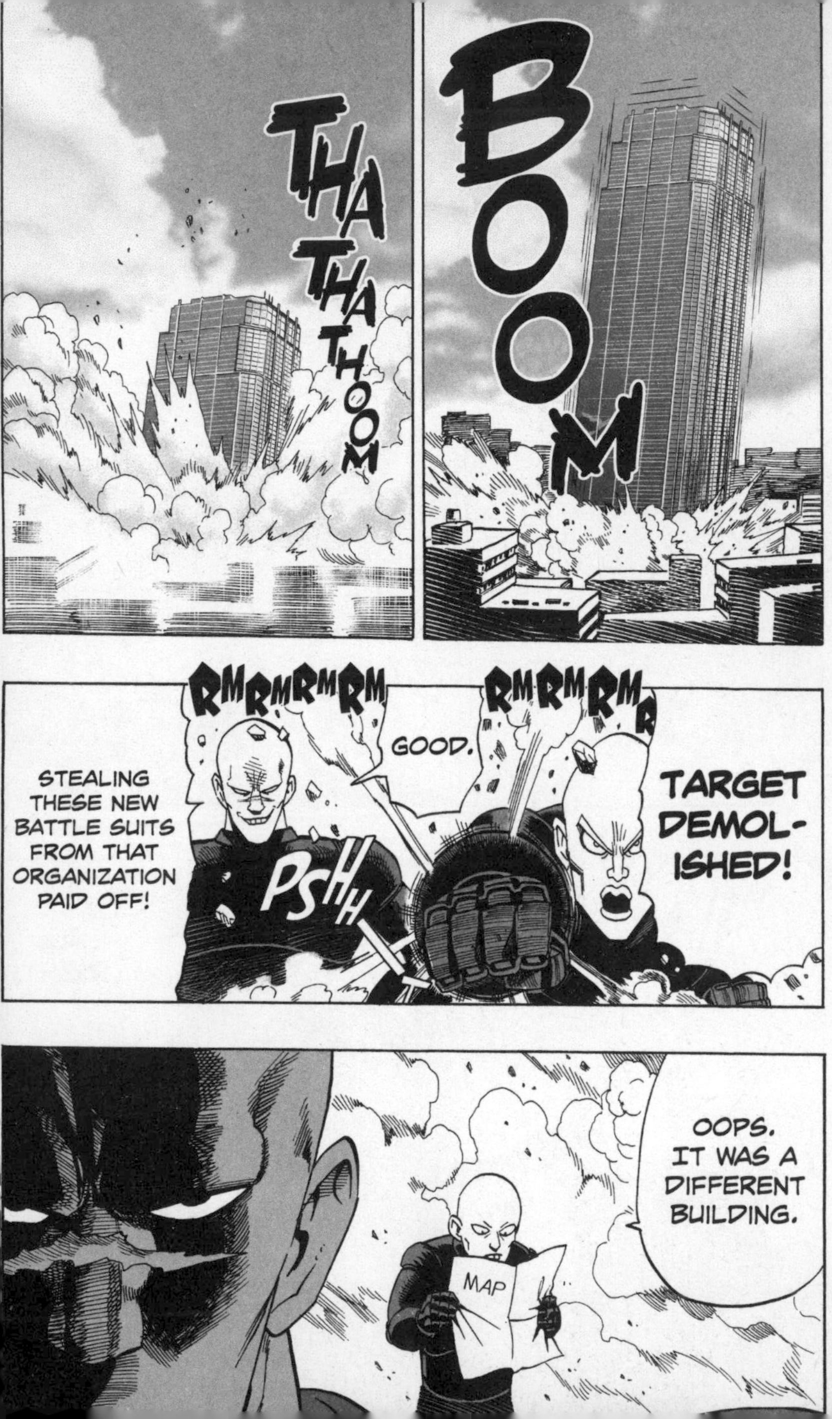
BOOOM
THATHATHOOM
RMRMRMRMR
TARGET DEMOL-ISHED!
RMRMRMRM
GOOD.
STEALING THESE NEW BATTLE SUITS FROM THAT ORGANIZATION PAID OFF!
PSHH
OOPS. IT WAS A DIFFERENT BUILDING.
MAP

READ THIS WAY

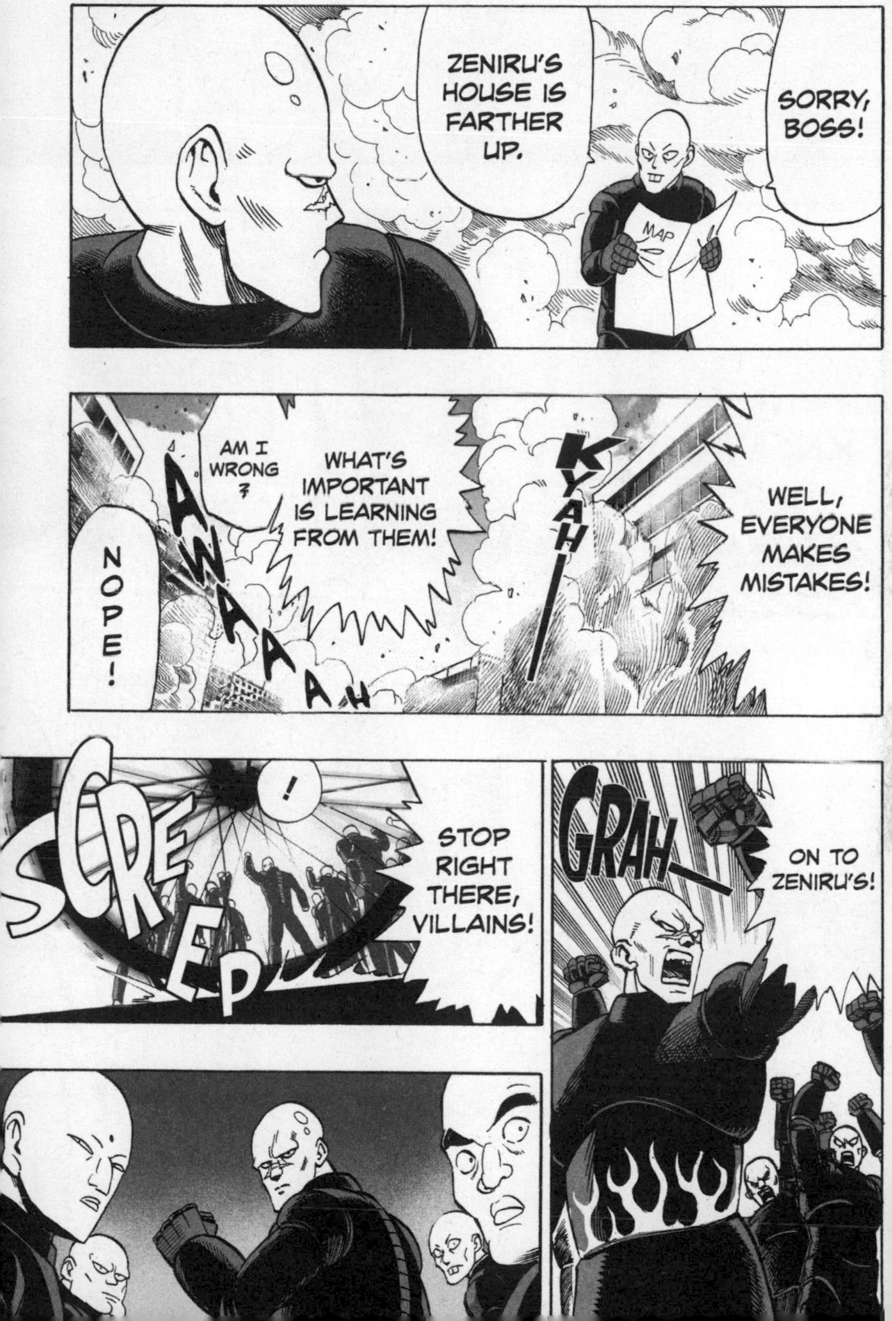
SORRY, BOSS!
ZENIRU'S HOUSE IS FARTHER UP.
MAP
WELL, EVERYONE MAKES MISTAKES!
KYAH!
WHAT'S IMPORTANT IS LEARNING FROM THEM!
AM I WRONG?
NOPE!
AWAAAAAH
ON TO ZENIRU'S!
GRAH—
STOP RIGHT THERE, VILLAINS!
!
SCREEP

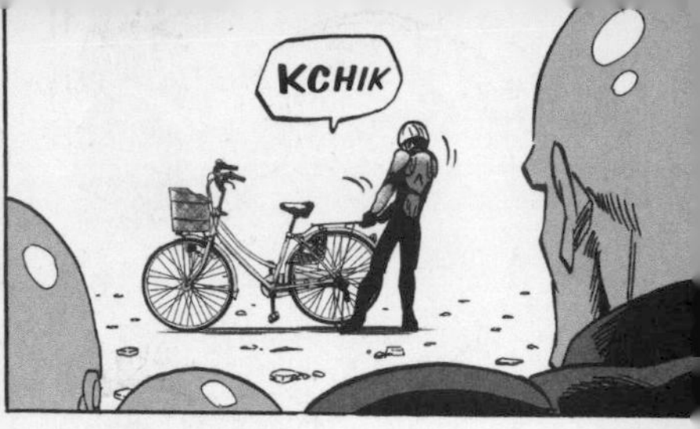
KCHIK

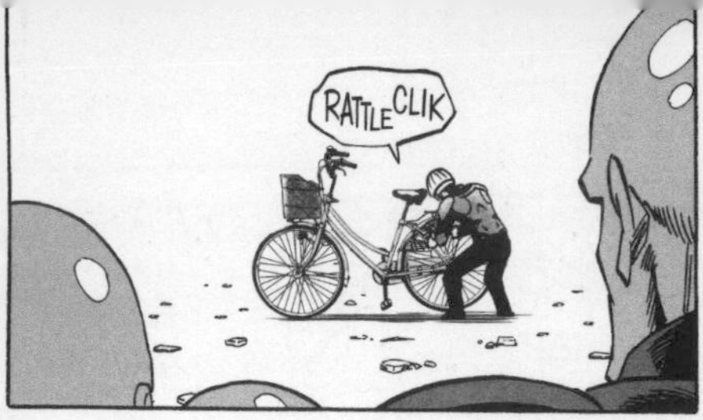
RATTLE CLIK

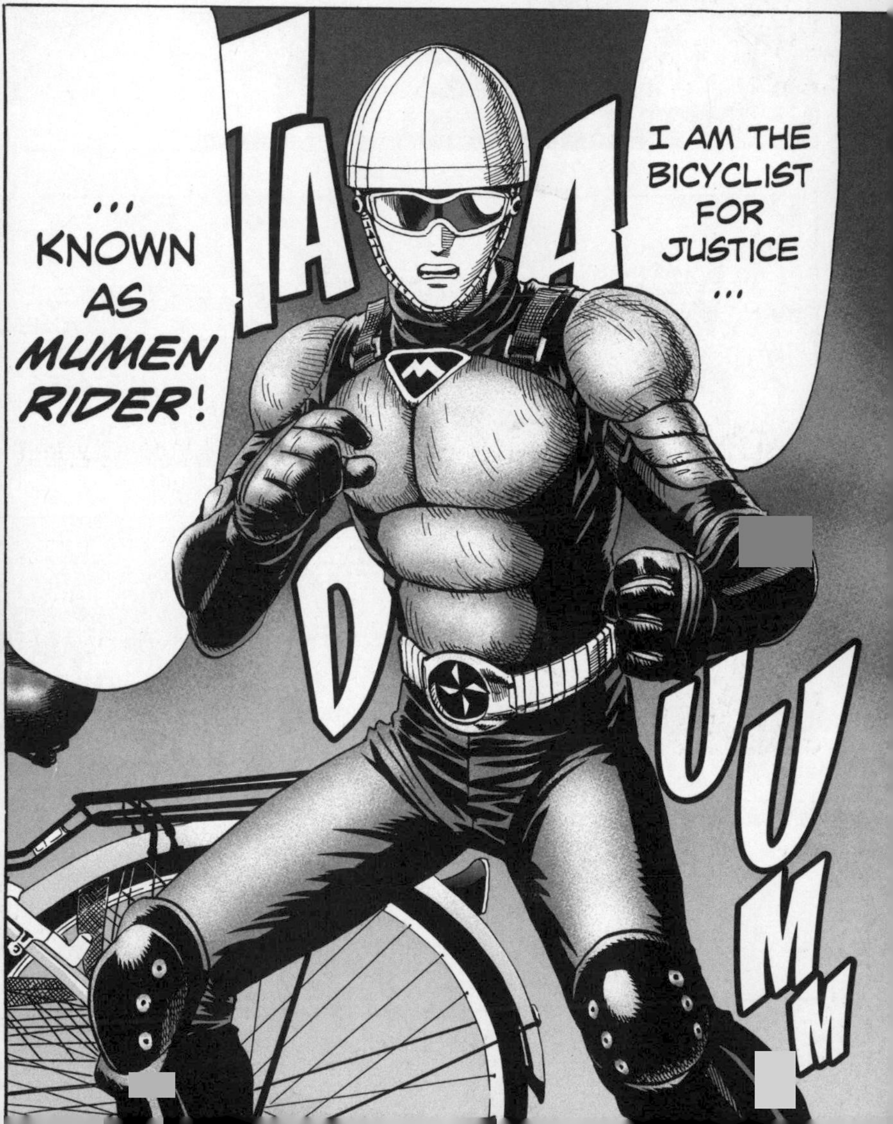
I AM THE BICYCLIST FOR JUSTICE ...
... KNOWN AS MUMEN RIDER!
TA
A
D
UUUMMM

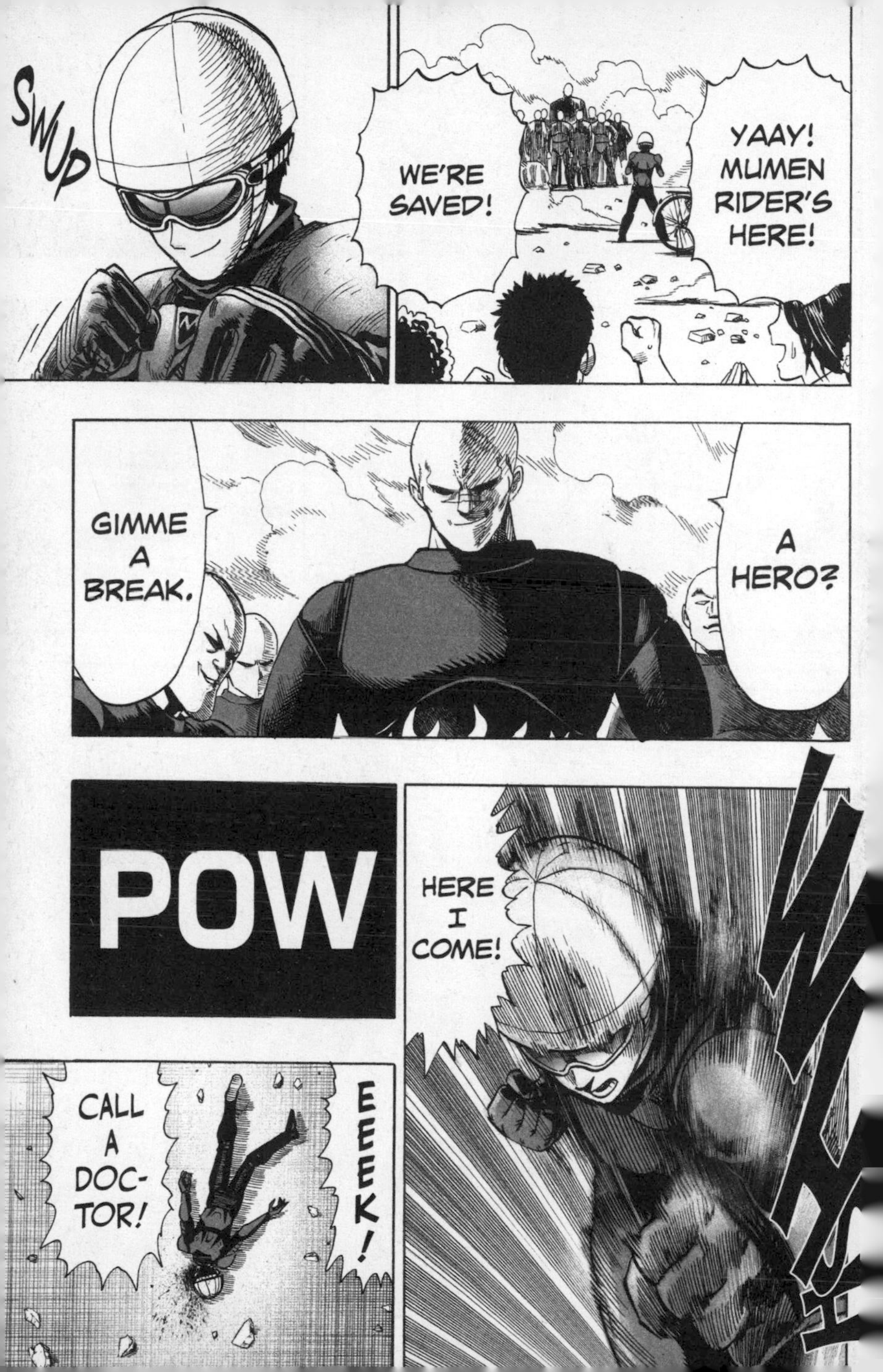
YAAY! MUMEN RIDER'S HERE!
WE'RE SAVED!
SWUP
A HERO?
GIMME A BREAK.
HERE I COME!
POW
EEEEK!
CALL A DOC-TOR!

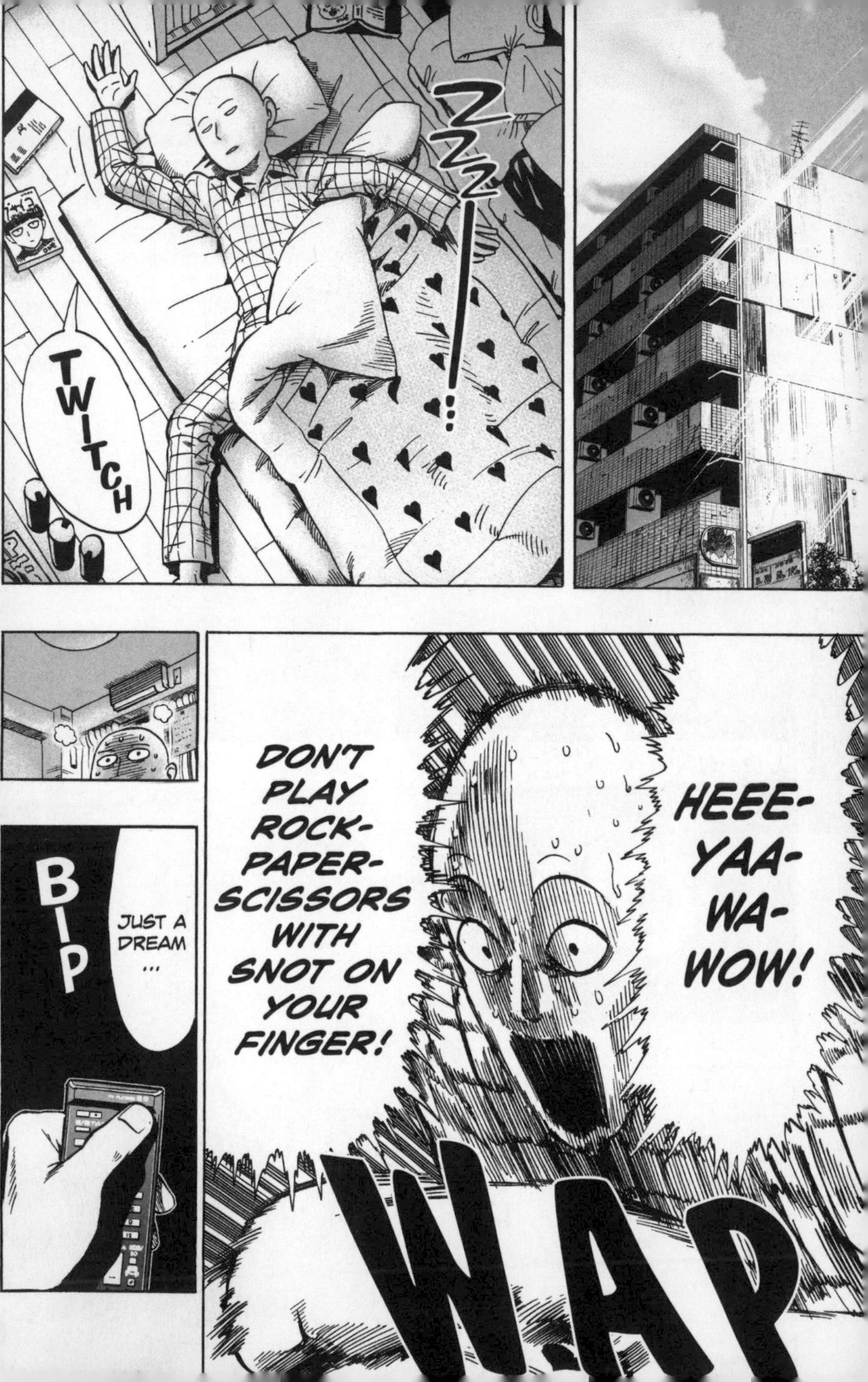
ZZZ!!
TWITCH
HEEE-YAA-WA-WOW!
DON'T PLAY ROCK-PAPER-SCISSORS WITH SNOT ON YOUR FINGER!
WAP
JUST A DREAM ...
BIP

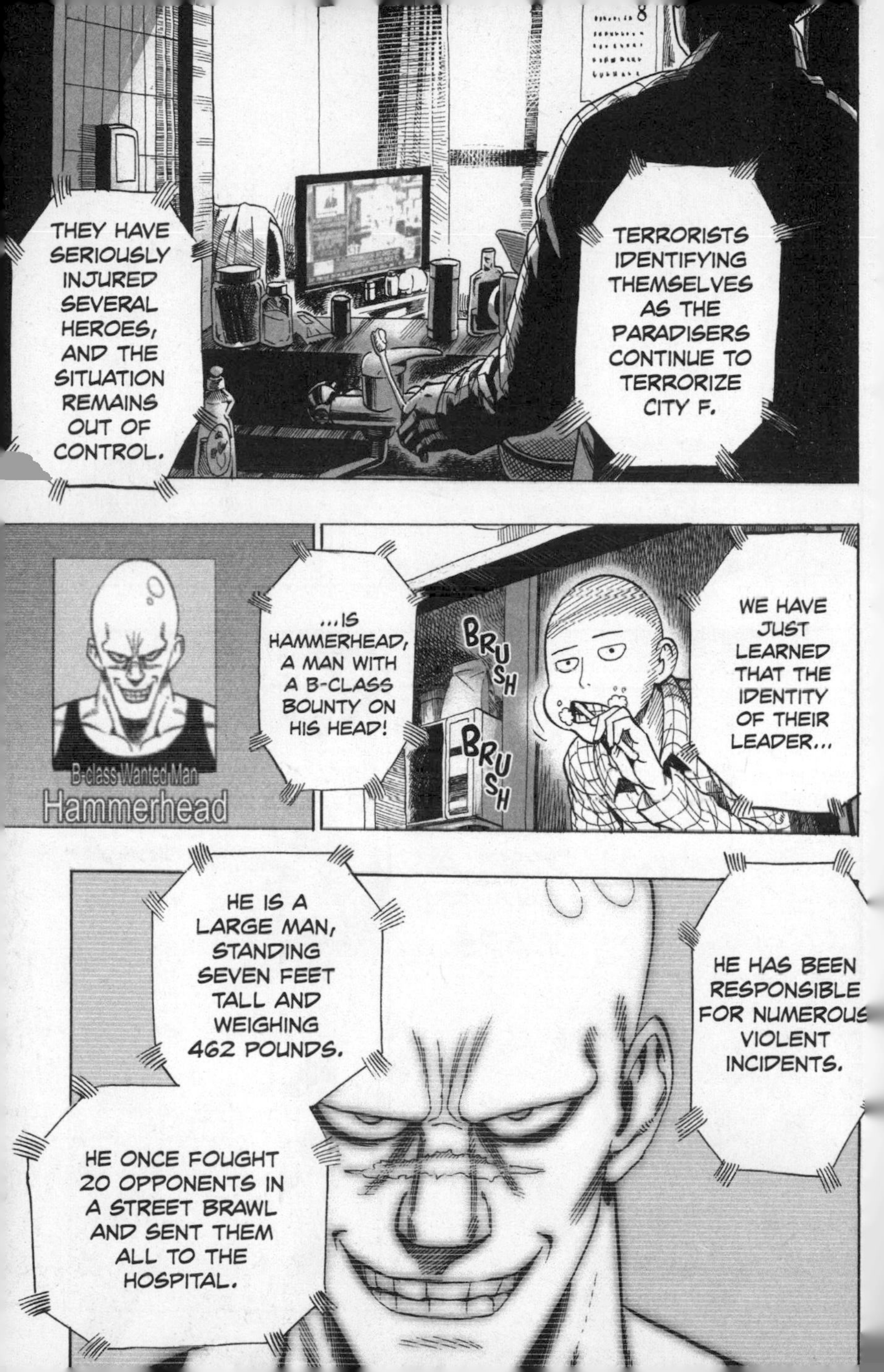
TERRORISTS IDENTIFYING THEMSELVES AS THE PARADISERS CONTINUE TO TERRORIZE CITY F.
THEY HAVE SERIOUSLY INJURED SEVERAL HEROES, AND THE SITUATION REMAINS OUT OF CONTROL.
WE HAVE JUST LEARNED THAT THE IDENTITY OF THEIR LEADER...
BRUSH
BRUSH
...IS HAMMERHEAD, A MAN WITH A B-CLASS BOUNTY ON HIS HEAD!
B-class Wanted Man
Hammerhead
HE HAS BEEN RESPONSIBLE FOR NUMEROUS VIOLENT INCIDENTS.
HE IS A LARGE MAN, STANDING SEVEN FEET TALL AND WEIGHING 462 POUNDS.
HE ONCE FOUGHT 20 OPPONENTS IN A STREET BRAWL AND SENT THEM ALL TO THE HOSPITAL.

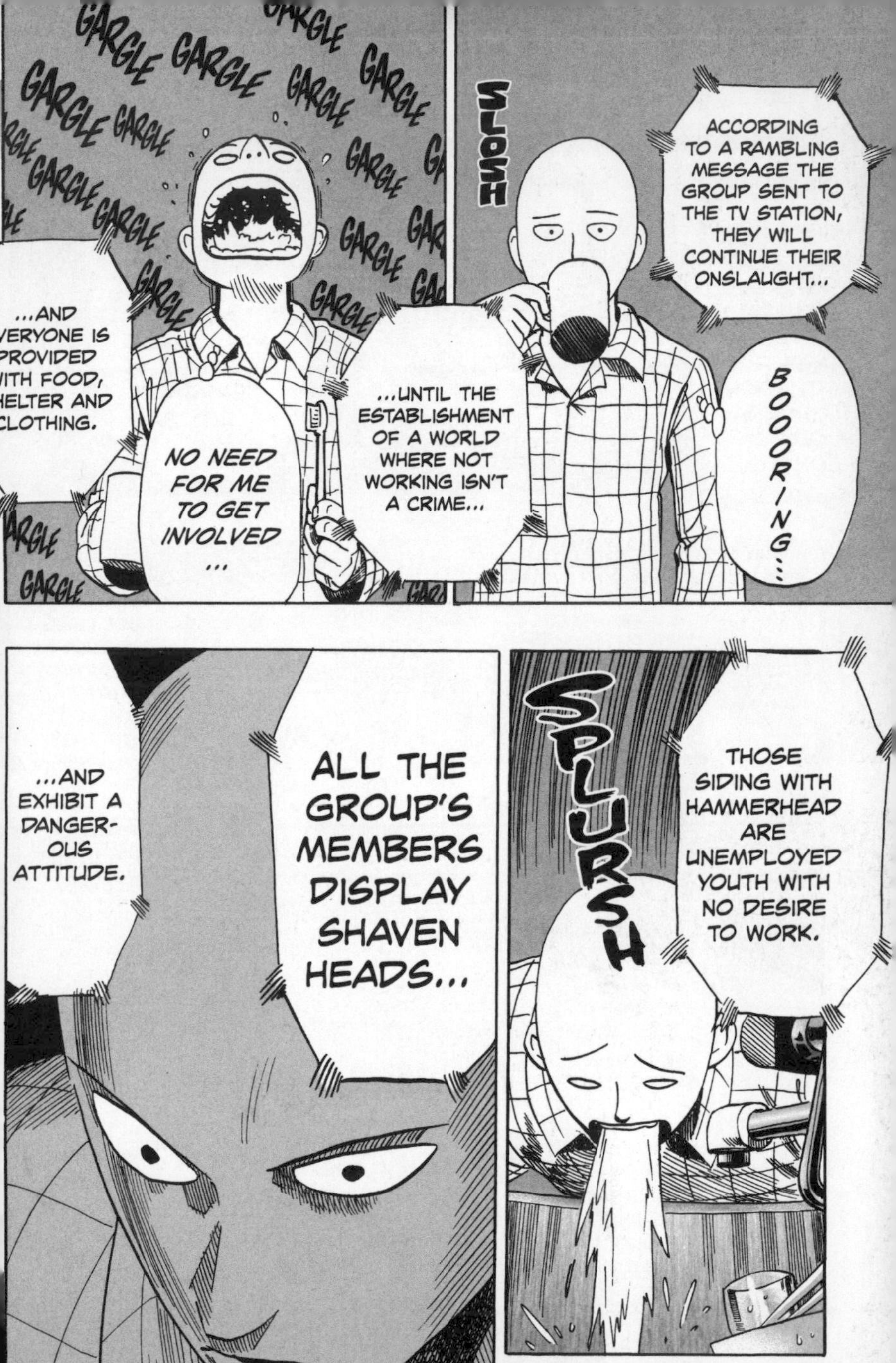
SLOSH
ACCORDING TO A RAMBLING MESSAGE THE GROUP SENT TO THE TV STATION, THEY WILL CONTINUE THEIR ONSLAUGHT...
BOOORING...
...UNTIL THE ESTABLISHMENT OF A WORLD WHERE NOT WORKING ISN'T A CRIME...
GARGLE GARGLE GARGLE GARGLE GARGLE GARGLE GARGLE GARGLE GARGLE GARGLE GARGLE GARGLE
NO NEED FOR ME TO GET INVOLVED ...
...AND EVERYONE IS PROVIDED WITH FOOD, SHELTER AND CLOTHING.
GARGLE GARGLE
THOSE SIDING WITH HAMMERHEAD ARE UNEMPLOYED YOUTH WITH NO DESIRE TO WORK.
SPLURSH
ALL THE GROUP'S MEMBERS DISPLAY SHAVEN HEADS...
...AND EXHIBIT A DANGER-OUS ATTITUDE.

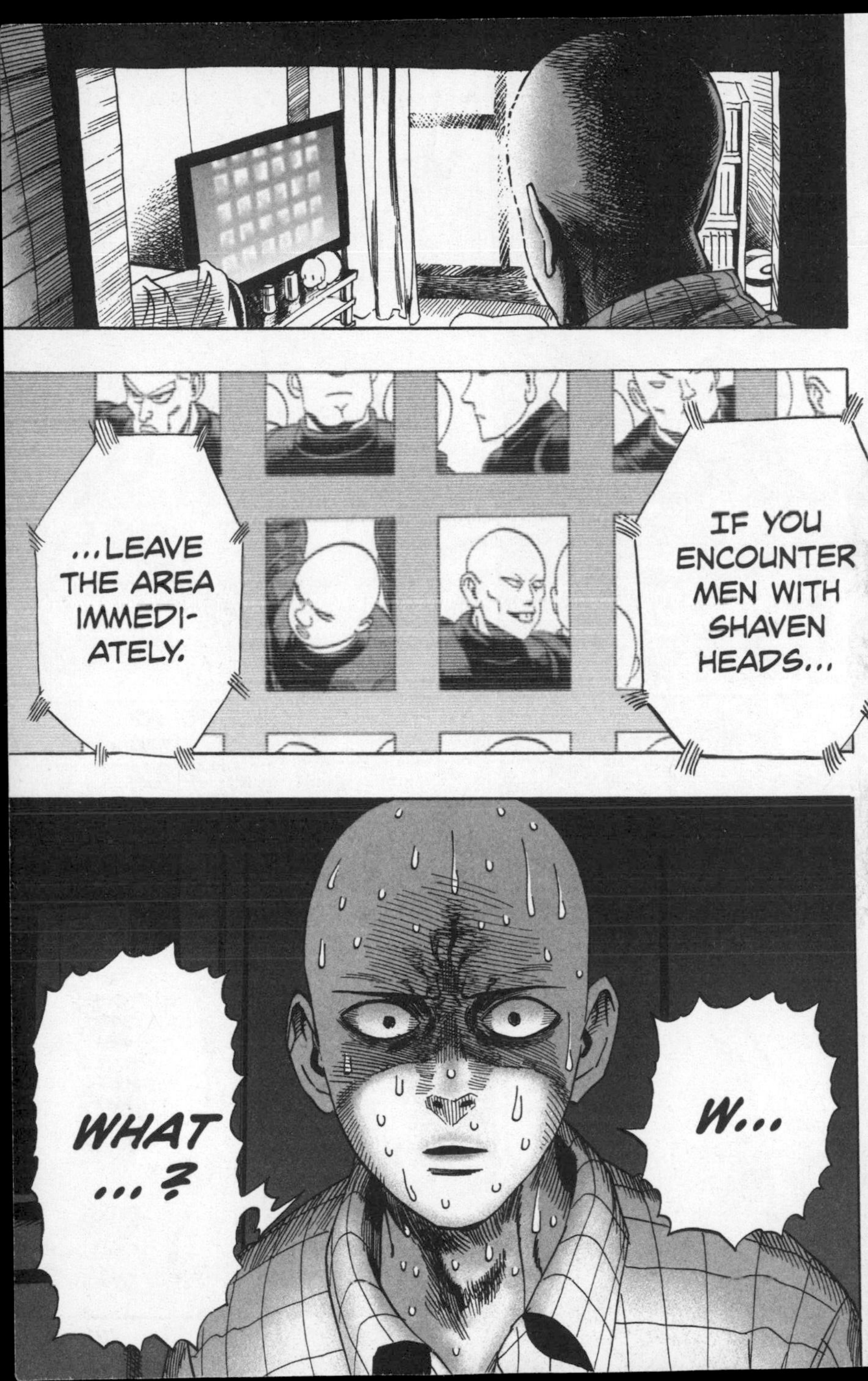
IF YOU ENCOUNTER MEN WITH SHAVEN HEADS...
...LEAVE THE AREA IMMEDI-ATELY.
W...
WHAT ...?

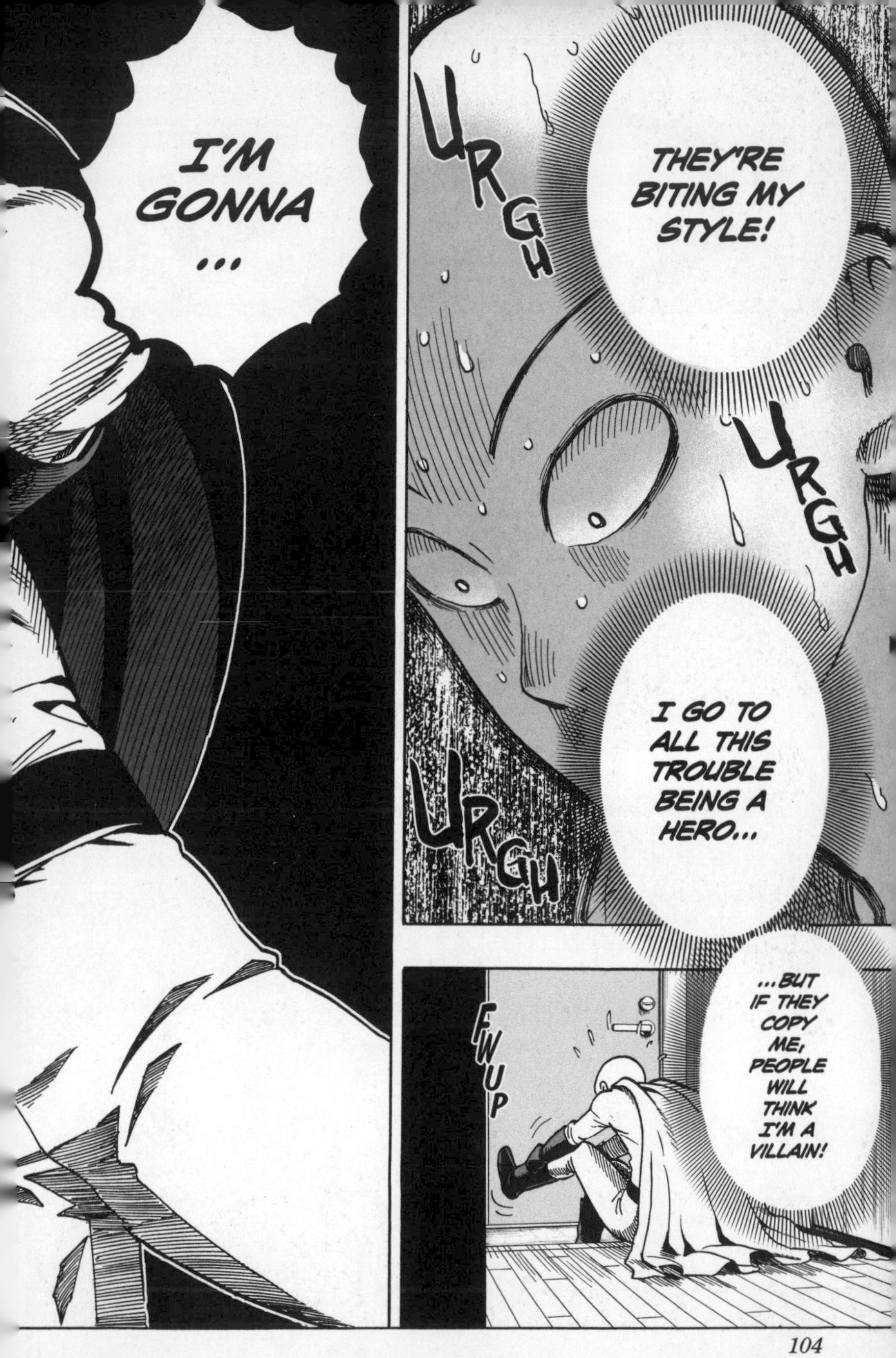
URGH
THEY'RE BITING MY STYLE!
URGH
URGH
I GO TO ALL THIS TROUBLE BEING A HERO...
...BUT IF THEY COPY ME, PEOPLE WILL THINK I'M A VILLAIN!
FWUP
I'M GONNA ...

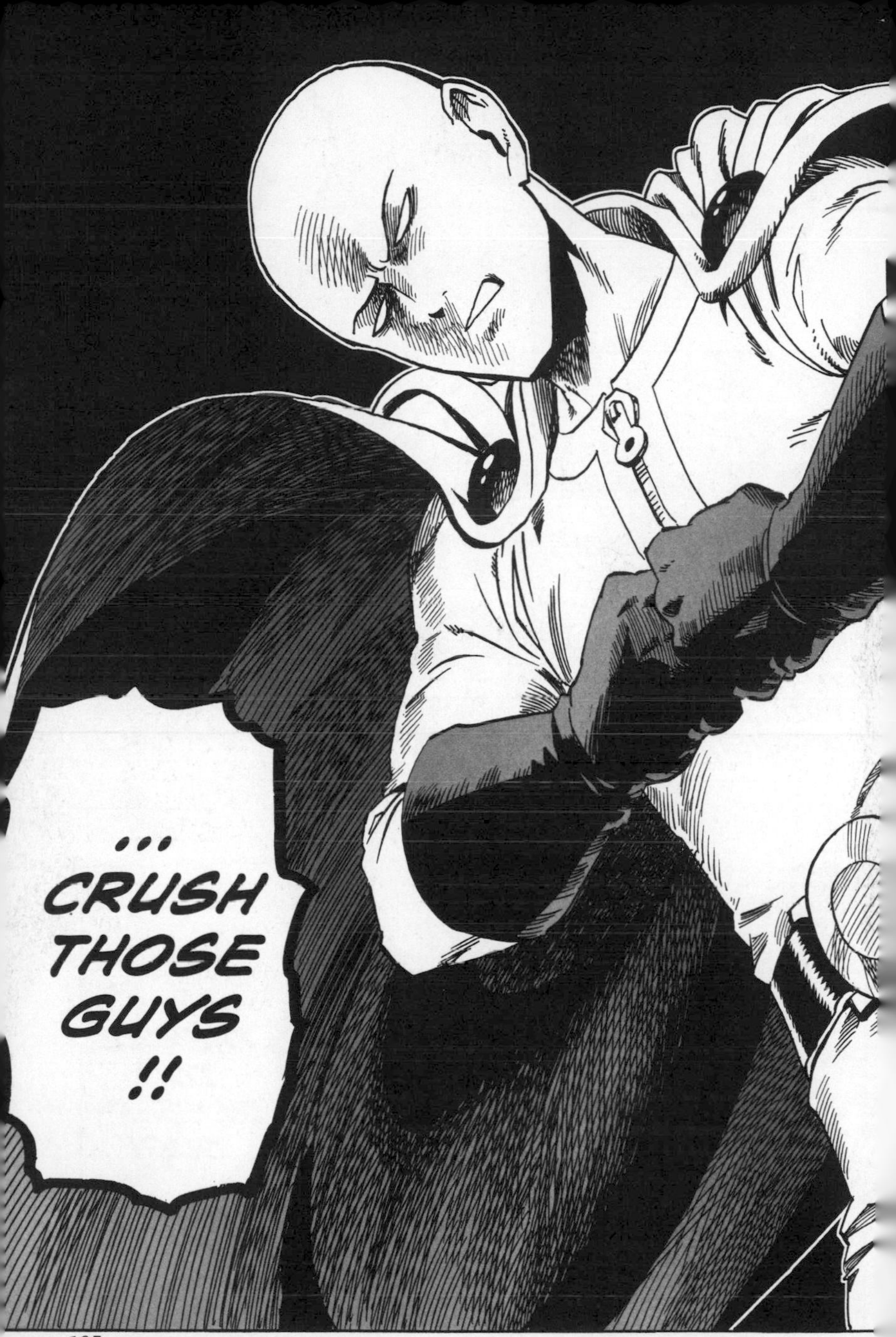
...CRUSH THOSE GUYS !!

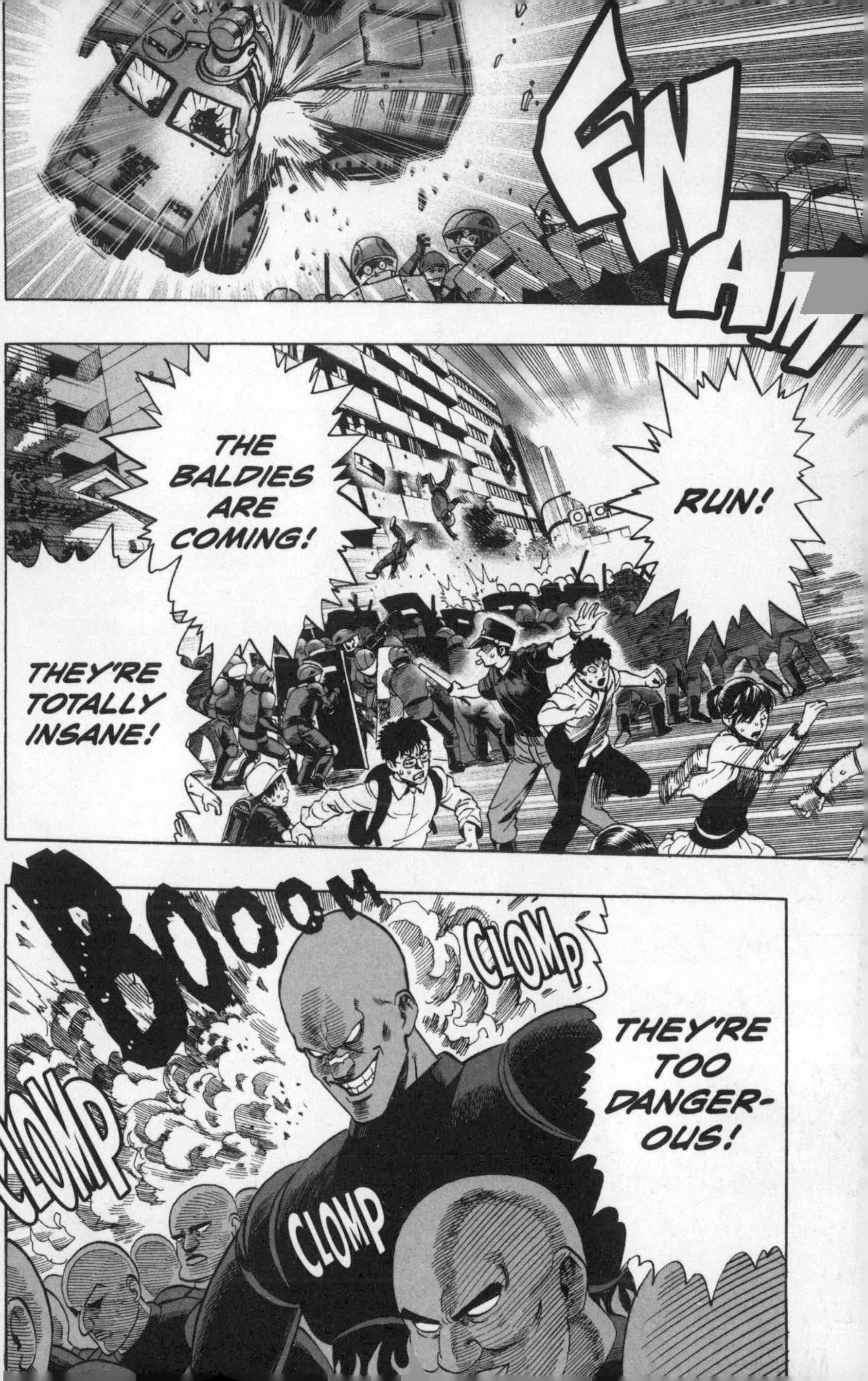
FWAM
RUN!
THE BALDIES ARE COMING!
THEY'RE TOTALLY INSANE!
CLOMP
THEY'RE TOO DANGER-OUS!
BOOOOM
CLOMP
CLOMP

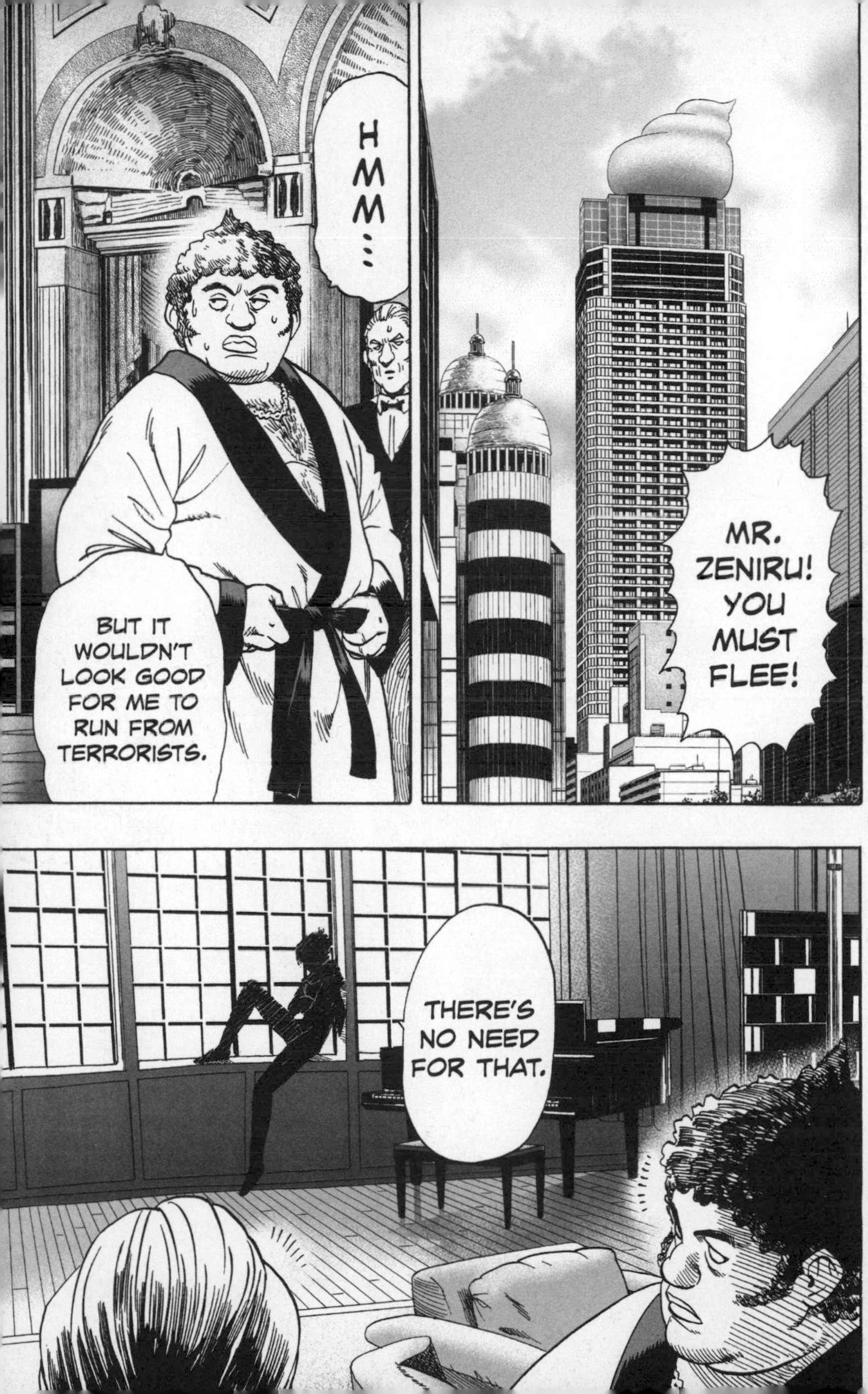
MR. ZENIRU! YOU MUST FLEE!
HMM...
BUT IT WOULDN'T LOOK GOOD FOR ME TO RUN FROM TERRORISTS.
THERE'S NO NEED FOR THAT.

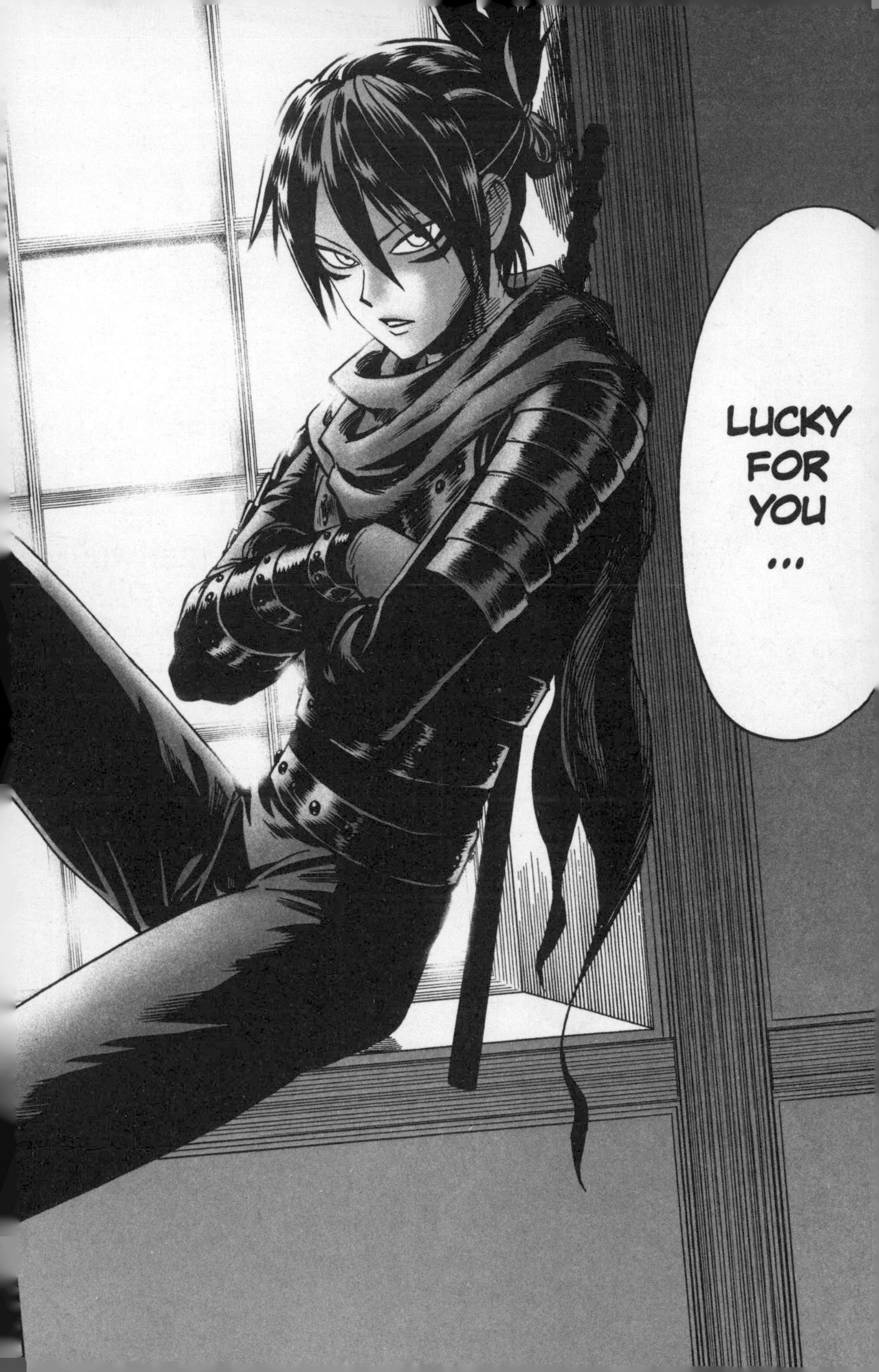
LUCKY FOR YOU ...

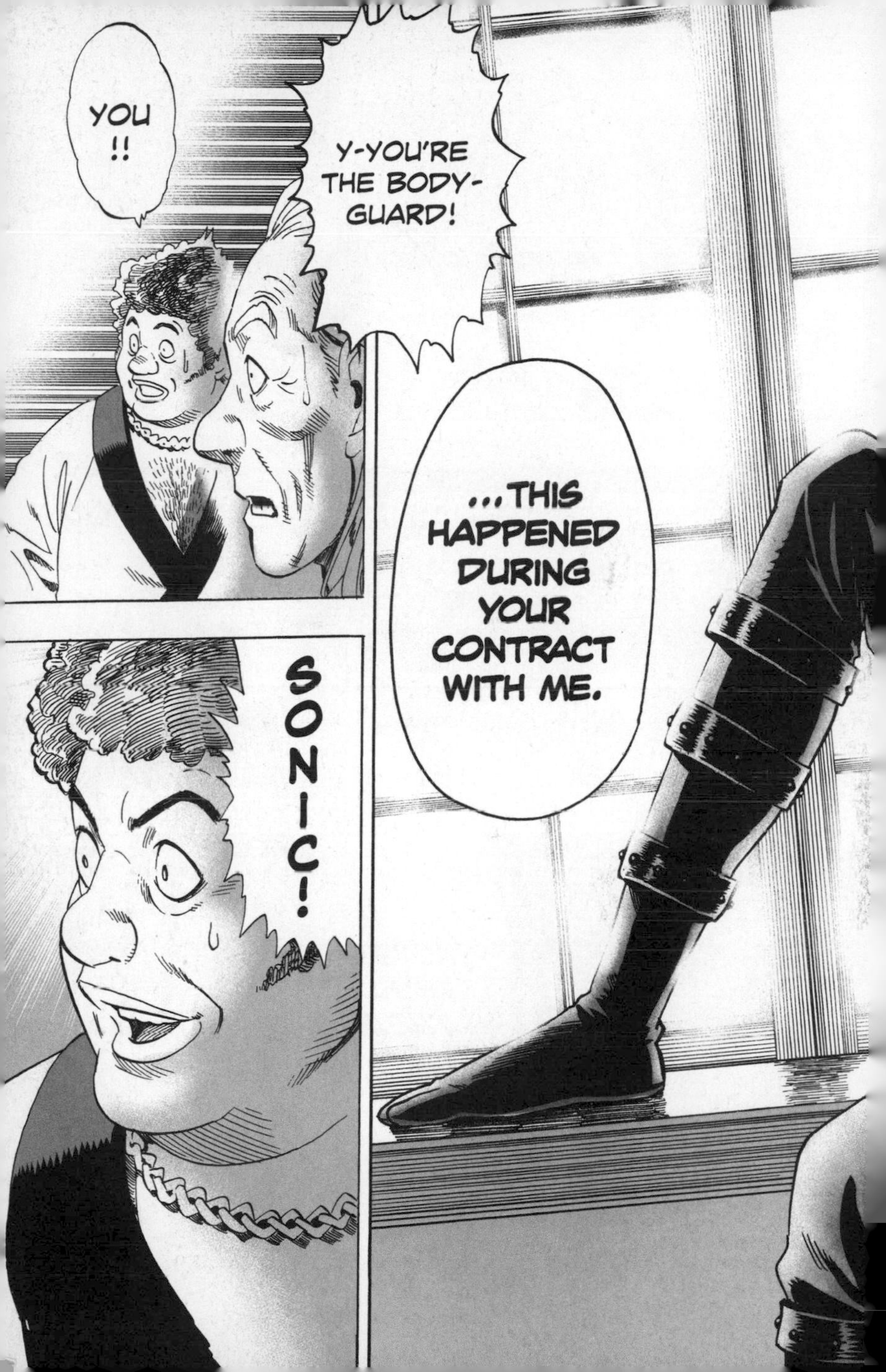
...THIS HAPPENED DURING YOUR CONTRACT WITH ME.
Y-YOU'RE THE BODY-GUARD!
YOU !!
SONIC!

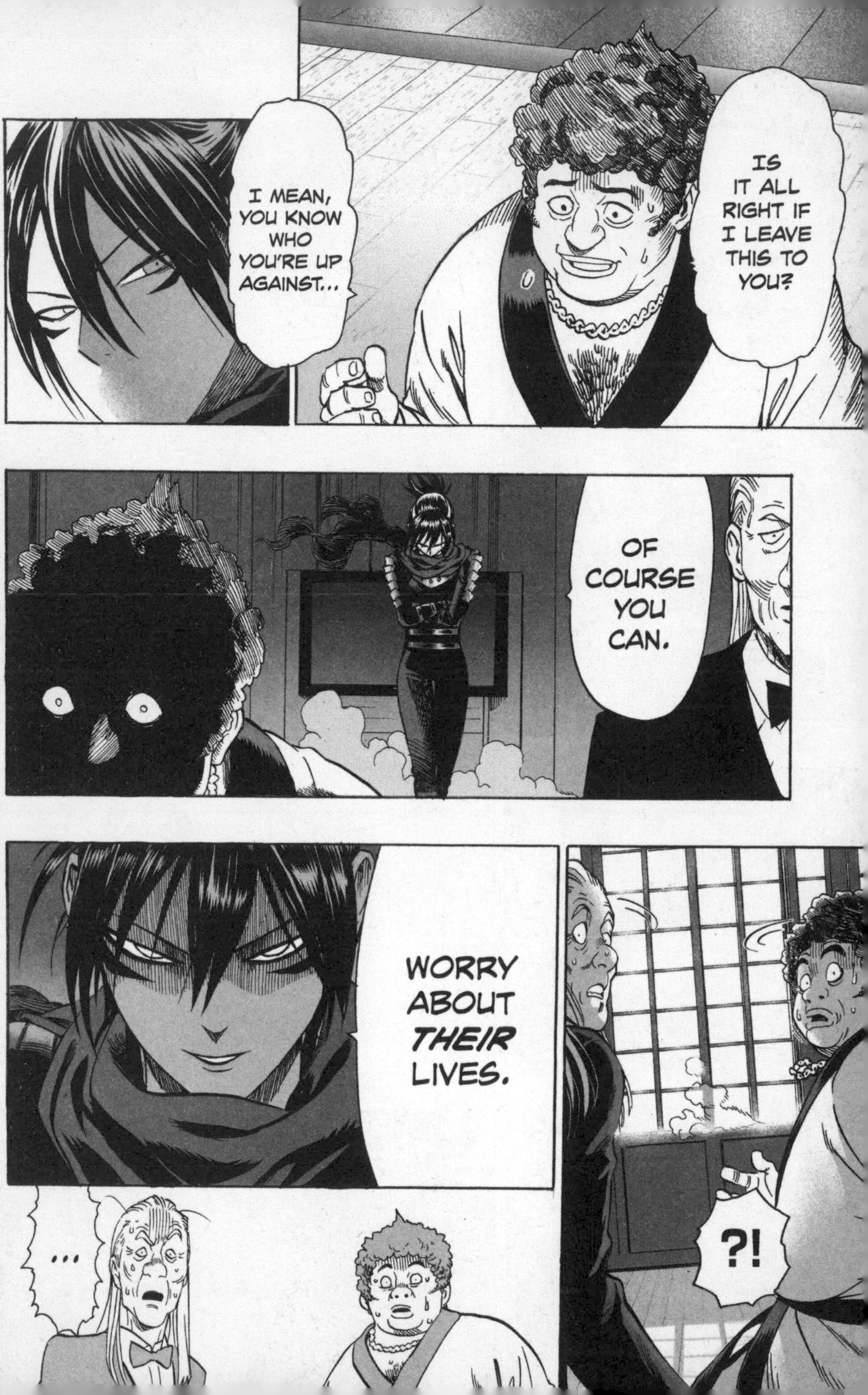
IS IT ALL RIGHT IF I LEAVE THIS TO YOU?
I MEAN, YOU KNOW WHO YOU'RE UP AGAINST...
OF COURSE YOU CAN.
WORRY ABOUT *THEIR* LIVES.
?!
...

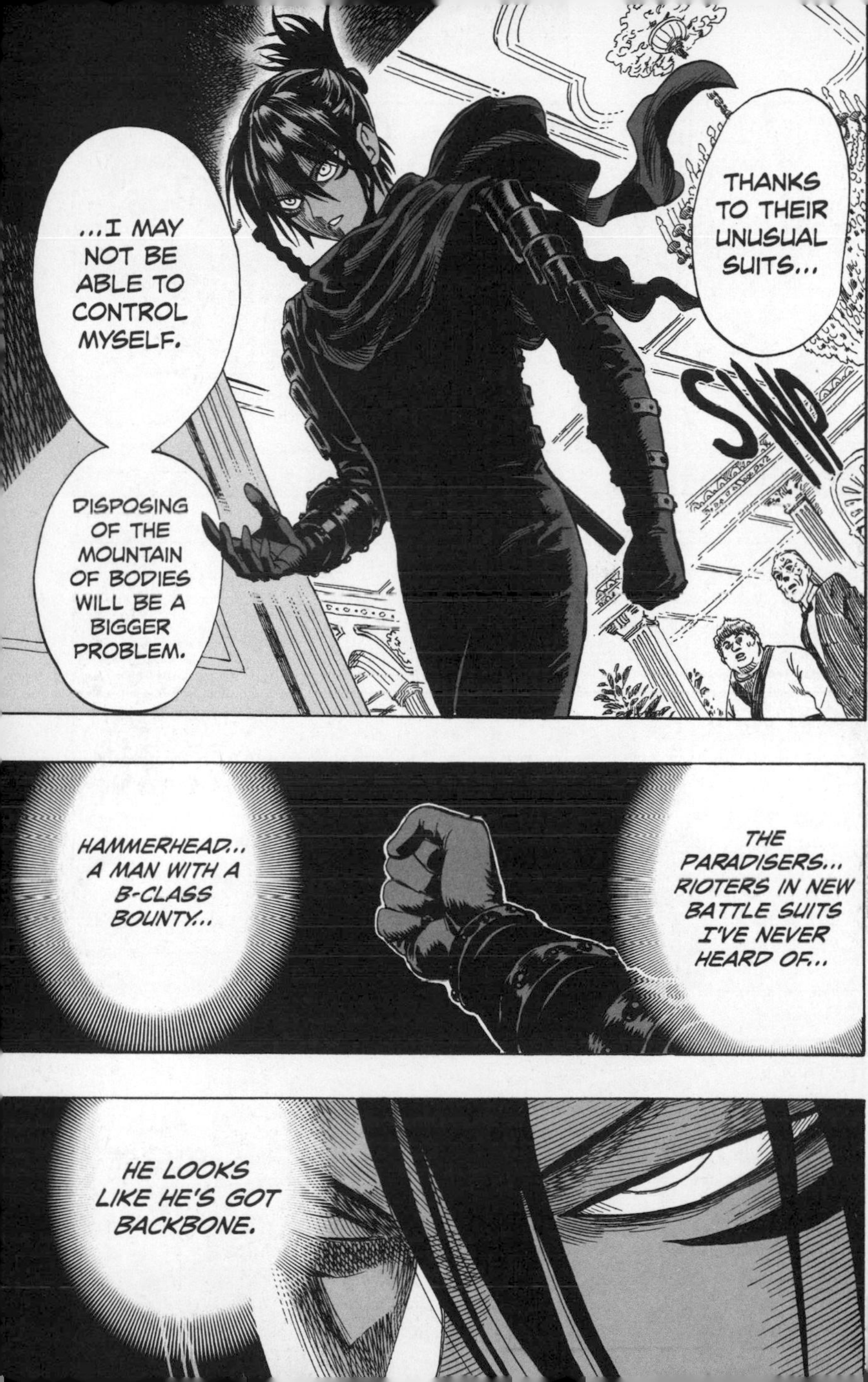
THANKS TO THEIR UNUSUAL SUITS...
SWP
...I MAY NOT BE ABLE TO CONTROL MYSELF.
DISPOSING OF THE MOUNTAIN OF BODIES WILL BE A BIGGER PROBLEM.
THE PARADISERS... RIOTERS IN NEW BATTLE SUITS I'VE NEVER HEARD OF...
HAMMERHEAD... A MAN WITH A B-CLASS BOUNTY...
HE LOOKS LIKE HE'S GOT BACKBONE.

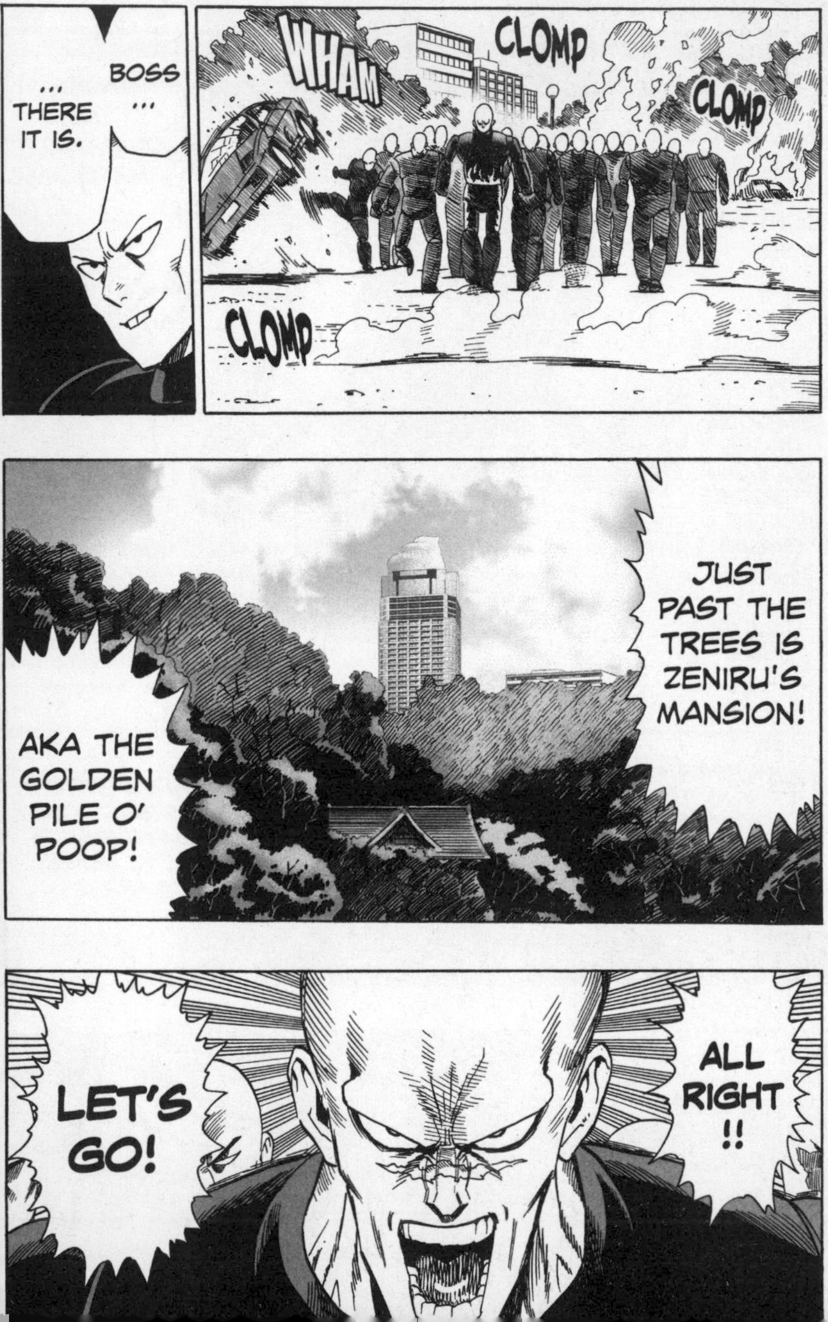
WHAM
CLOMP
CLOMP
CLOMP
BOSS ...
... THERE IT IS.
JUST PAST THE TREES IS ZENIRU'S MANSION!
AKA THE GOLDEN PILE O' POOP!
ALL RIGHT !!
LET'S GO!

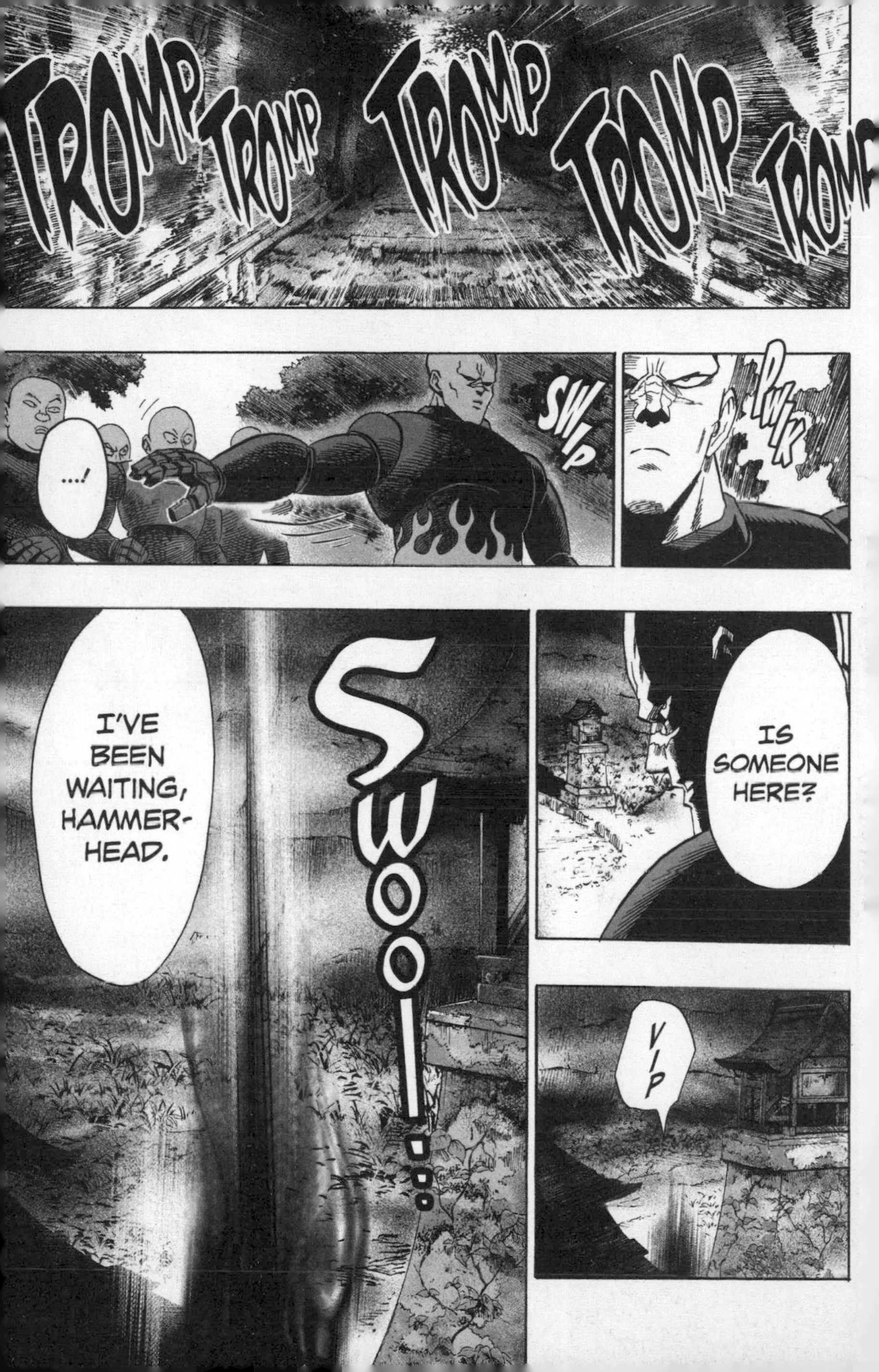
TROMP TROMP TROMP TROMP TROMP
PWIK
SWIP
...!
IS SOMEONE HERE?
VIP
I'VE BEEN WAITING, HAMMER-HEAD.
SWOO!...

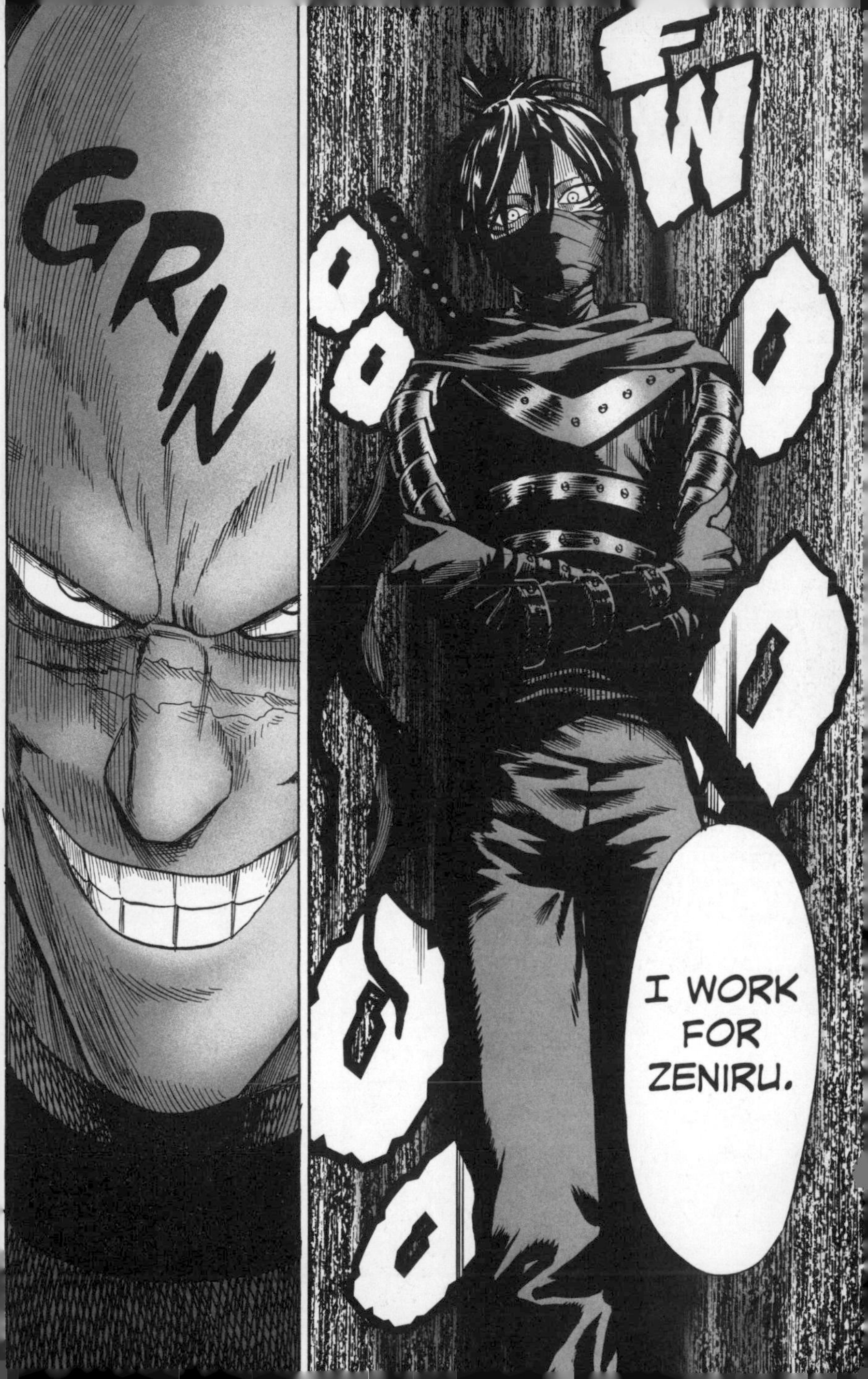
FWOOOOOOO
I WORK FOR ZENIRU.
GRIN

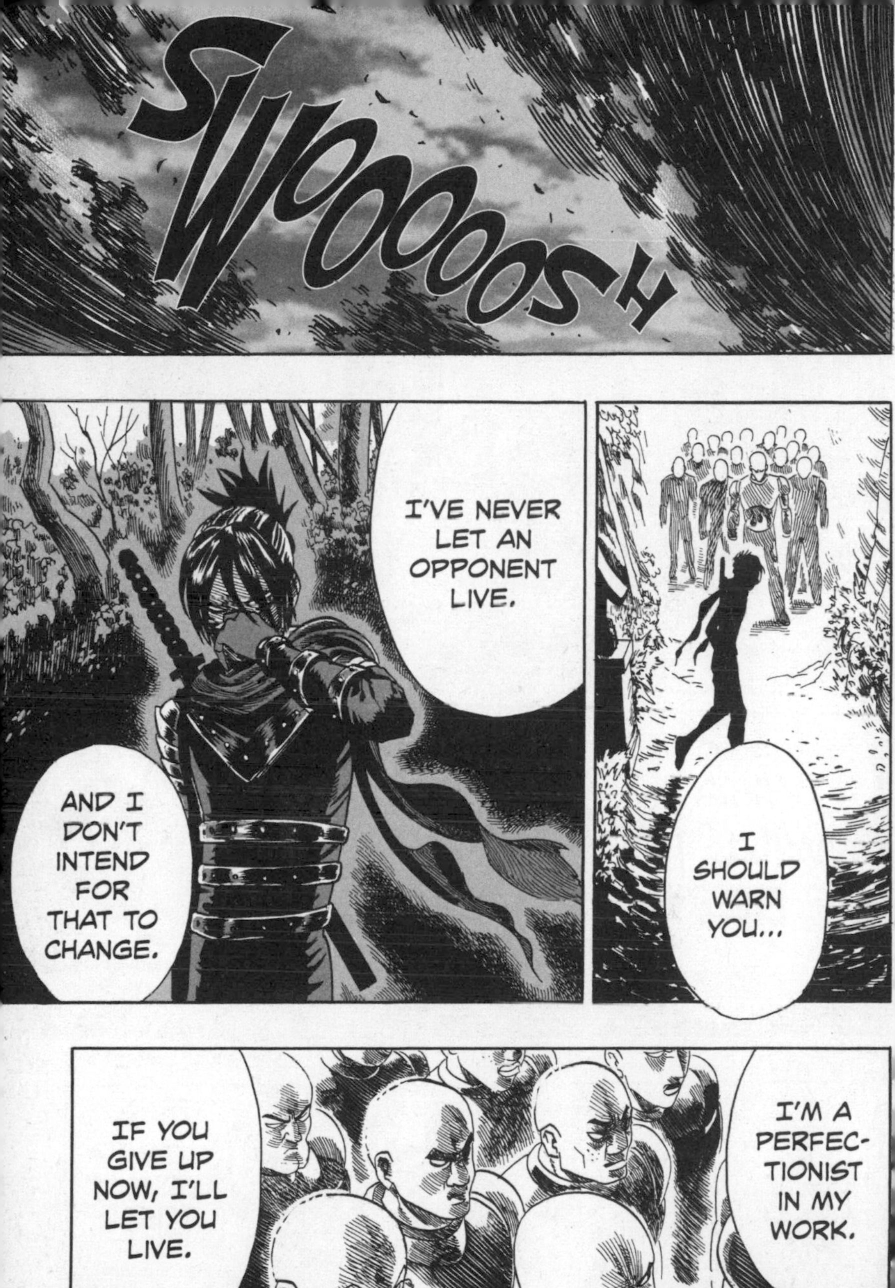
SWOOOOOSH
I SHOULD WARN YOU...
I'VE NEVER LET AN OPPONENT LIVE.
AND I DON'T INTEND FOR THAT TO CHANGE.
I'M A PERFECTIONIST IN MY WORK.
IF YOU GIVE UP NOW, I'LL LET YOU LIVE.

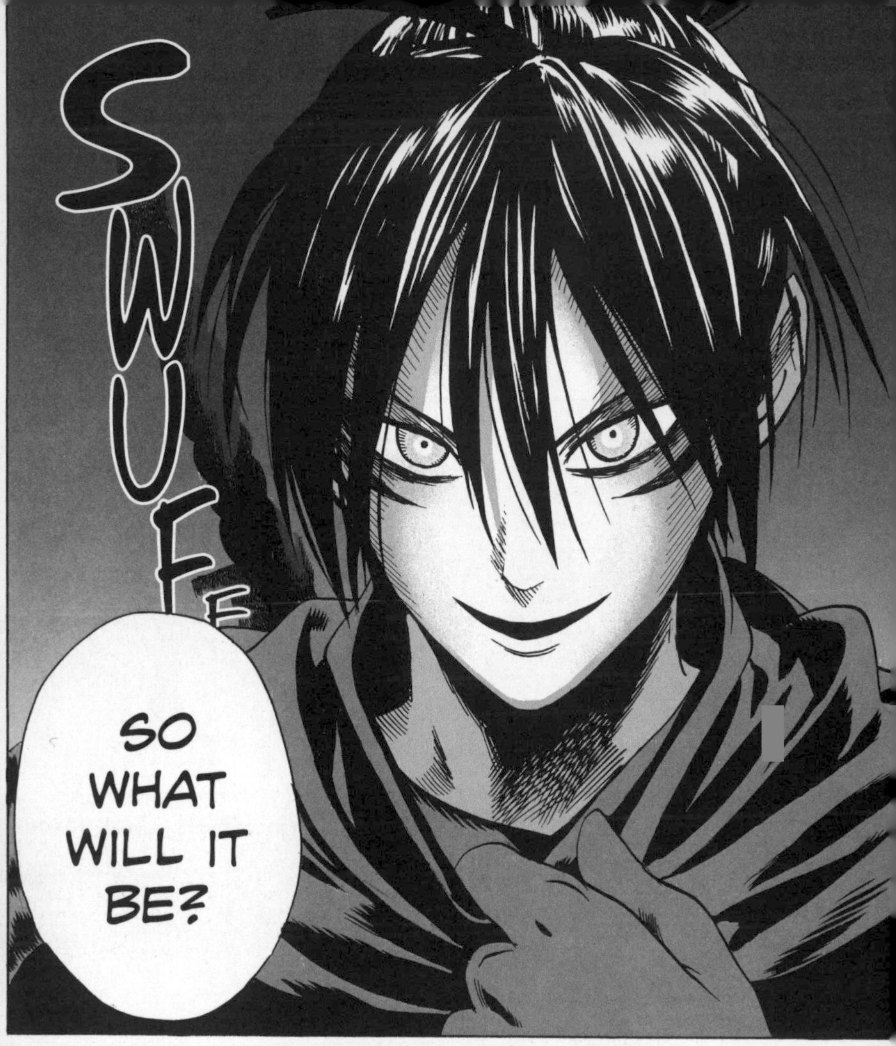
SWUFF
SO WHAT WILL IT BE?

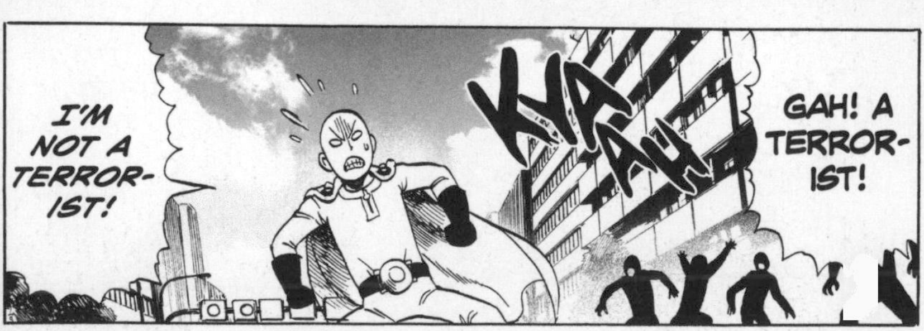
GAH! A TERROR-IST!
KYAAH
I'M NOT A TERROR-IST!

PUNCH 13: SPEED

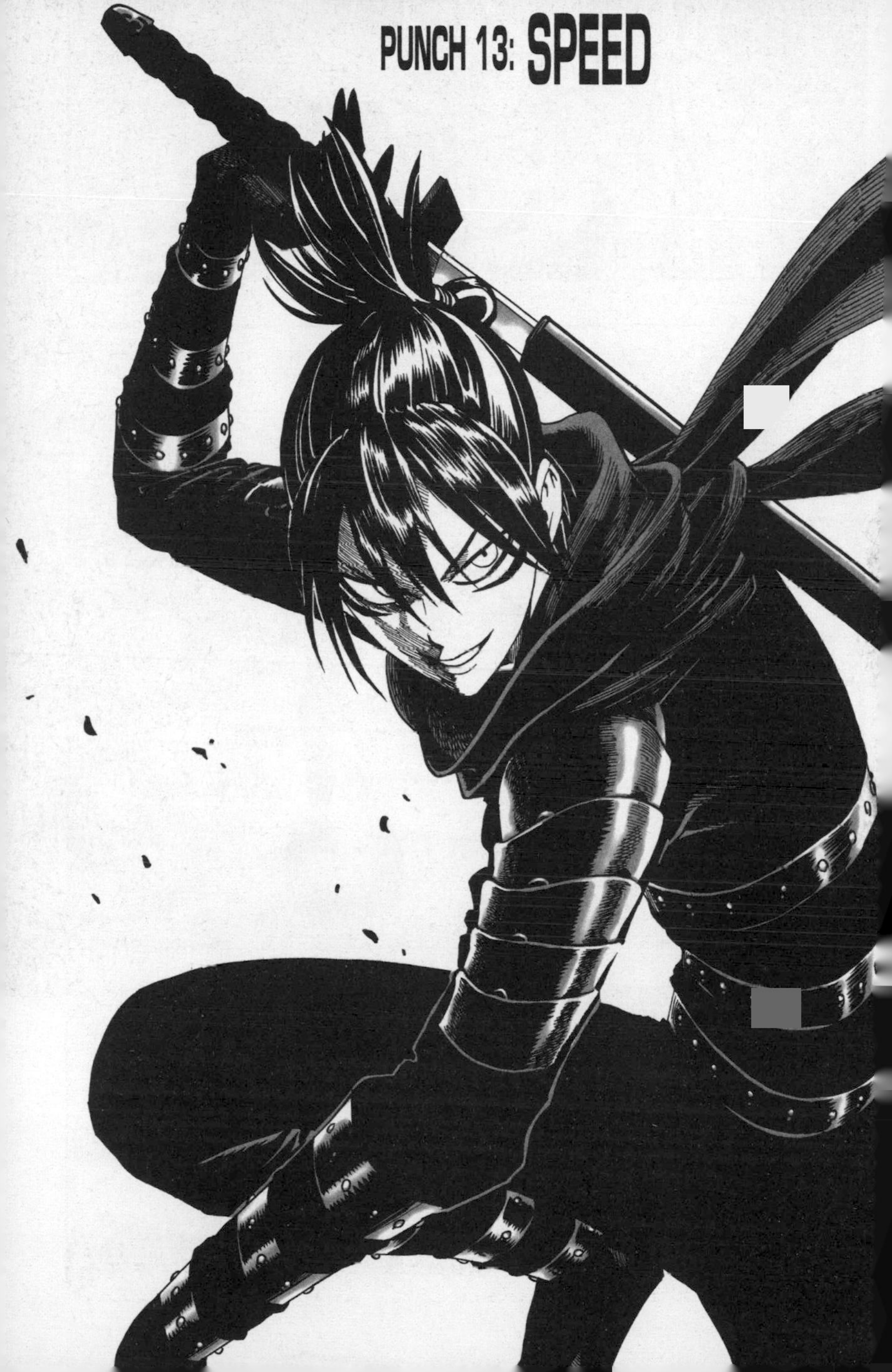

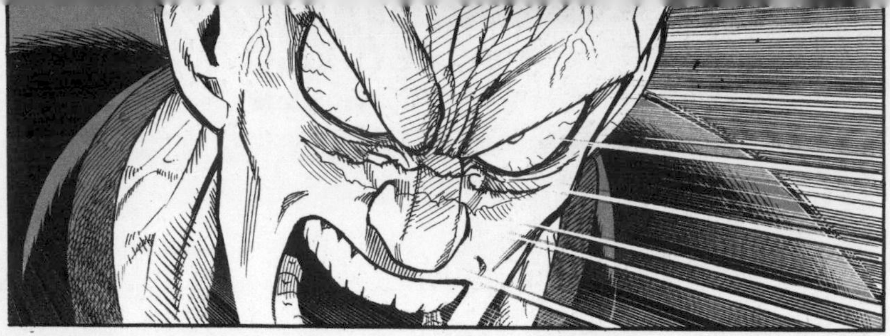
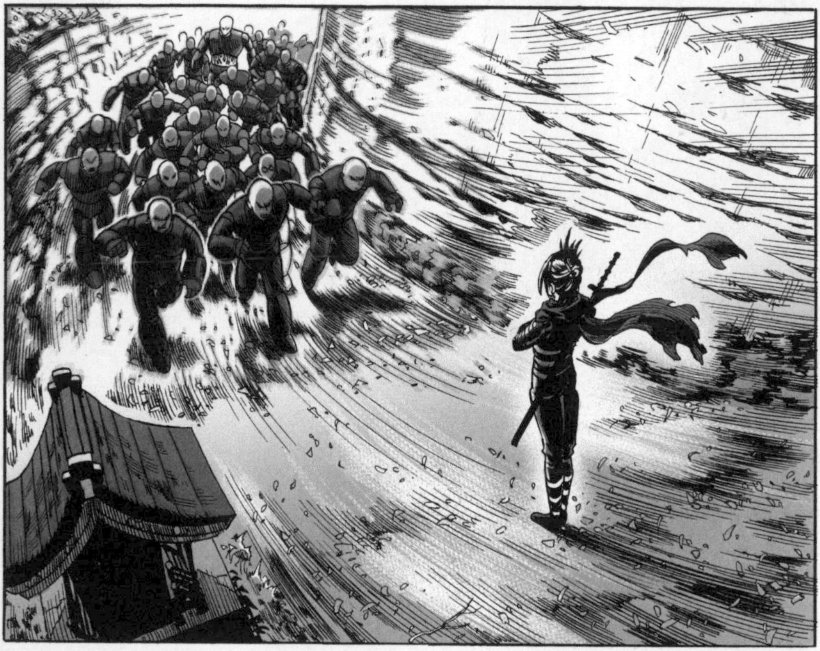
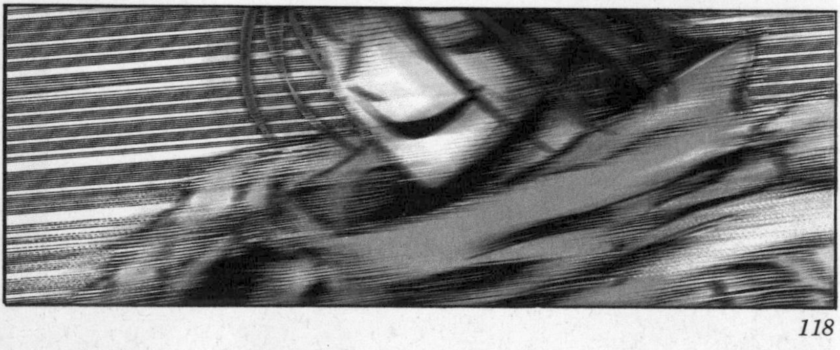

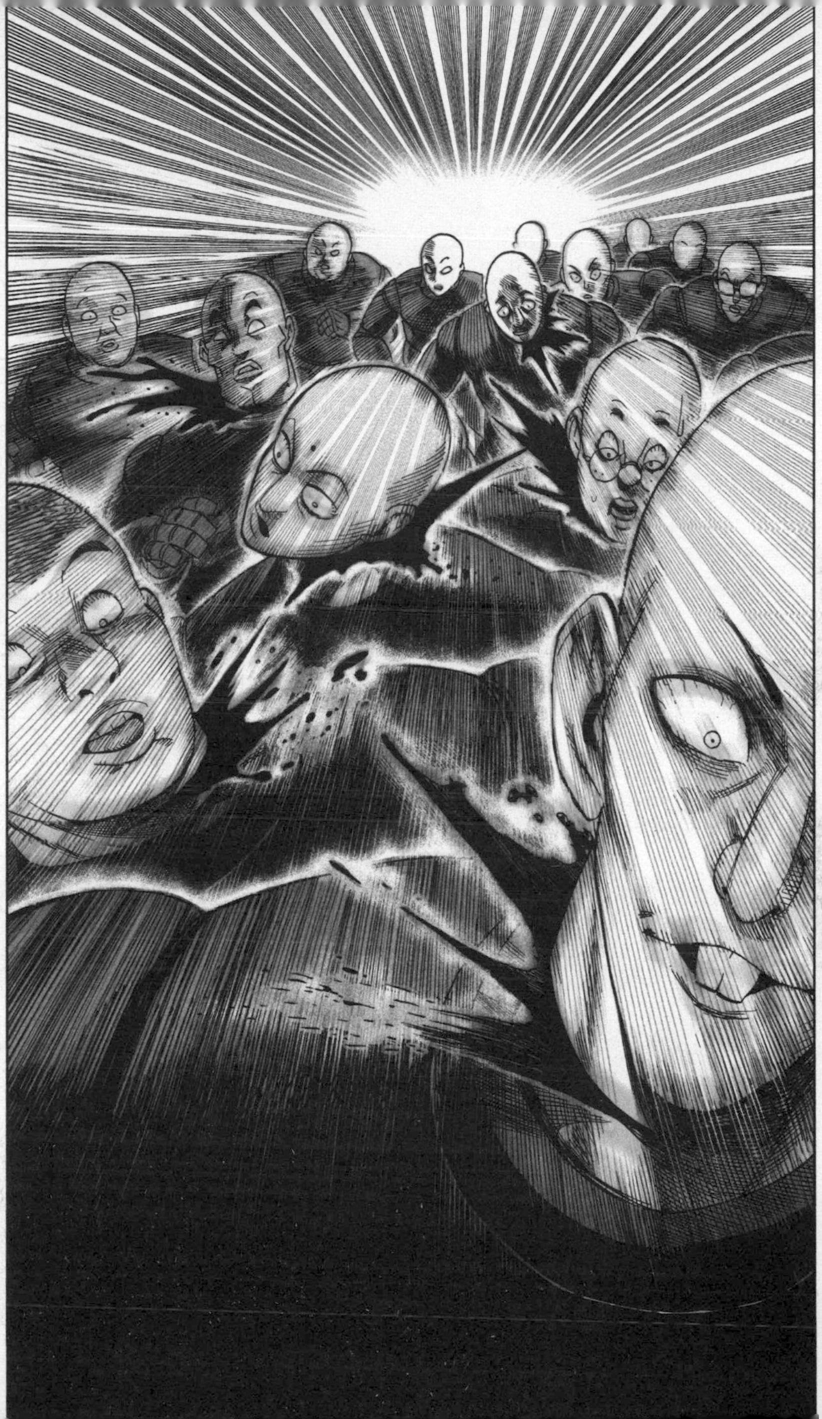

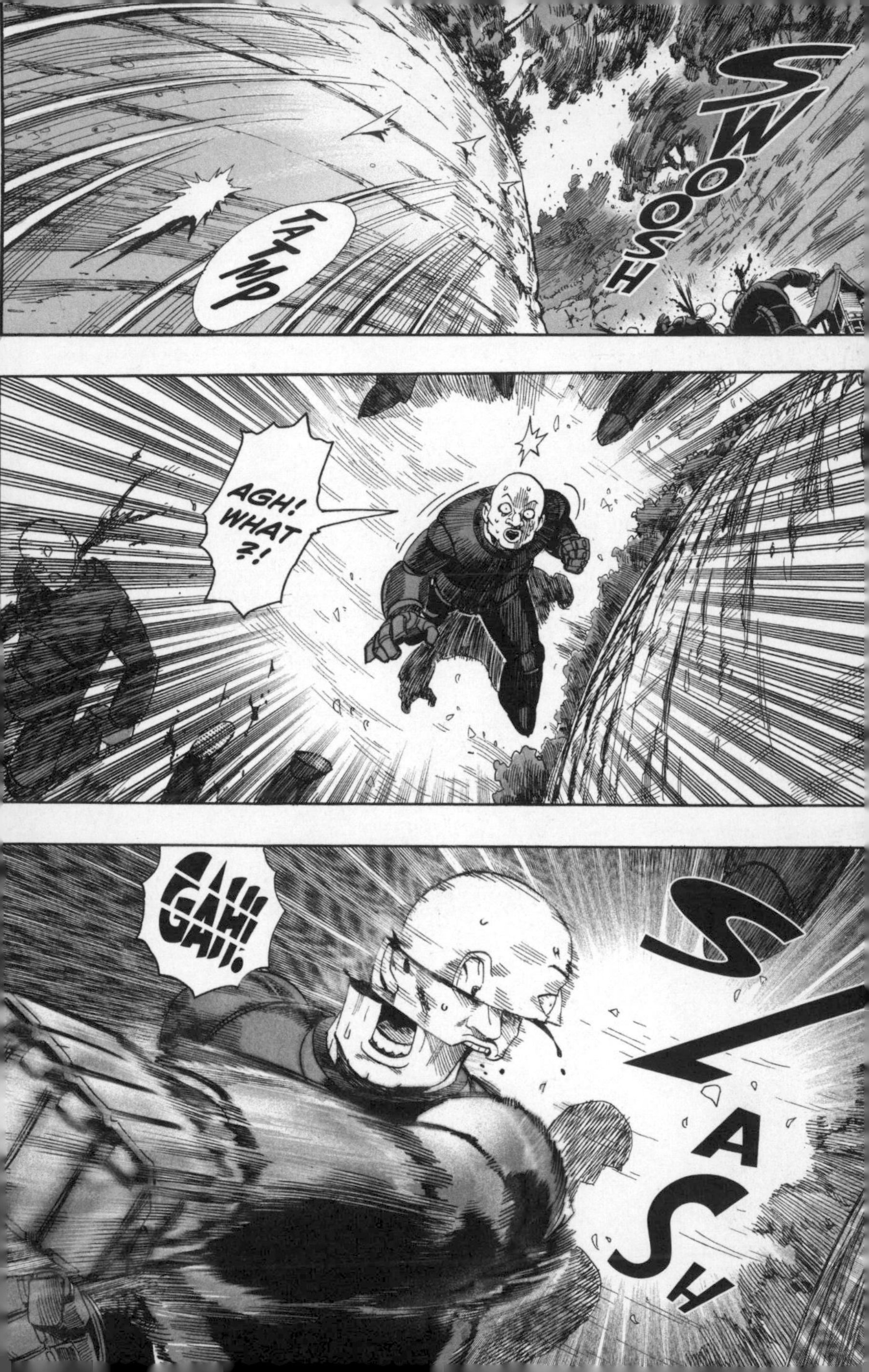
SWOOSH
TATMP
AGH! WHAT ?!
GAH! GAH!
SWASH

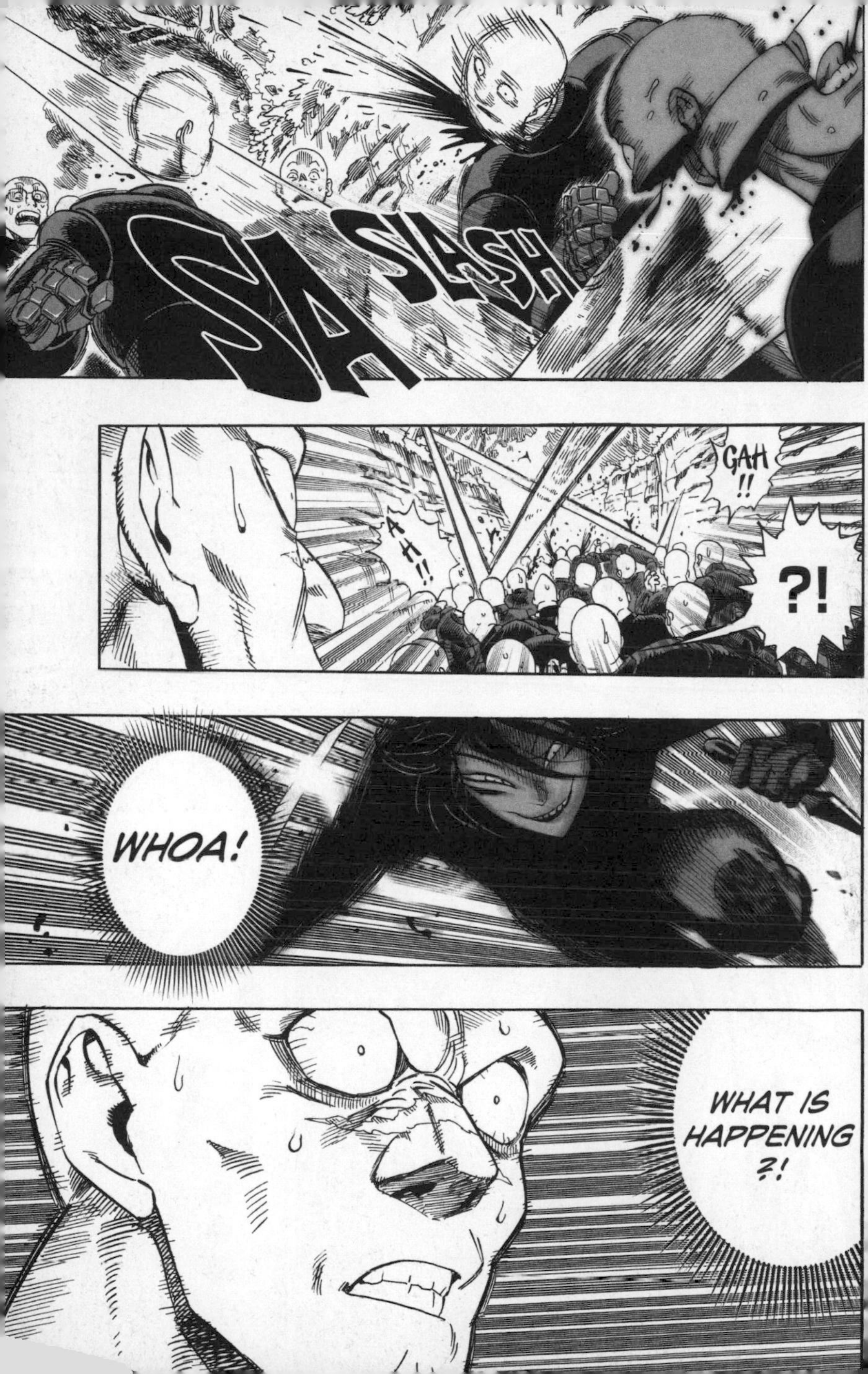
SLASH
GAH!!
AH!!
?!
WHOA!
WHAT IS HAPPENING?!

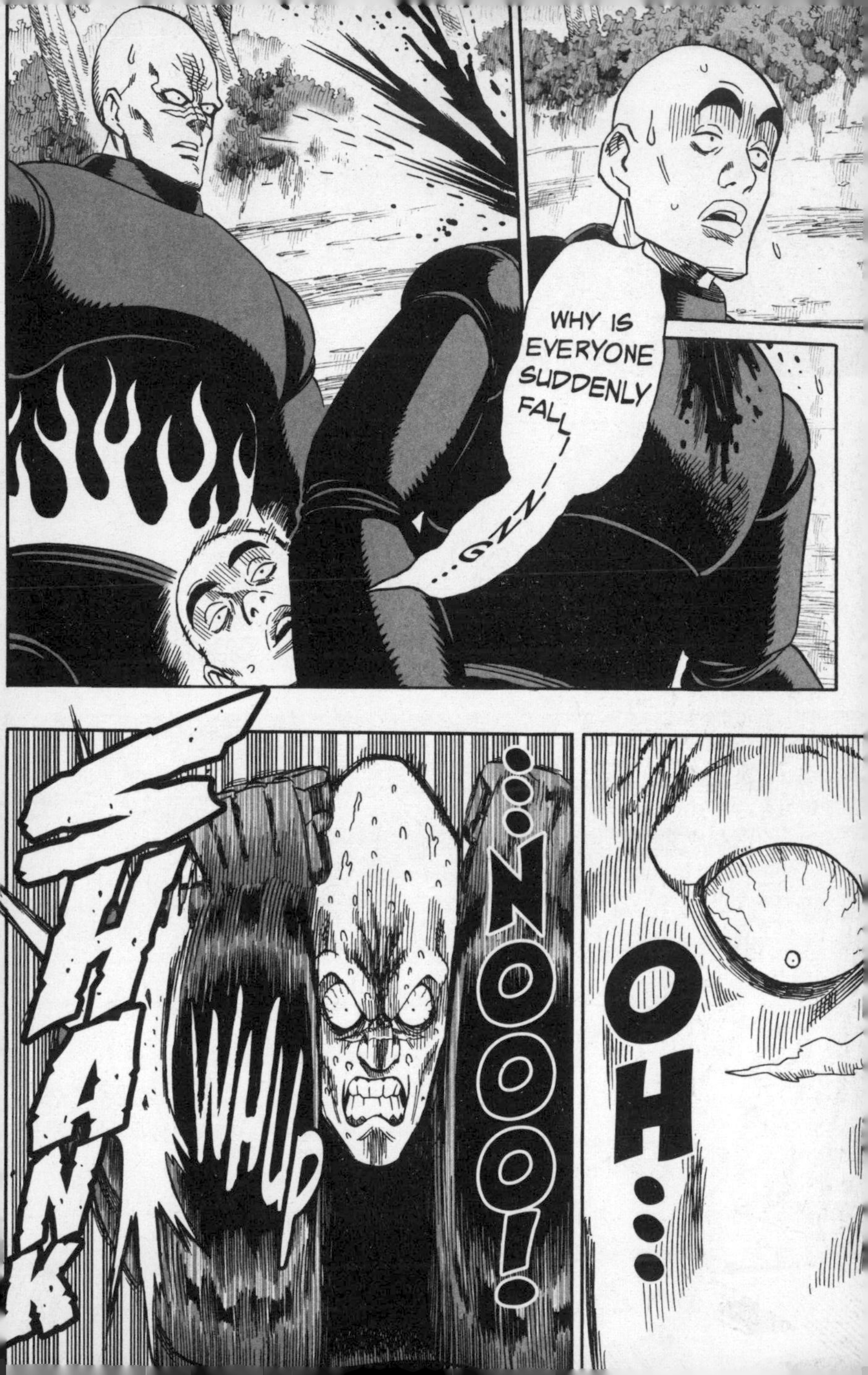
WHY IS EVERYONE SUDDENLY FALL
...GZZ
OH...
...NOOOO!
WHUP

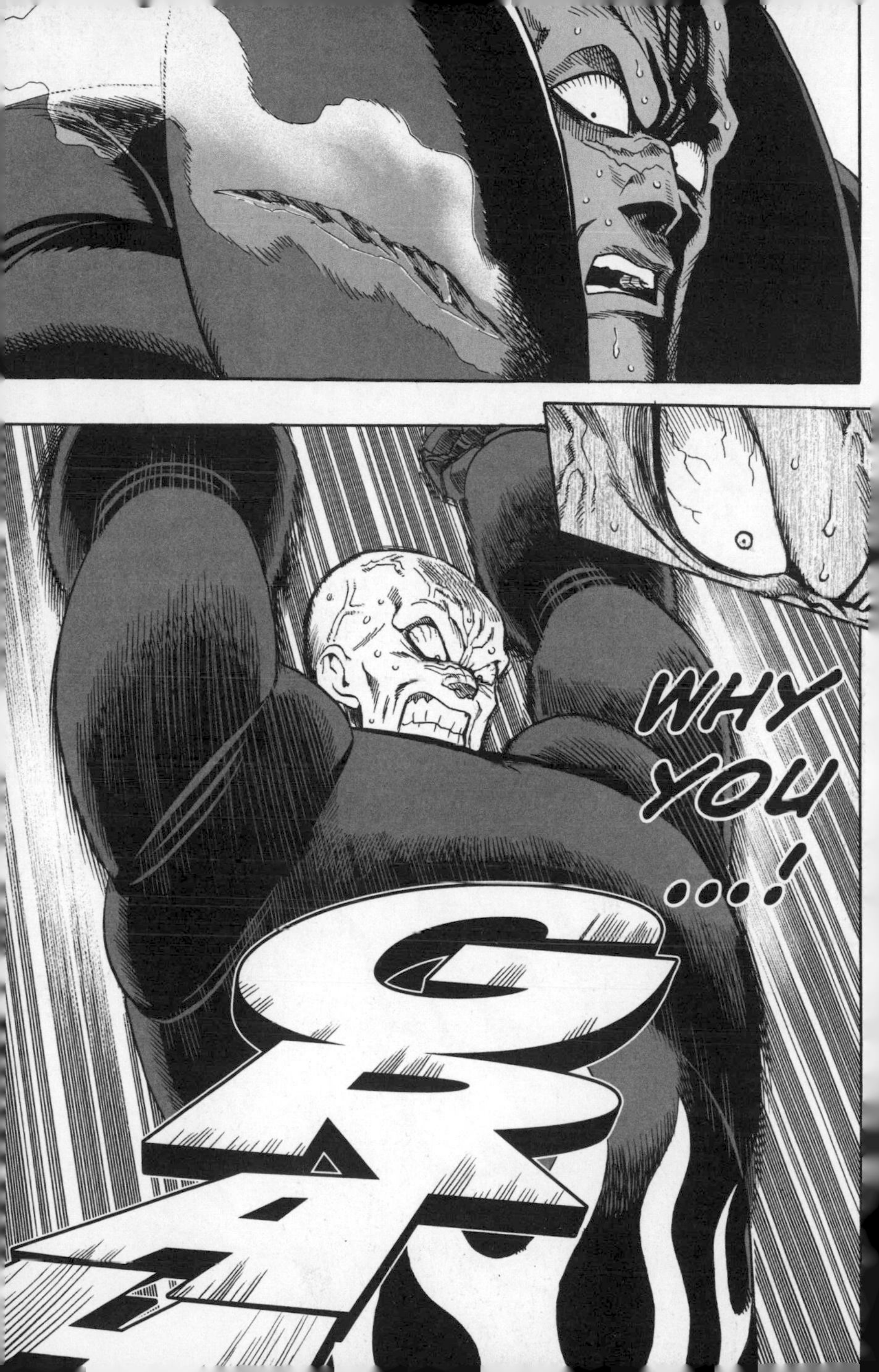
WHY YOU ...!

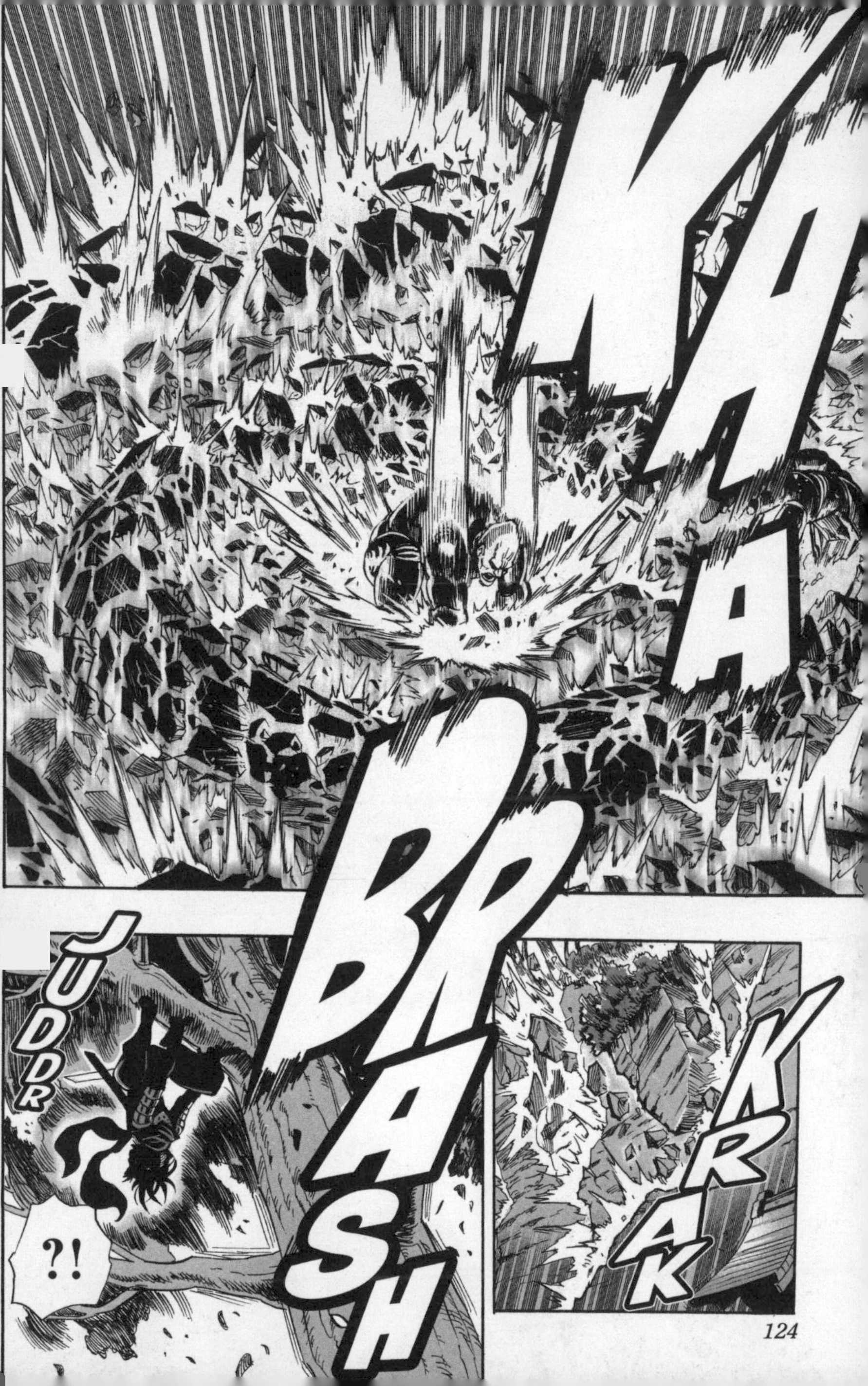
KRAK
JUDDR
?!

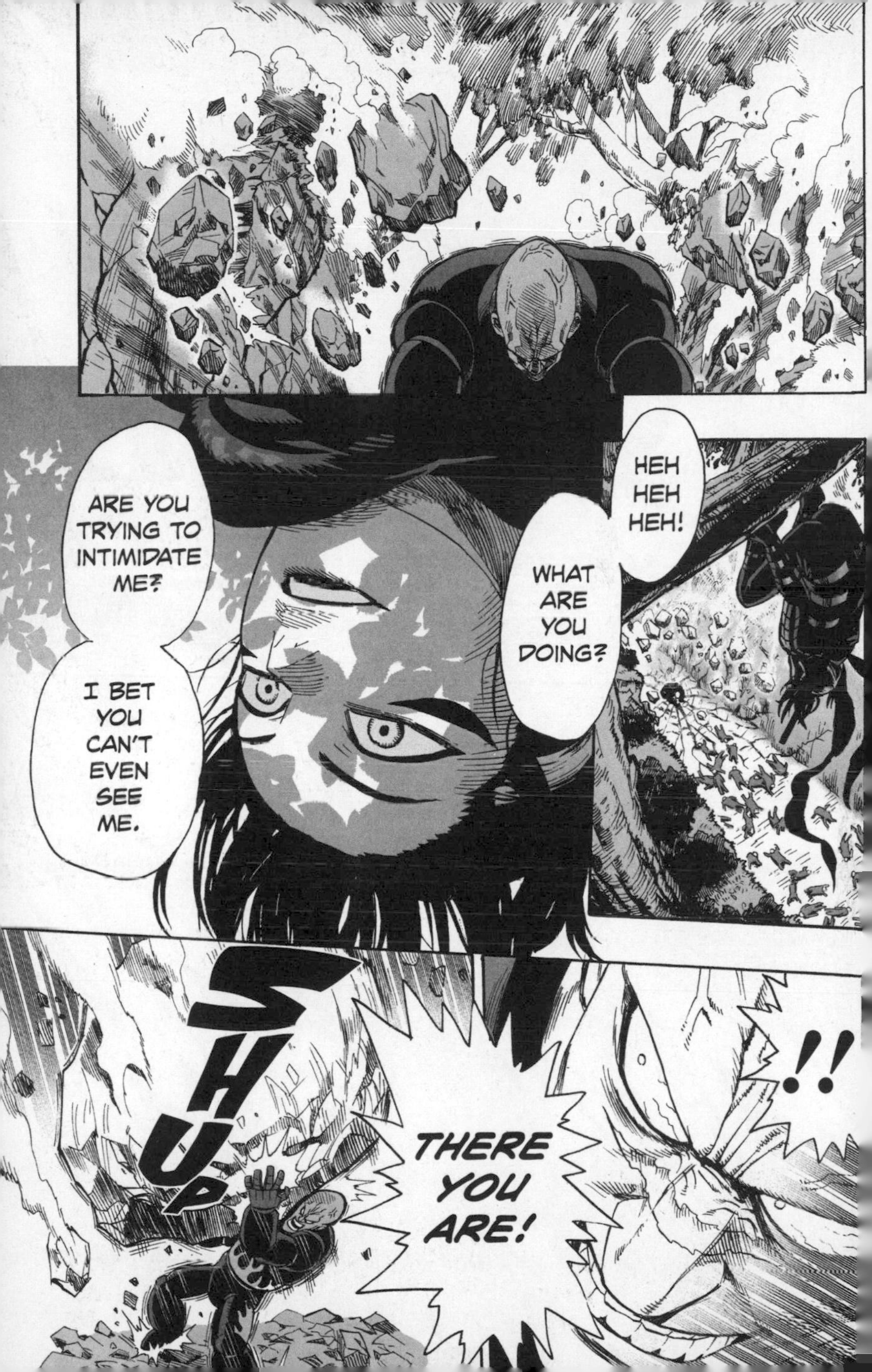
HEH HEH HEH!
WHAT ARE YOU DOING?
ARE YOU TRYING TO INTIMIDATE ME?
I BET YOU CAN'T EVEN SEE ME.
!!
THERE YOU ARE!
SHUP

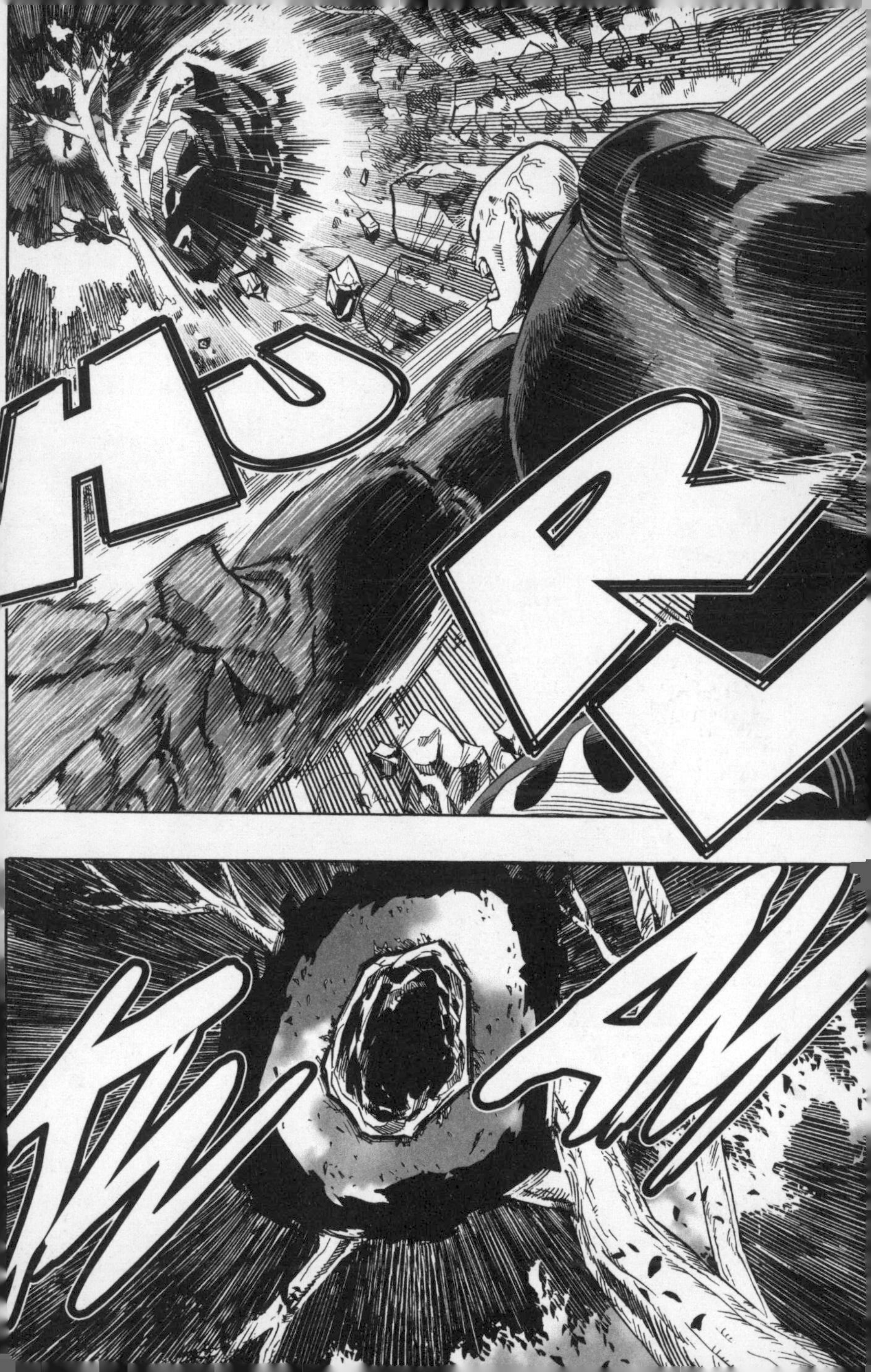

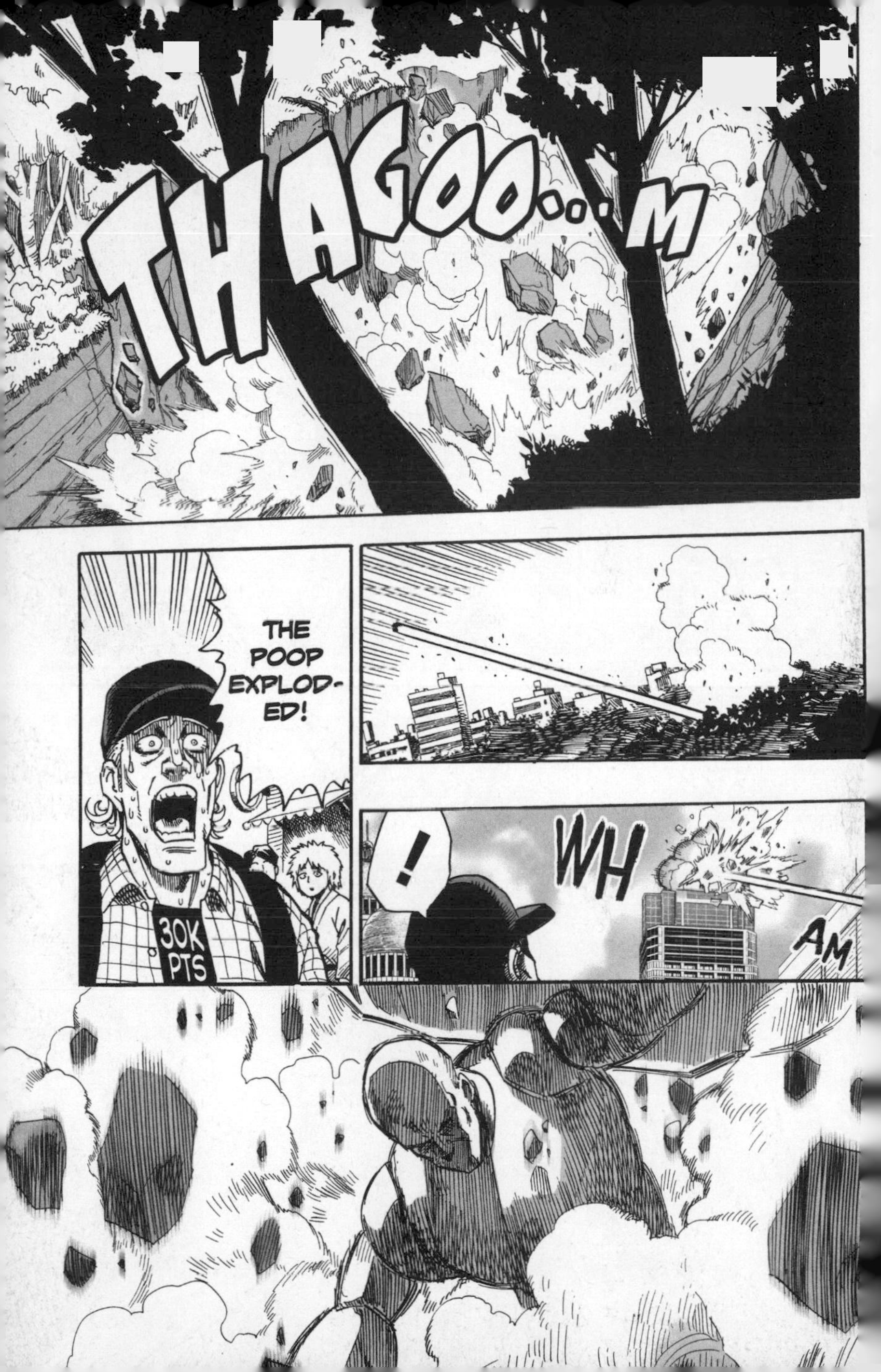
THAGOO...M
!
WH
AM
THE POOP EXPLODED!
30K PTS

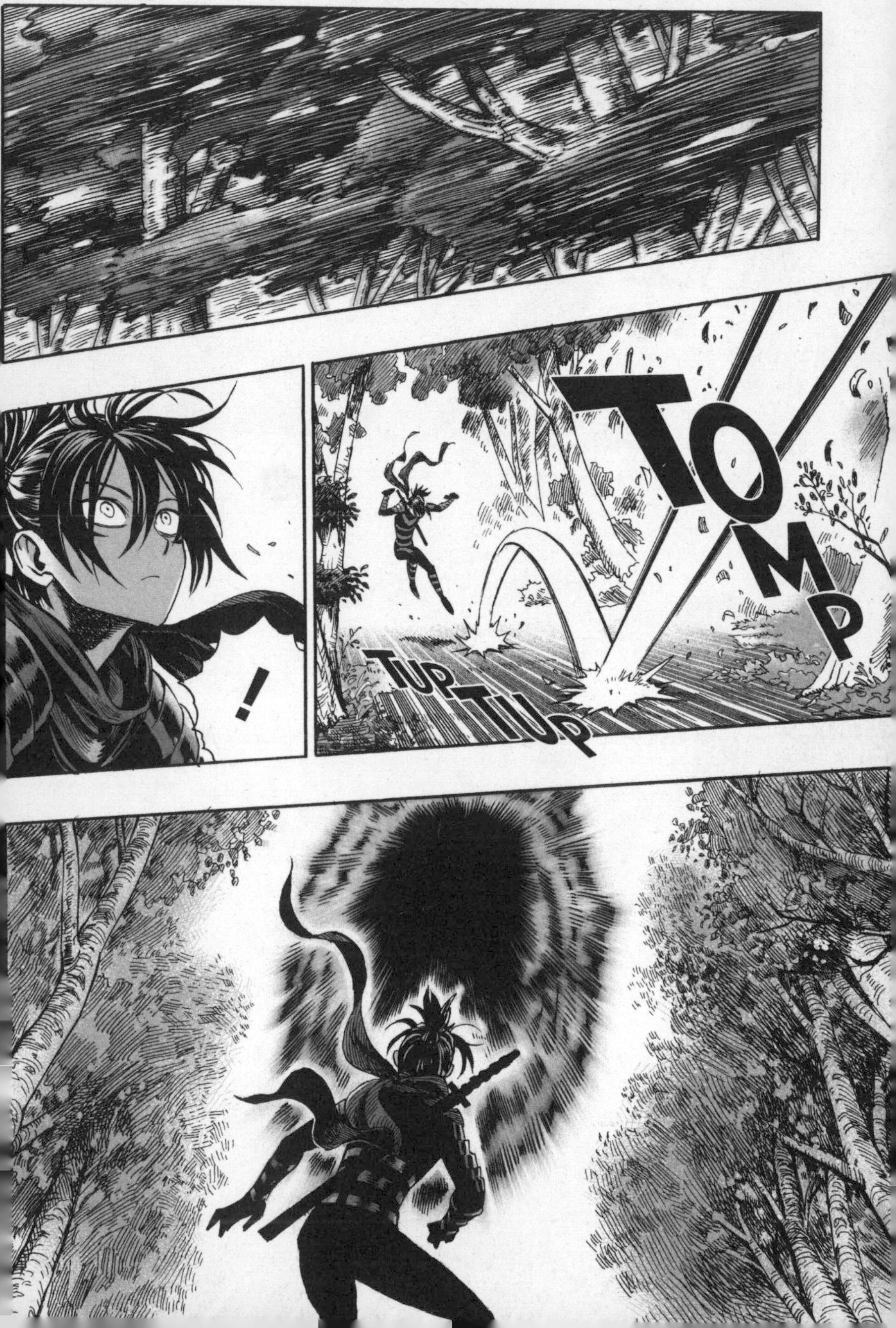
TOMP
TUP TUUP
!

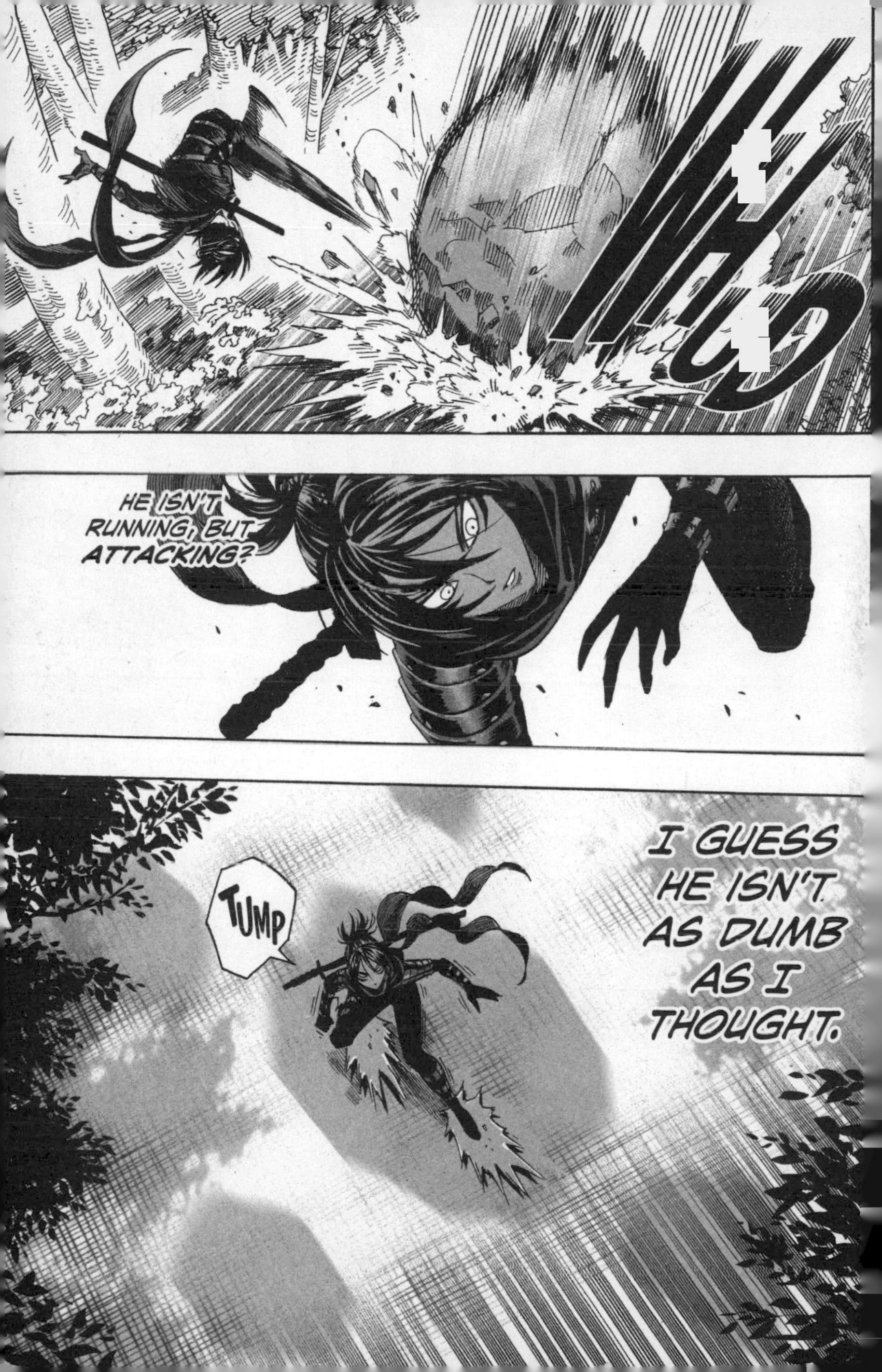
WHUD
HE ISN'T RUNNING, BUT ATTACKING?
I GUESS HE ISN'T AS DUMB AS I THOUGHT.
TUMP

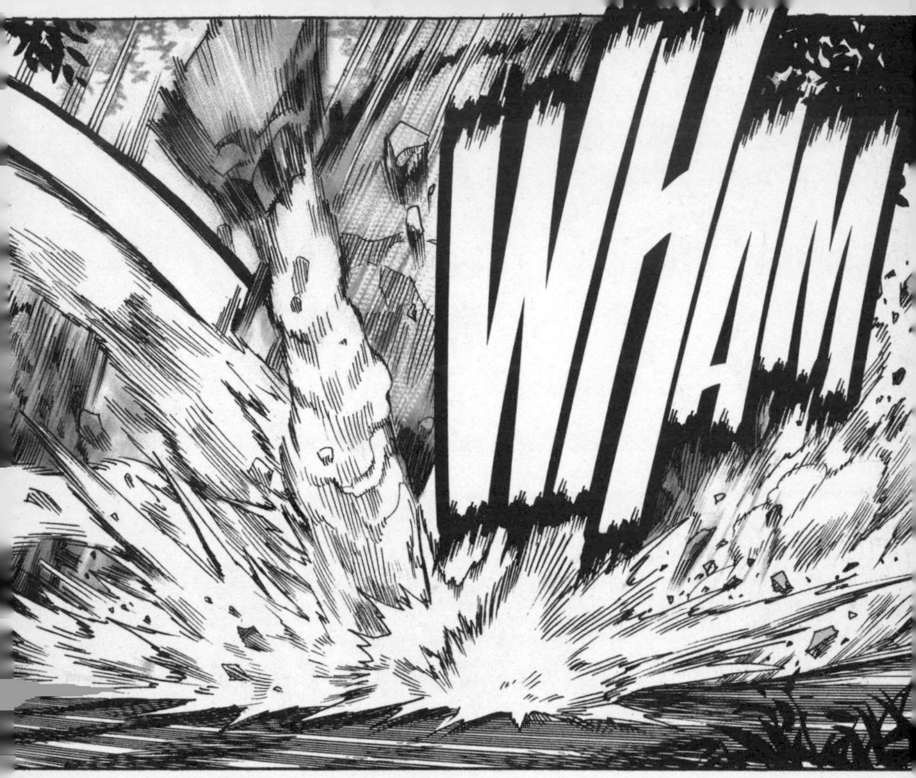
WHAM
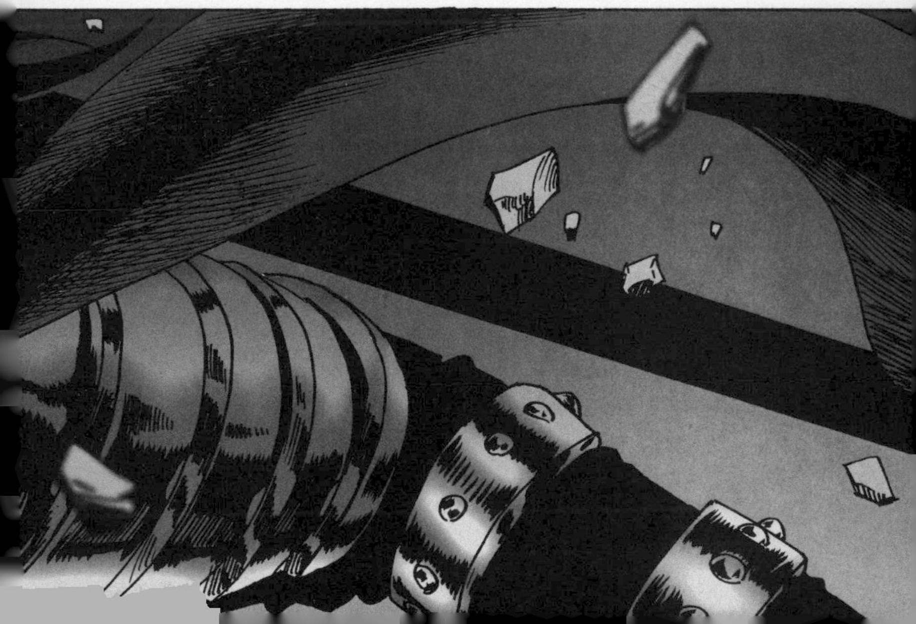

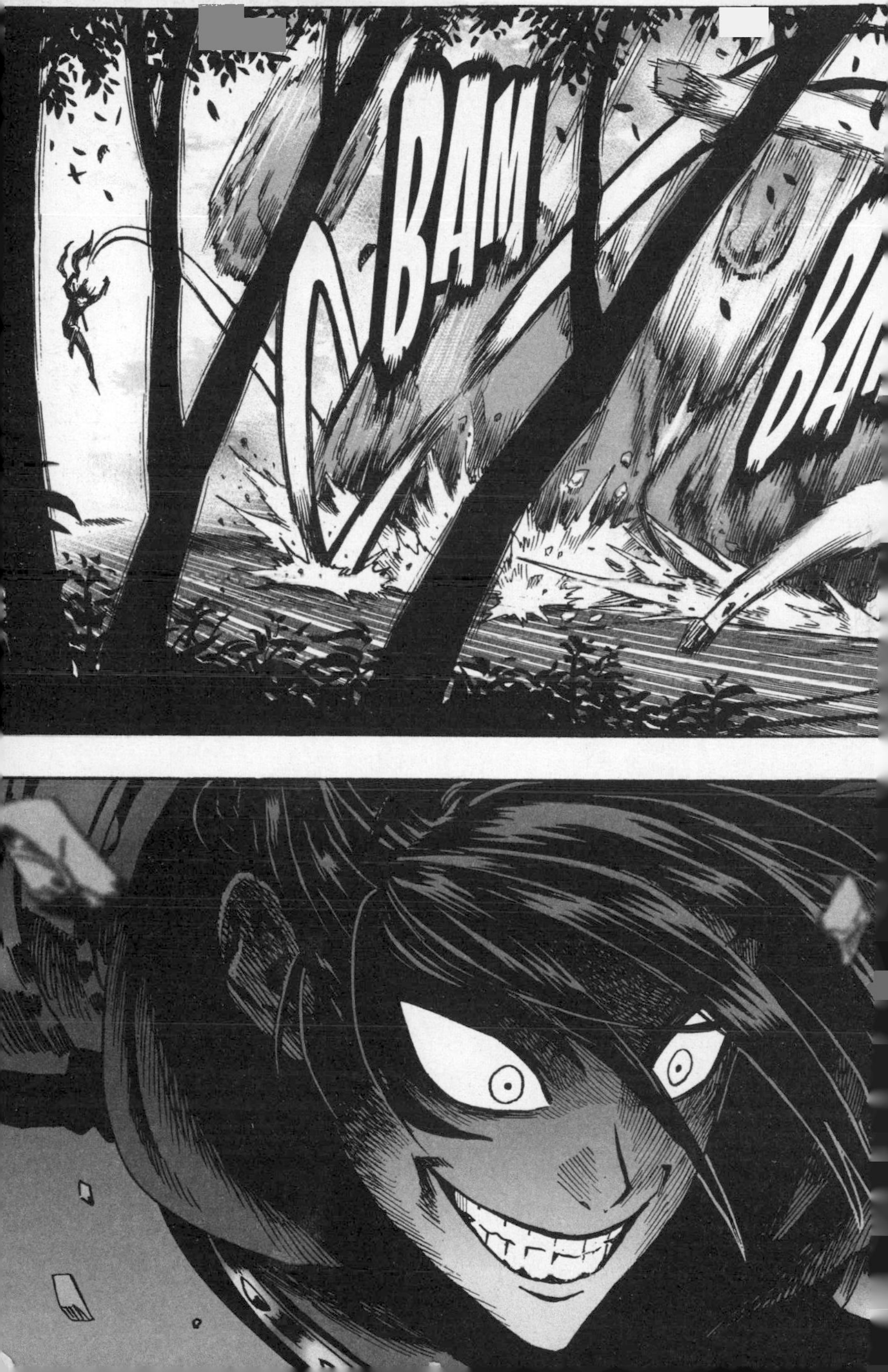
BAM

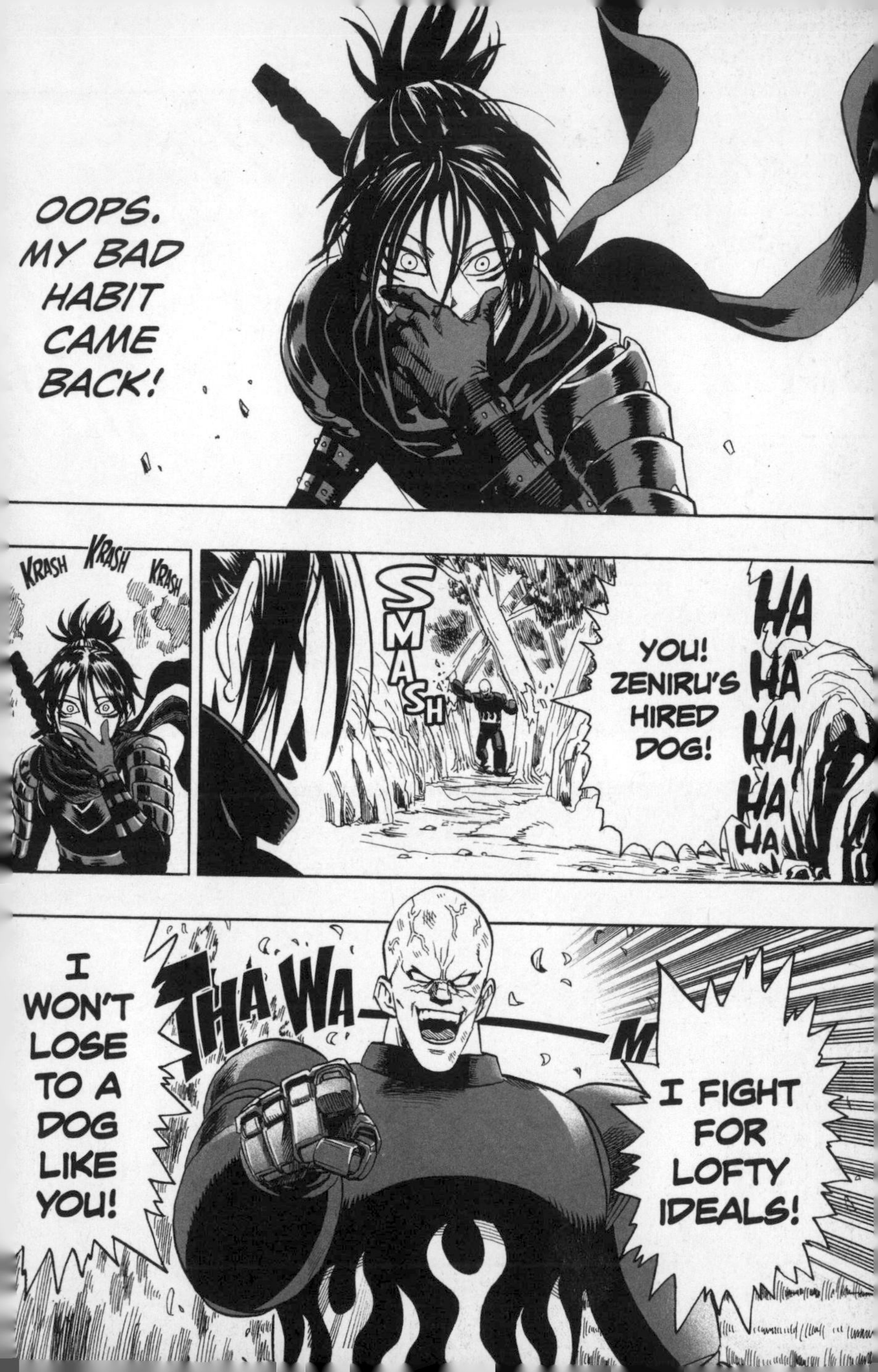
OOPS. MY BAD HABIT CAME BACK!
KRASH KRASH KRASH
HA HA HA HA HA HA
YOU! ZENIRU'S HIRED DOG!
SMASH
THA WA—M
I FIGHT FOR LOFTY IDEALS!
I WON'T LOSE TO A DOG LIKE YOU!

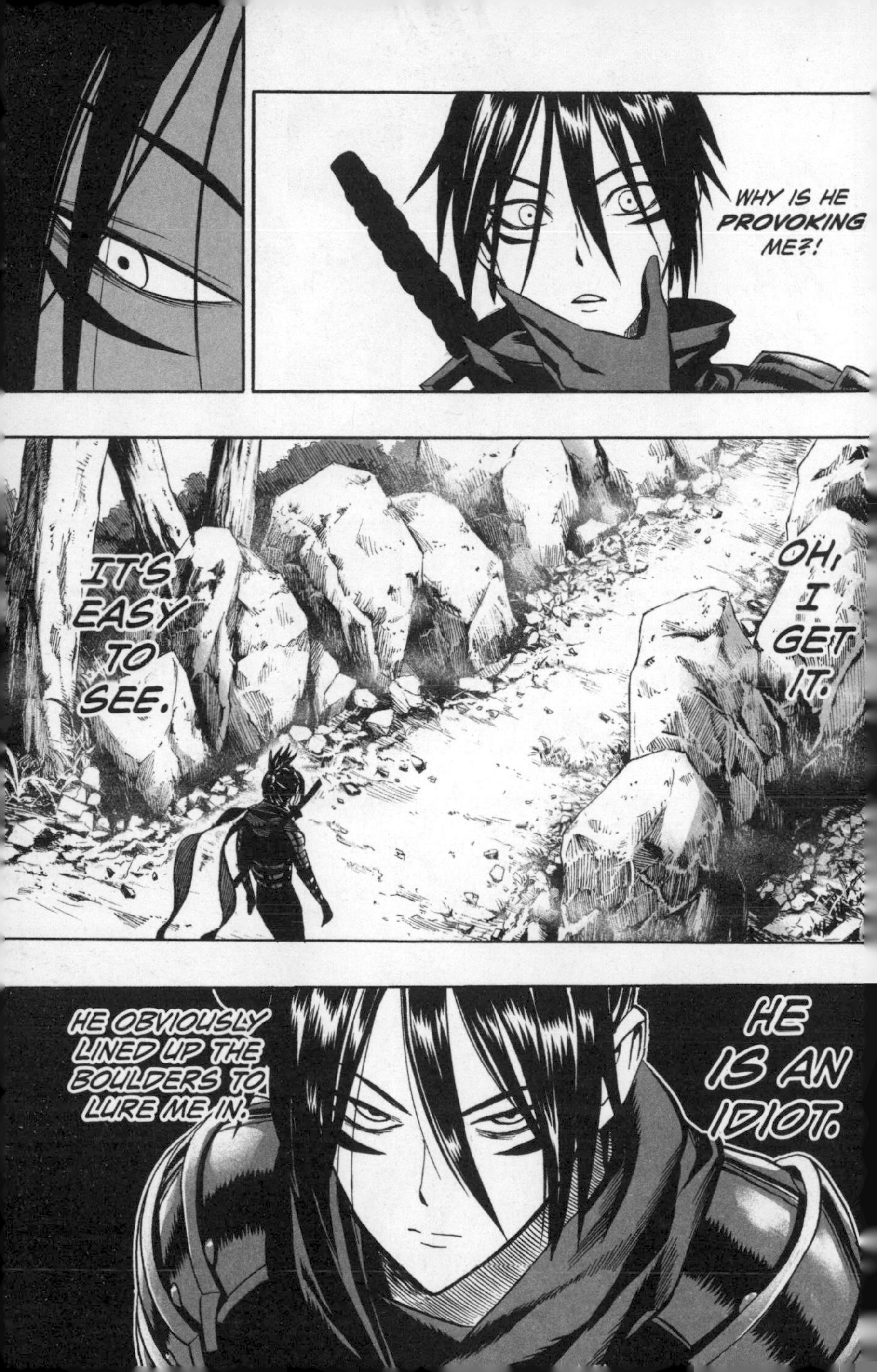
WHY IS HE PROVOKING ME?!
OH, I GET IT.
IT'S EASY TO SEE.
HE IS AN IDIOT.
HE OBVIOUSLY LINED UP THE BOULDERS TO LURE ME IN.

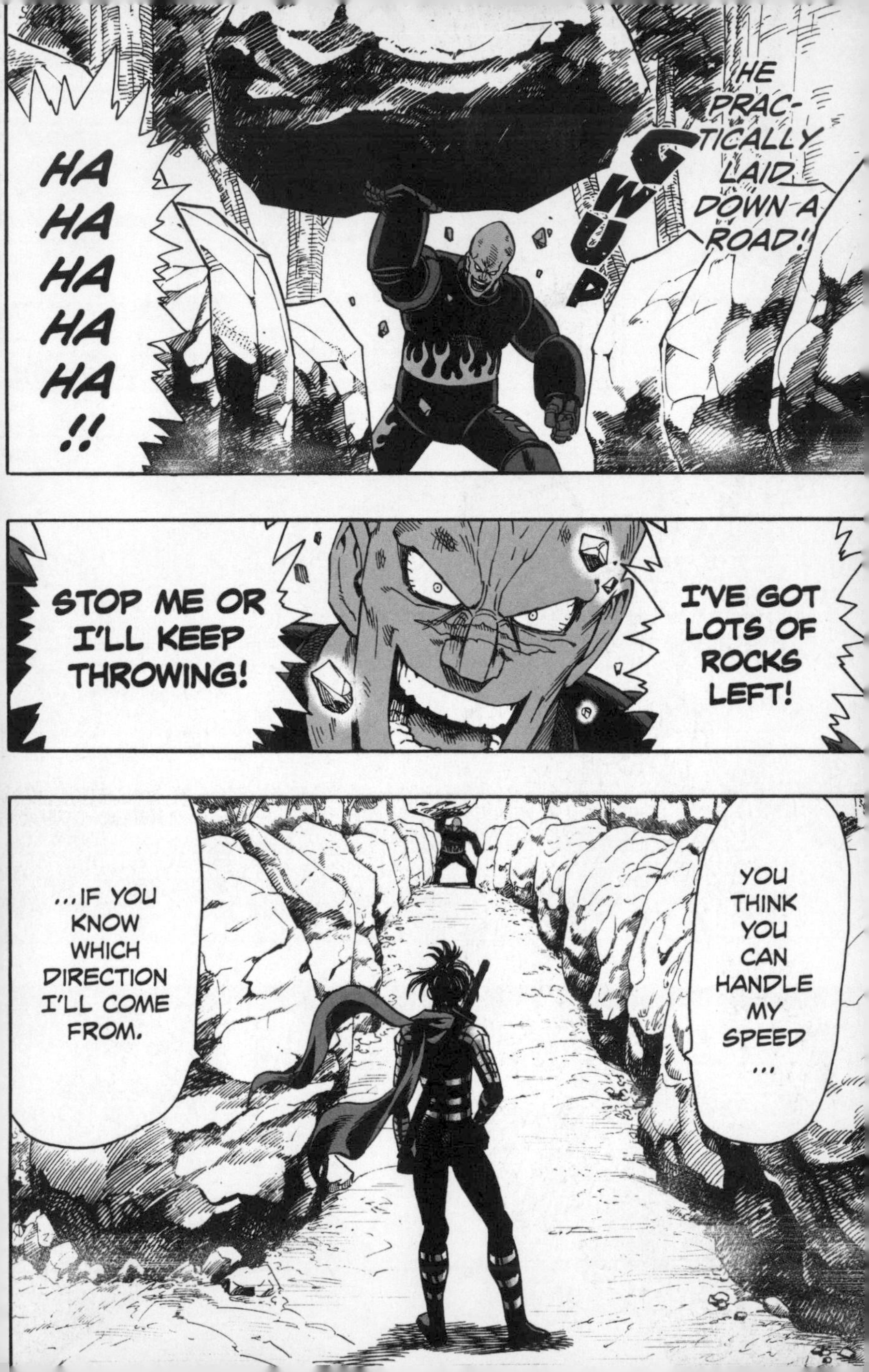
HE PRAC-TICALLY LAID DOWN A ROAD!
GWUD
HA HA HA HA HA!!
I'VE GOT LOTS OF ROCKS LEFT!
STOP ME OR I'LL KEEP THROWING!
YOU THINK YOU CAN HANDLE MY SPEED...
...IF YOU KNOW WHICH DIRECTION I'LL COME FROM.

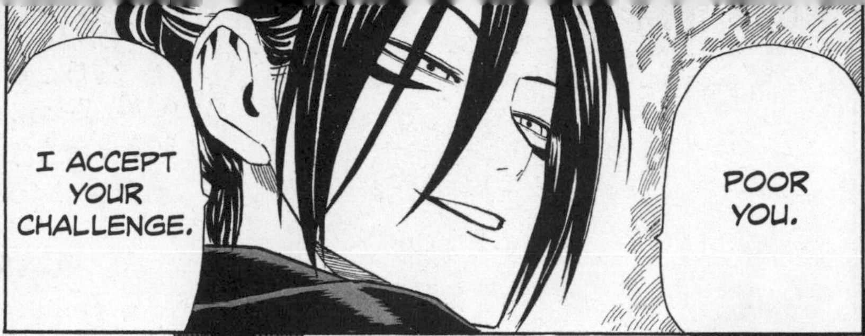
POOR YOU.
I ACCEPT YOUR CHALLENGE.
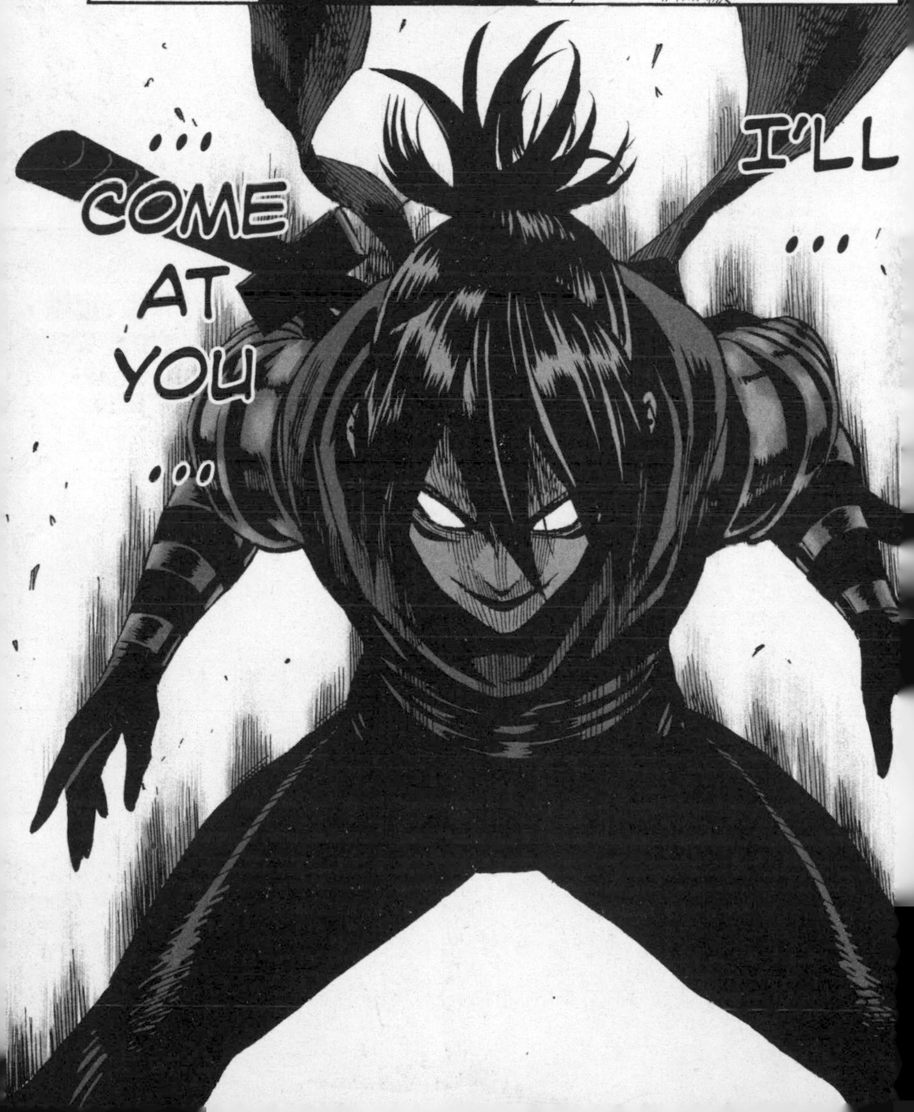
I'LL ...
... COME AT YOU ...

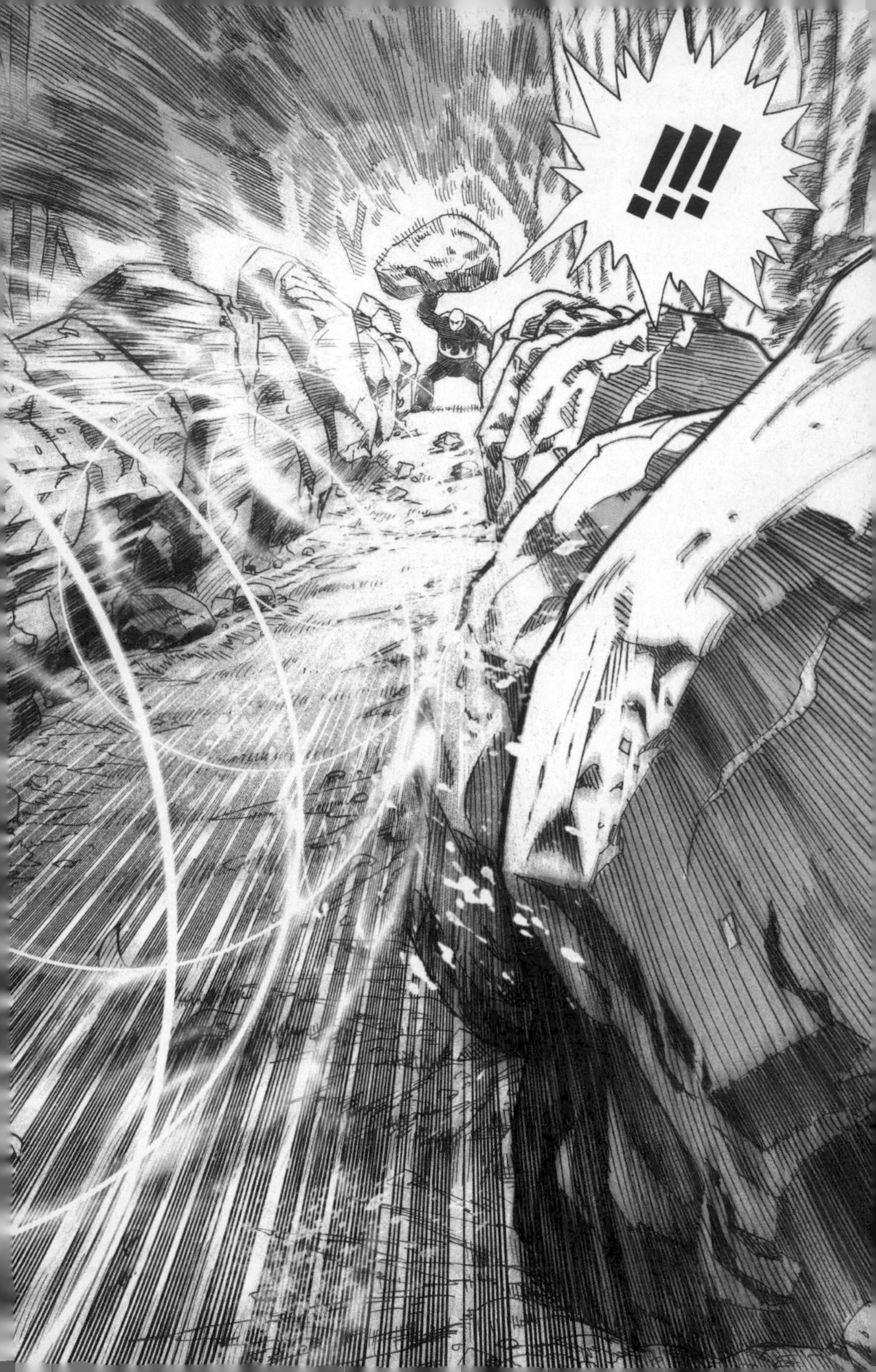
!!!

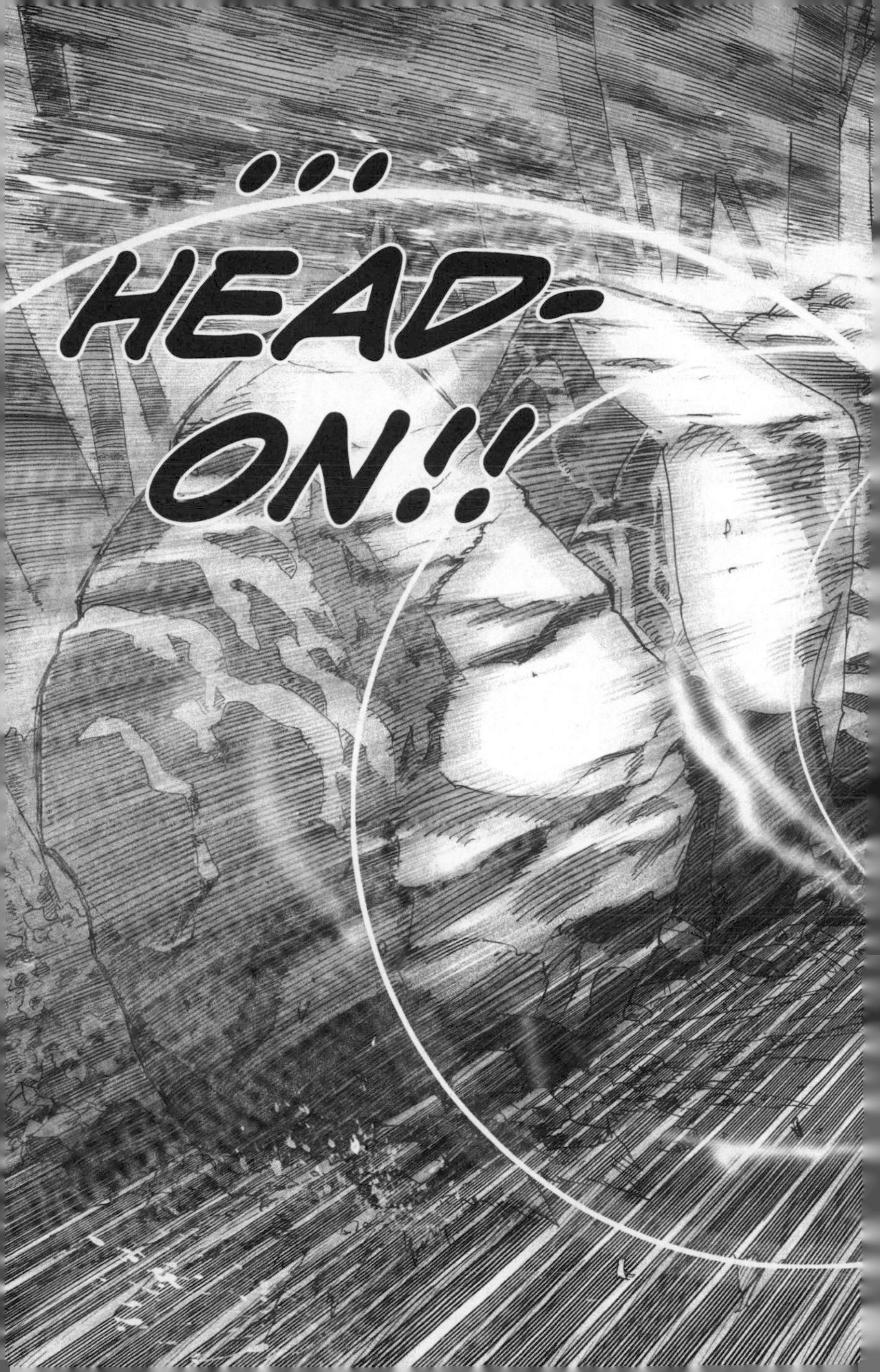
HEAD-ON!!

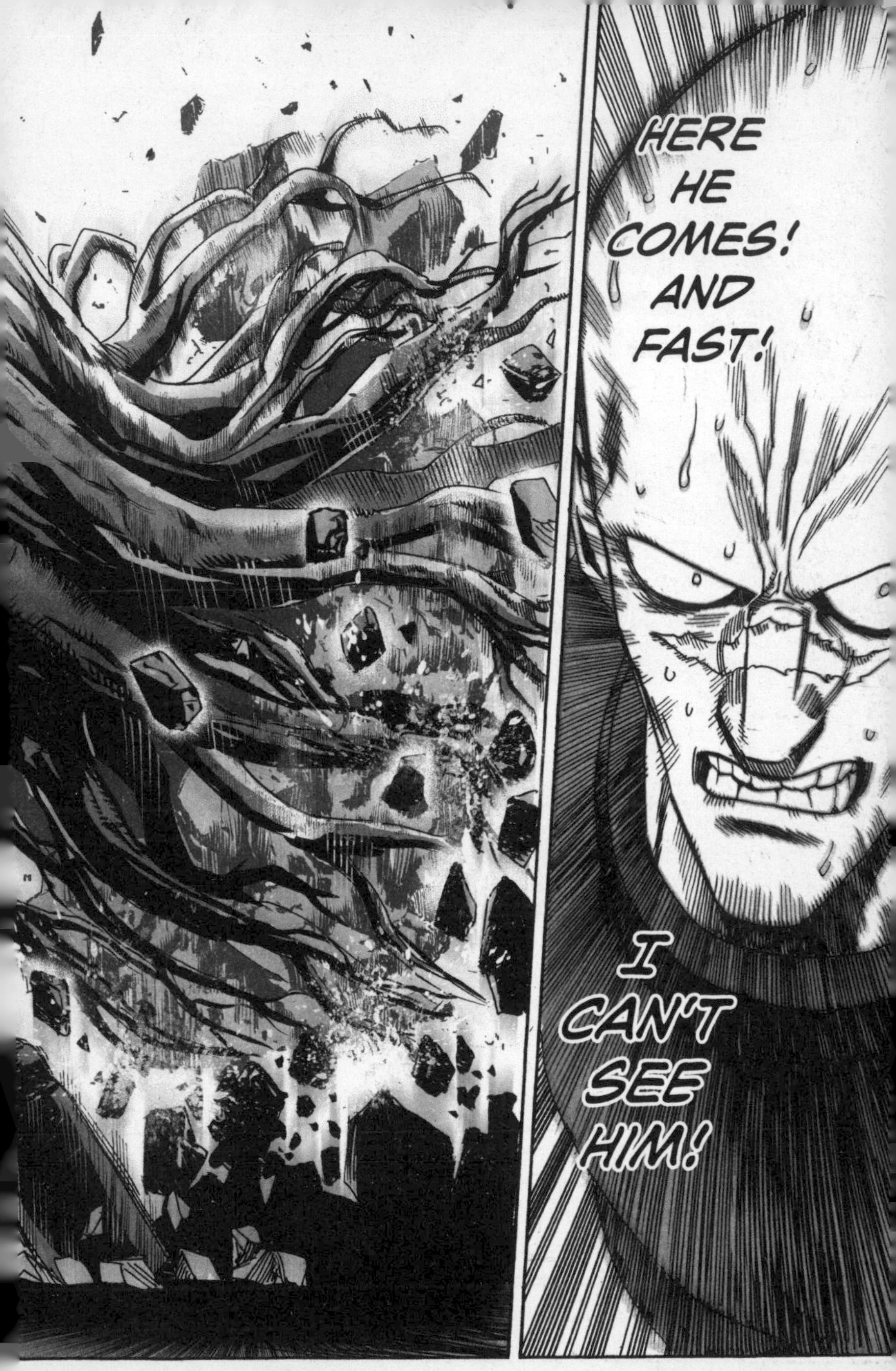
HERE HE COMES! AND FAST!
I CAN'T SEE HIM!

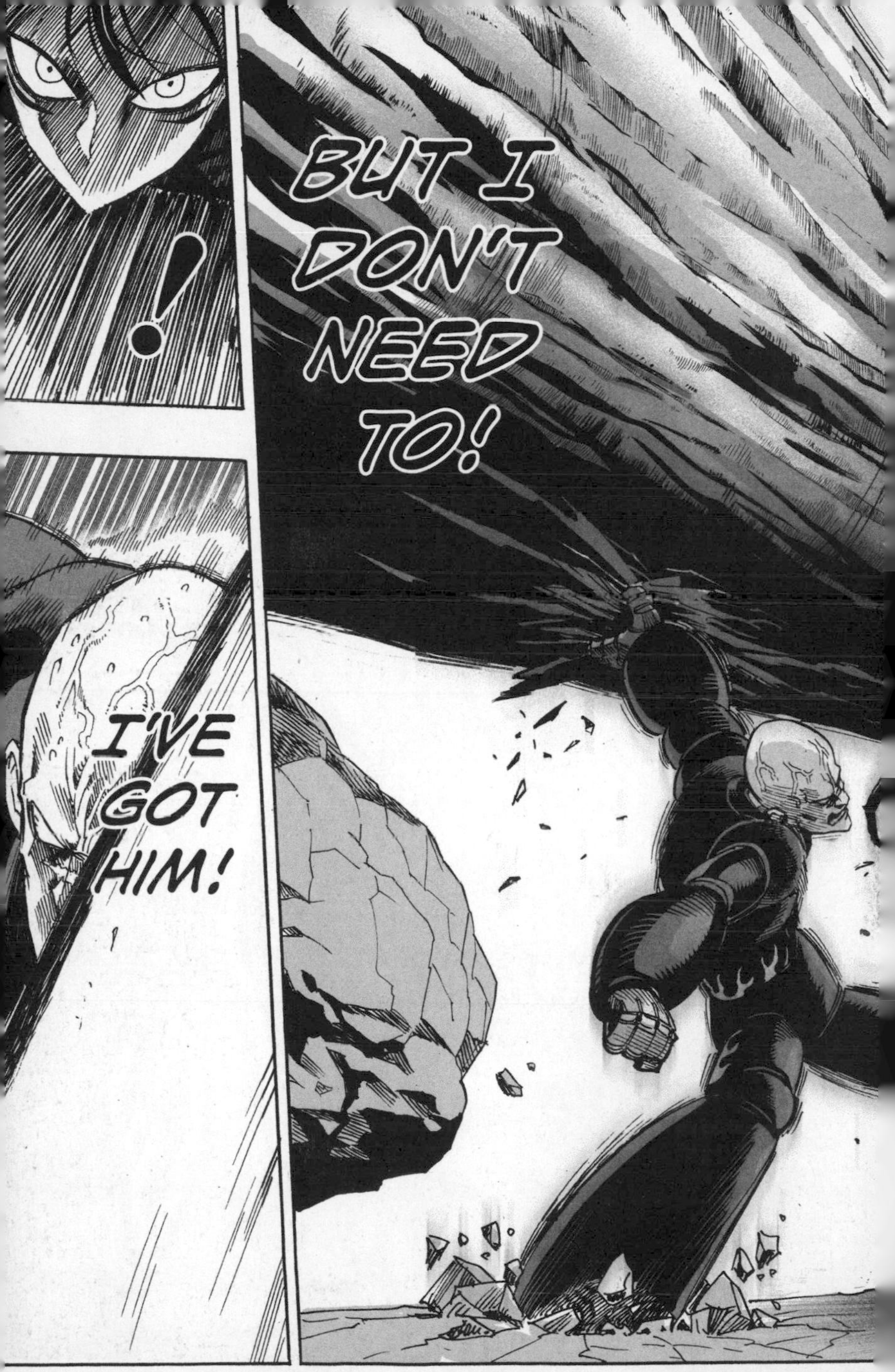
BUT I DON'T NEED TO!
!
I'VE GOT HIM!

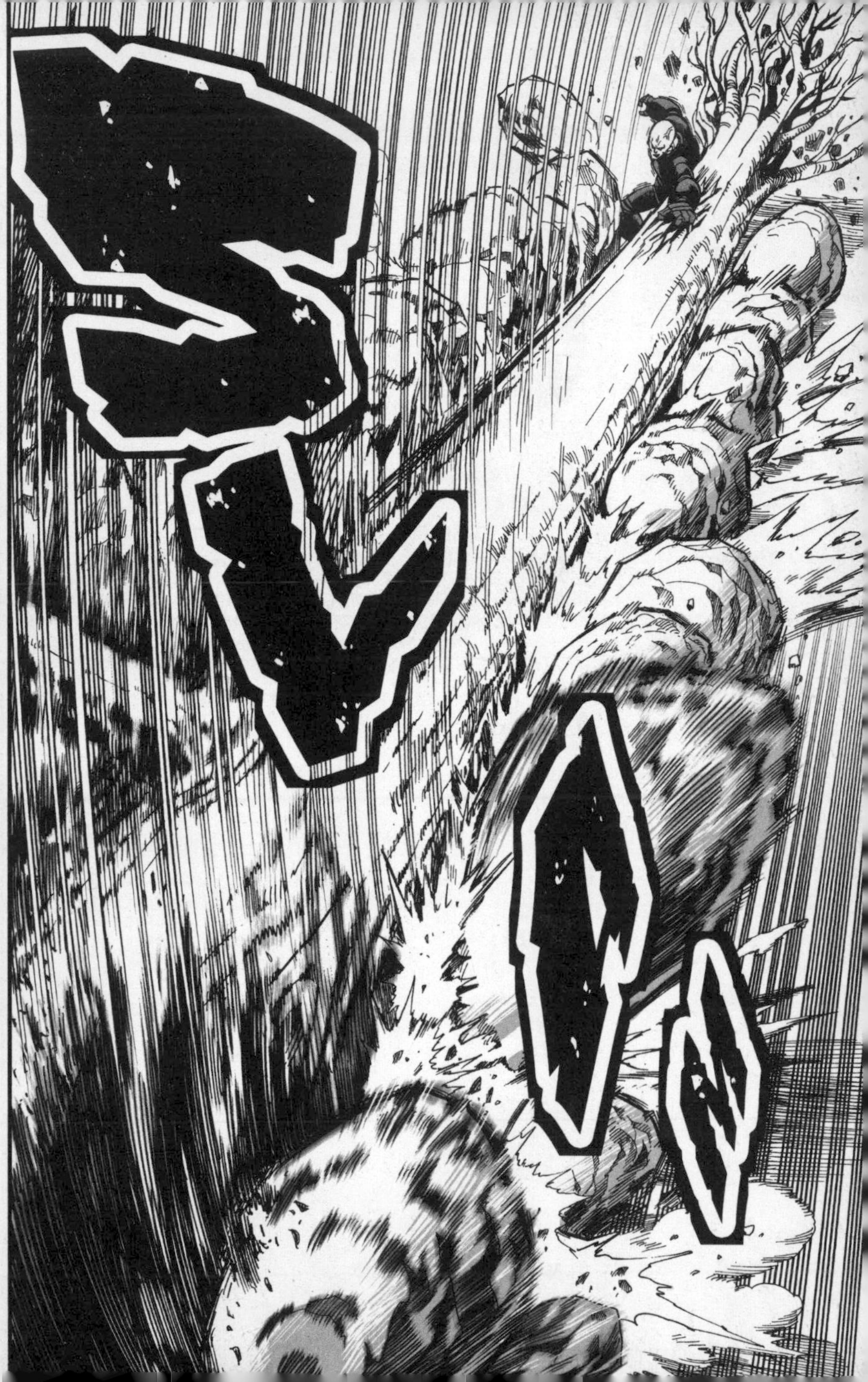

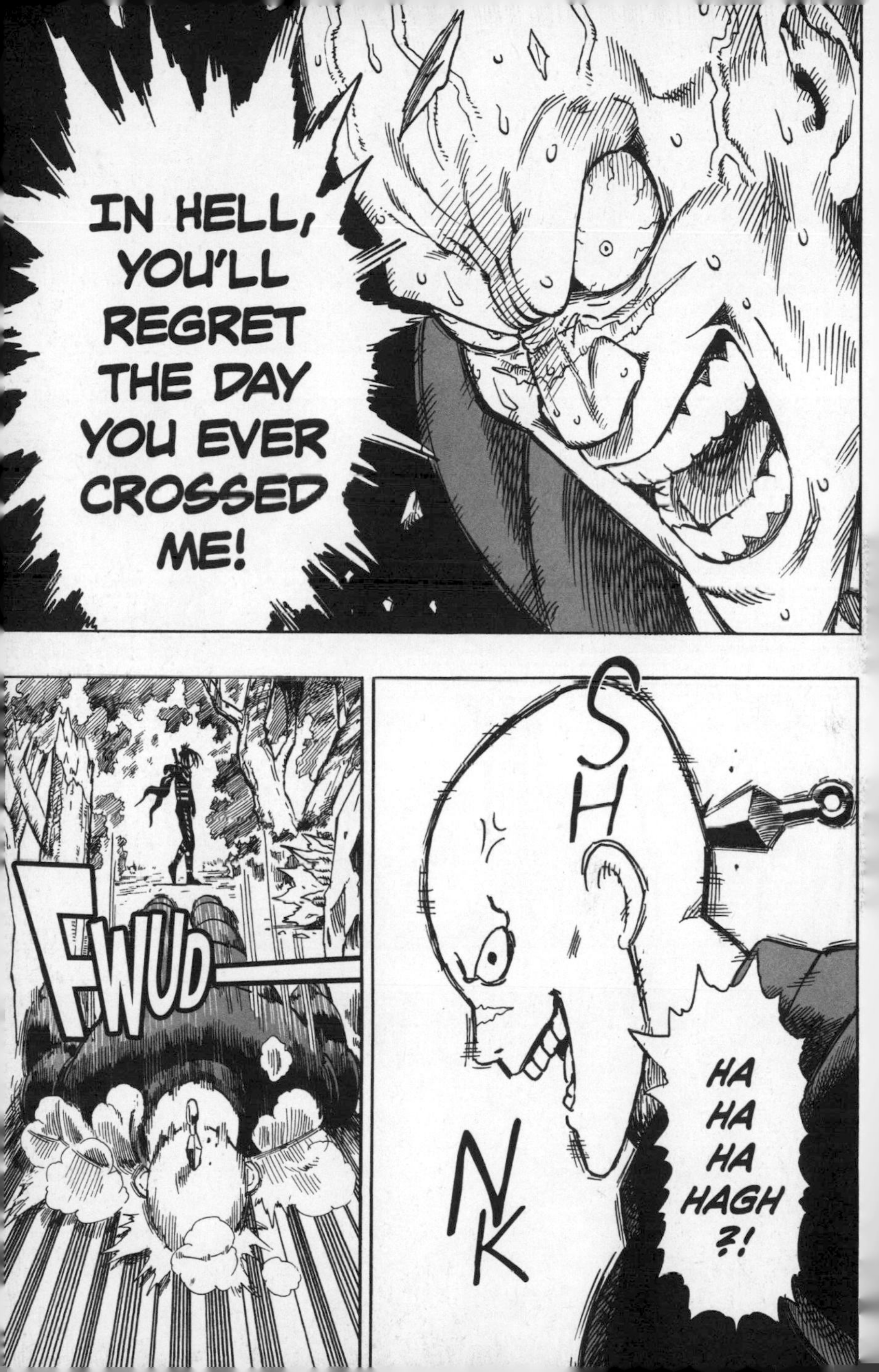
IN HELL, YOU'LL REGRET THE DAY YOU EVER CROSSED ME!
SHNK
HA HA HA HAGH ?!
F-WUD

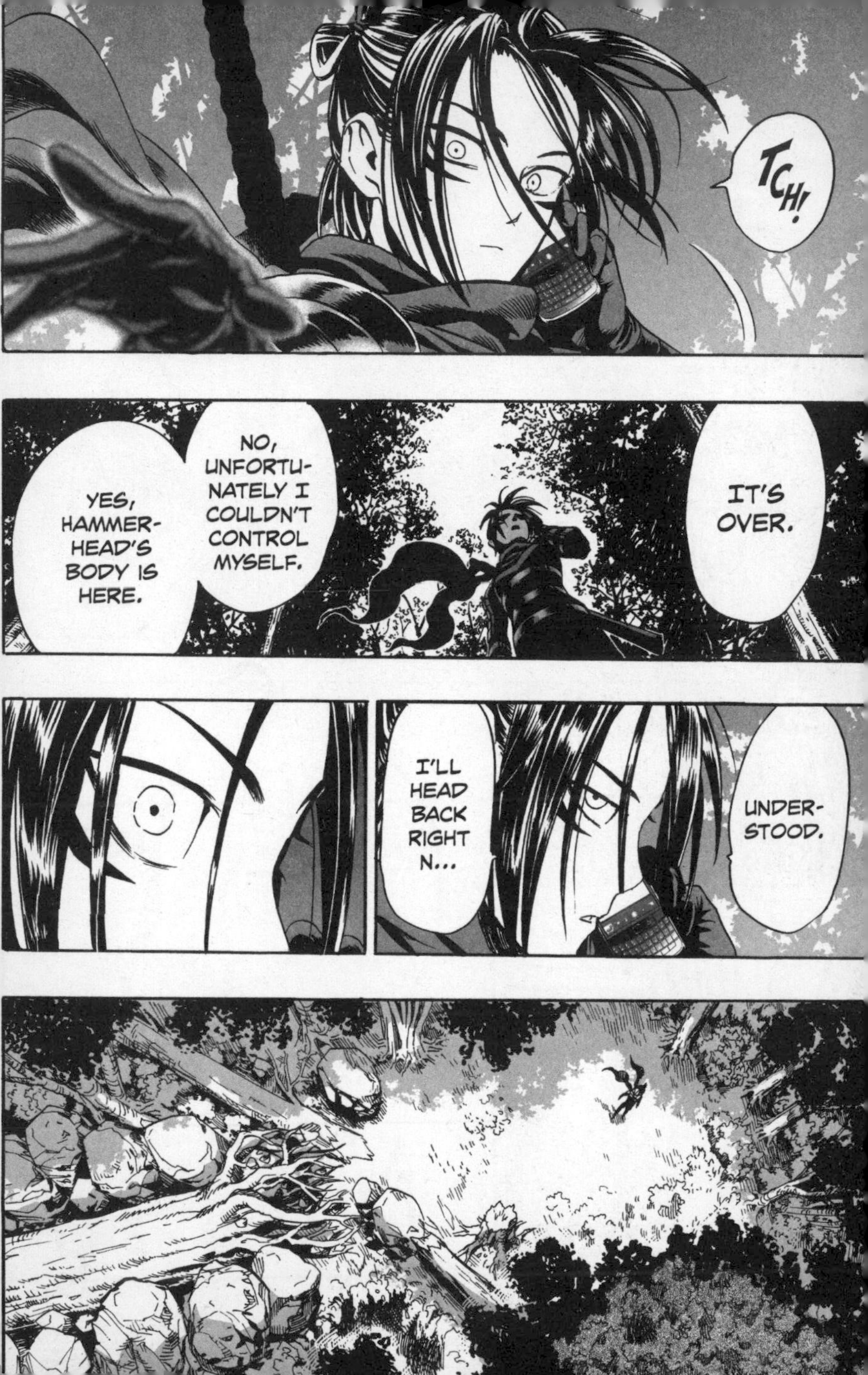
TCH!
IT'S OVER.
NO, UNFORTUNATELY I COULDN'T CONTROL MYSELF.
YES, HAMMERHEAD'S BODY IS HERE.
UNDERSTOOD.
I'LL HEAD BACK RIGHT N...

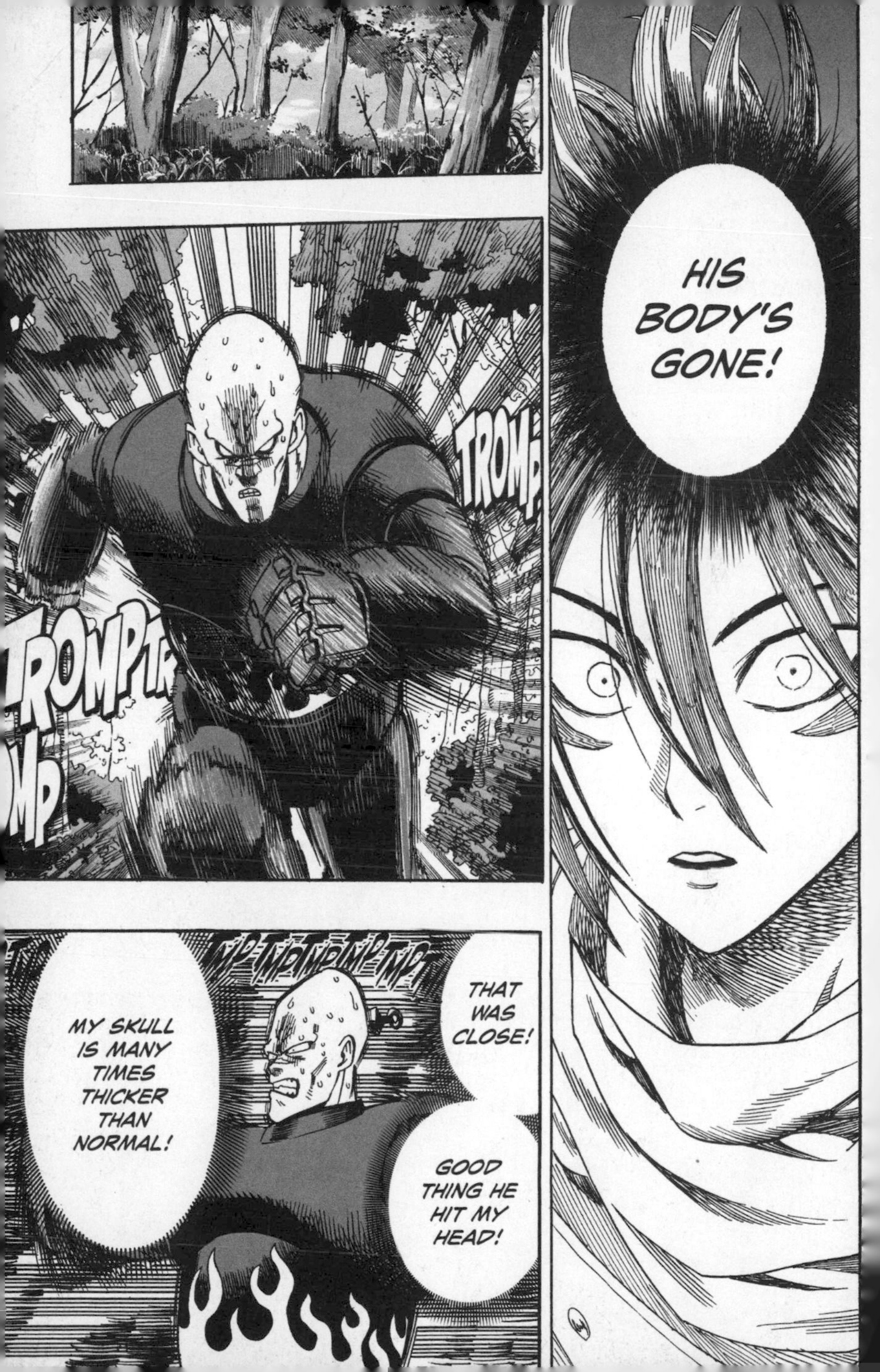
HIS BODY'S GONE!
TROMP
TROMPTR
MP
THAT WAS CLOSE!
GOOD THING HE HIT MY HEAD!
MY SKULL IS MANY TIMES THICKER THAN NORMAL!

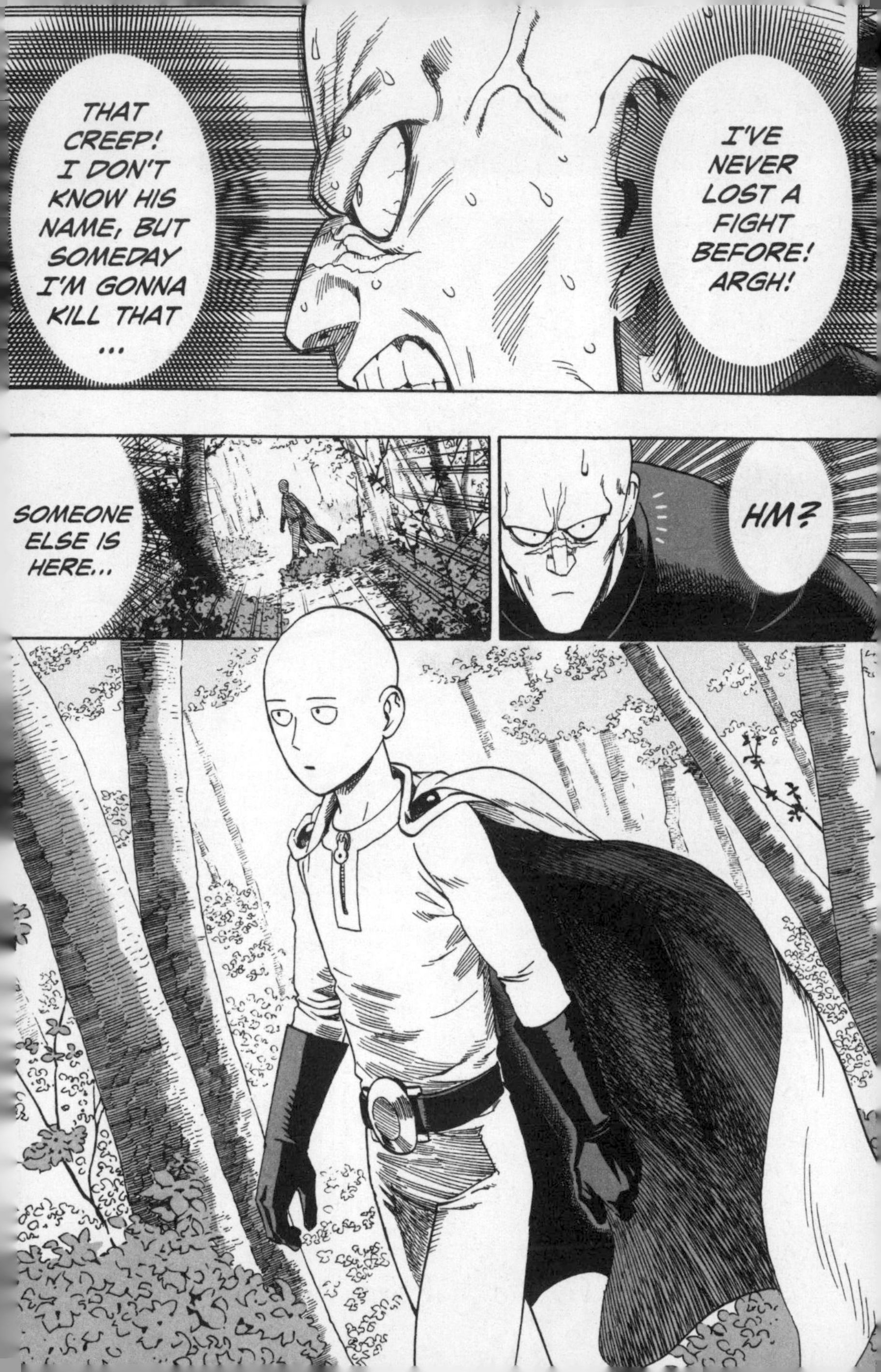
I'VE NEVER LOST A FIGHT BEFORE! ARGH!
THAT CREEP! I DON'T KNOW HIS NAME, BUT SOMEDAY I'M GONNA KILL THAT ...
HM?
SOMEONE ELSE IS HERE...

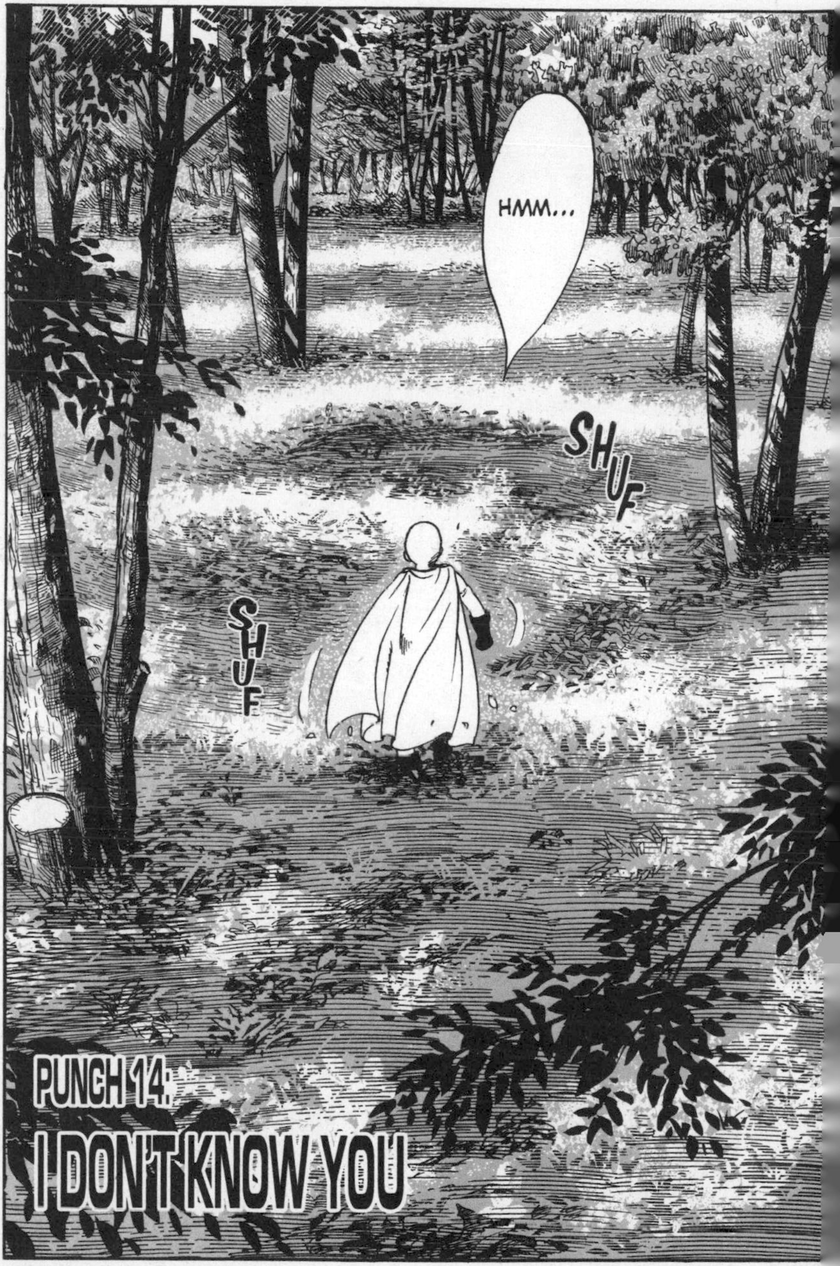
HMM...
SHUF
SHUF
PUNCH 14:
I DON'T KNOW YOU

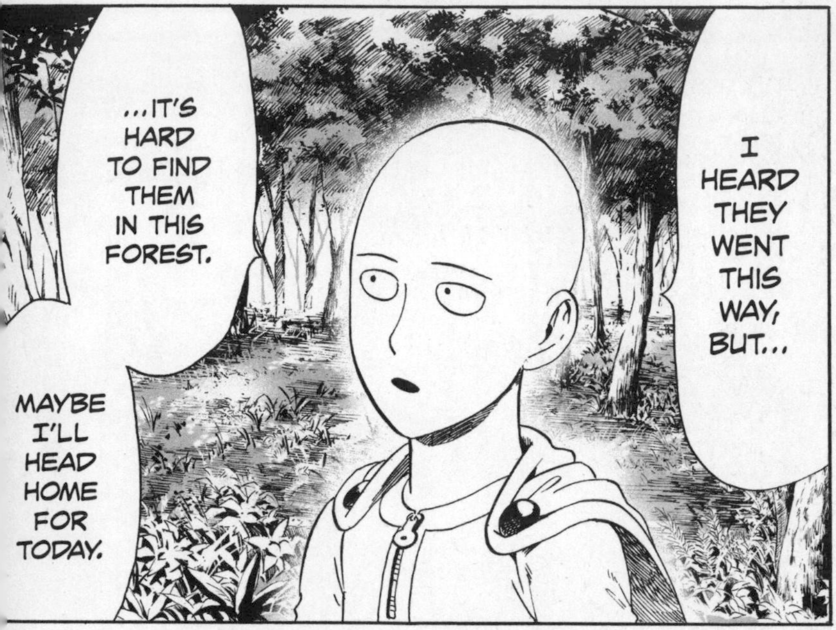
I HEARD THEY WENT THIS WAY, BUT...
...IT'S HARD TO FIND THEM IN THIS FOREST.
MAYBE I'LL HEAD HOME FOR TODAY.

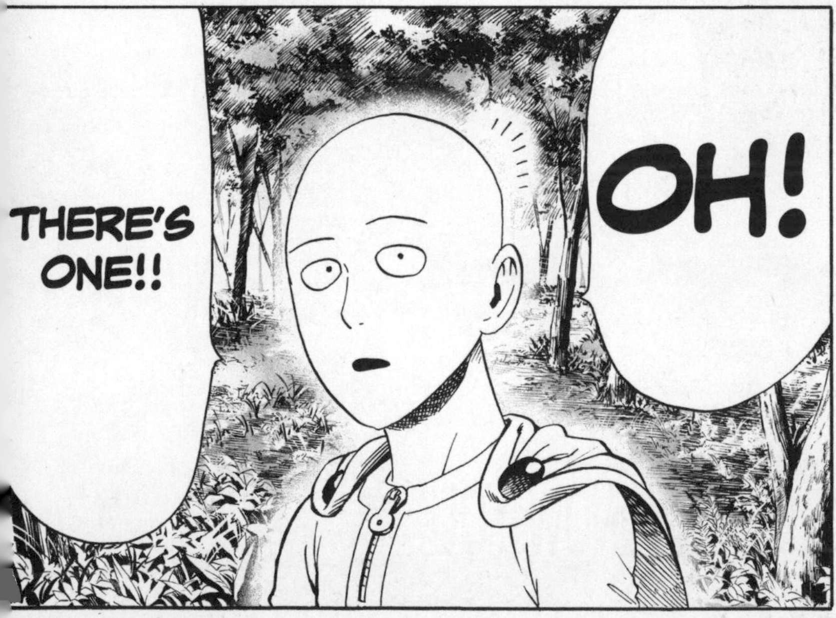
OH!
THERE'S ONE!!

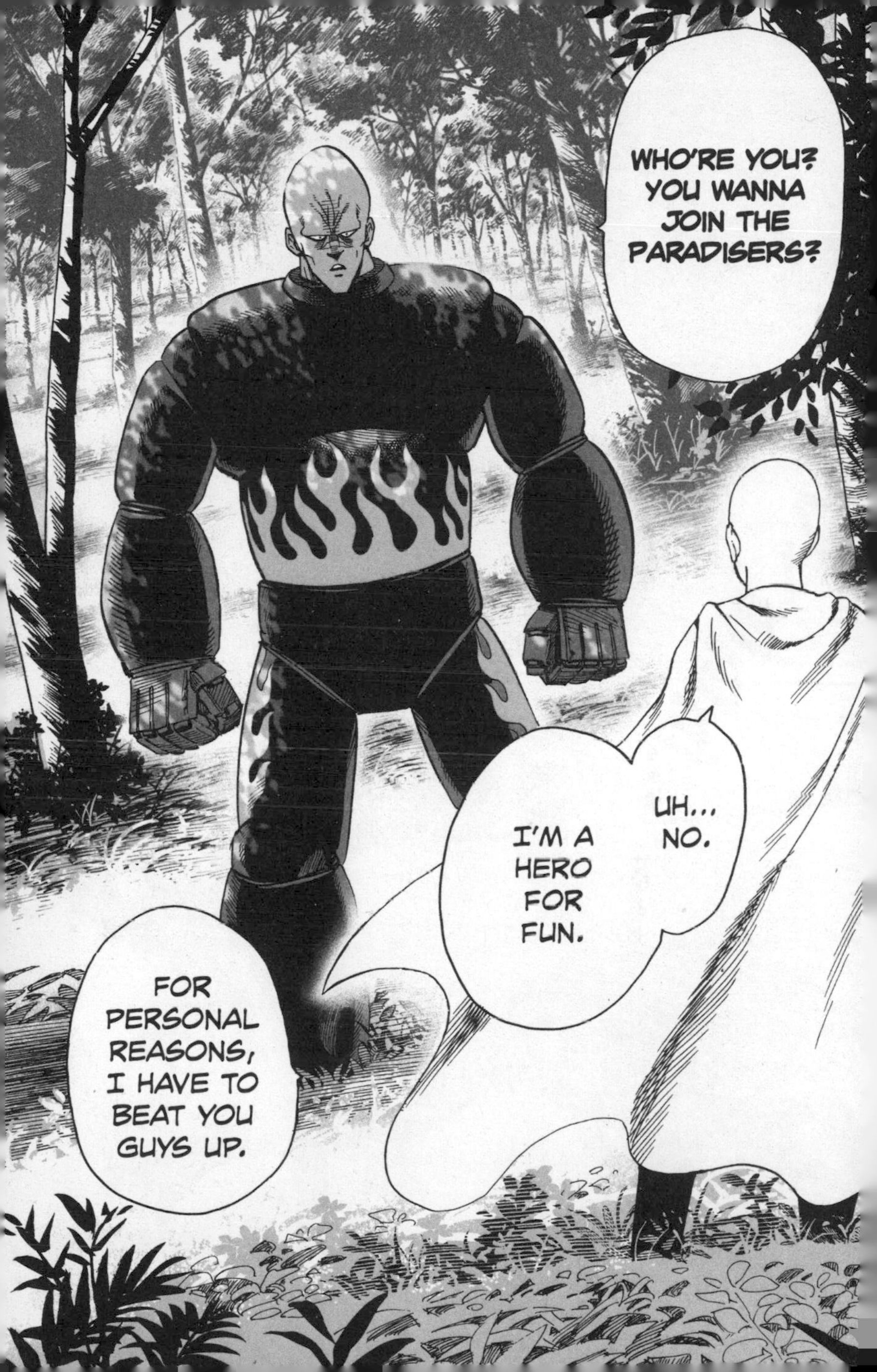
WHO'RE YOU? YOU WANNA JOIN THE PARADISERS?
UH... NO.
I'M A HERO FOR FUN.
FOR PERSONAL REASONS, I HAVE TO BEAT YOU GUYS UP.

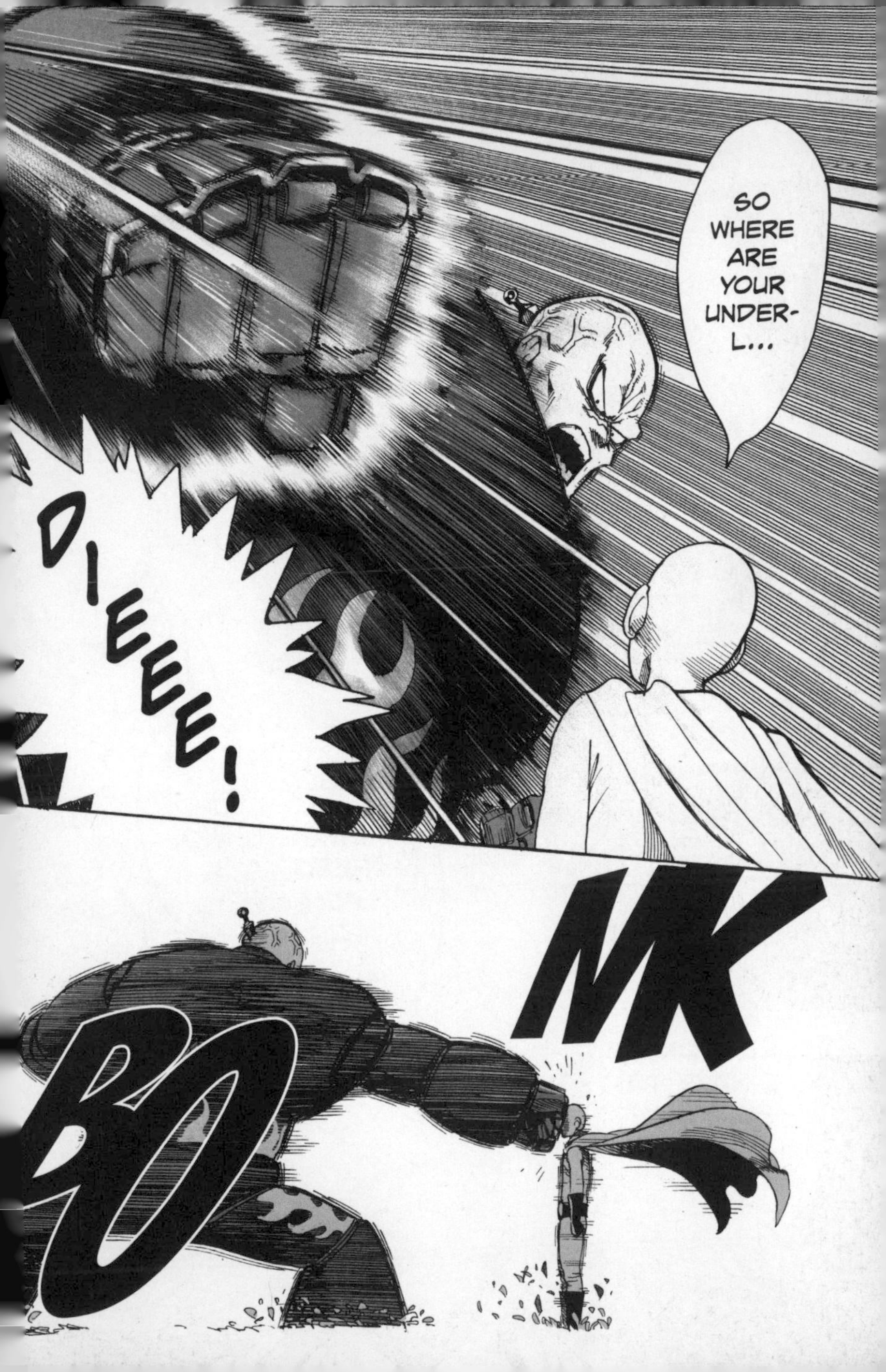
SO WHERE ARE YOUR UNDER-L...
DIEEE!
BOMK

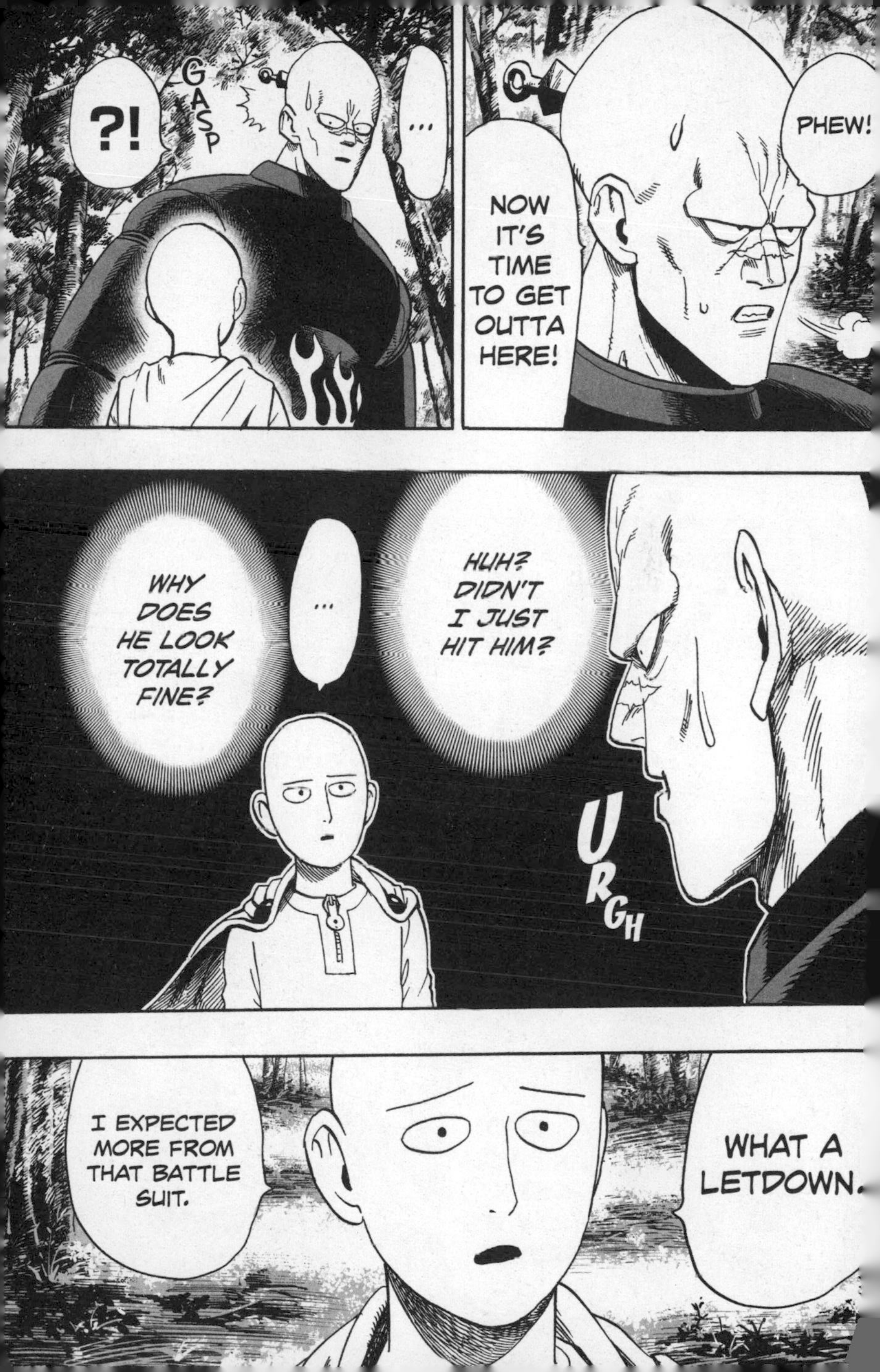
PHEW!
NOW IT'S TIME TO GET OUTTA HERE!
...
GASP
?!
HUH? DIDN'T I JUST HIT HIM?
...
WHY DOES HE LOOK TOTALLY FINE?
URGH
WHAT A LETDOWN.
I EXPECTED MORE FROM THAT BATTLE SUIT.

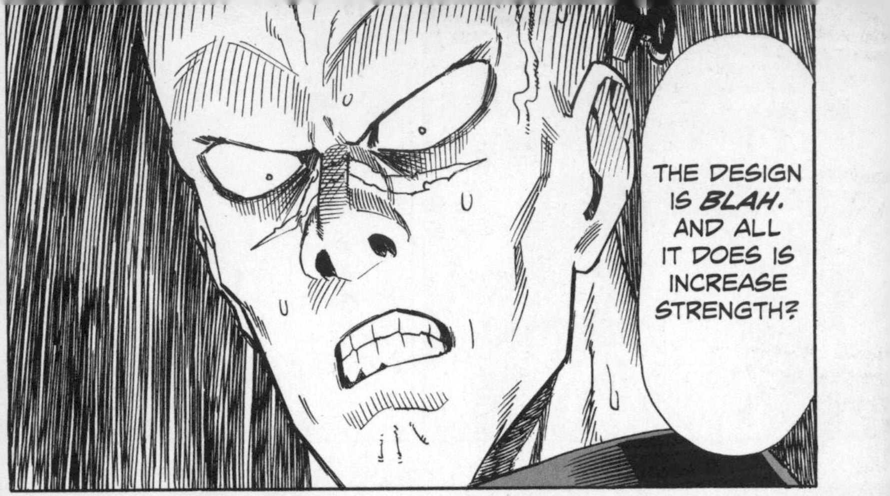
THE DESIGN IS *BLAH.* AND ALL IT DOES IS INCREASE STRENGTH?

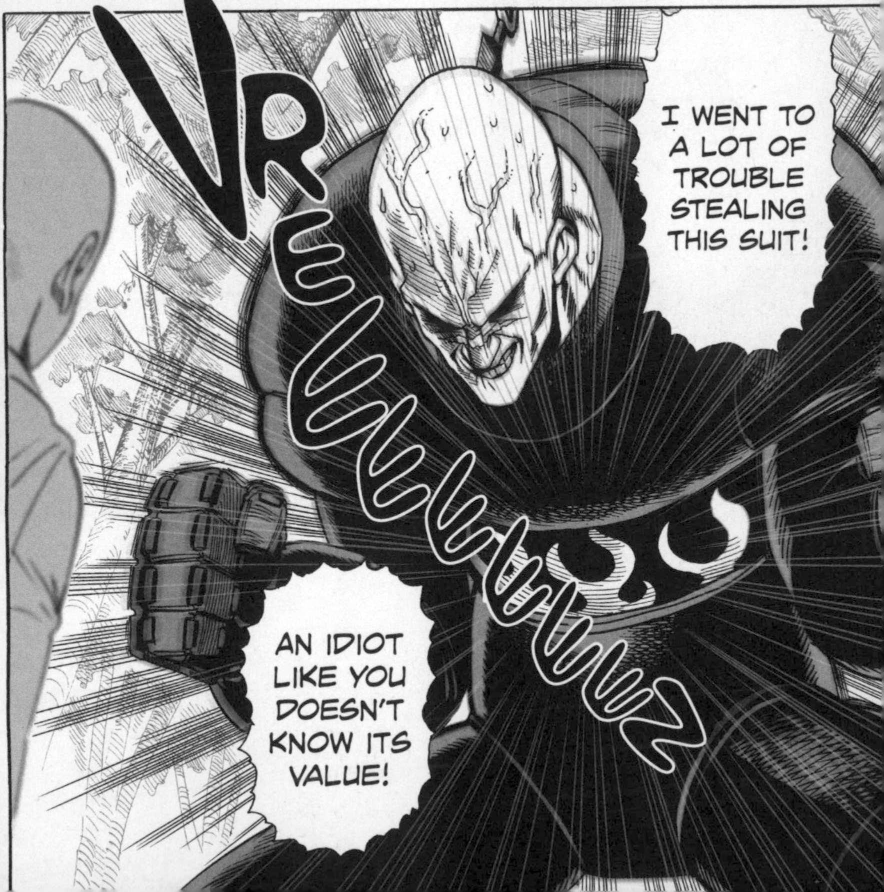
I WENT TO A LOT OF TROUBLE STEALING THIS SUIT!
VRRRRRRRRRRRRRRMMMZ
AN IDIOT LIKE YOU DOESN'T KNOW ITS VALUE!

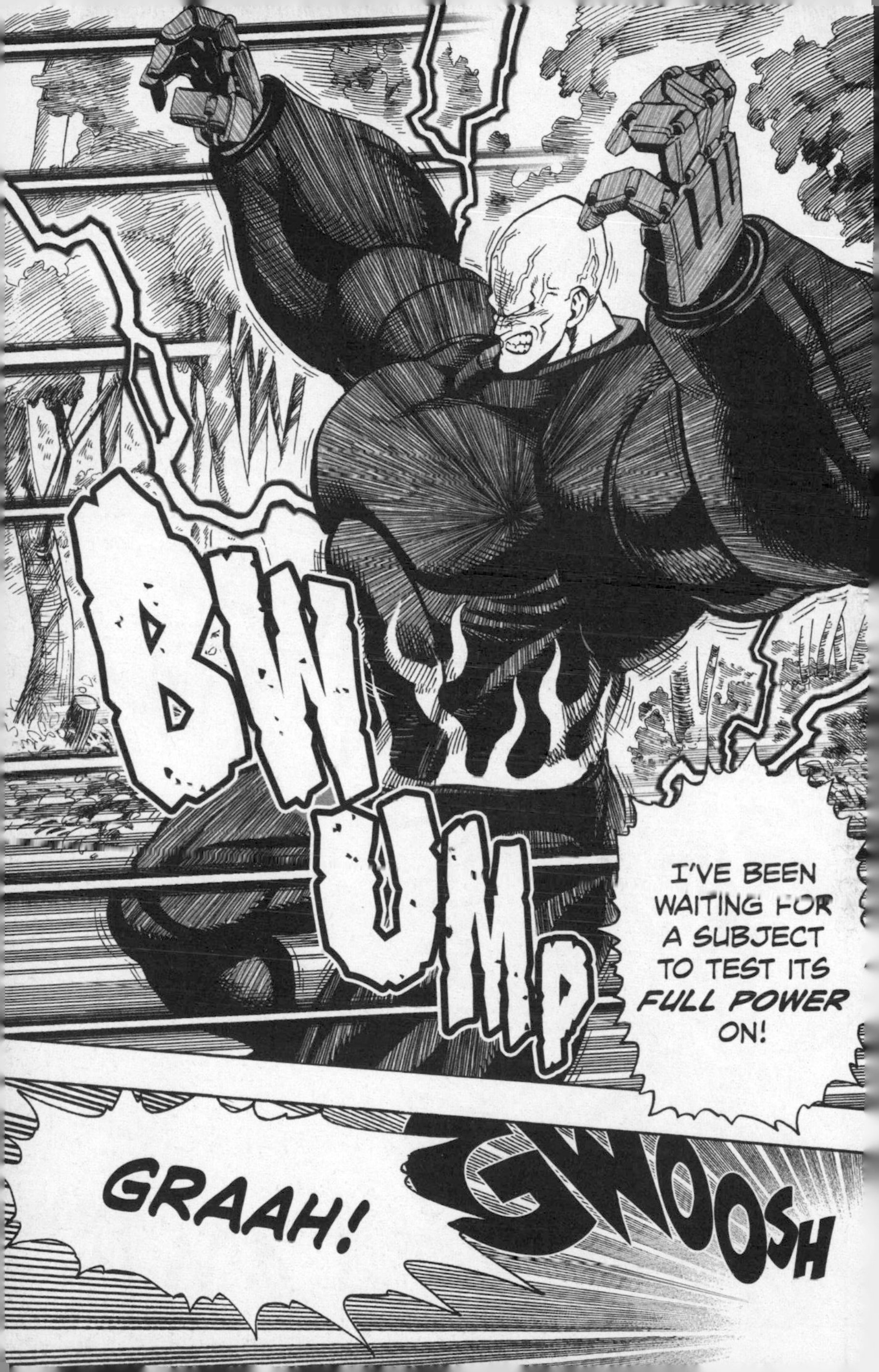
I'VE BEEN WAITING FOR A SUBJECT TO TEST ITS *FULL POWER* ON!
BWUMP
GWOOSH
GRAAH!

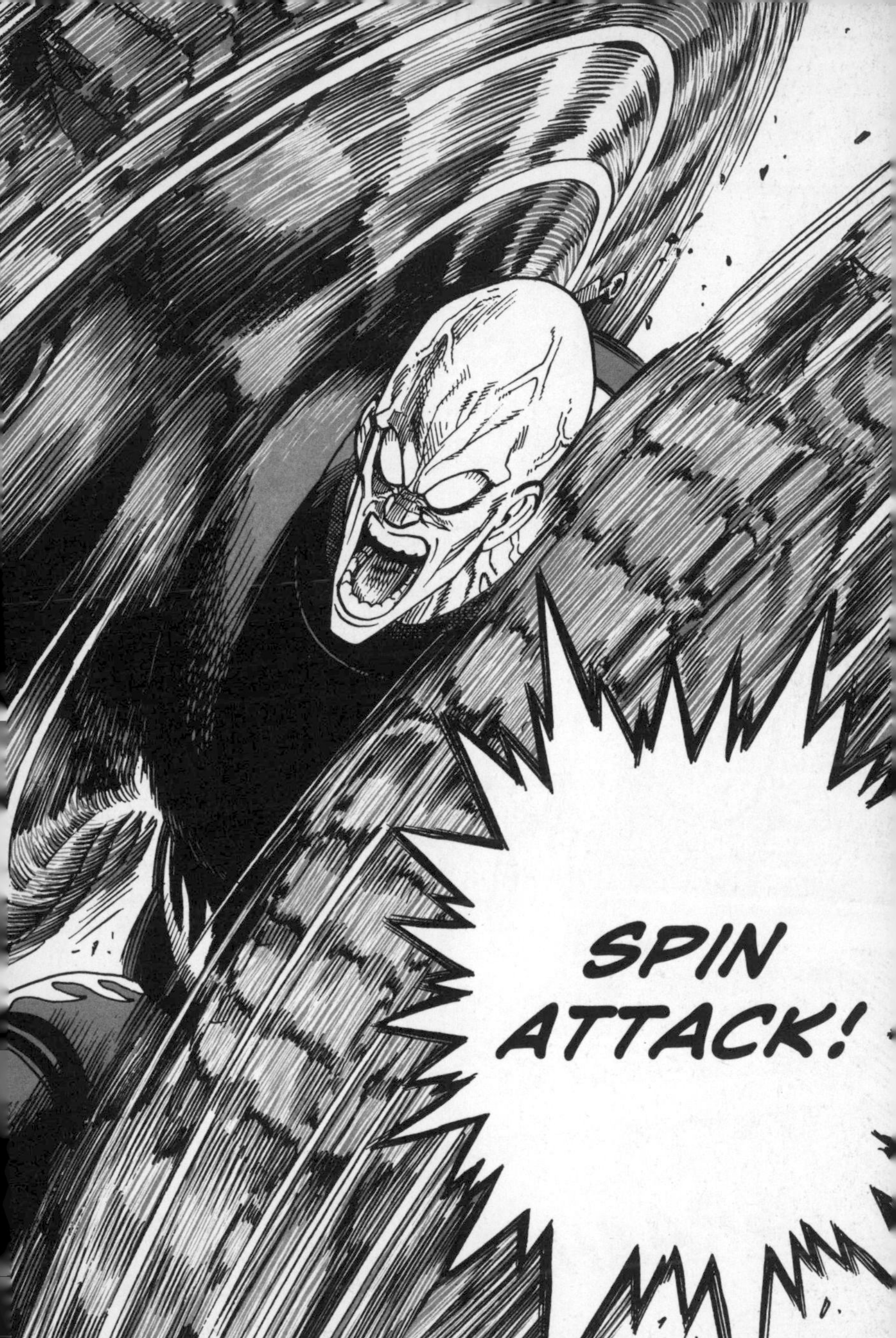
SPIN ATTACK!

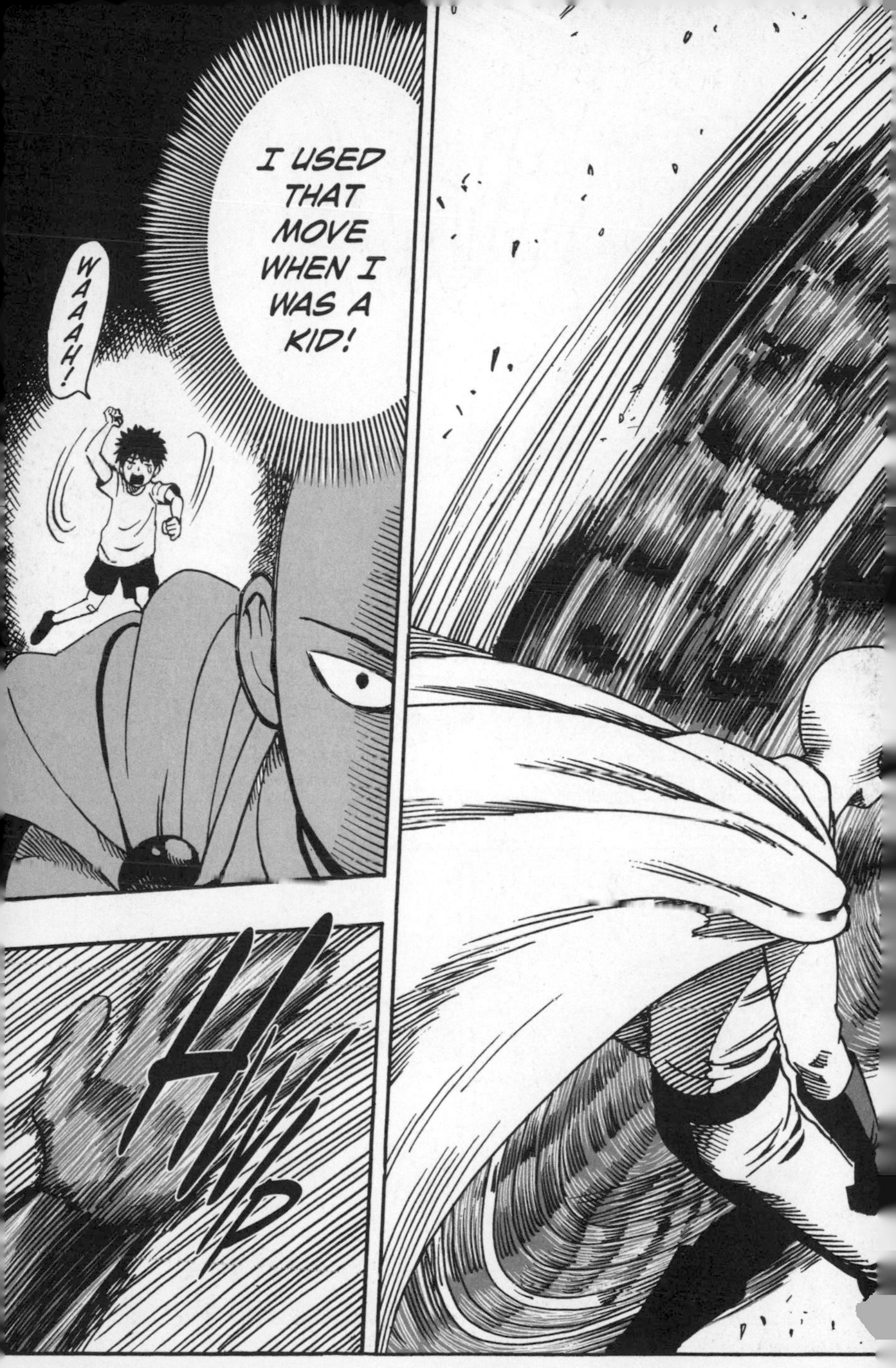
I USED THAT MOVE WHEN I WAS A KID!
WAAAH!
HWP

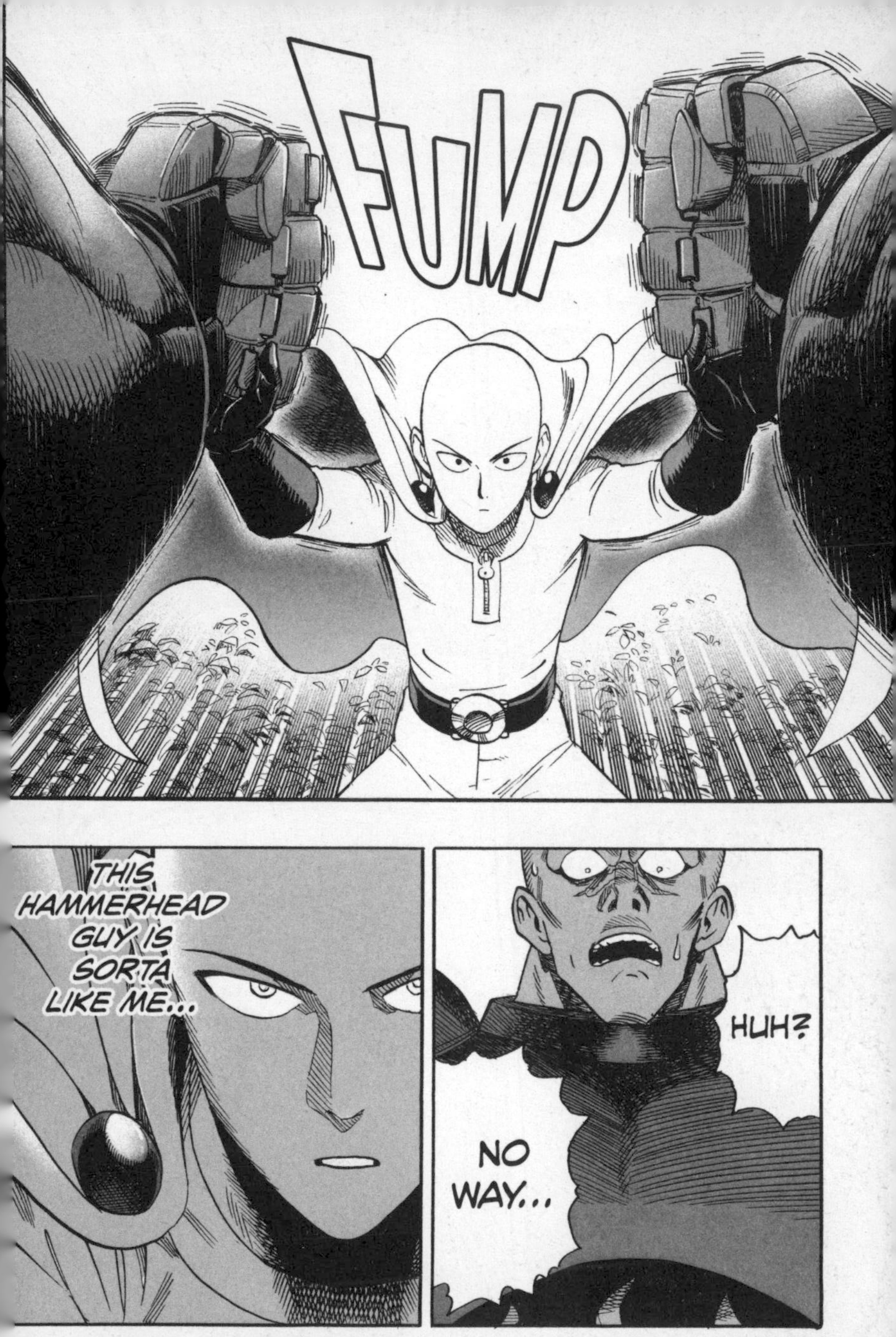
FUMP
HUH?
NO WAY...
THIS HAMMERHEAD GUY IS SORTA LIKE ME...

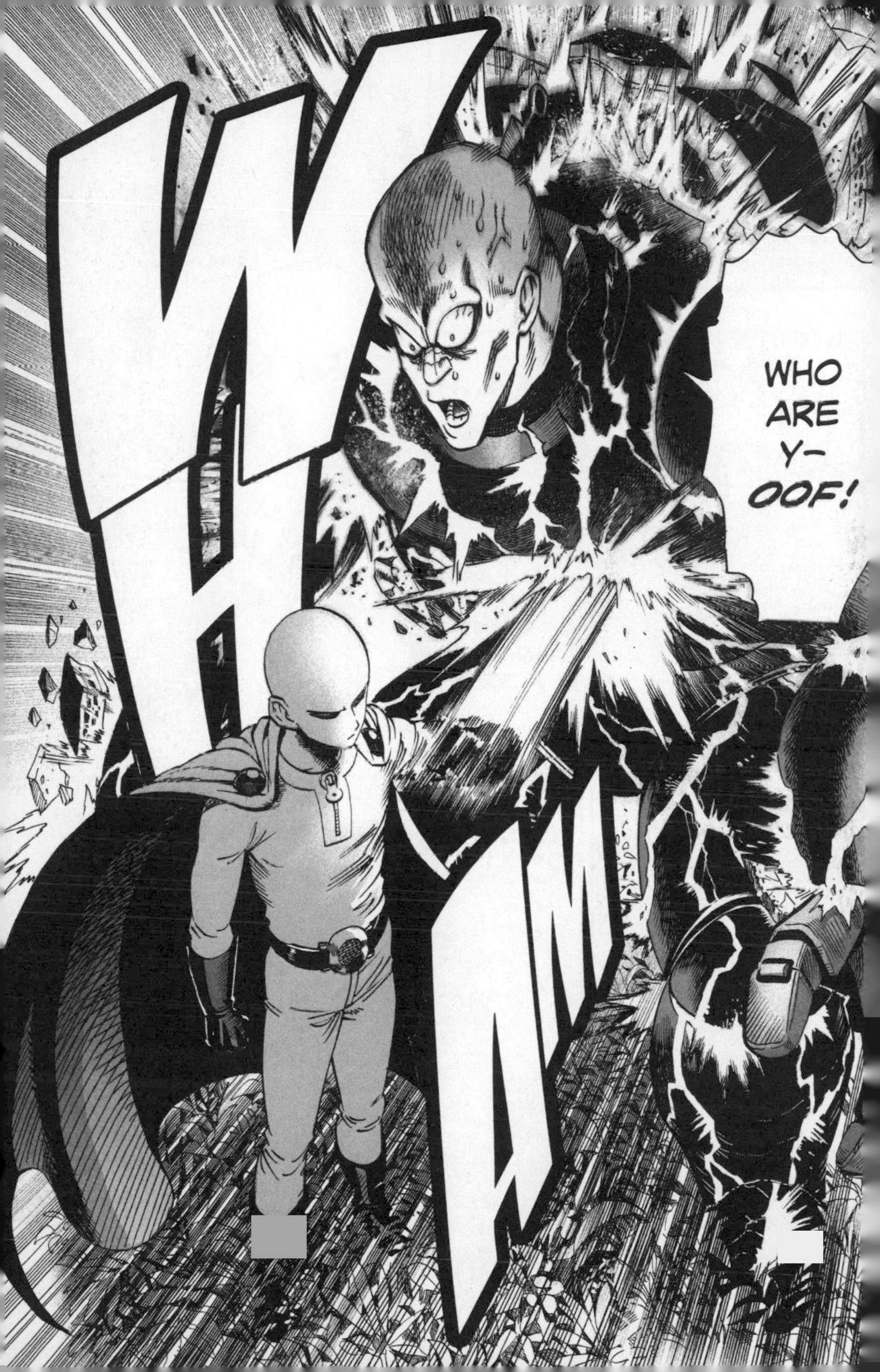
WHO ARE Y— OOF!
WHAM

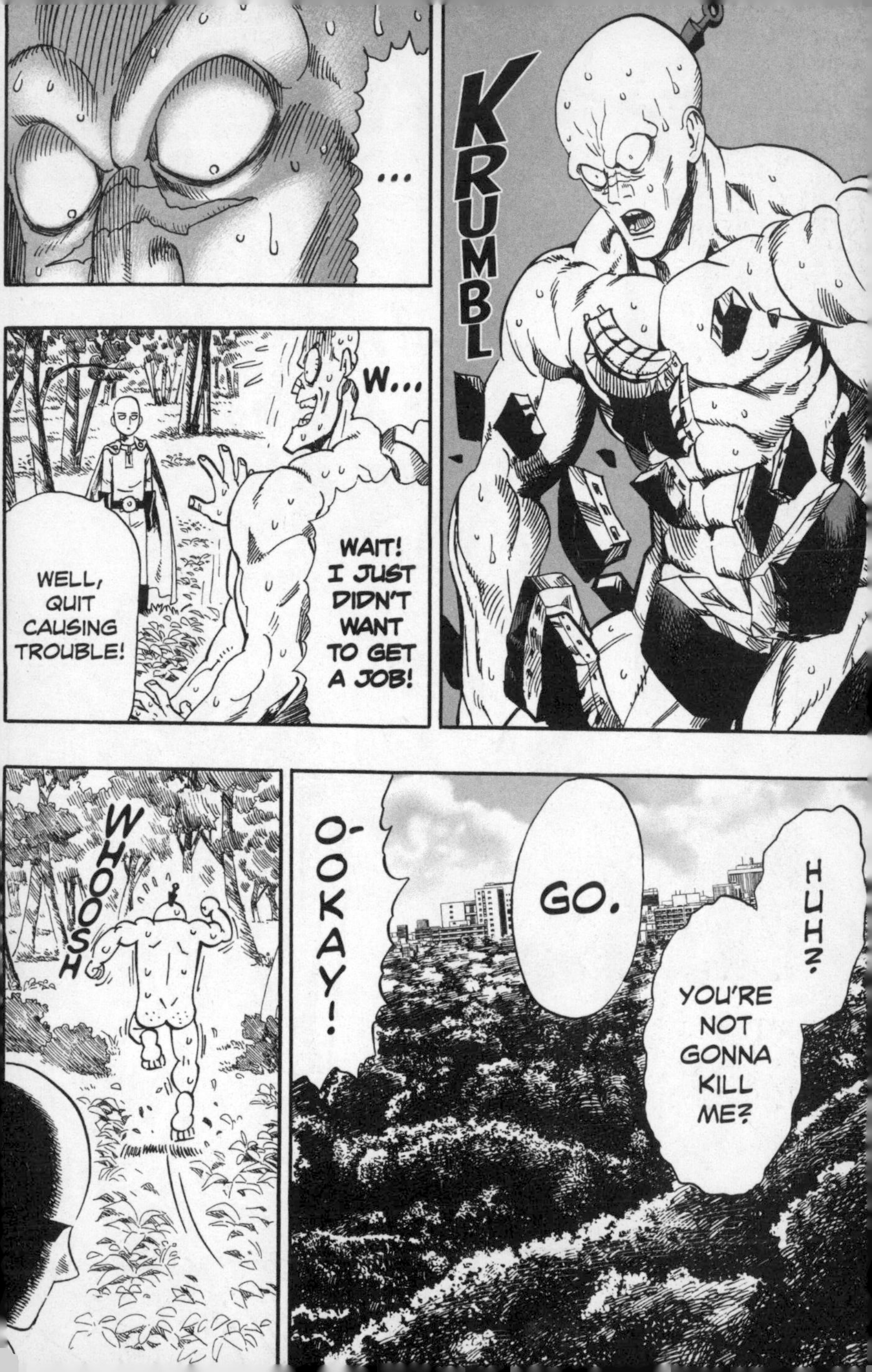
KRUMBL
...
W...
WAIT! I JUST DIDN'T WANT TO GET A JOB!
WELL, QUIT CAUSING TROUBLE!
HUH?
YOU'RE NOT GONNA KILL ME?
GO.
O-OOKAY!
WHOOOSH

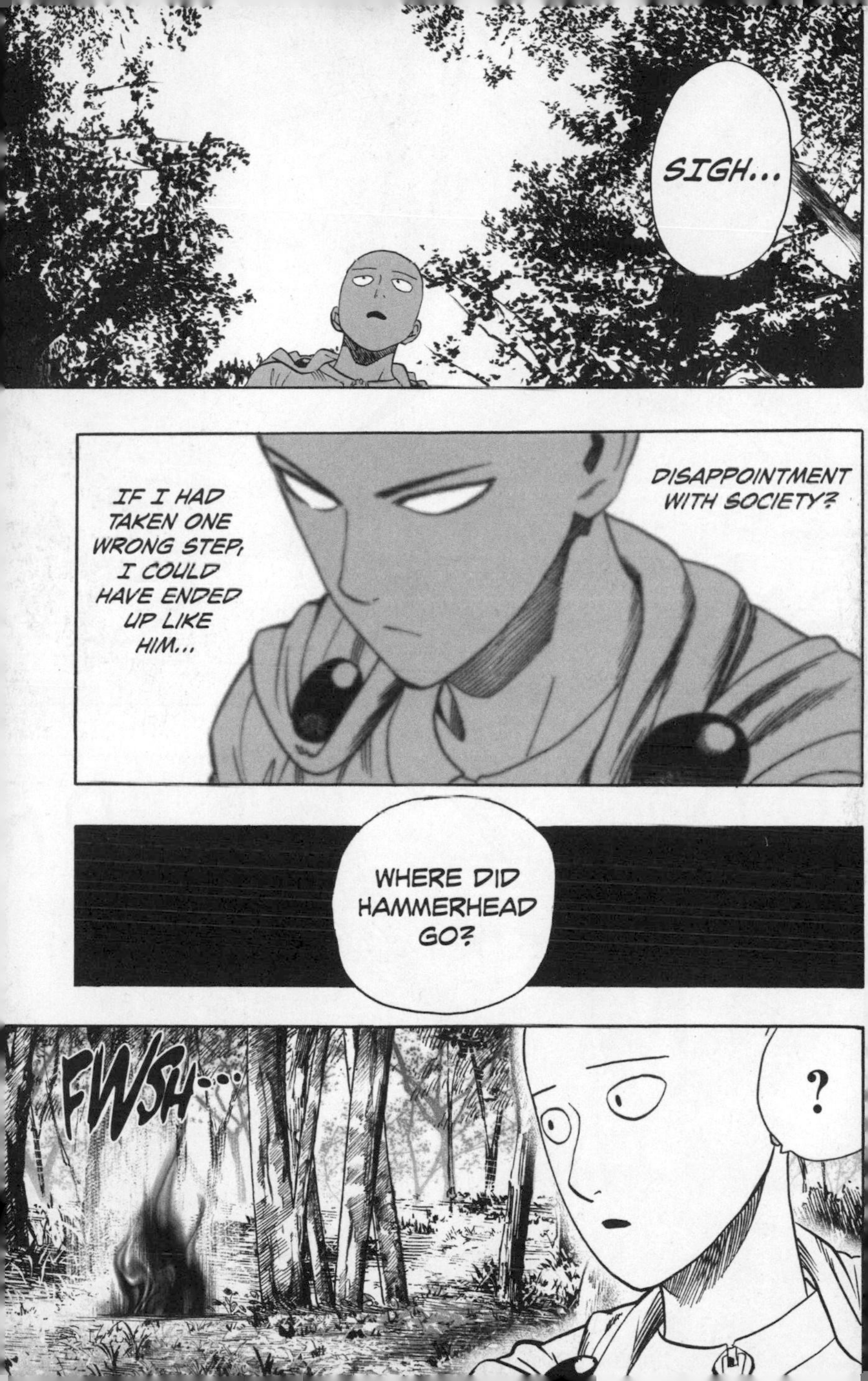
SIGH...
DISAPPOINTMENT WITH SOCIETY?
IF I HAD TAKEN ONE WRONG STEP, I COULD HAVE ENDED UP LIKE HIM...
WHERE DID HAMMERHEAD GO?
?
FWSH...

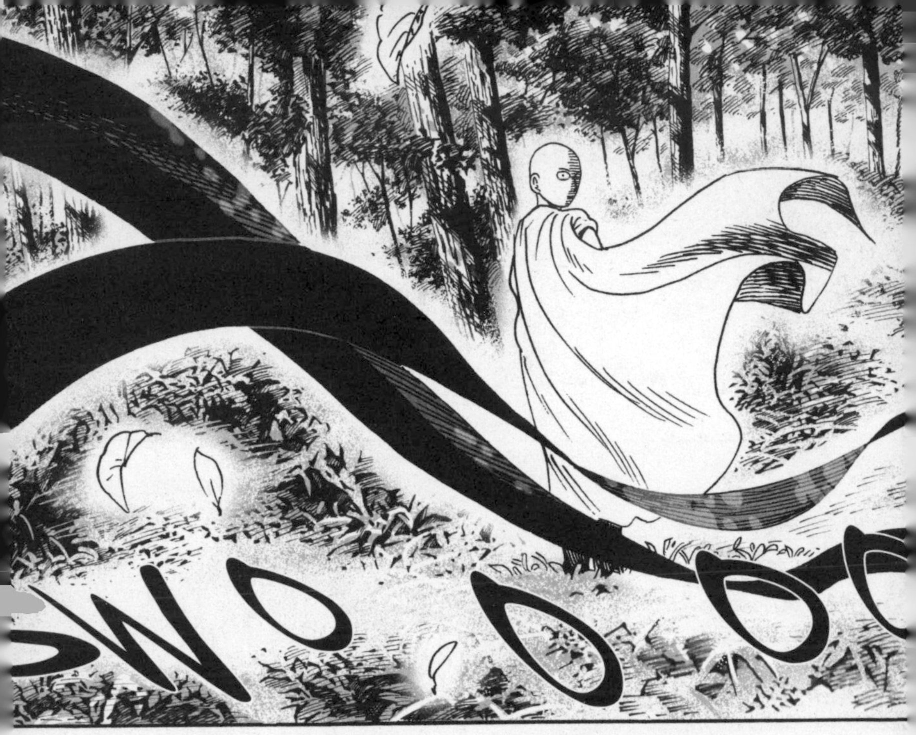
WOOOO
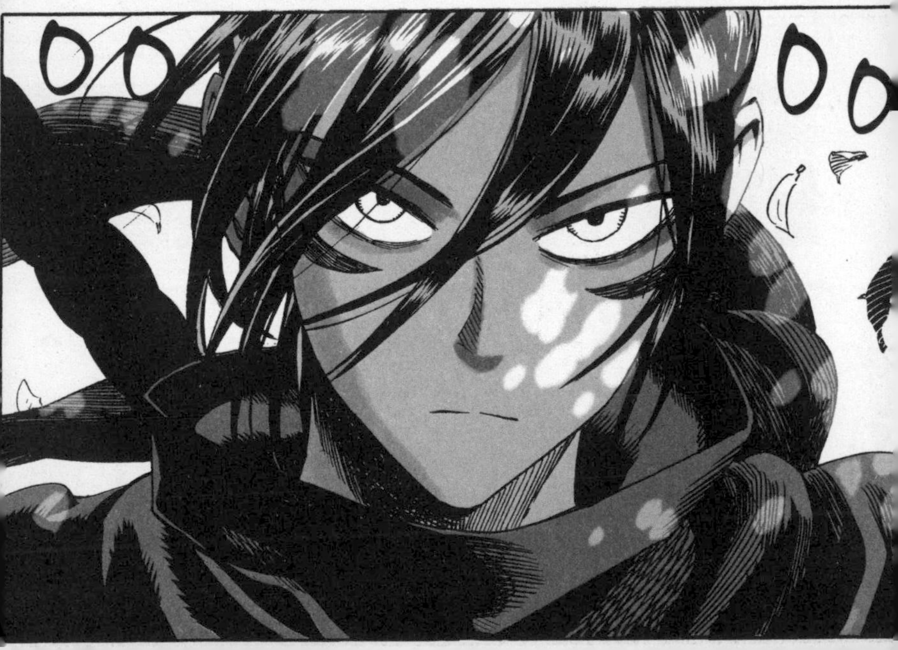
OOOO

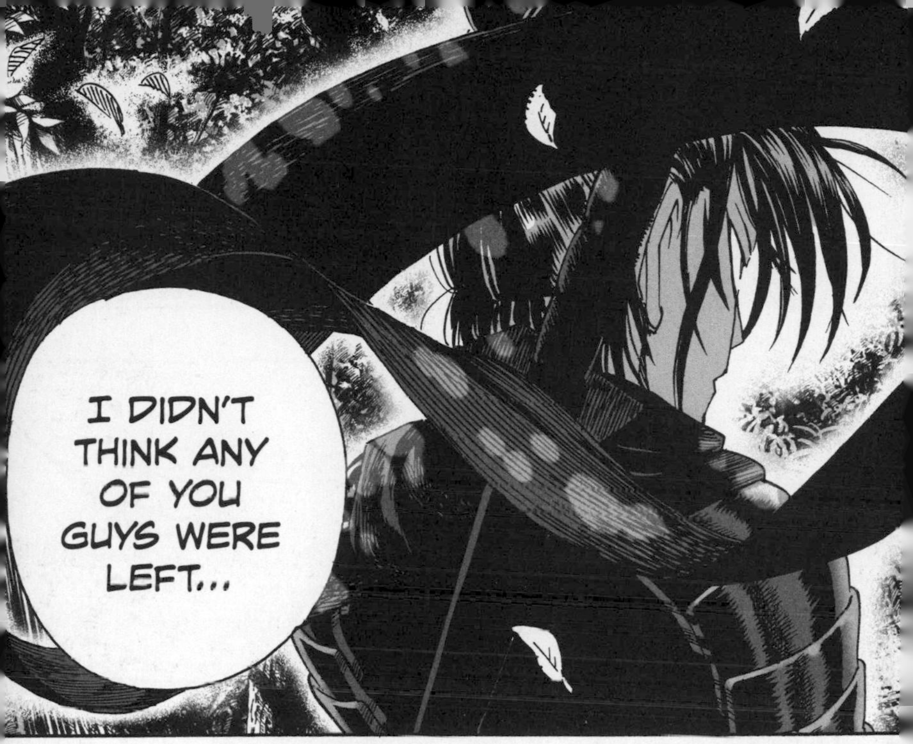
I DIDN'T THINK ANY OF YOU GUYS WERE LEFT...

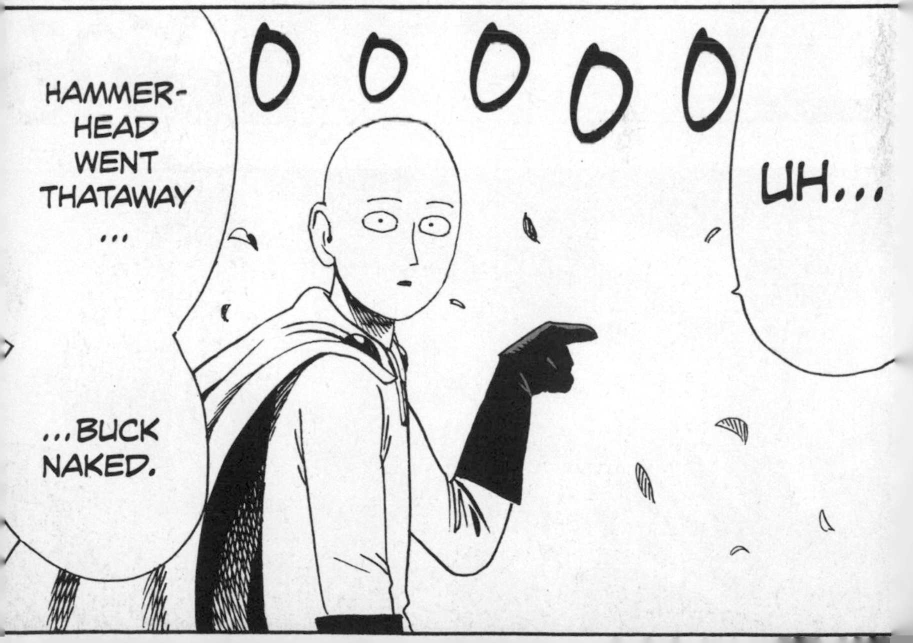
UH...
OOOOO
HAMMER-HEAD WENT THATAWAY ...
...BUCK NAKED.

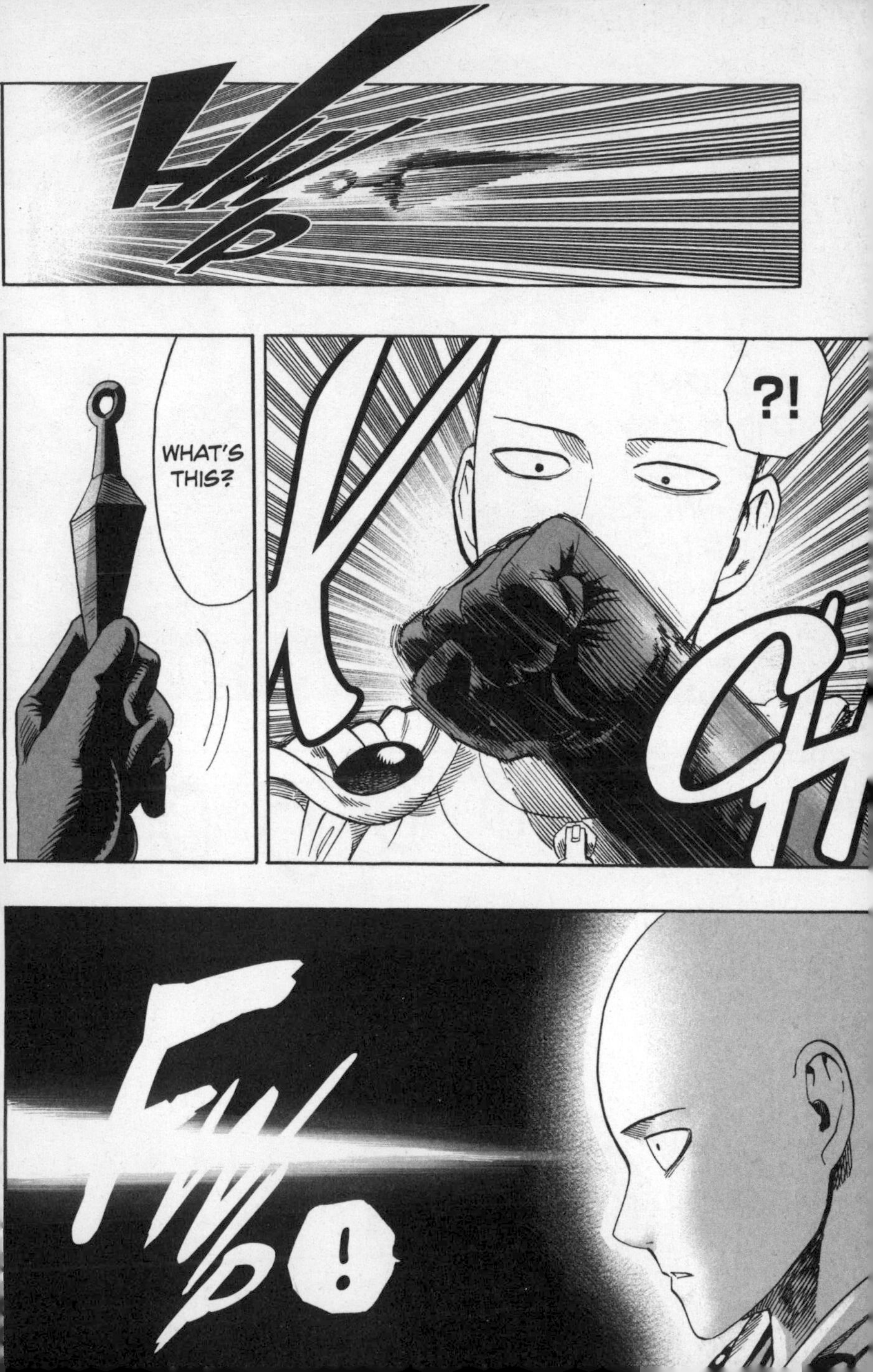
WHIP
?!
WHAT'S THIS?
FWIP
!

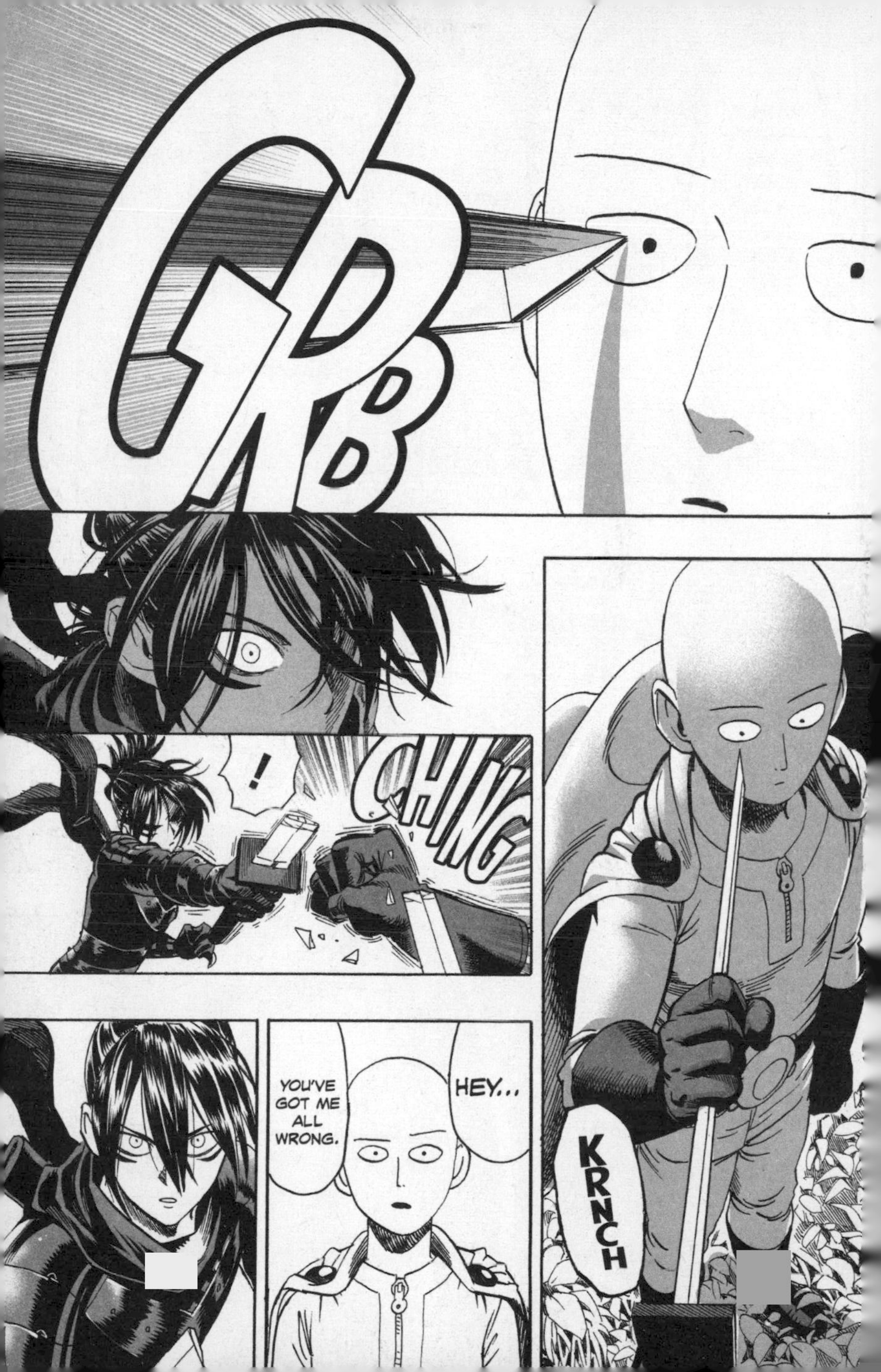
GRB
KRNCH
!
CHING
HEY...
YOU'VE GOT ME ALL WRONG.

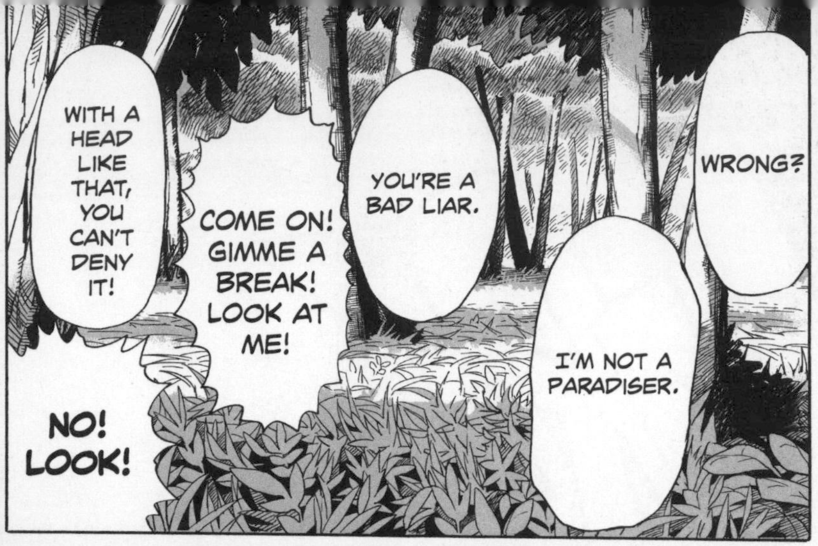
WRONG?
I'M NOT A PARADISER.
YOU'RE A BAD LIAR.
COME ON! GIMME A BREAK! LOOK AT ME!
WITH A HEAD LIKE THAT, YOU CAN'T DENY IT!
NO! LOOK!

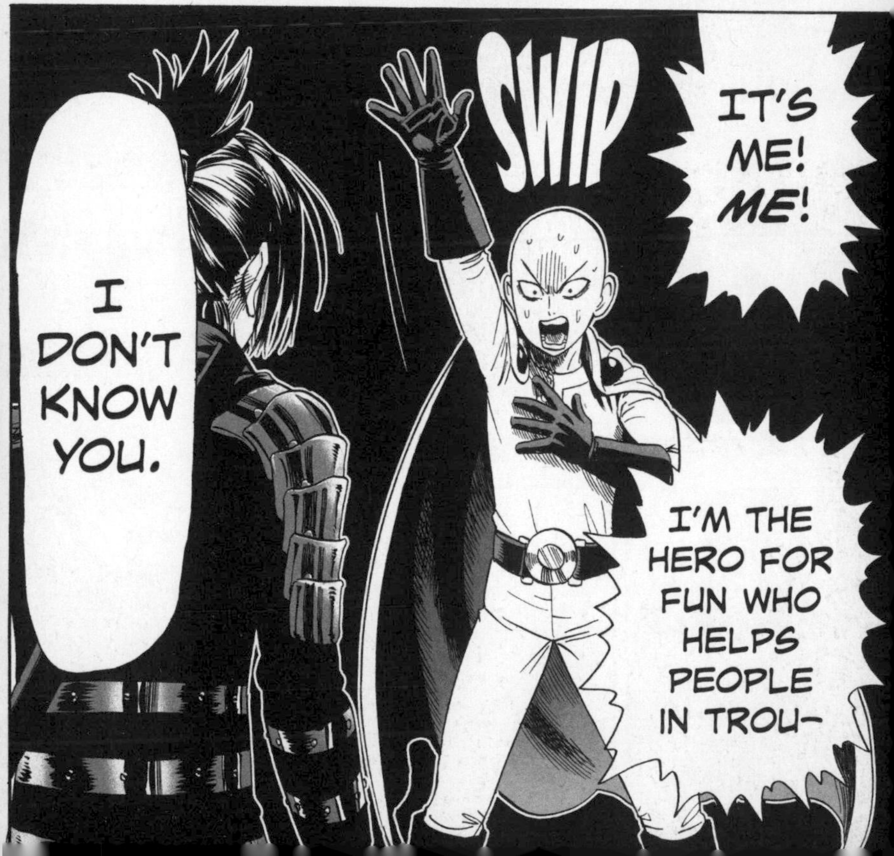
SWIP
IT'S ME! *ME*!
I'M THE HERO FOR FUN WHO HELPS PEOPLE IN TROU-
I DON'T KNOW YOU.

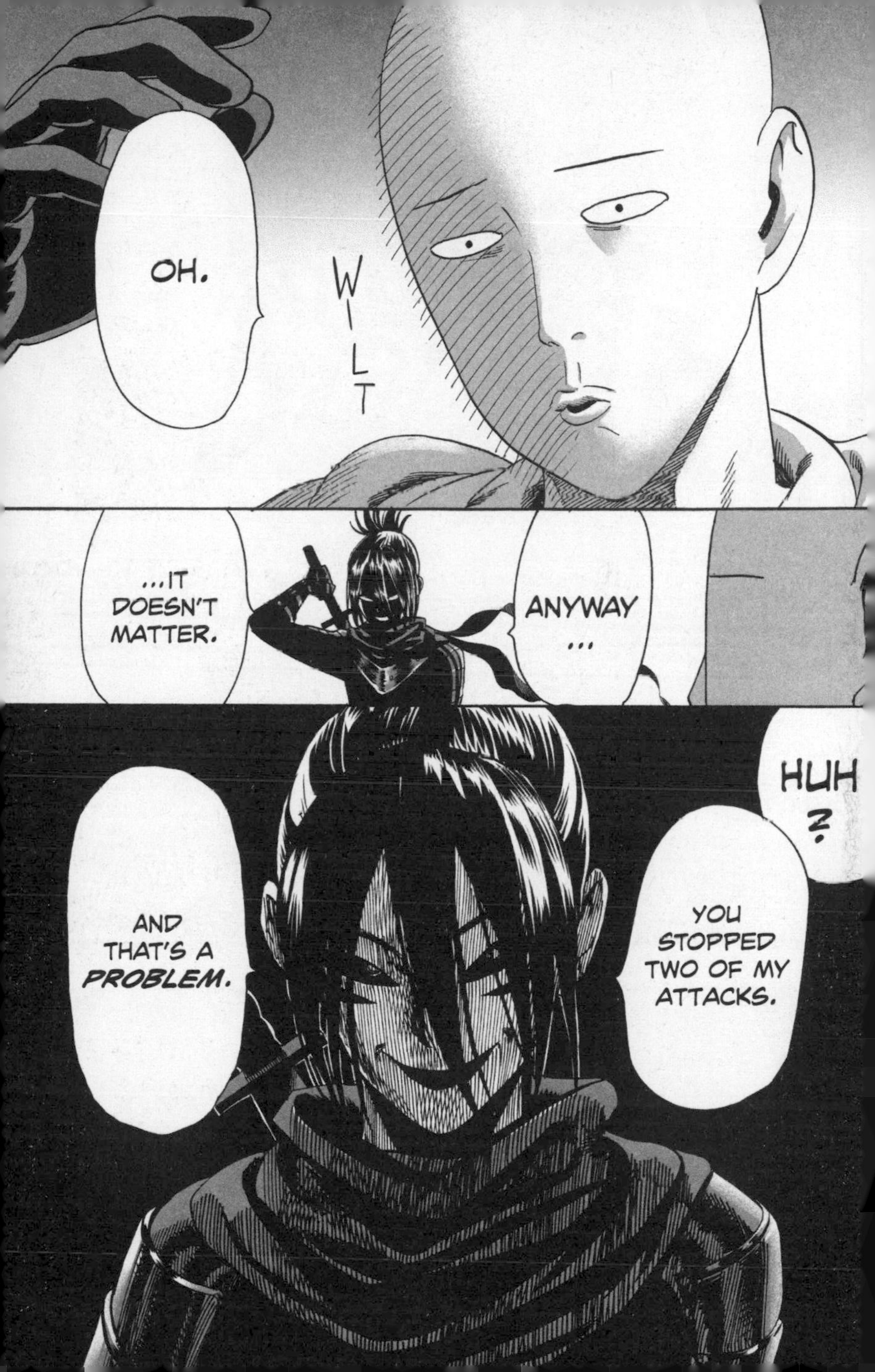
WILT
OH.
ANYWAY ...
...IT DOESN'T MATTER.
HUH ?
YOU STOPPED TWO OF MY ATTACKS.
AND THAT'S A *PROBLEM.*

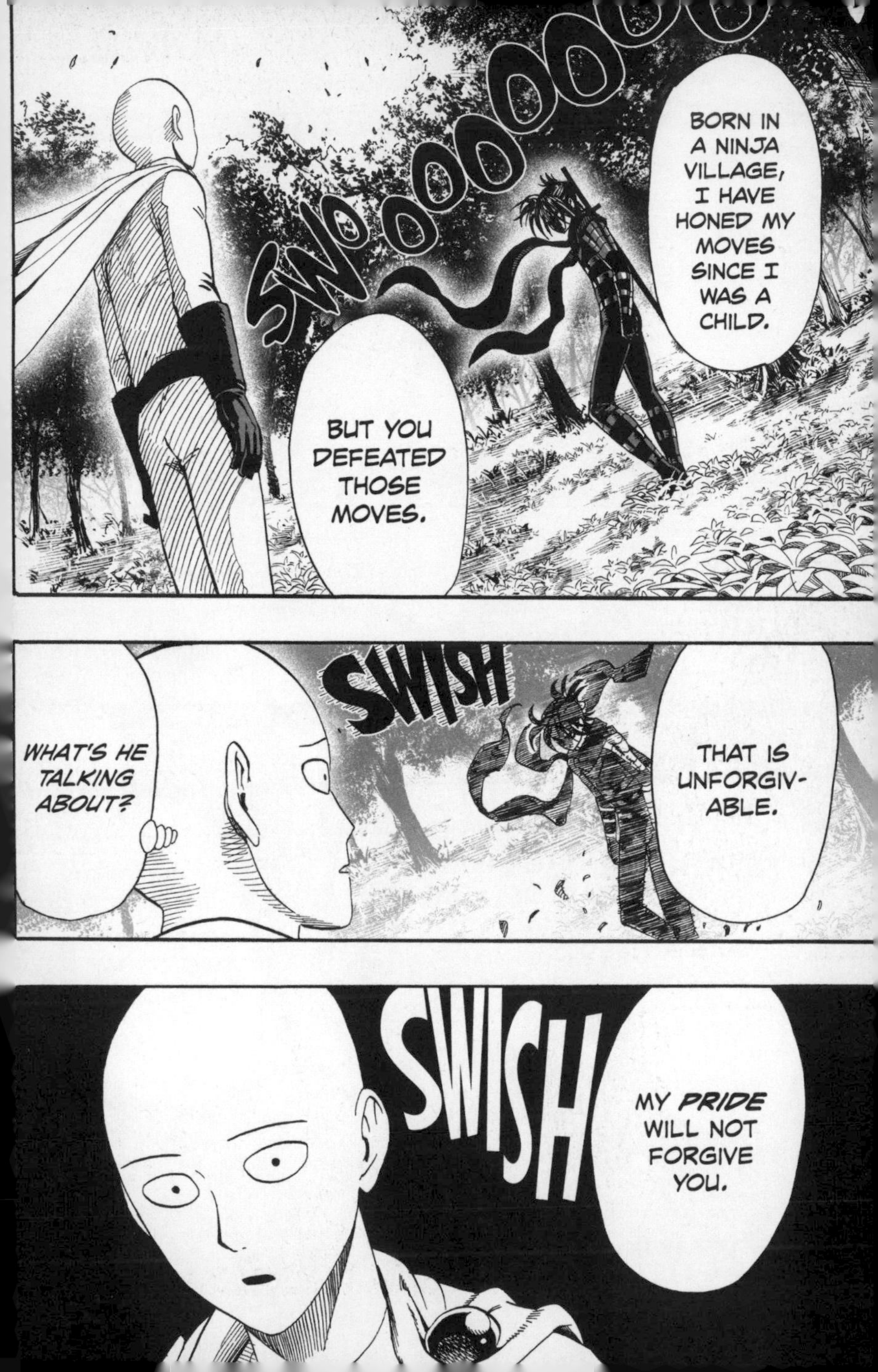
BORN IN A NINJA VILLAGE, I HAVE HONED MY MOVES SINCE I WAS A CHILD.
SWOOOOOOOOO
BUT YOU DEFEATED THOSE MOVES.
THAT IS UNFORGIV-ABLE.
SWISH
WHAT'S HE TALKING ABOUT?
MY *PRIDE* WILL NOT FORGIVE YOU.
SWISH

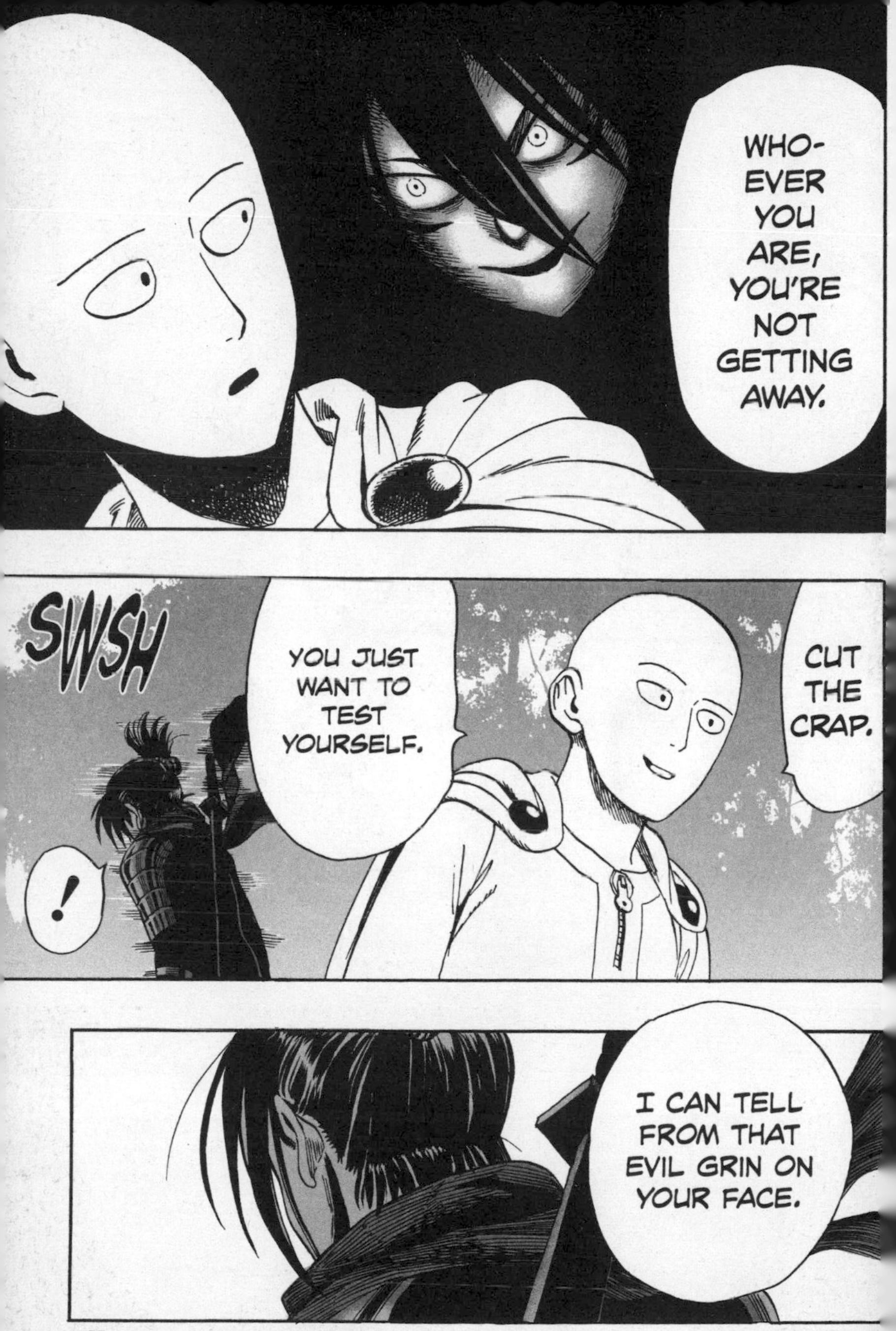
WHO-EVER YOU ARE, YOU'RE NOT GETTING AWAY.
CUT THE CRAP.
YOU JUST WANT TO TEST YOURSELF.
SWSH
!
I CAN TELL FROM THAT EVIL GRIN ON YOUR FACE.

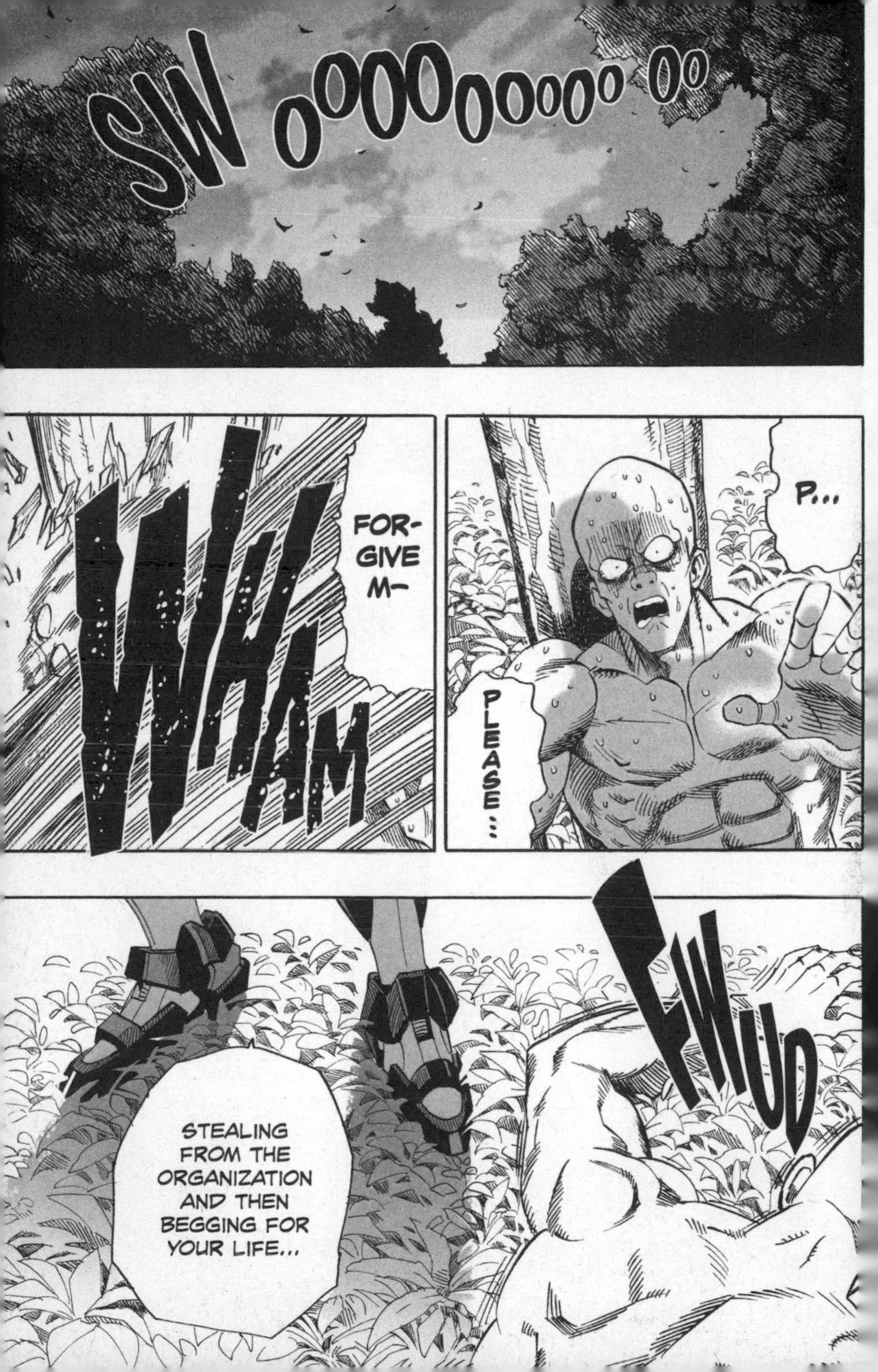
SWOOOOOOOOOOO
P...
PLEASE...
FOR-GIVE M-
WHAM
FWUD
STEALING FROM THE ORGANIZATION AND THEN BEGGING FOR YOUR LIFE...

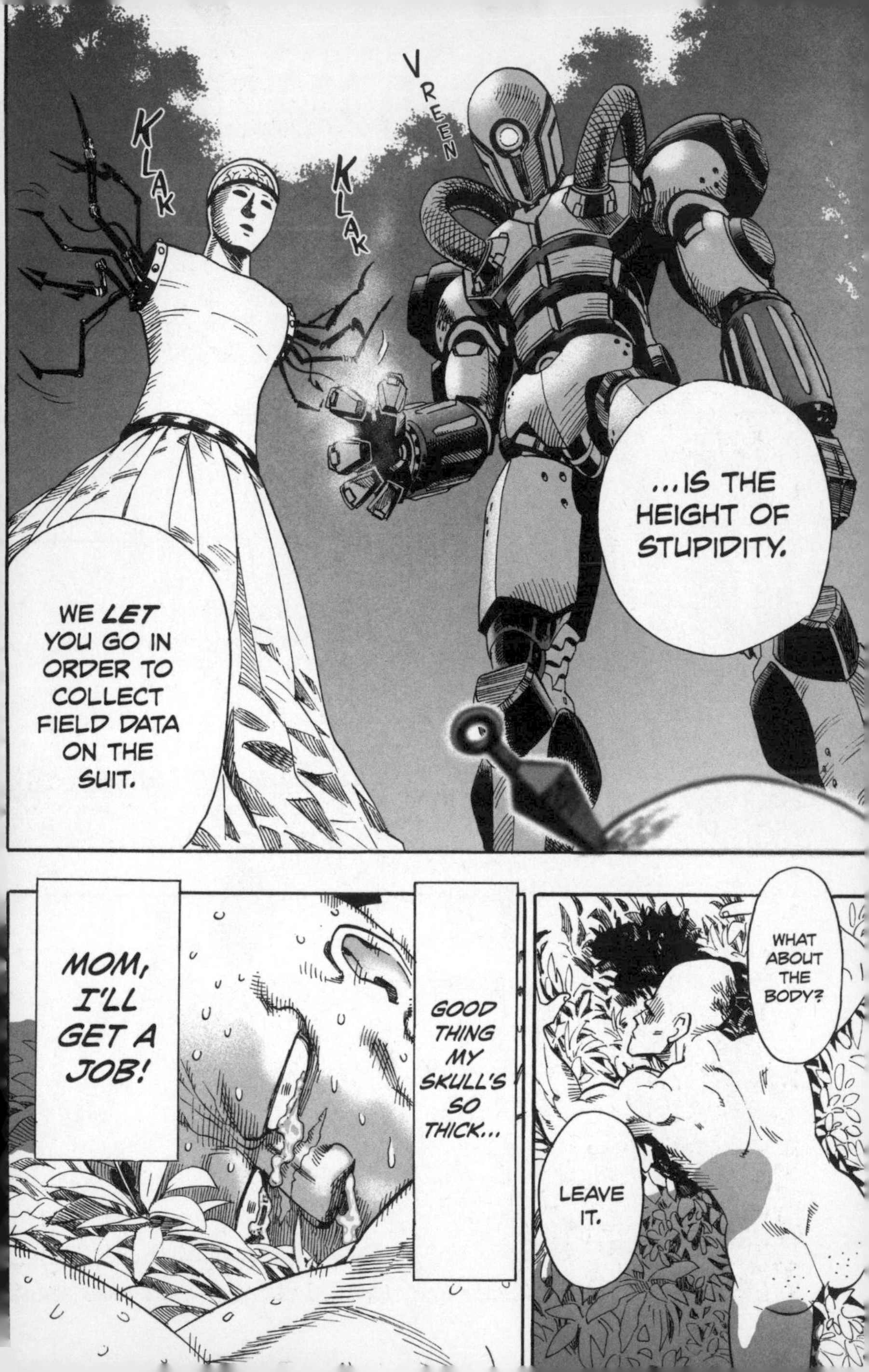
VREEN
KLAK
KLAK
...IS THE HEIGHT OF STUPIDITY.
WE *LET* YOU GO IN ORDER TO COLLECT FIELD DATA ON THE SUIT.
WHAT ABOUT THE BODY?
LEAVE IT.
GOOD THING MY SKULL'S SO THICK...
MOM, I'LL GET A JOB!

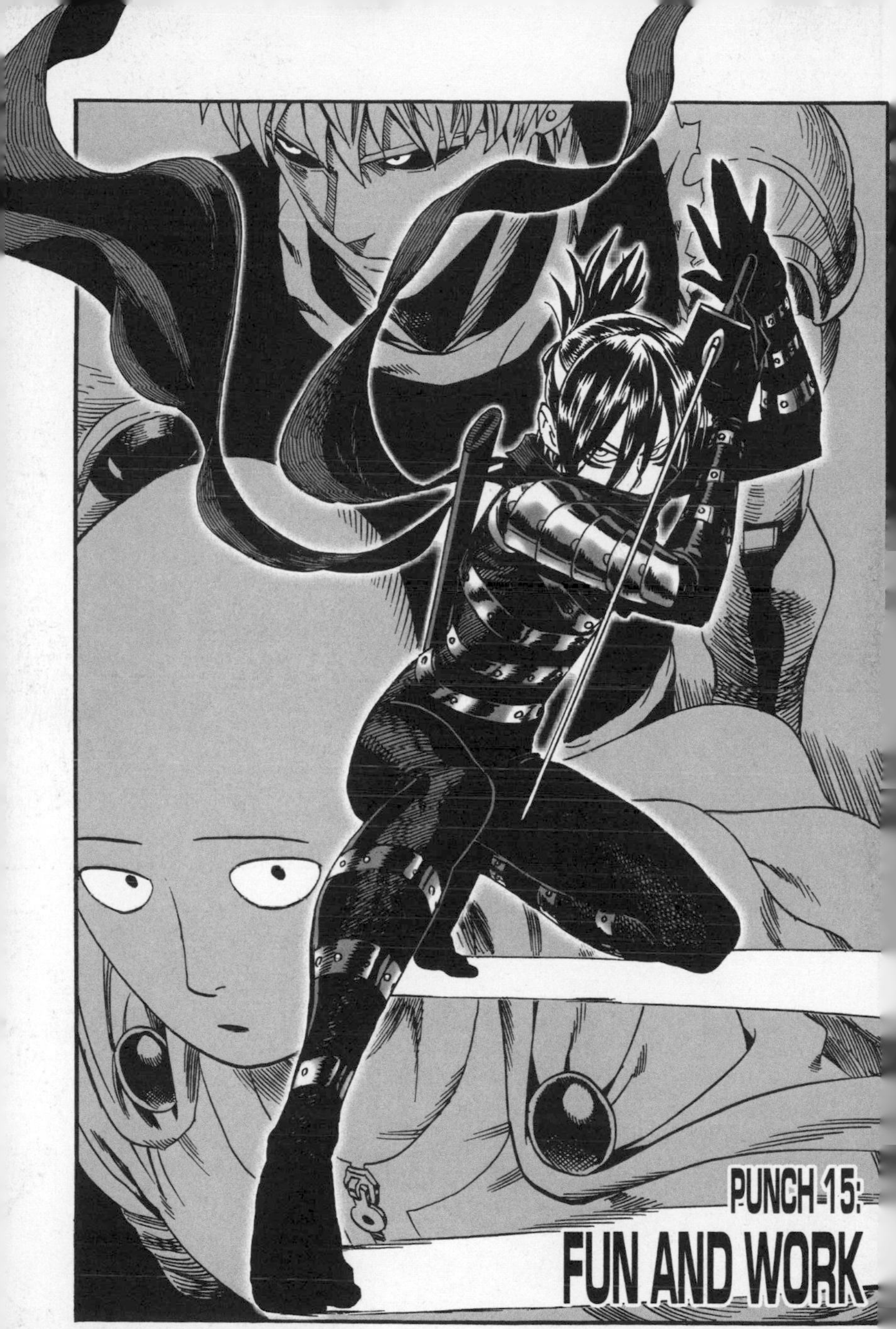
PUNCH 15:
FUN AND WORK

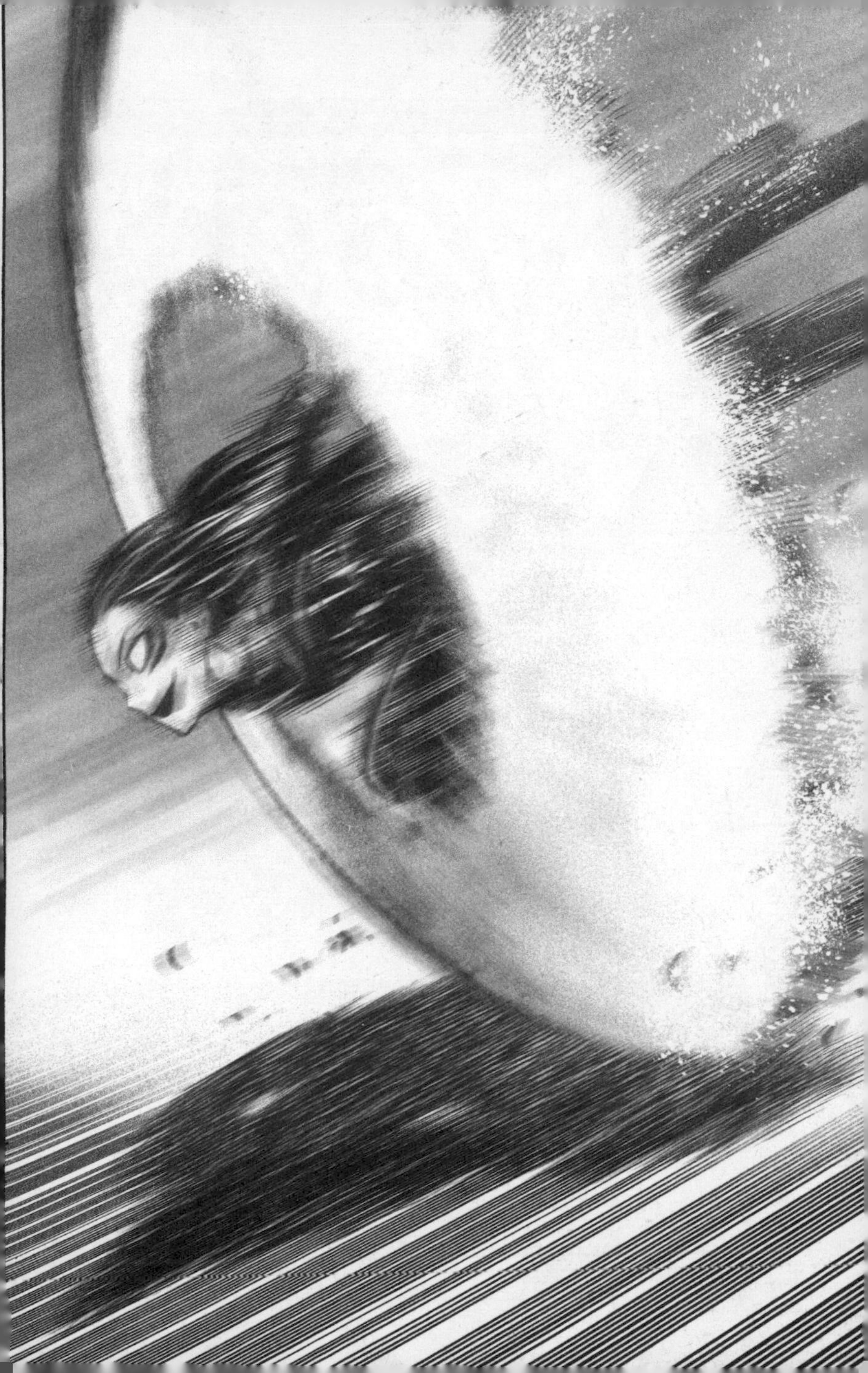

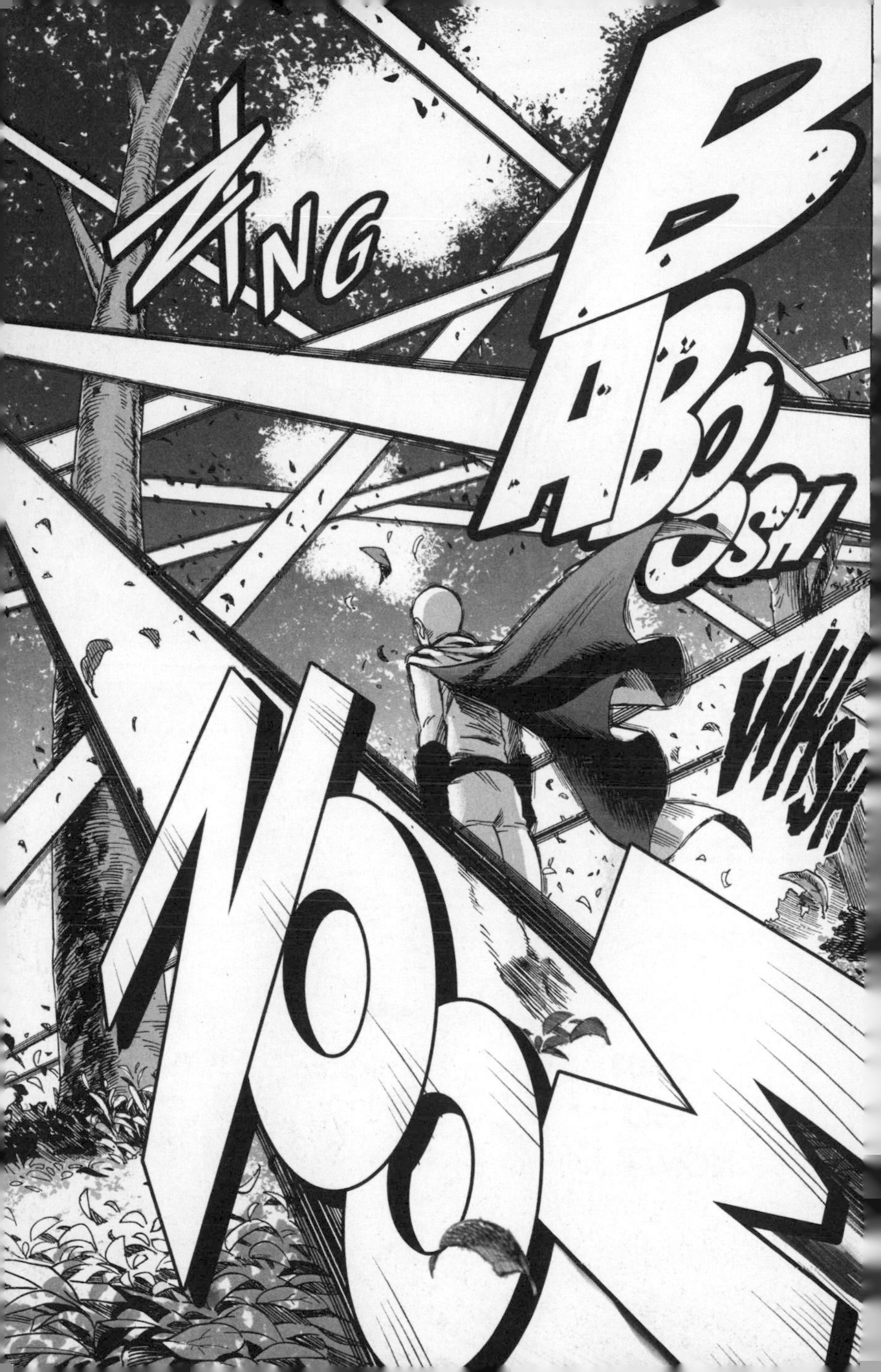
ZING
BABOOSH
WHISH

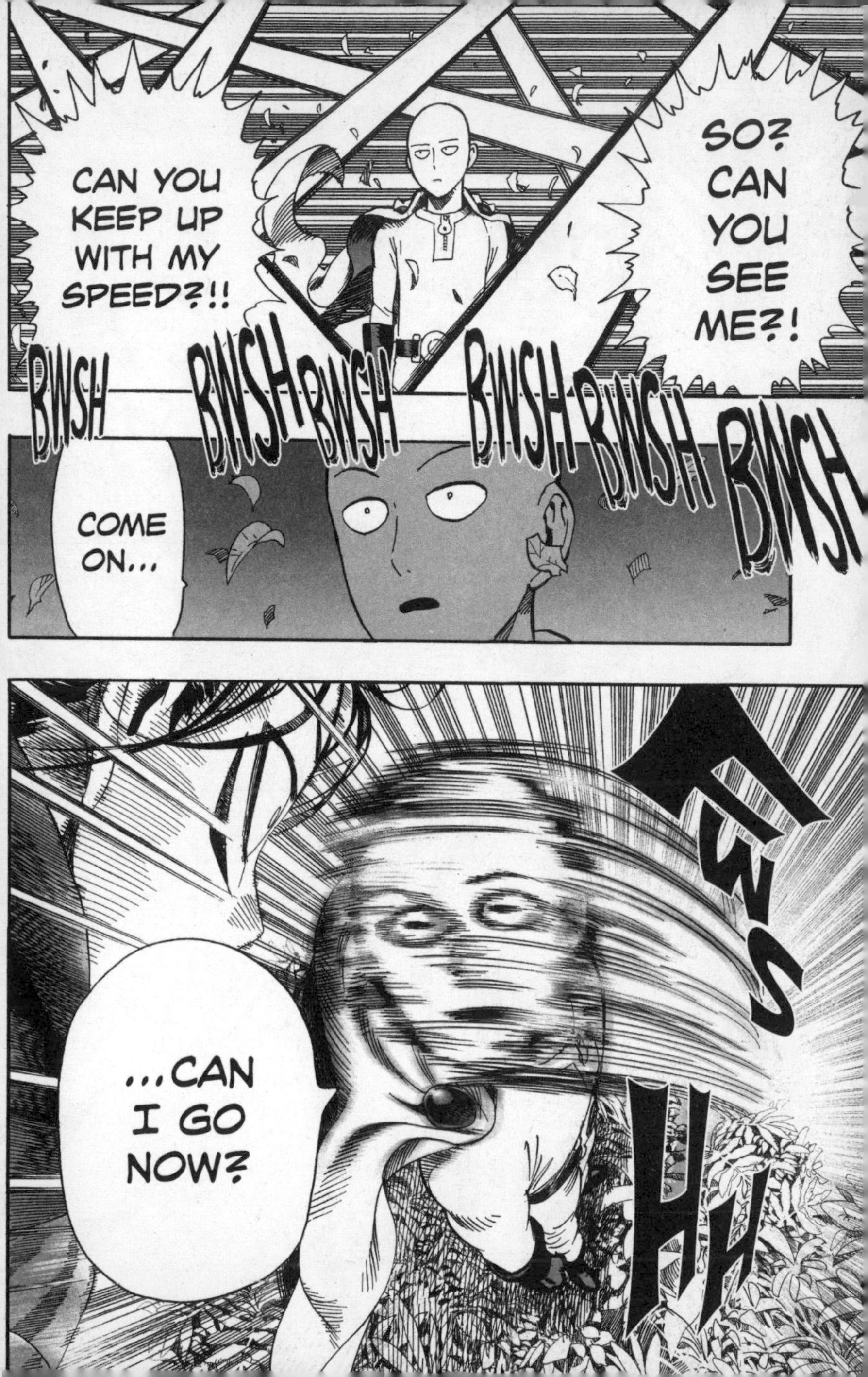
SO? CAN YOU SEE ME?!
CAN YOU KEEP UP WITH MY SPEED?!!
BWSH
BWSH
BWSH
BWSH
BWSH
BWSH
BWSH
COME ON...
...CAN I GO NOW?

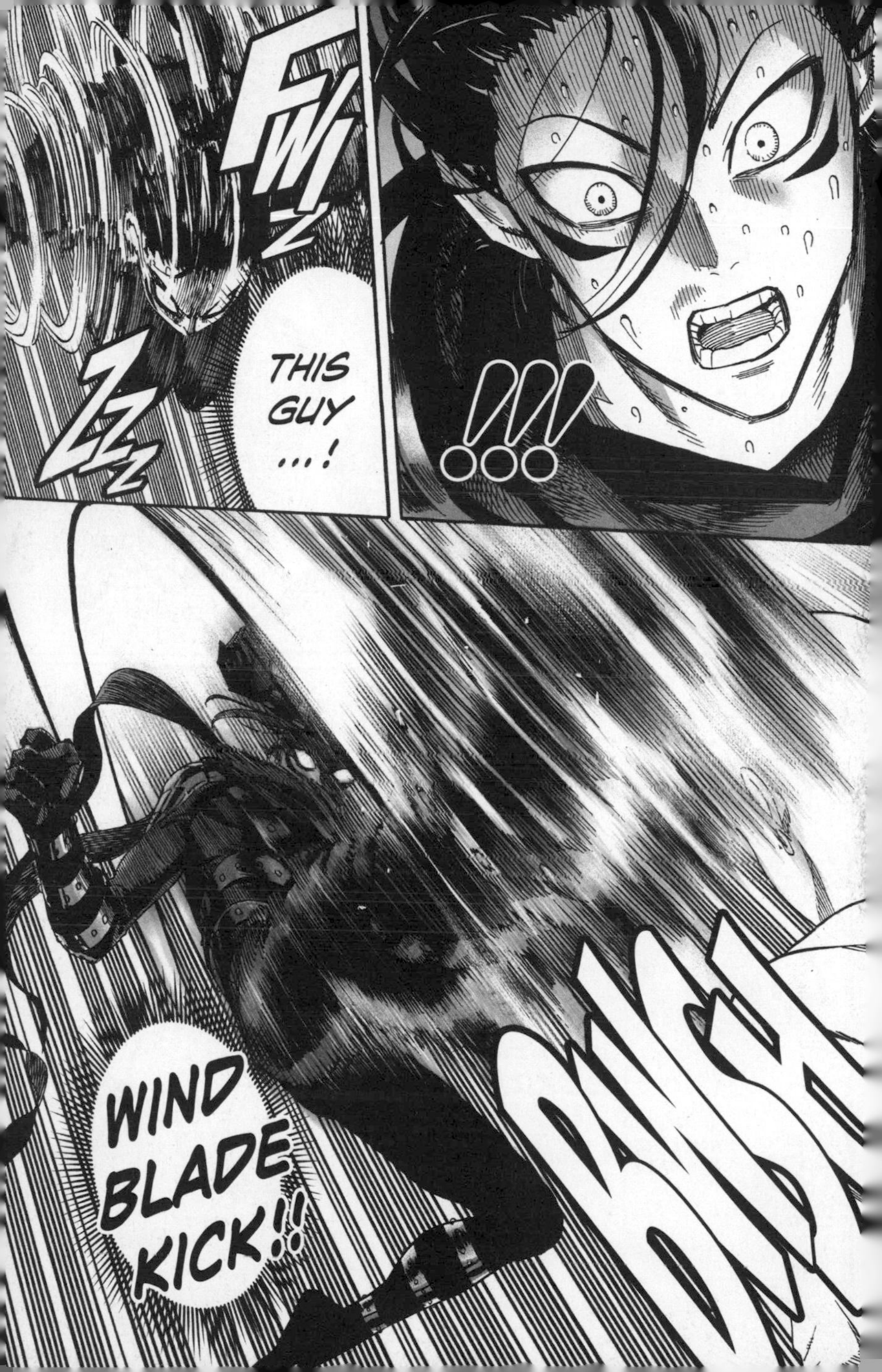
!!!
THIS GUY ...!
WIND BLADE KICK!!

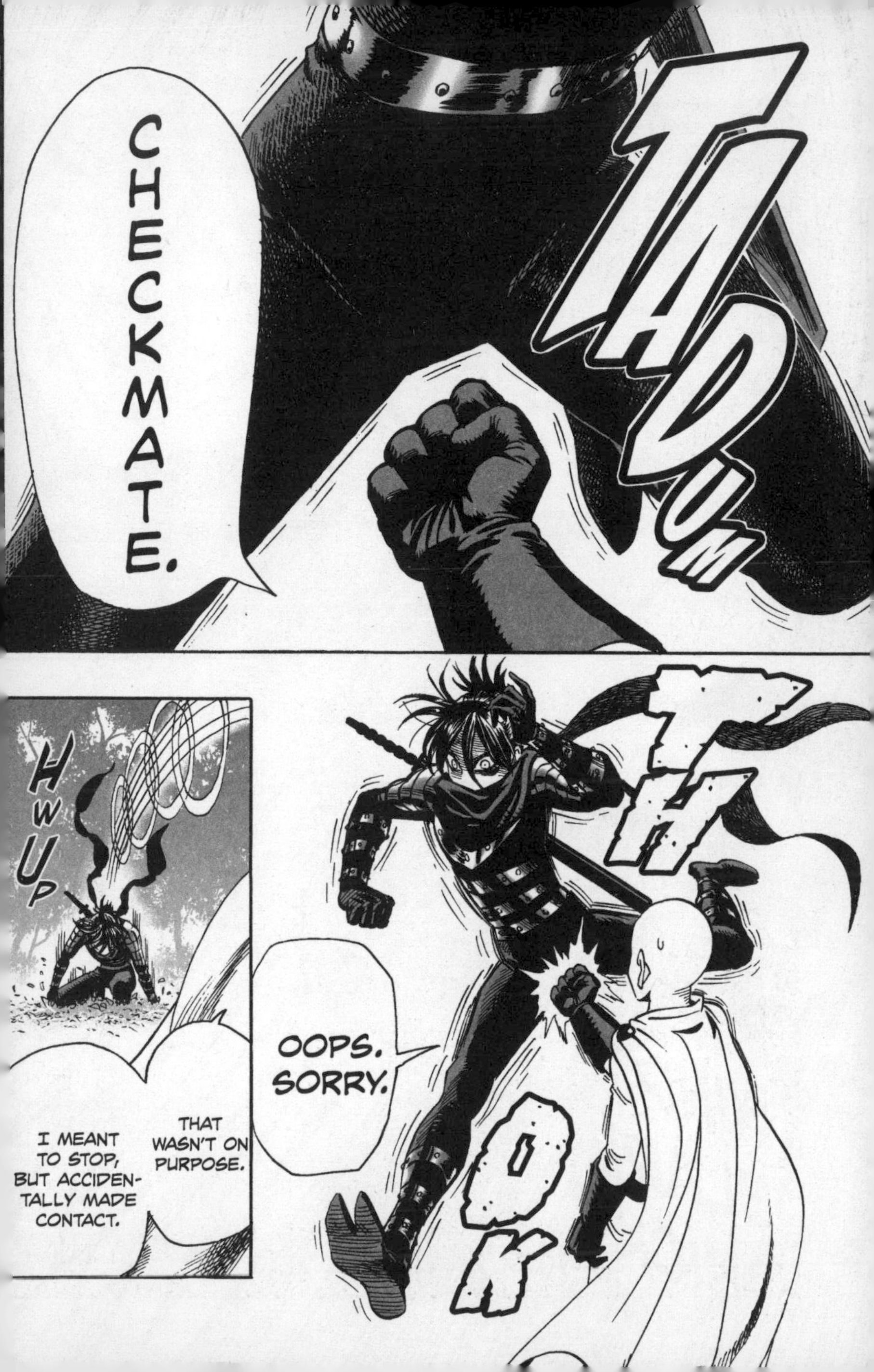
CHECKMATE.
THDUM
THOK
OOPS. SORRY.
HWUP
THAT WASN'T ON PURPOSE.
I MEANT TO STOP, BUT ACCIDENTALLY MADE CONTACT.

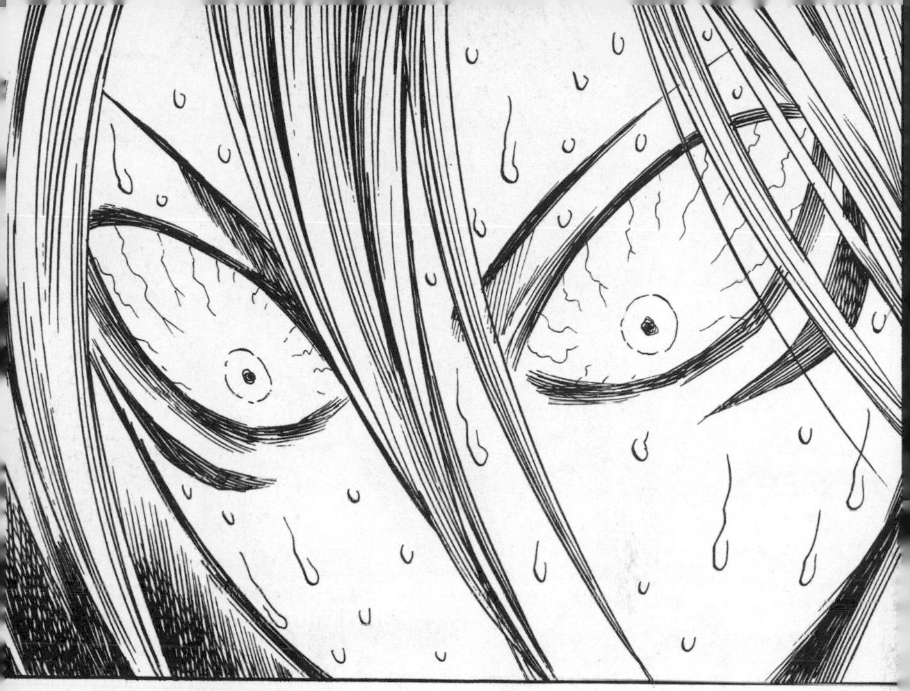

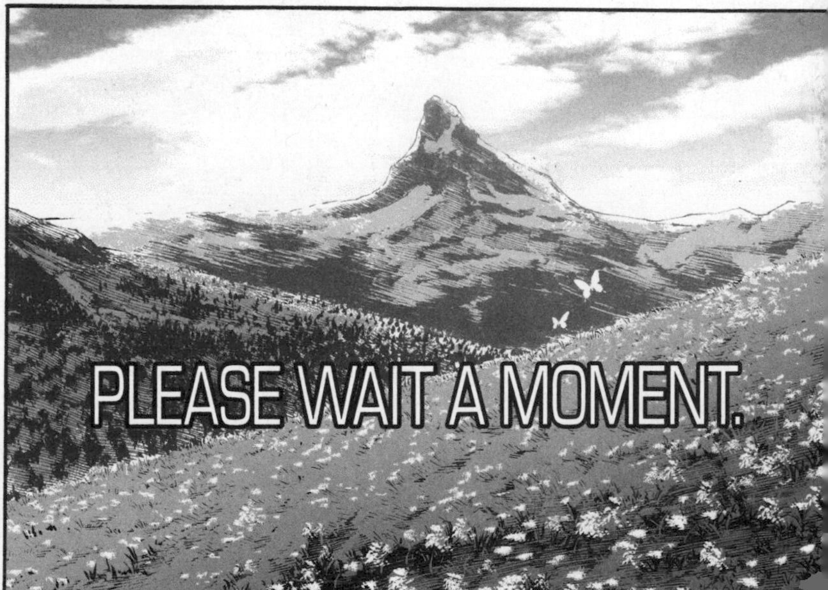
PLEASE WAIT A MOMENT.

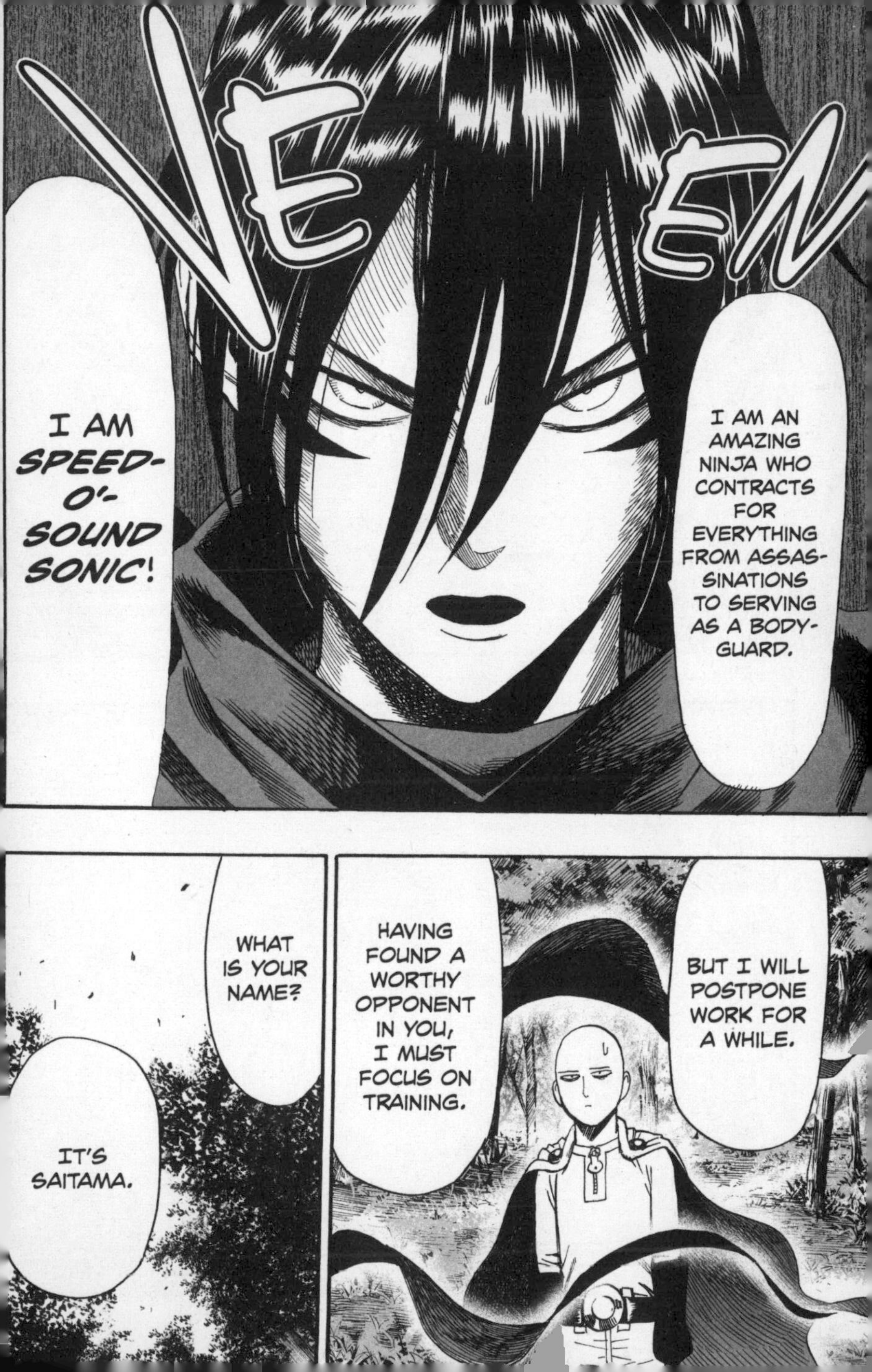
VEEN
I AM AN AMAZING NINJA WHO CONTRACTS FOR EVERYTHING FROM ASSAS-SINATIONS TO SERVING AS A BODY-GUARD.
I AM SPEED-O'-SOUND SONIC!
BUT I WILL POSTPONE WORK FOR A WHILE.
HAVING FOUND A WORTHY OPPONENT IN YOU, I MUST FOCUS ON TRAINING.
WHAT IS YOUR NAME?
IT'S SAITAMA.

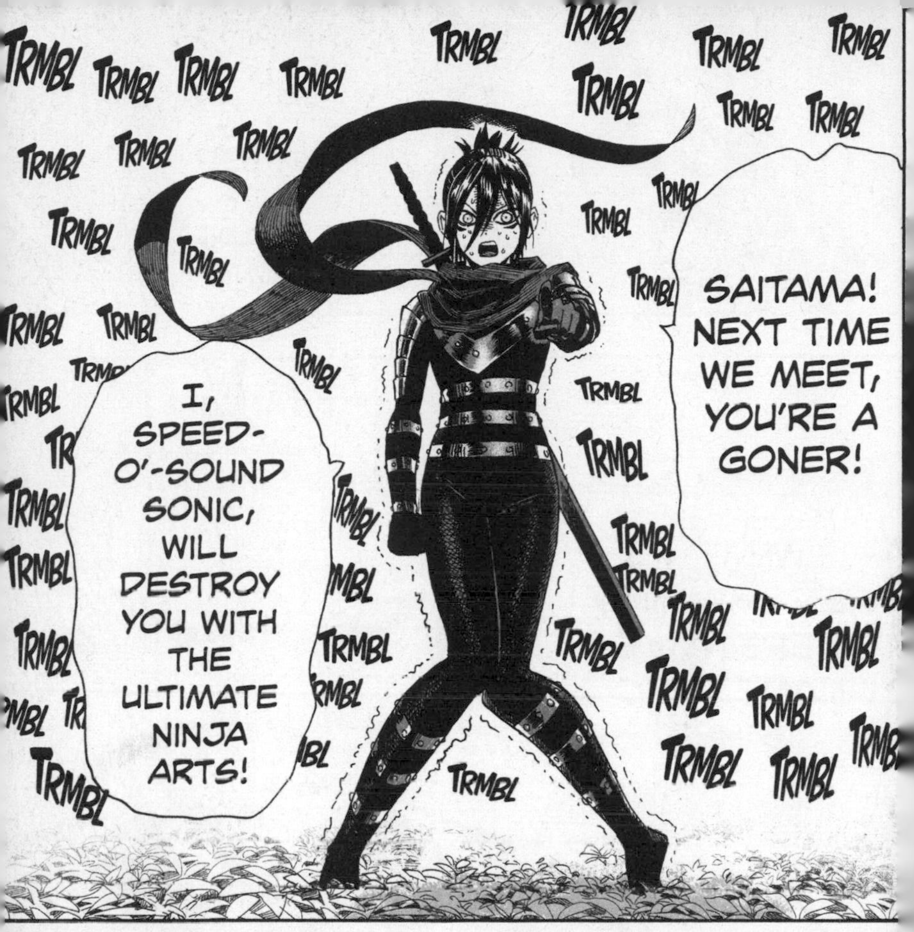
TRMBL
SAITAMA! NEXT TIME WE MEET, YOU'RE A GONER!
I, SPEED-O'-SOUND SONIC, WILL DESTROY YOU WITH THE ULTIMATE NINJA ARTS!

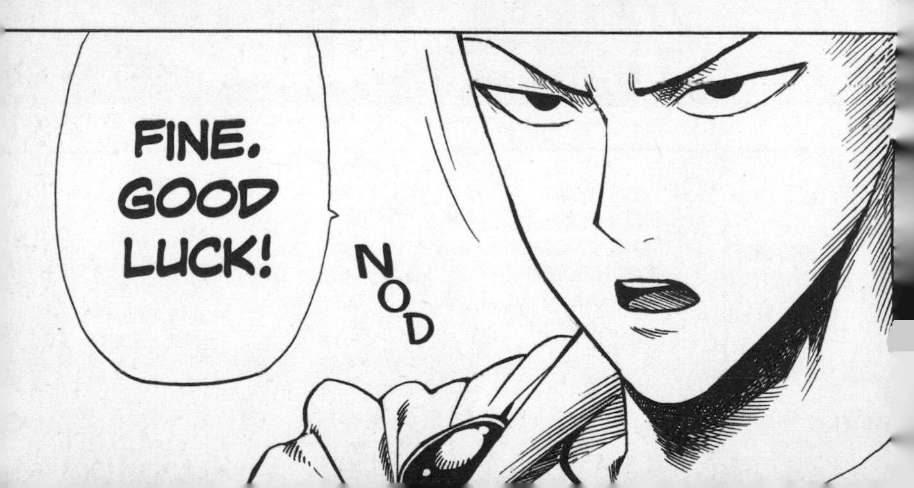
NOD
FINE. GOOD LUCK!

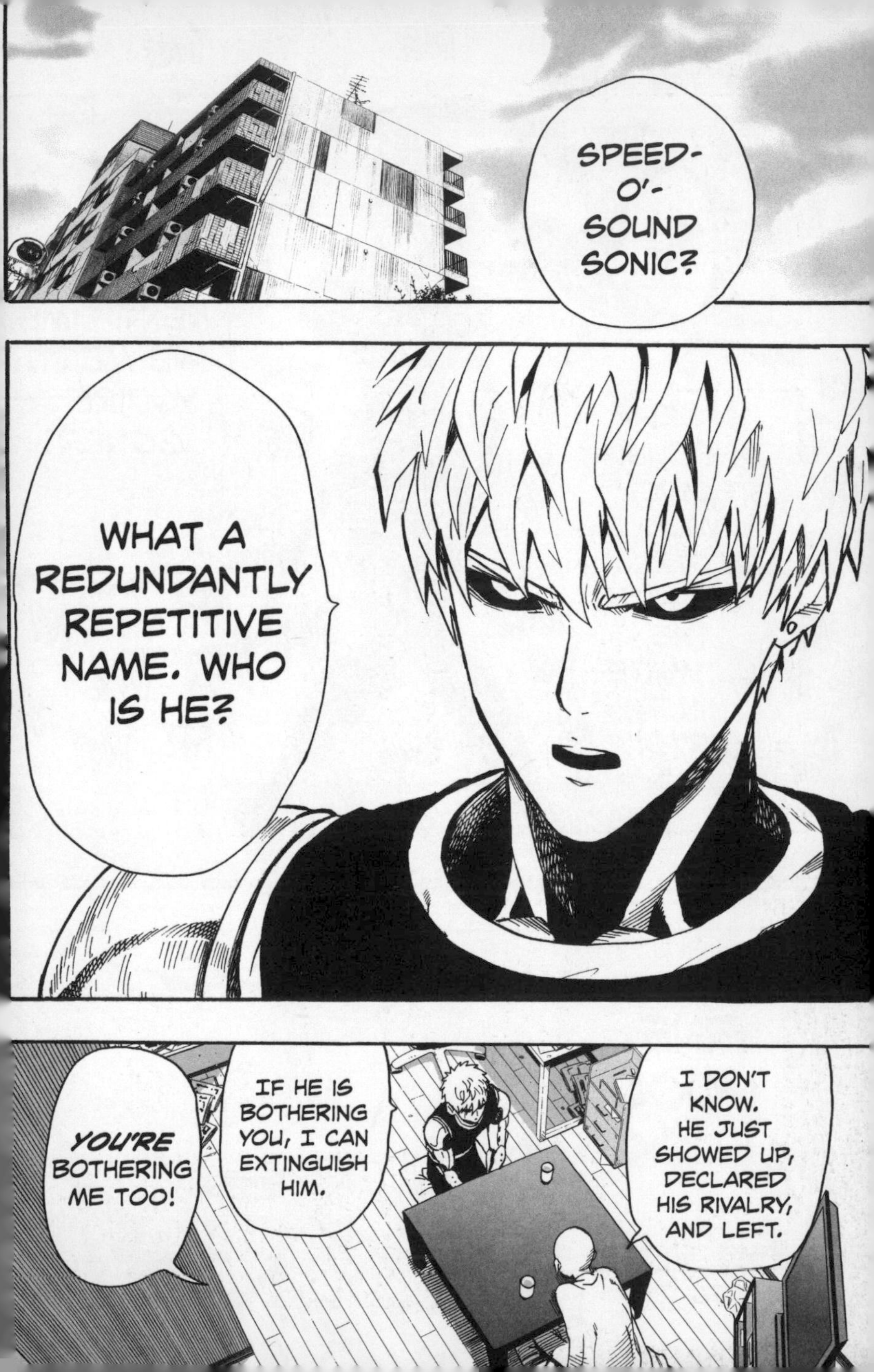
SPEED-O'-SOUND SONIC?
WHAT A REDUNDANTLY REPETITIVE NAME. WHO IS HE?
I DON'T KNOW. HE JUST SHOWED UP, DECLARED HIS RIVALRY, AND LEFT.
IF HE IS BOTHERING YOU, I CAN EXTINGUISH HIM.
YOU'RE BOTHERING ME TOO!

READ THIS WAY

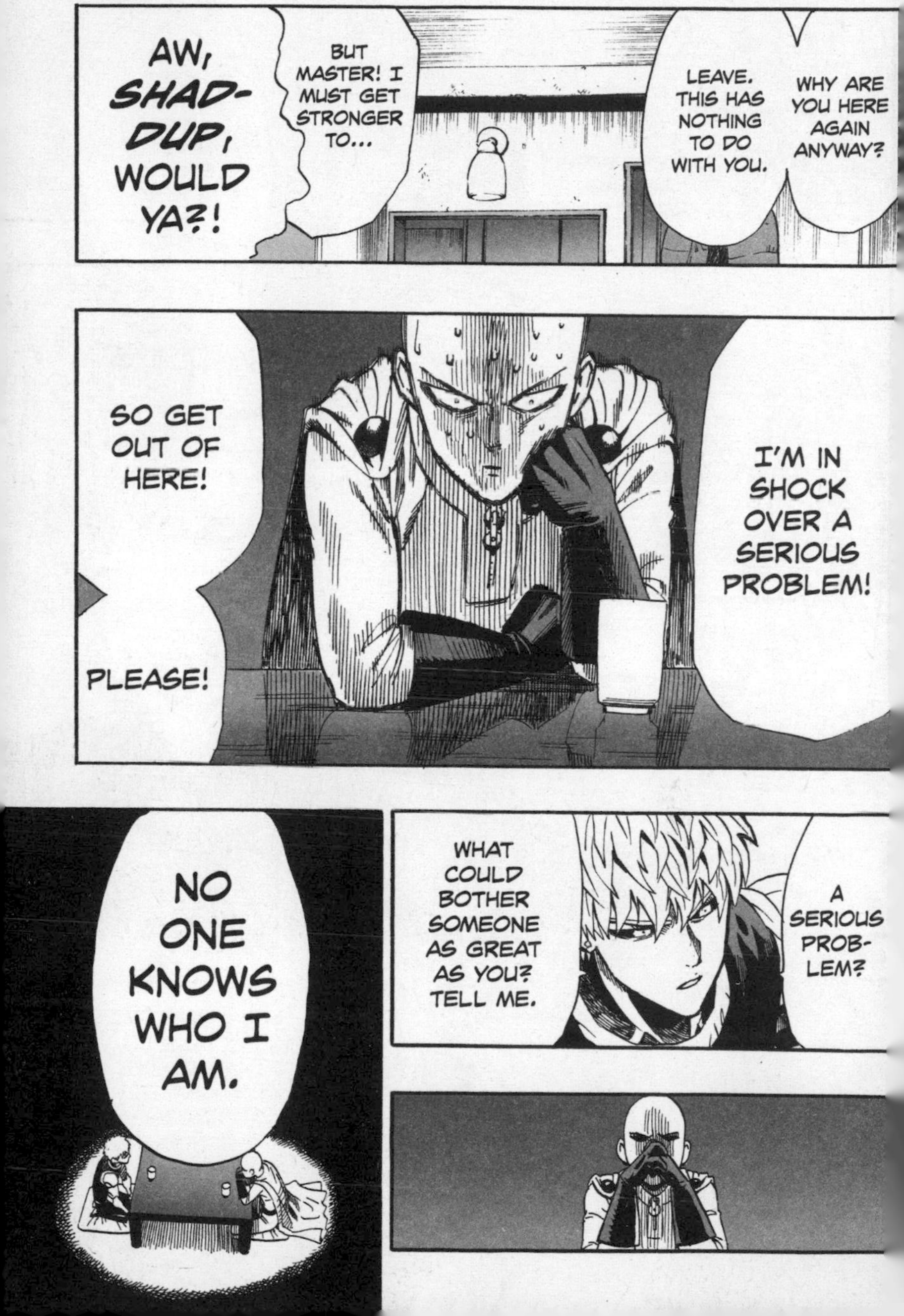
WHY ARE YOU HERE AGAIN ANYWAY?
LEAVE. THIS HAS NOTHING TO DO WITH YOU.
BUT MASTER! I MUST GET STRONGER TO...
AW, SHAD-DUP, WOULD YA?!
I'M IN SHOCK OVER A SERIOUS PROBLEM!
SO GET OUT OF HERE!
PLEASE!
A SERIOUS PROB-LEM?
WHAT COULD BOTHER SOMEONE AS GREAT AS YOU? TELL ME.
NO ONE KNOWS WHO I AM.

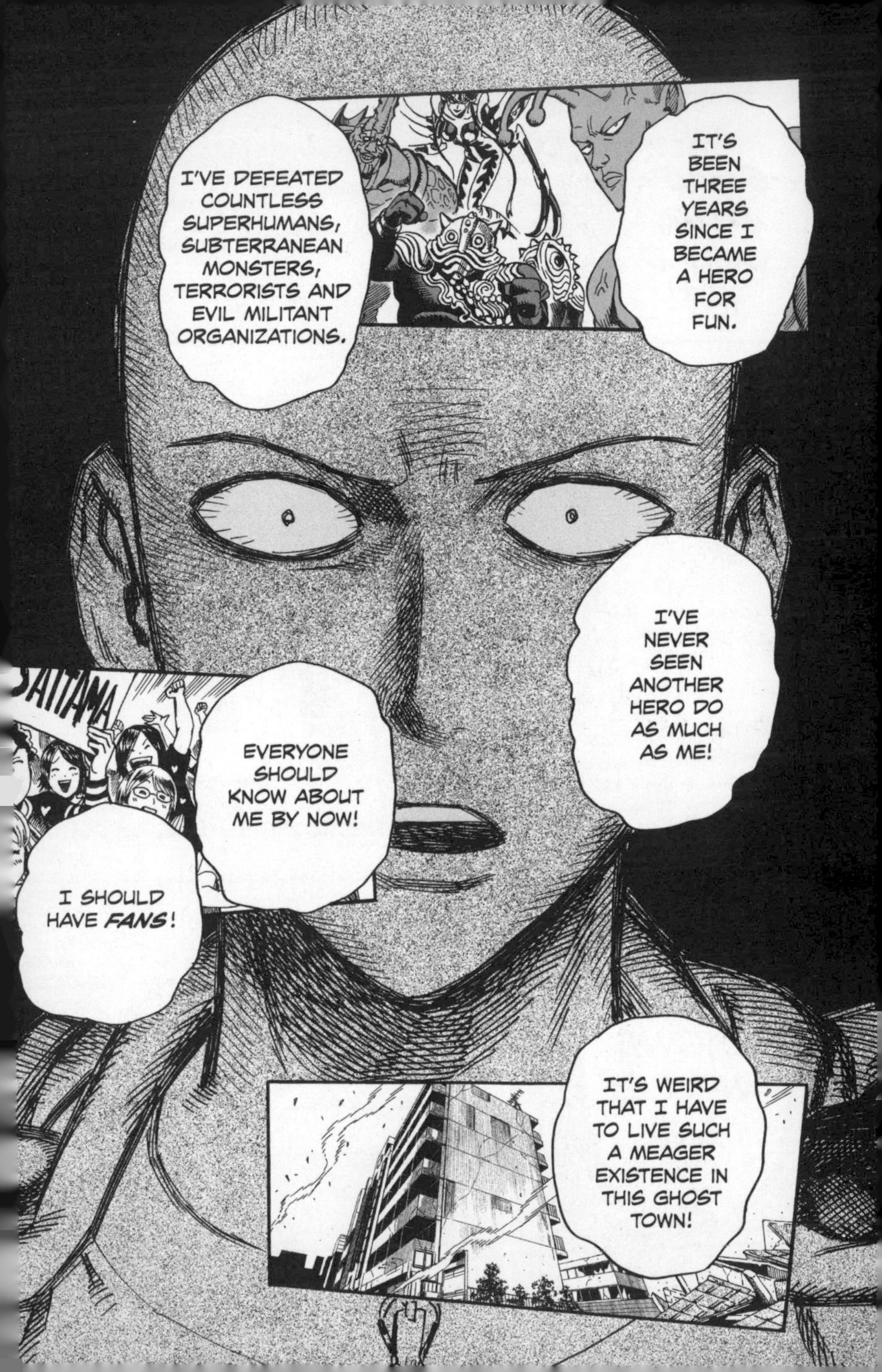
IT'S BEEN THREE YEARS SINCE I BECAME A HERO FOR FUN.
I'VE DEFEATED COUNTLESS SUPERHUMANS, SUBTERRANEAN MONSTERS, TERRORISTS AND EVIL MILITANT ORGANIZATIONS.
I'VE NEVER SEEN ANOTHER HERO DO AS MUCH AS ME!
SAITAMA
EVERYONE SHOULD KNOW ABOUT ME BY NOW!
I SHOULD HAVE *FANS*!
IT'S WEIRD THAT I HAVE TO LIVE SUCH A MEAGER EXISTENCE IN THIS GHOST TOWN!

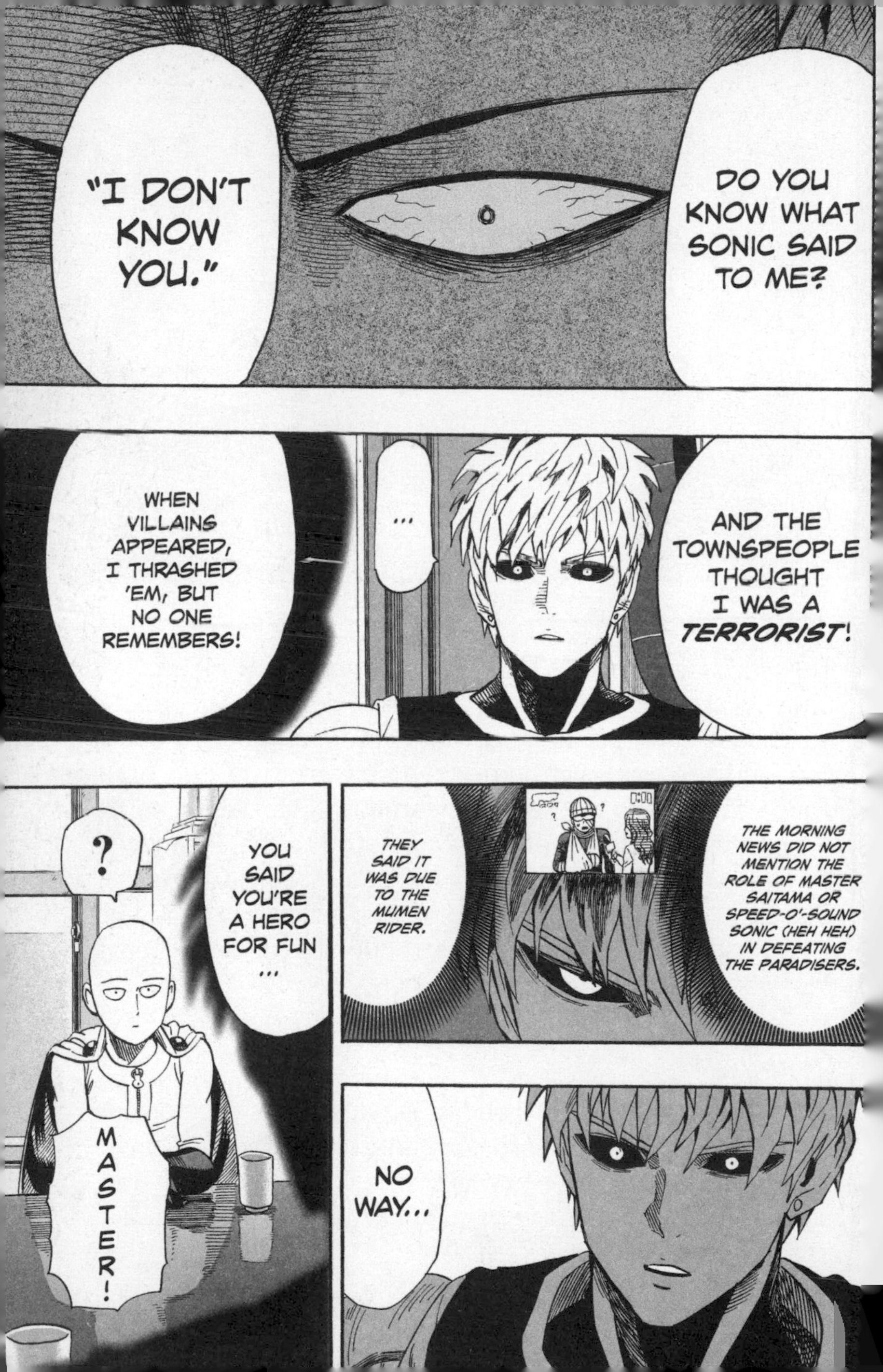
DO YOU KNOW WHAT SONIC SAID TO ME?
"I DON'T KNOW YOU."
AND THE TOWNSPEOPLE THOUGHT I WAS A TERRORIST!
...
WHEN VILLAINS APPEARED, I THRASHED 'EM, BUT NO ONE REMEMBERS!
THE MORNING NEWS DID NOT MENTION THE ROLE OF MASTER SAITAMA OR SPEED-O'-SOUND SONIC (HEH HEH) IN DEFEATING THE PARADISERS.
THEY SAID IT WAS DUE TO THE MUMEN RIDER.
NO WAY...
YOU SAID YOU'RE A HERO FOR FUN ...
?
MASTER!

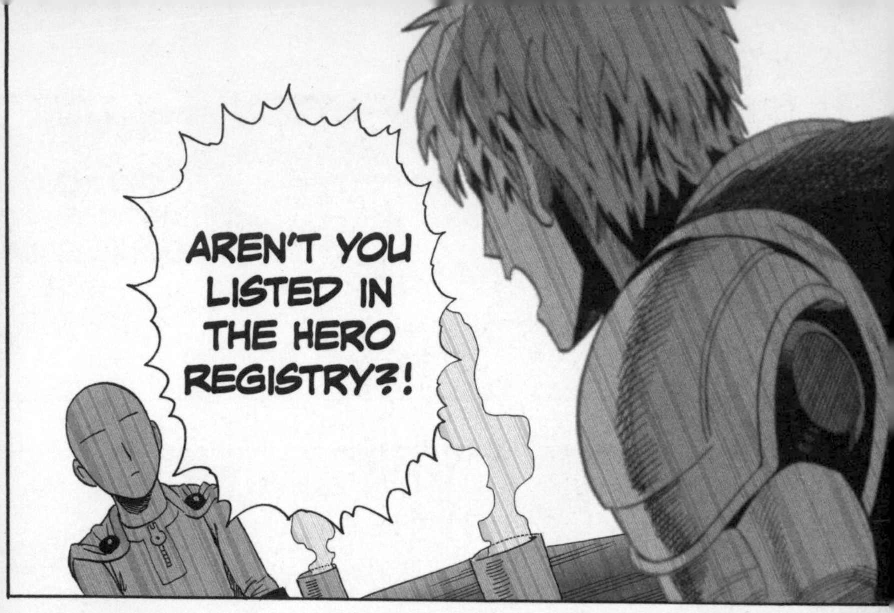
AREN'T YOU LISTED IN THE HERO REGISTRY?!

The Hero Registry lists the names of heroes who have taken physical strength and justice tests at Hero Association facilities around the country, met certain standards, and received permission to name themselves official heroes. Those recognized by the association as professional heroes may receive funds out of money donated to the association through its fundraising efforts. Heroes listed in the Hero Registry may also appear in ability and popularity rankings. The world pays a great deal of attention to those heroes, and many of them have fan clubs.

Note

What the world refers to as heroes are those professional heroes listed in the registry. Any unlisted individual claiming to be a hero, no matter how active, is viewed askance and considered nothing more than a pervy freak who spouts irresponsible nonsense.

READ THIS WAY

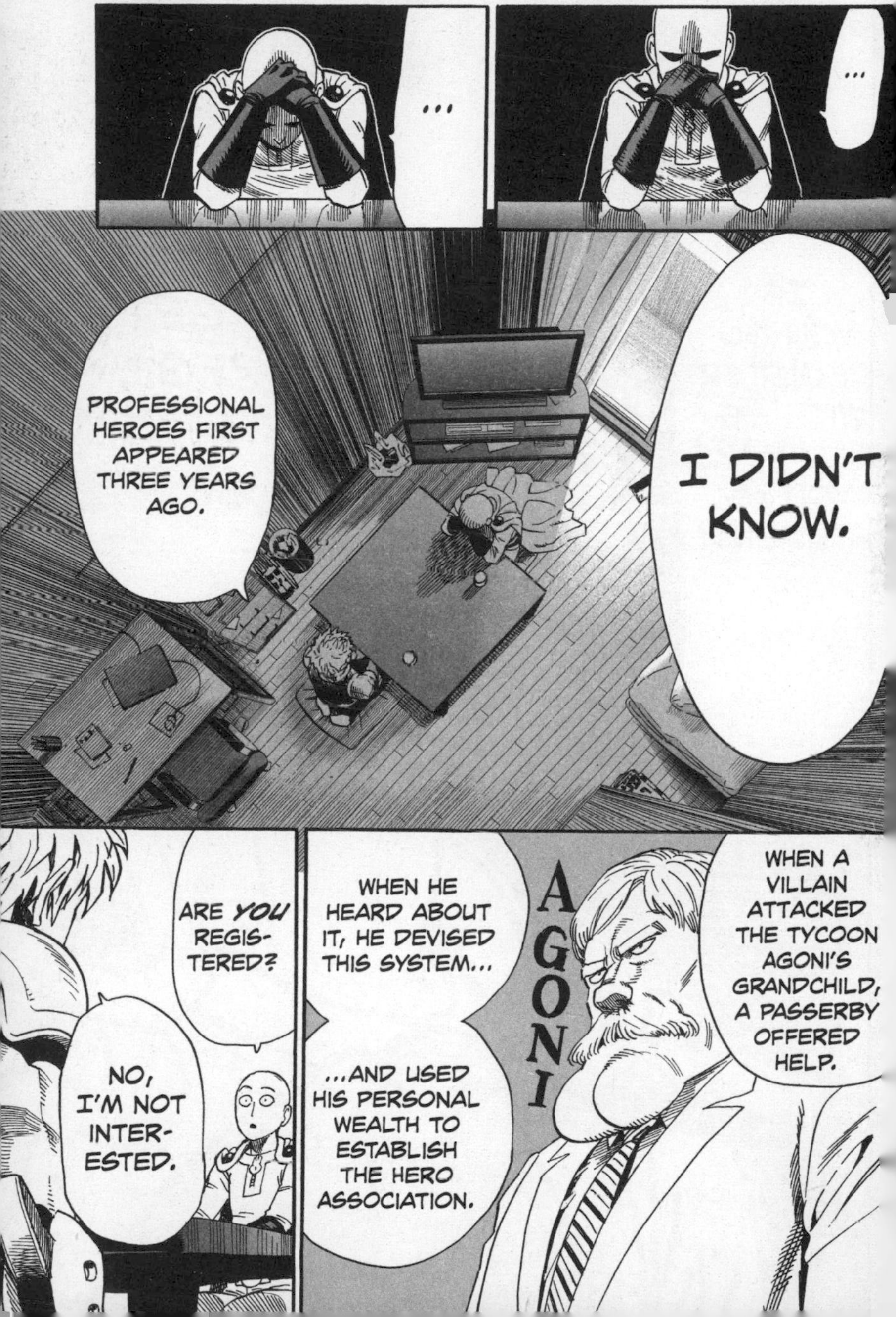
...
...
I DIDN'T KNOW.
PROFESSIONAL HEROES FIRST APPEARED THREE YEARS AGO.
WHEN A VILLAIN ATTACKED THE TYCOON AGONI'S GRANDCHILD, A PASSERBY OFFERED HELP.
AGONI
WHEN HE HEARD ABOUT IT, HE DEVISED THIS SYSTEM...
...AND USED HIS PERSONAL WEALTH TO ESTABLISH THE HERO ASSOCIATION.
ARE *YOU* REGISTERED?
NO, I'M NOT INTERESTED.

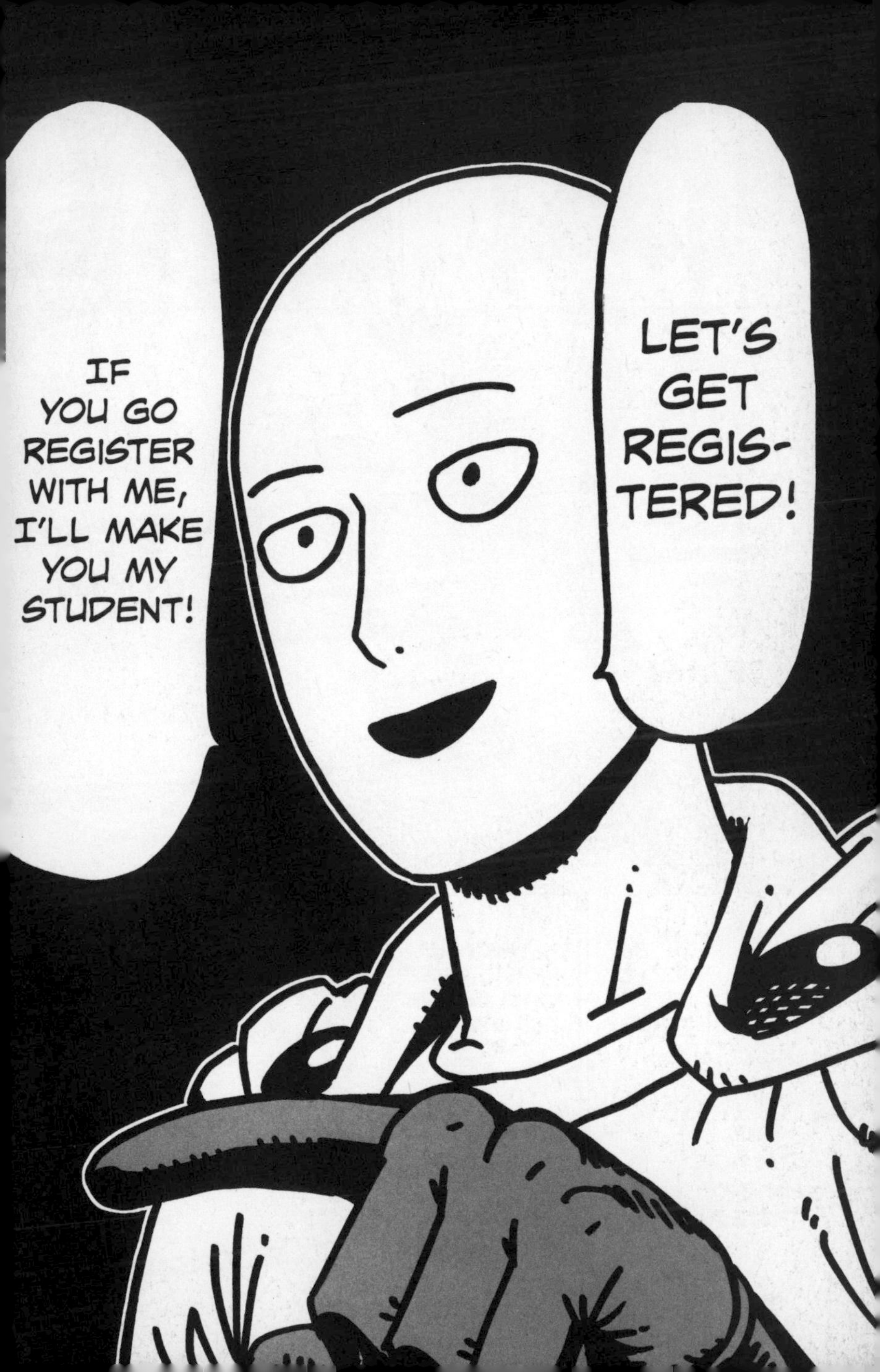
LET'S GET REGIS- TERED!
IF YOU GO REGISTER WITH ME, I'LL MAKE YOU MY STUDENT!

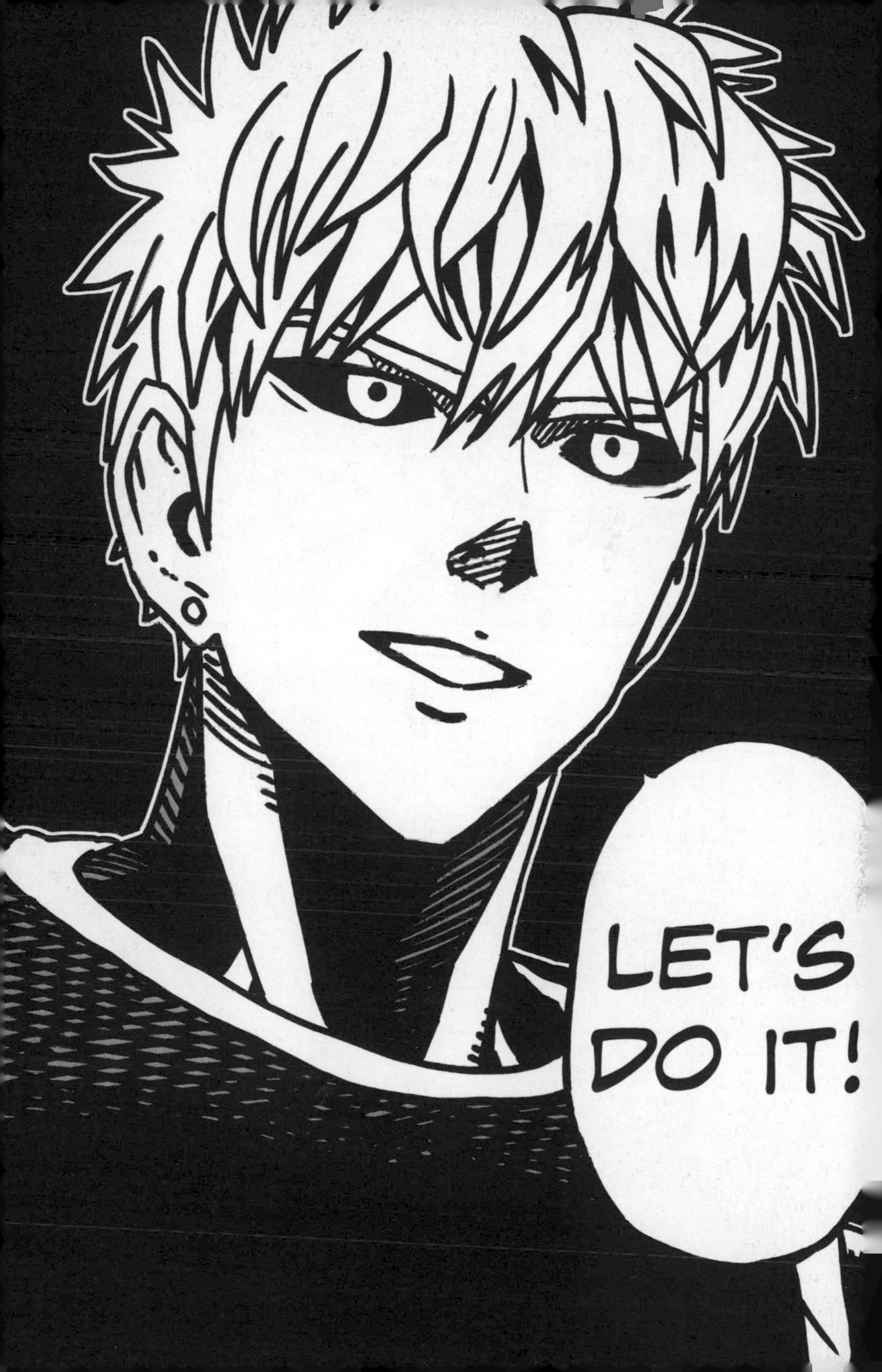
LET'S DO IT!

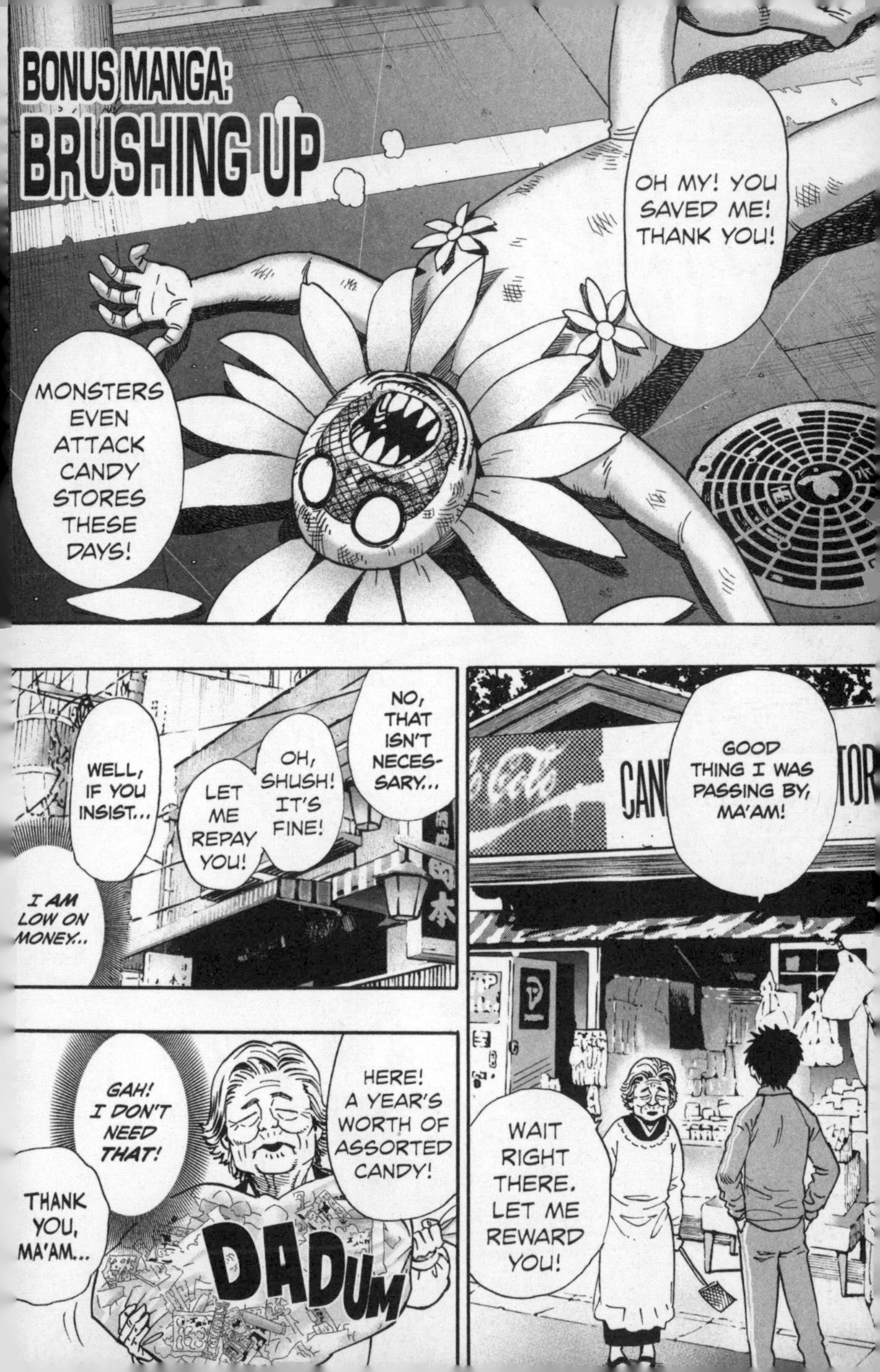
BONUS MANGA:
BRUSHING UP
OH MY! YOU SAVED ME! THANK YOU!
MONSTERS EVEN ATTACK CANDY STORES THESE DAYS!
GOOD THING I WAS PASSING BY, MA'AM!
WAIT RIGHT THERE. LET ME REWARD YOU!
NO, THAT ISN'T NECES-SARY...
OH, SHUSH! IT'S FINE!
LET ME REPAY YOU!
WELL, IF YOU INSIST...
I AM LOW ON MONEY...
HERE! A YEAR'S WORTH OF ASSORTED CANDY!
GAH! I DON'T NEED THAT!
THANK YOU, MA'AM...
DADUM

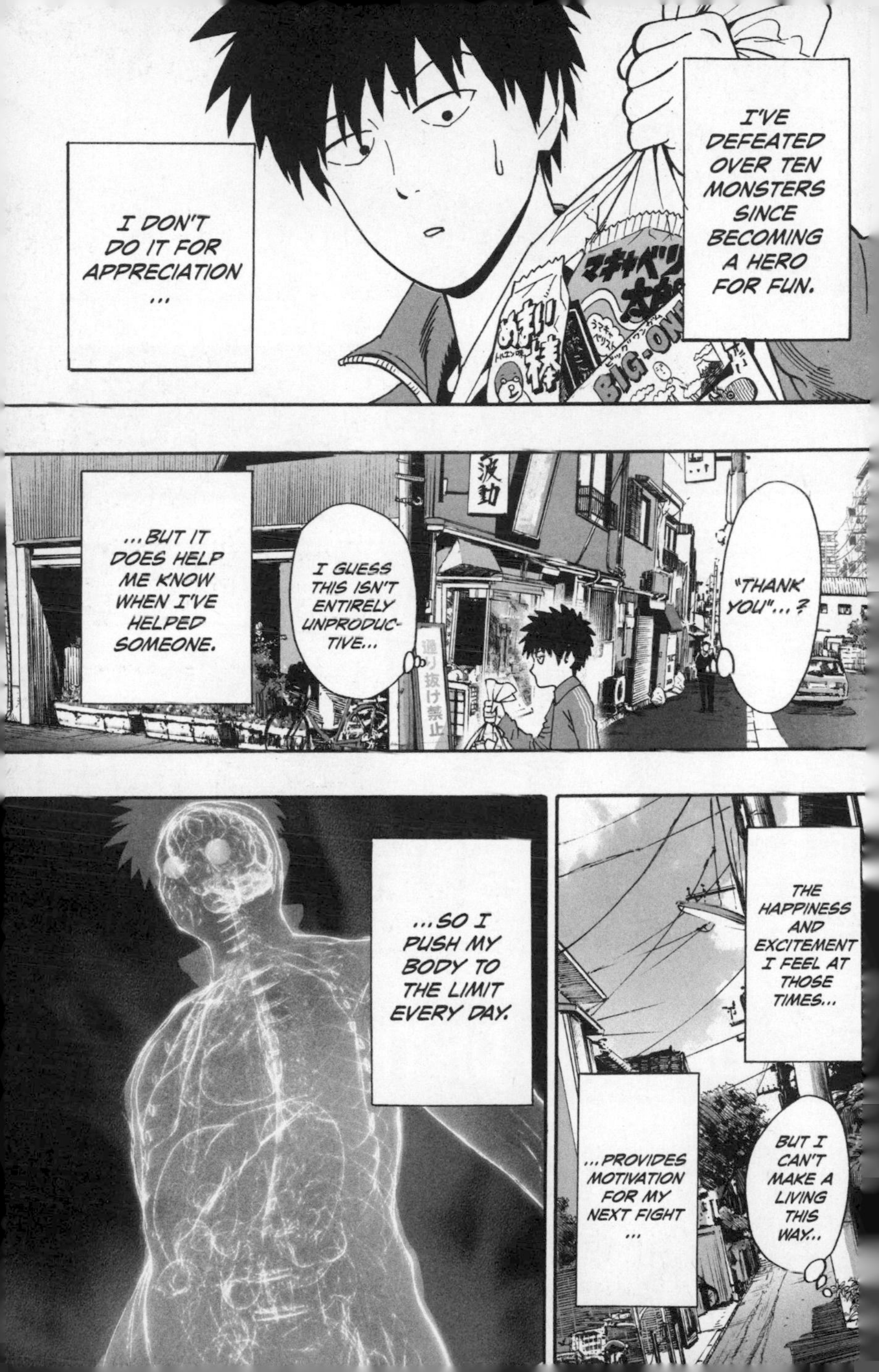
I'VE DEFEATED OVER TEN MONSTERS SINCE BECOMING A HERO FOR FUN.
I DON'T DO IT FOR APPRECIATION ...
"THANK YOU"...?
I GUESS THIS ISN'T ENTIRELY UNPRODUC-TIVE...
...BUT IT DOES HELP ME KNOW WHEN I'VE HELPED SOMEONE.
THE HAPPINESS AND EXCITEMENT I FEEL AT THOSE TIMES...
...PROVIDES MOTIVATION FOR MY NEXT FIGHT ...
BUT I CAN'T MAKE A LIVING THIS WAY..
...SO I PUSH MY BODY TO THE LIMIT EVERY DAY.

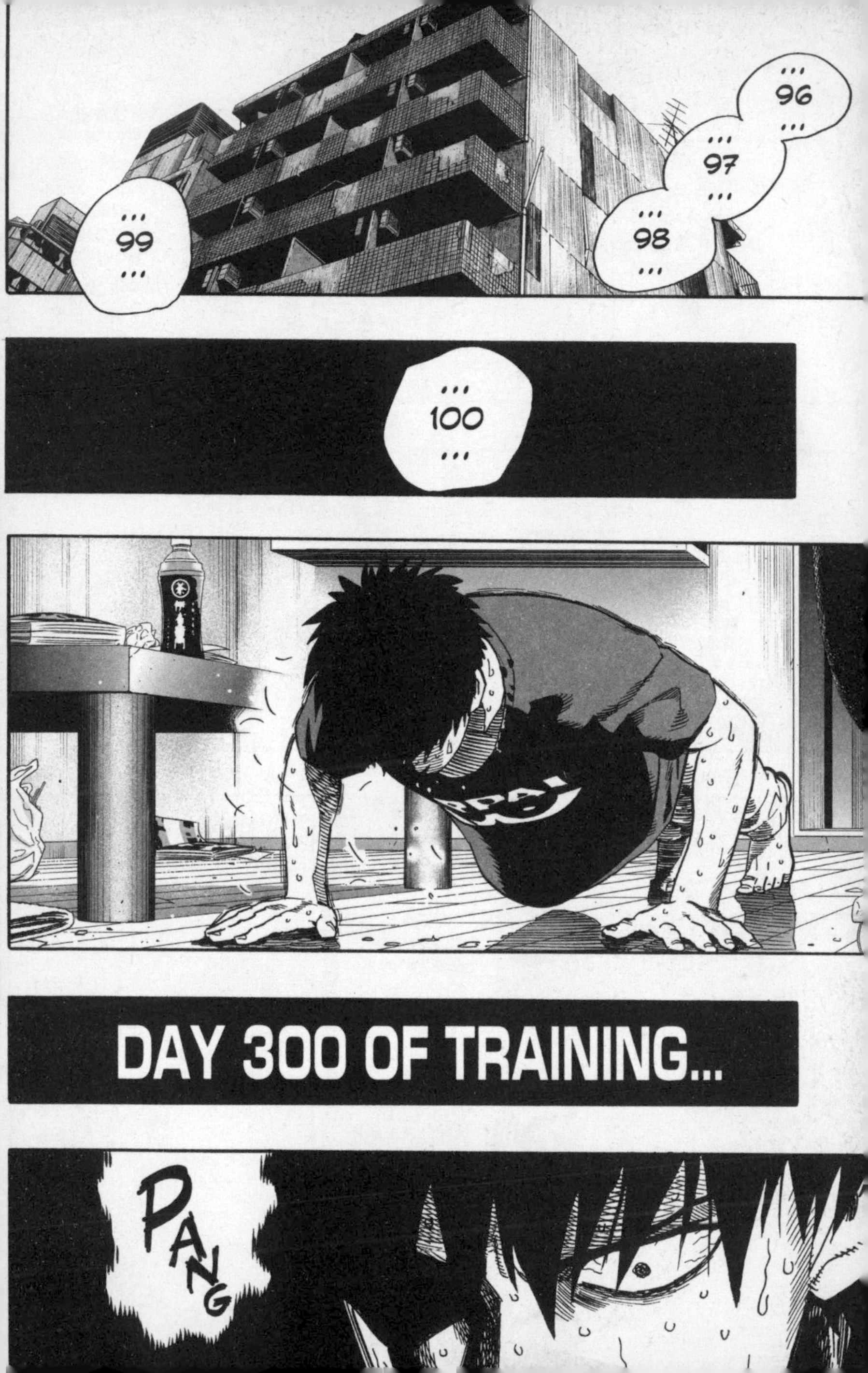
...96...
...97...
...98...
...99...
...100...
DAY 300 OF TRAINING...
PANG

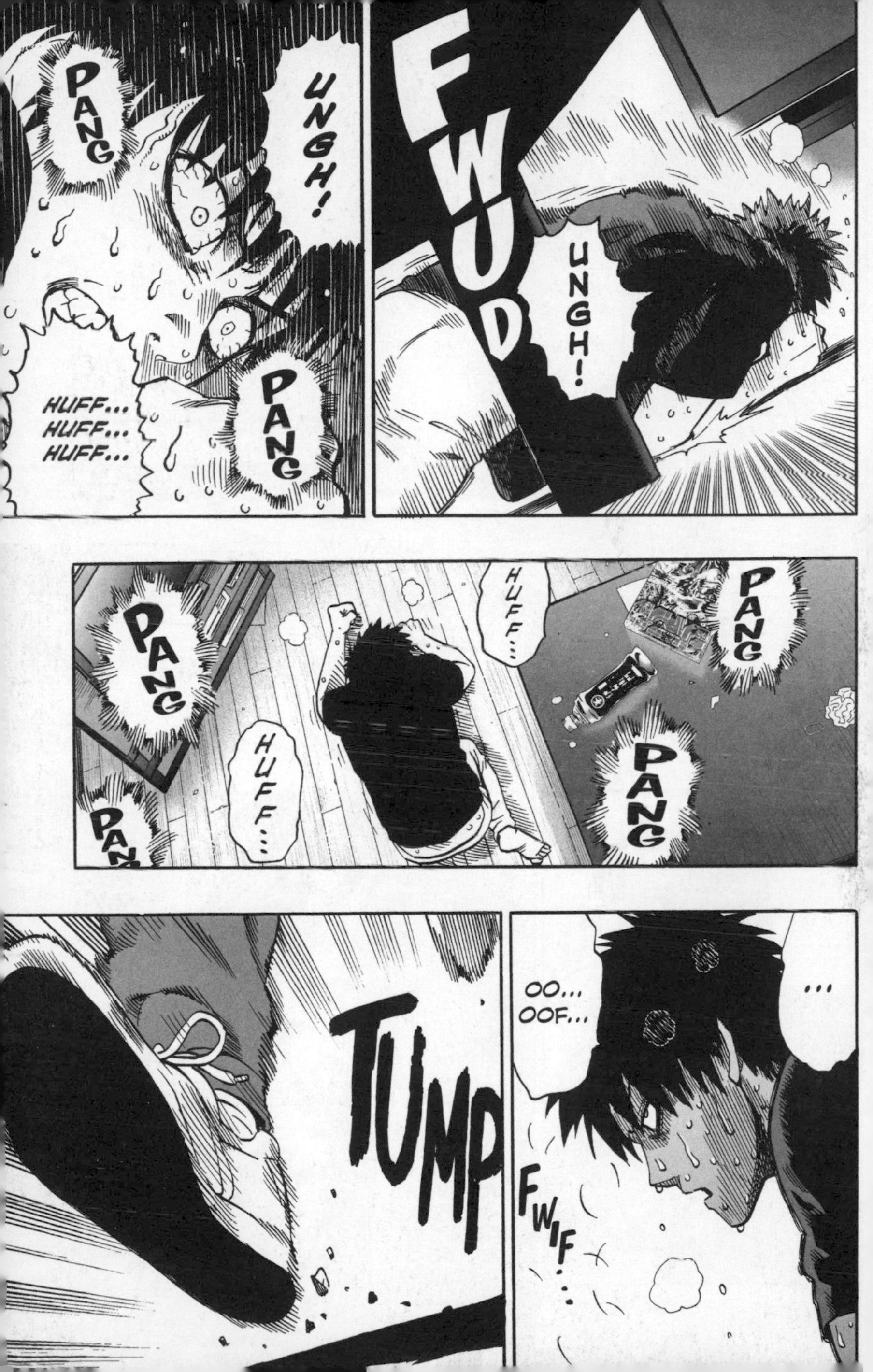
FWUD
UNGH!
UNGH!
PANG
PANG
HUFF... HUFF... HUFF...
PANG
PANG
HUFF...
HUFF...
PANG
PANG
...
OO... OOF...
FWIF...
TUMP

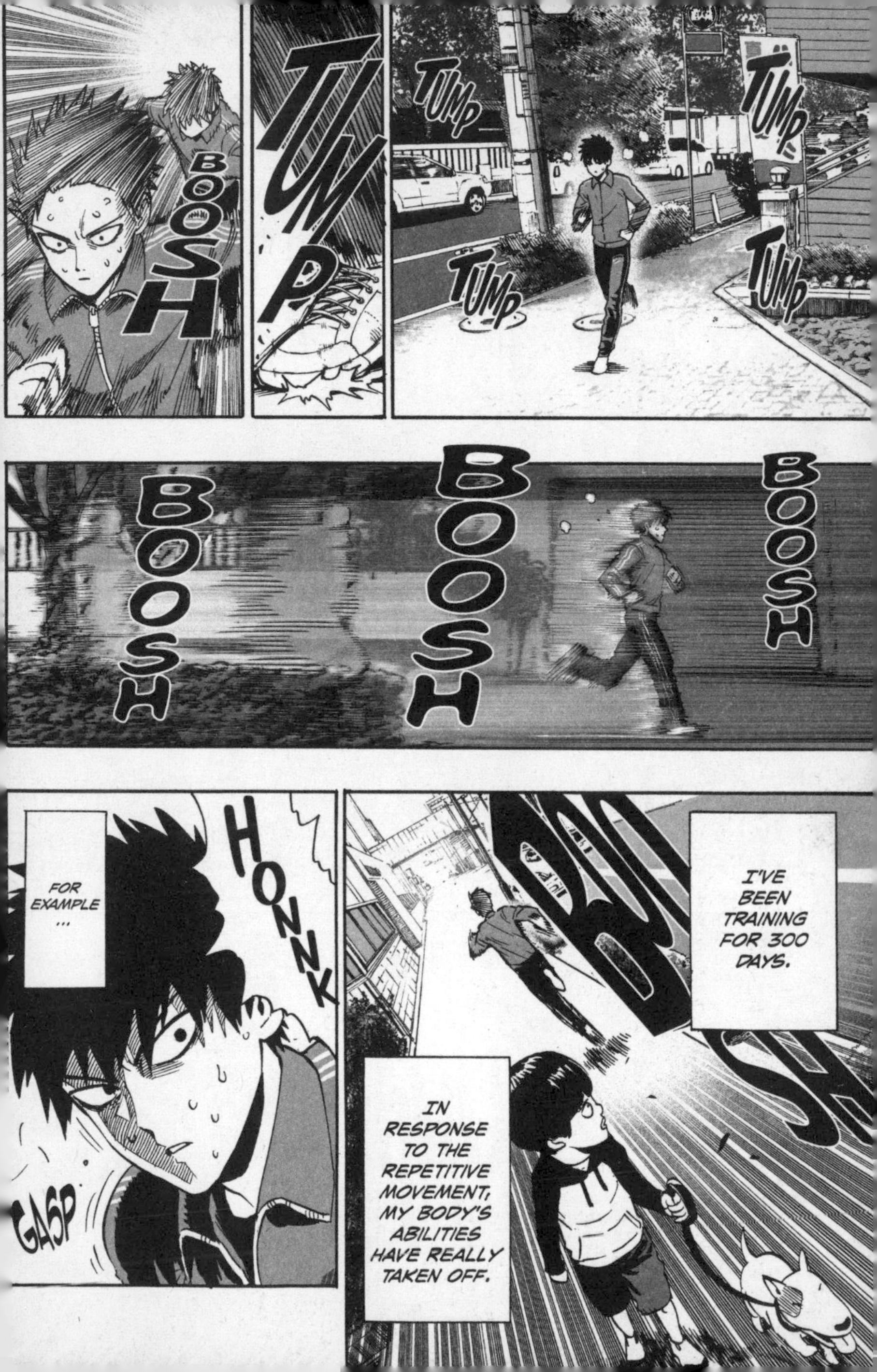
TUMP
TUMP
TUMP
TUMP
TUMP
BOOSH
BOOSH
BOOSH
BOOSH
I'VE BEEN TRAINING FOR 300 DAYS.
IN RESPONSE TO THE REPETITIVE MOVEMENT, MY BODY'S ABILITIES HAVE REALLY TAKEN OFF.
FOR EXAMPLE ...
HONNK
GASP

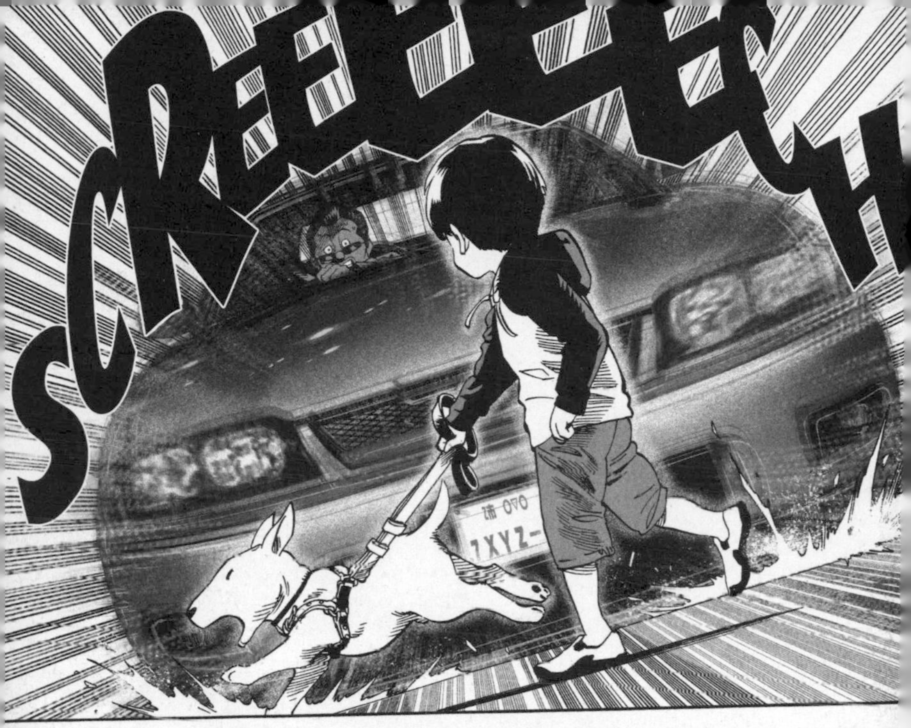
SCREEEEECH
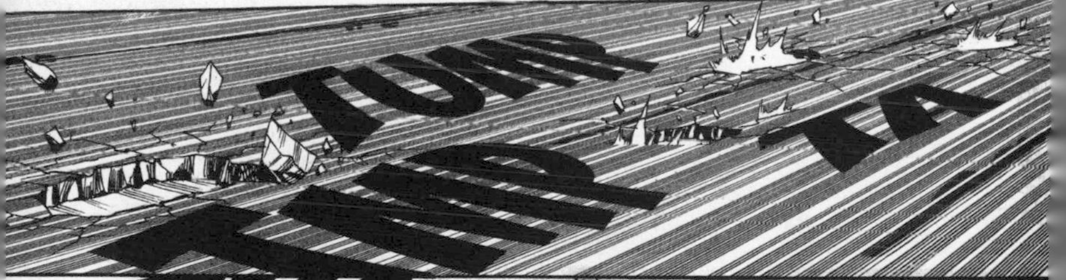
TA
TUMP
TMP
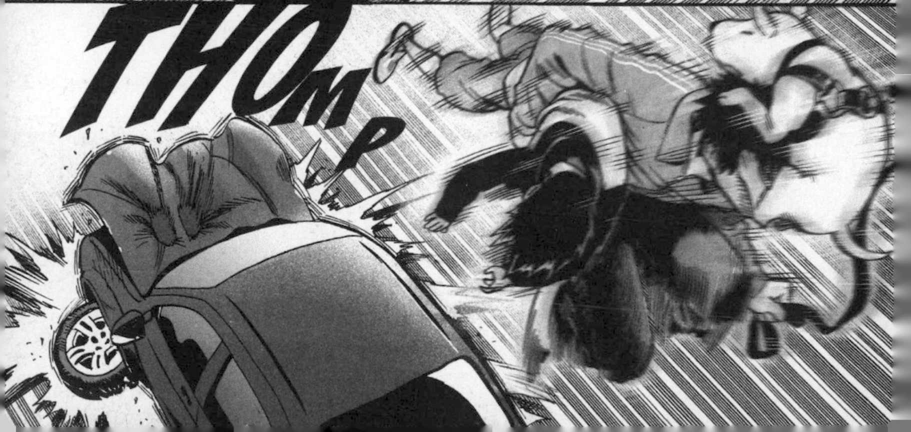
THOMP

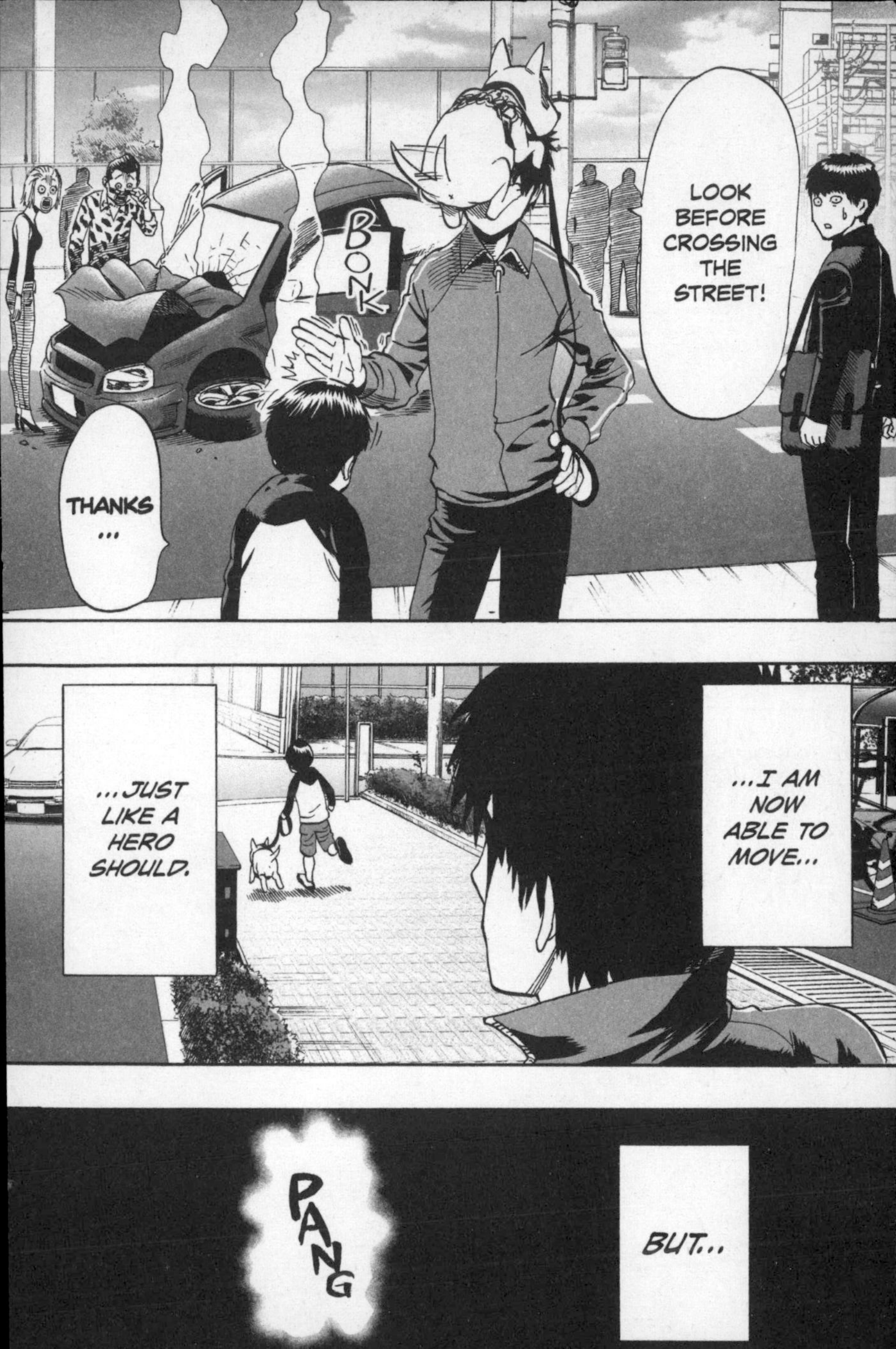
LOOK BEFORE CROSSING THE STREET!
BONK
THANKS...
...I AM NOW ABLE TO MOVE...
...JUST LIKE A HERO SHOULD.
BUT...
PANG

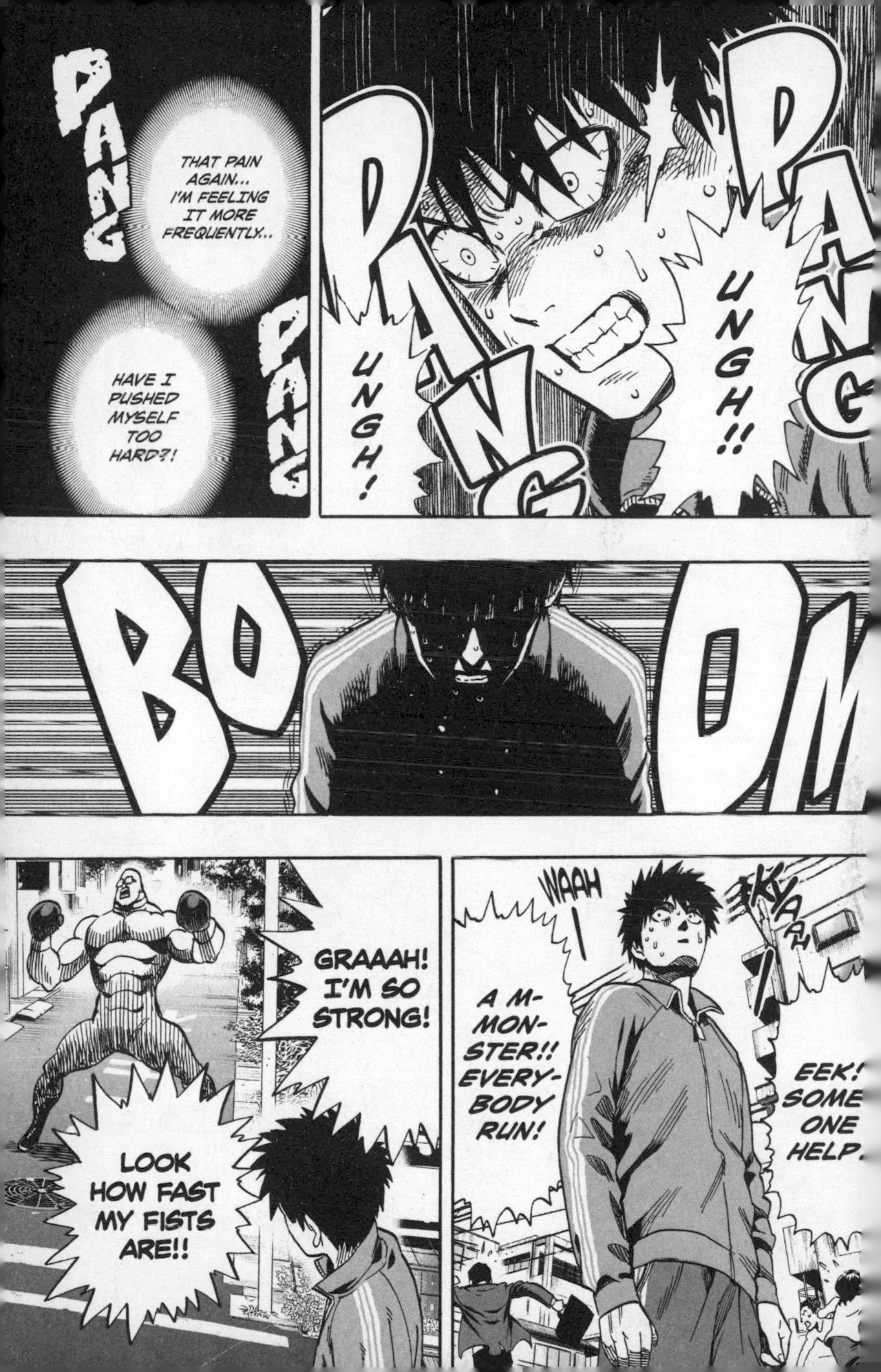
PANG
UNGH!!
PANG
UNGH!
PANG
THAT PAIN AGAIN... I'M FEELING IT MORE FREQUENTLY...
HAVE I PUSHED MYSELF TOO HARD?!
PANG
BOOM
KYAAH
WAAH
EEK! SOME ONE HELP.
A M-MONSTER!! EVERYBODY RUN!
GRAAAH! I'M SO STRONG!
LOOK HOW FAST MY FISTS ARE!!

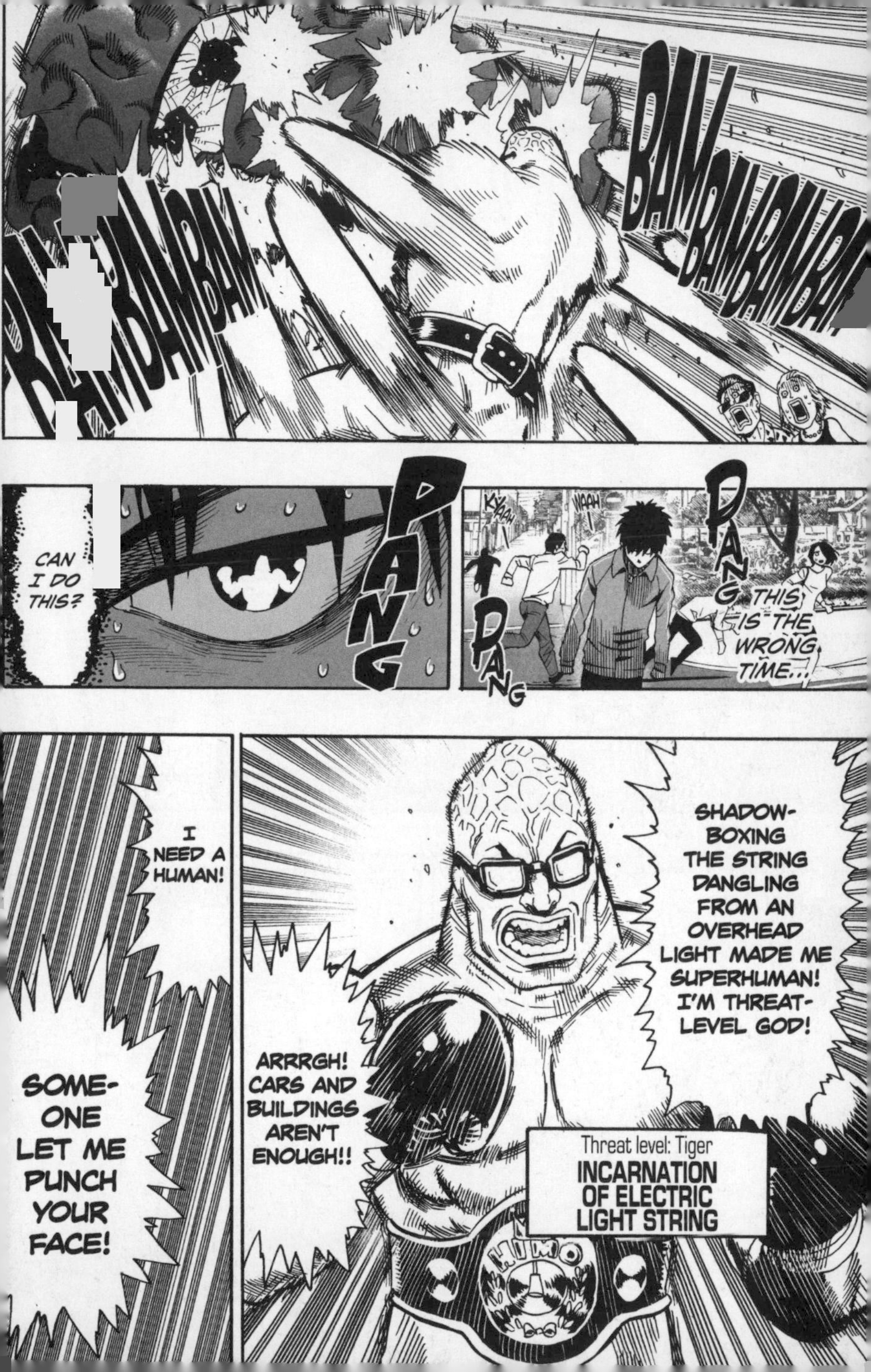
BAMBAMBAMBAM
KYAAH
WAAH
DANG
DANG
THIS IS THE WRONG TIME...
DANG
CAN I DO THIS?
SHADOW-BOXING THE STRING DANGLING FROM AN OVERHEAD LIGHT MADE ME SUPERHUMAN! I'M THREAT-LEVEL GOD!
ARRRGH! CARS AND BUILDINGS AREN'T ENOUGH!!
Threat level: Tiger
INCARNATION OF ELECTRIC LIGHT STRING
HIMO
I NEED A HUMAN!
SOME-ONE LET ME PUNCH YOUR FACE!

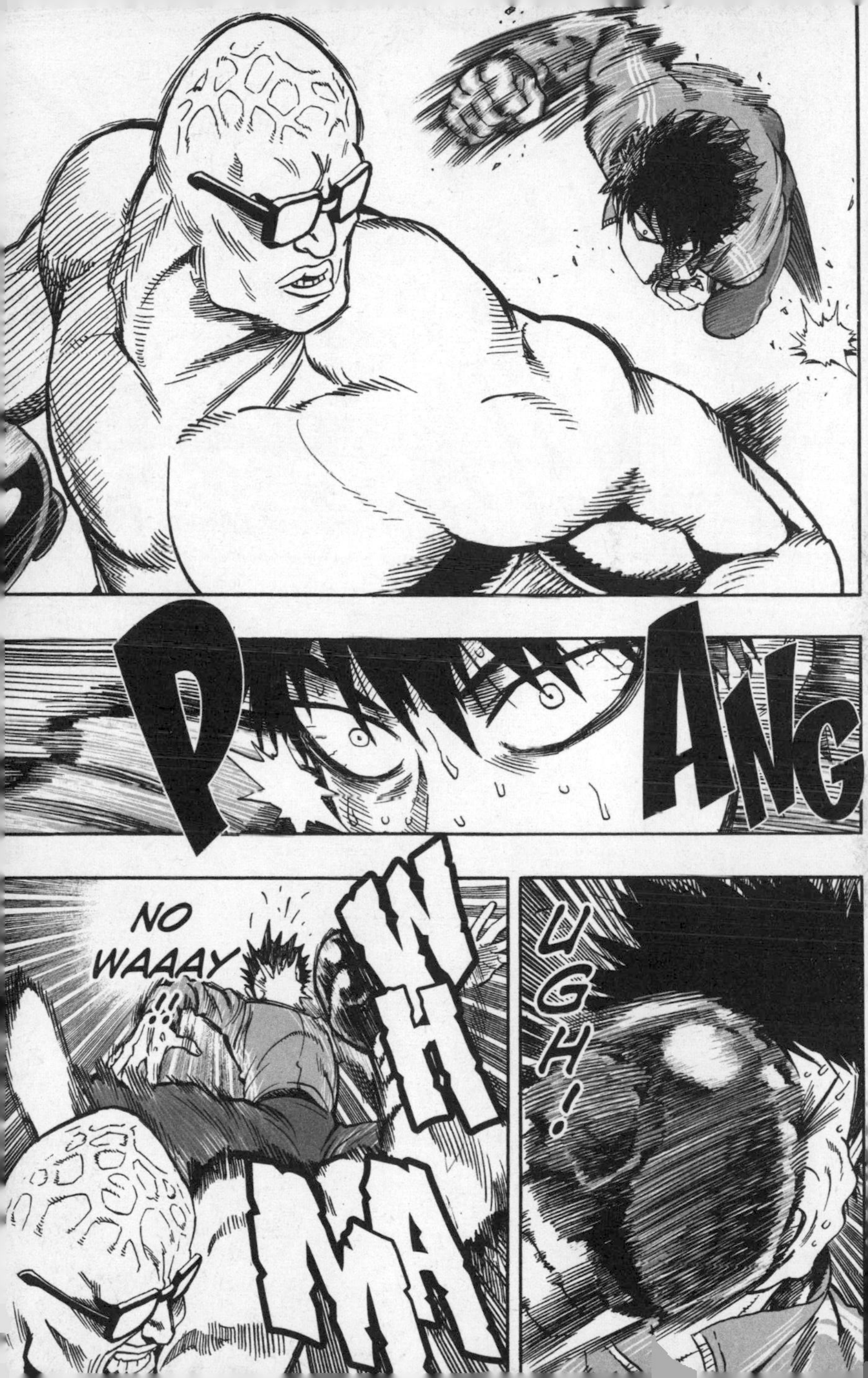
PANG
UGH!
NO WAAAY!!
WHAM

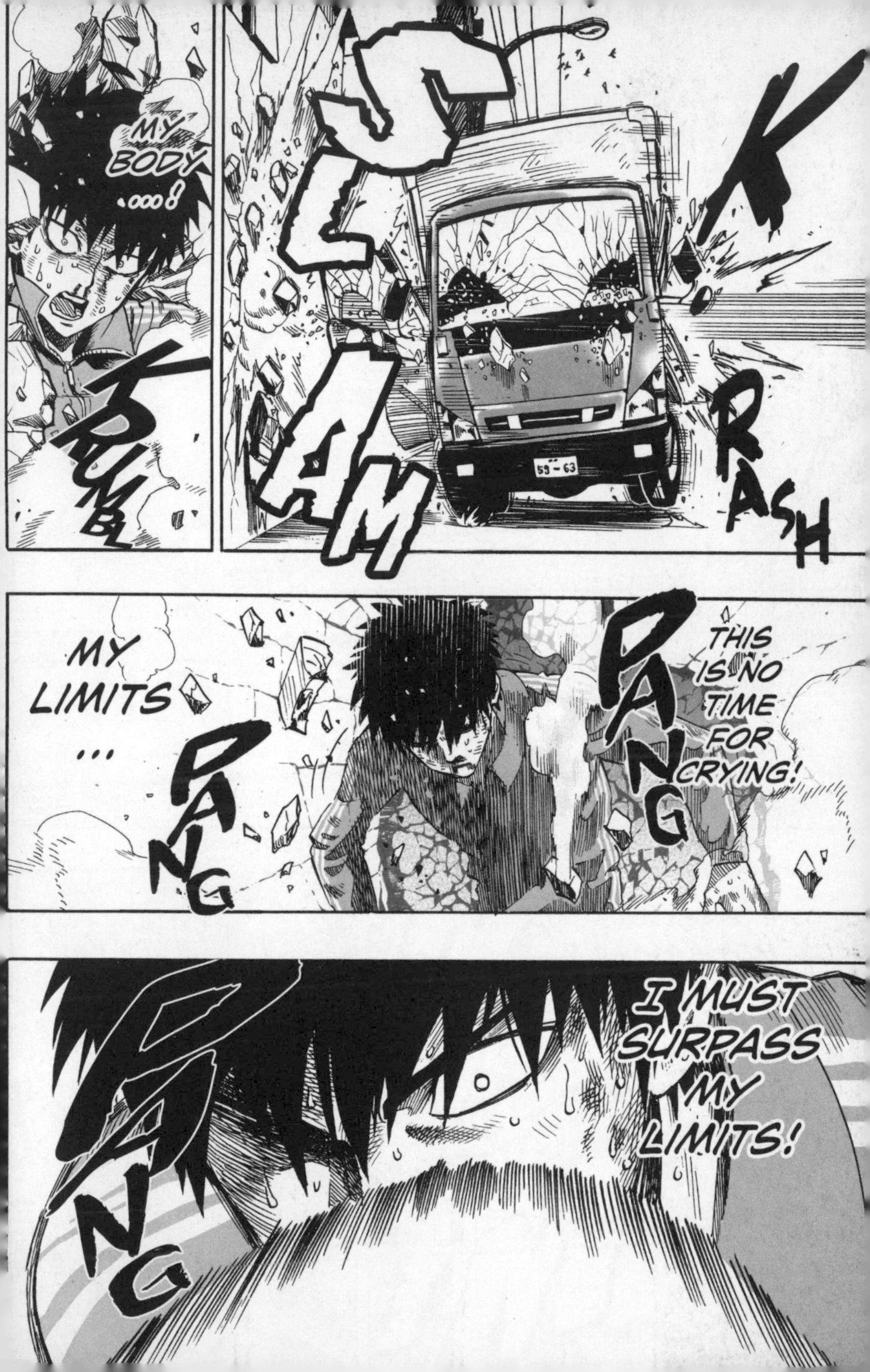
KRASH
LAM
MY BODY...!
KRUMBL
PANG
THIS IS NO TIME FOR CRYING!
MY LIMITS...
PANG
I MUST SURPASS MY LIMITS!
NG

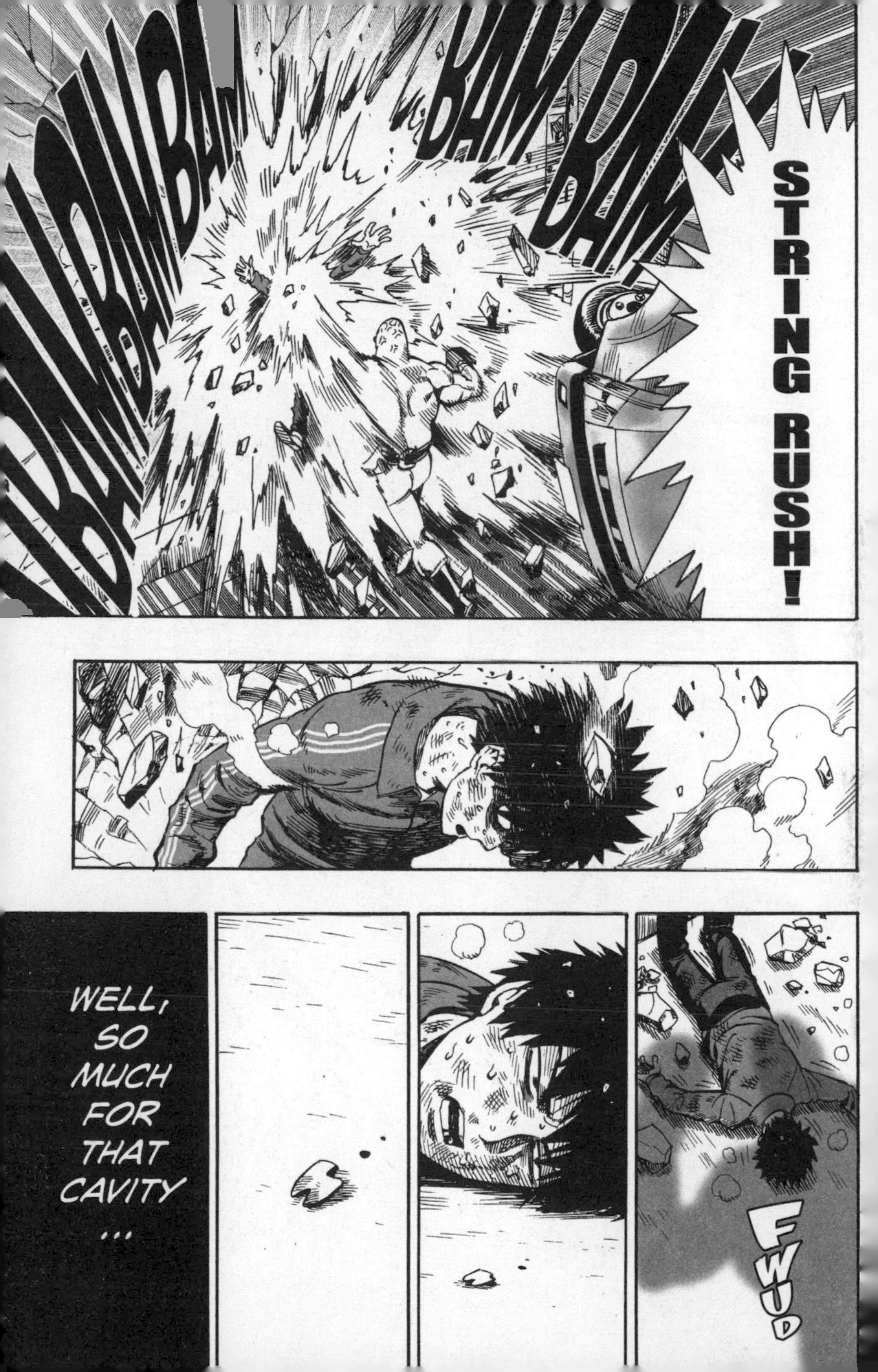
STRING RUSH!
BAM BAM BAM
BAMBAMBAM
FWUD
WELL, SO MUCH FOR THAT CAVITY...

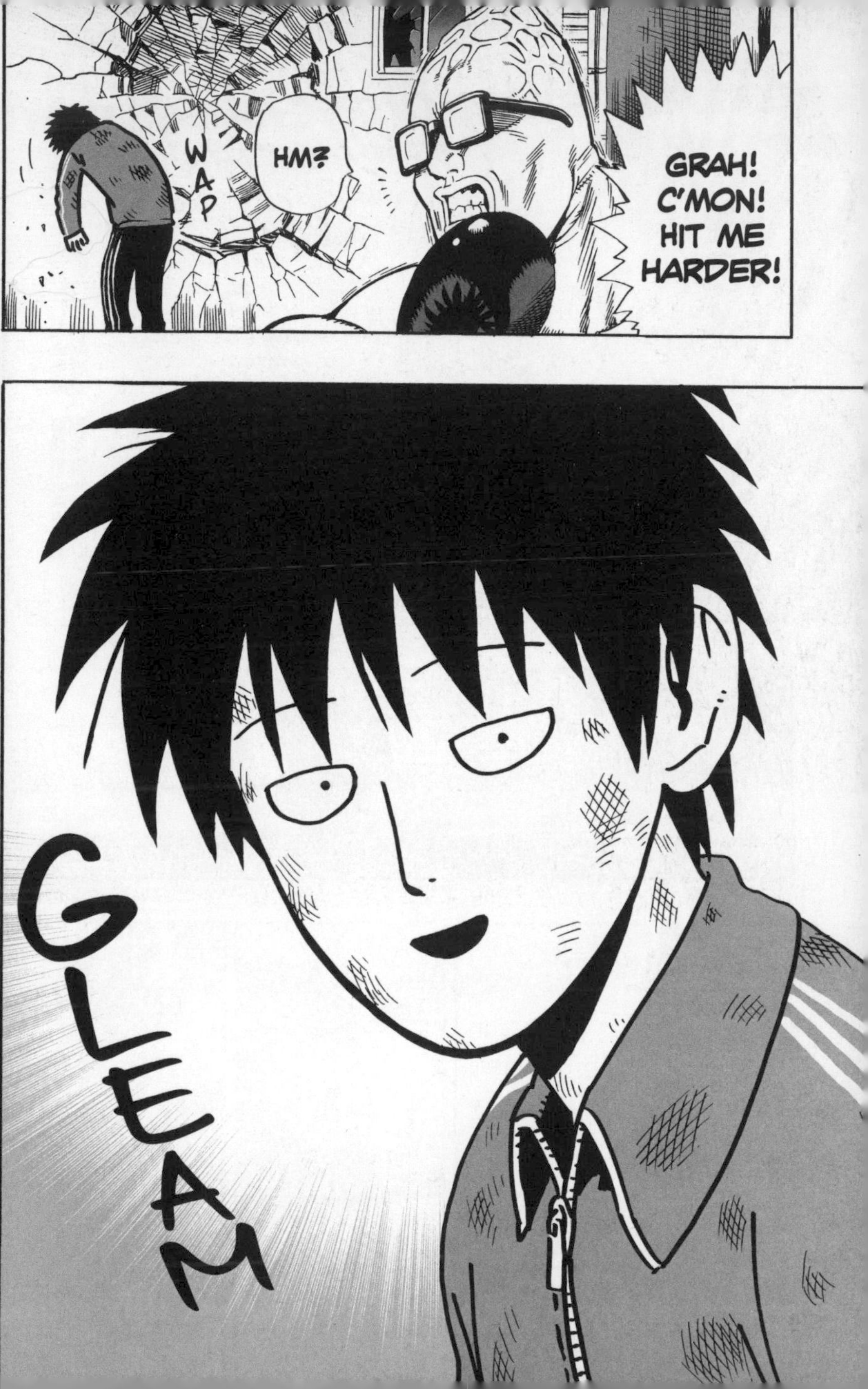
GRAH! C'MON! HIT ME HARDER!
HM?
WAP
GLEAM

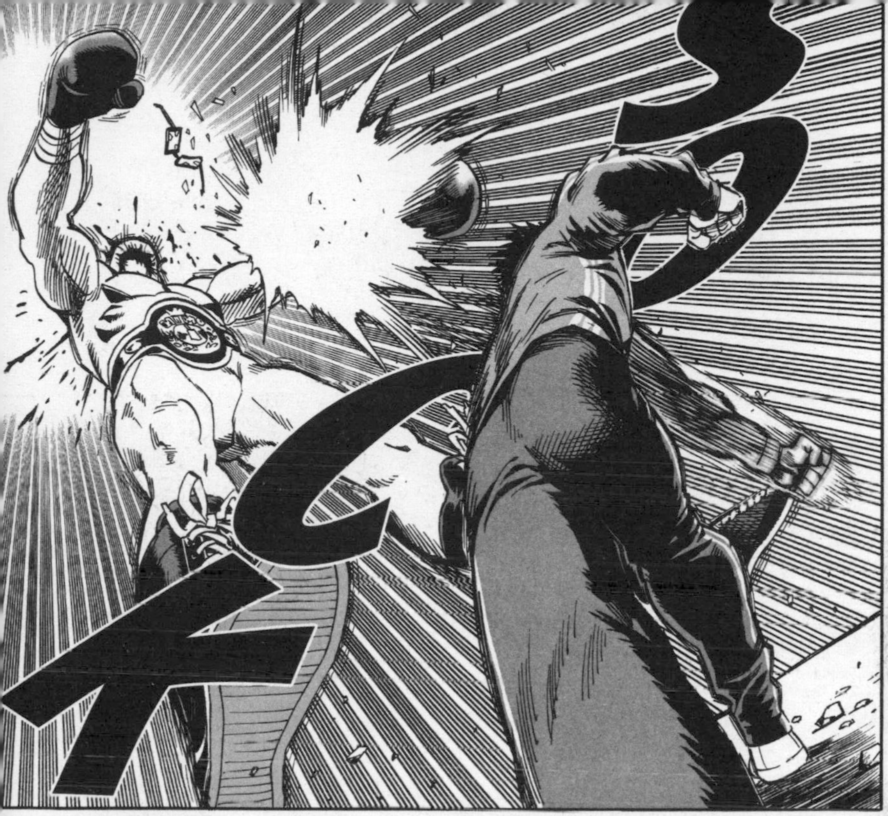

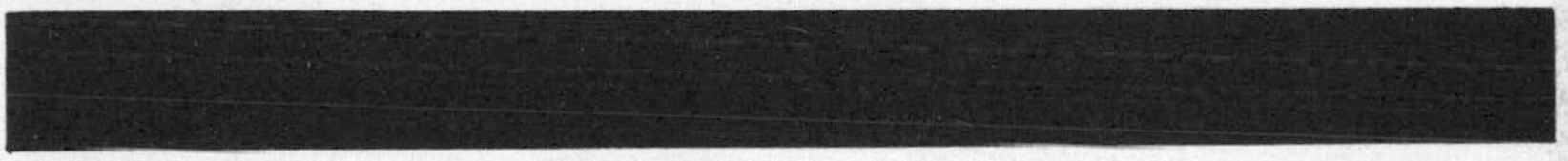

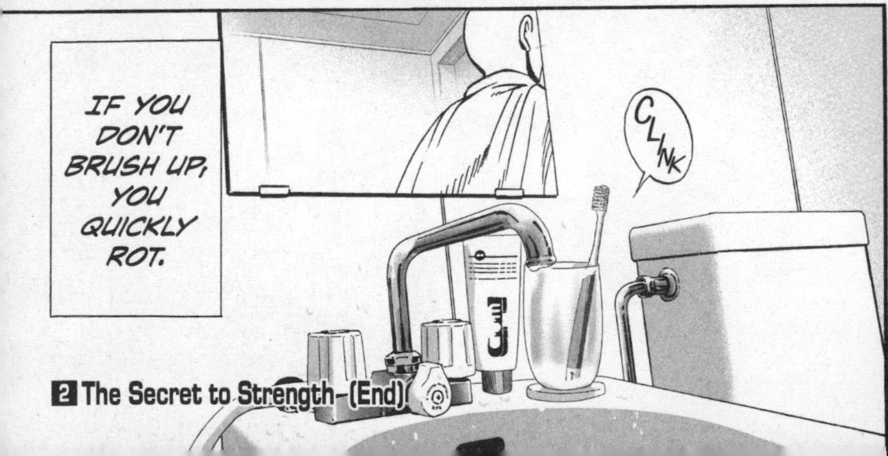
IF YOU DON'T BRUSH UP, YOU QUICKLY ROT.
CLINK

2 The Secret to Strength (End)

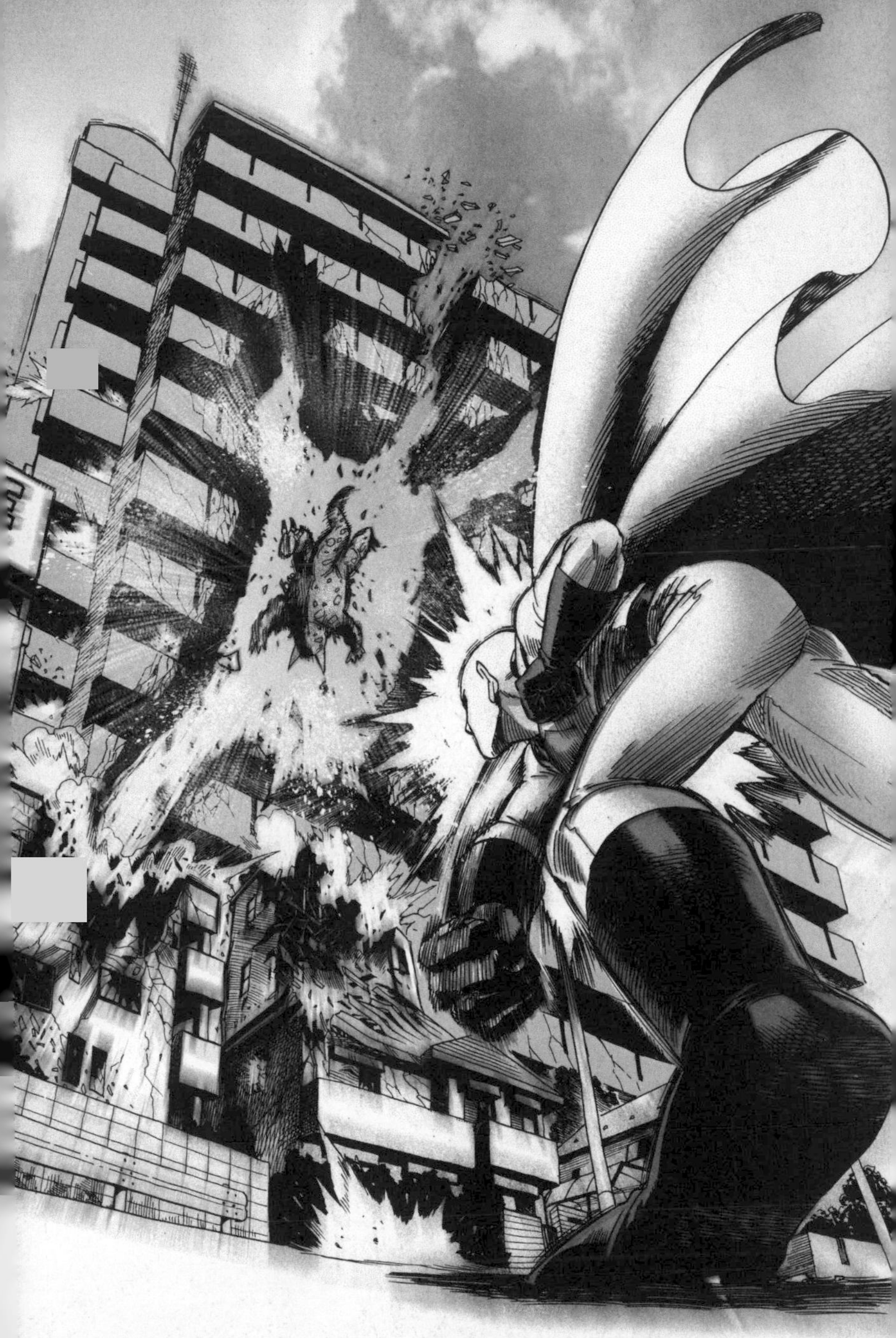

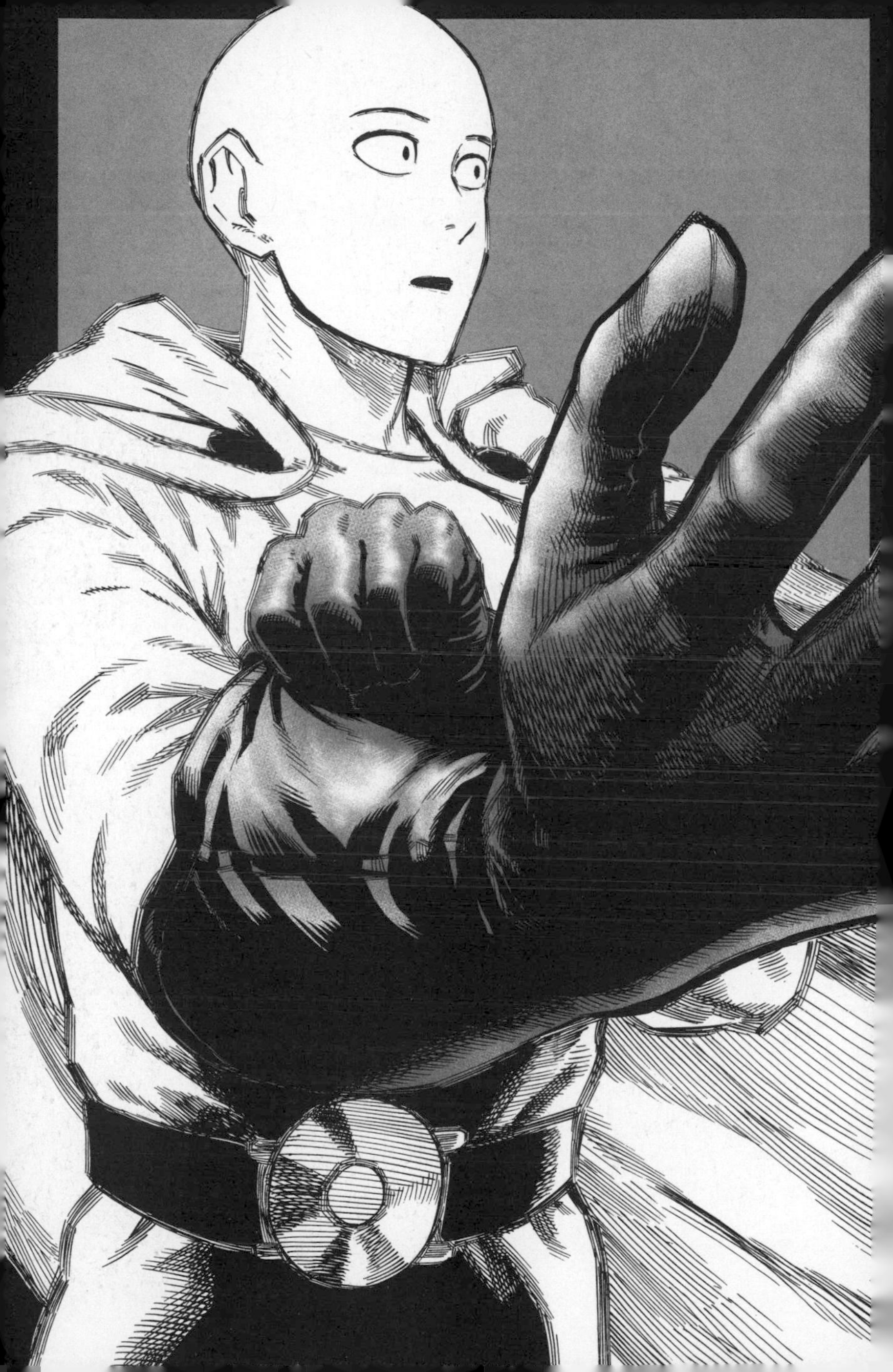

END NOTES

PAGE 3:
   The kanji on the bird's chest means "sparrow."

PAGE 98, PANEL 3:
   "Mumen" in Japanese means "no driver's license"
      and is a parody of *Kamen Rider*.

PAGE 100, PANEL 2:
   The graphic novel in this panel is ONE Sensei's very own
      series, *Mob Psycho 100*.

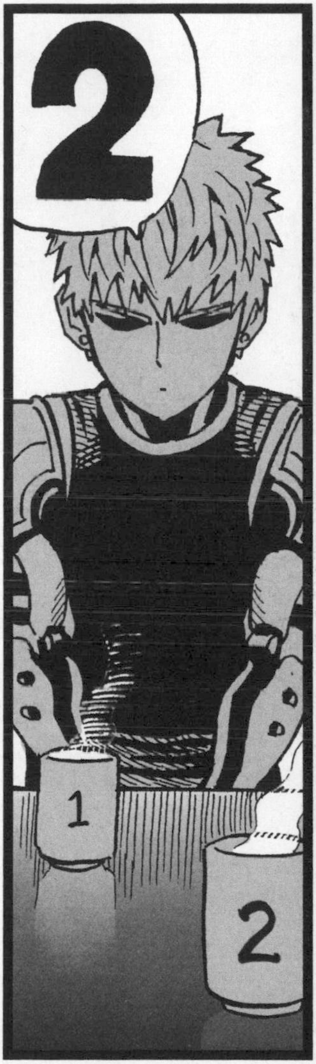
2
1
2

ONE-PUNCH MAN

VOLUME 2

SHONEN JUMP MANGA EDITION

STORY BY | ONE
ART BY | YUSUKE MURATA

TRANSLATION | JOHN WERRY
TOUCH-UP ART AND LETTERING | JAMES GAUBATZ
DESIGN | FAWN LAU
SHONEN JUMP SERIES EDITOR | JOHN BAE
GRAPHIC NOVEL EDITOR | JENNIFER LEBLANC

First published in Japan in 2012 by SHUEISHA Inc., Tokyo.
English translation rights arranged by SHUEISHA Inc.

Printed in the U.S.A.

Published by VIZ Media, LLC
P.O. Box 77010
San Francisco, CA 94107

10 9 8 7 6 5 4 3 2
First printing, September 2015
Second printing, November 2015

RATED T FOR TEEN

PARENTAL ADVISORY
ONE-PUNCH MAN is rated T for Teen and is recommended for ages 13 and up. This volume contains realistic and fantasy violence.

ratings.viz.com

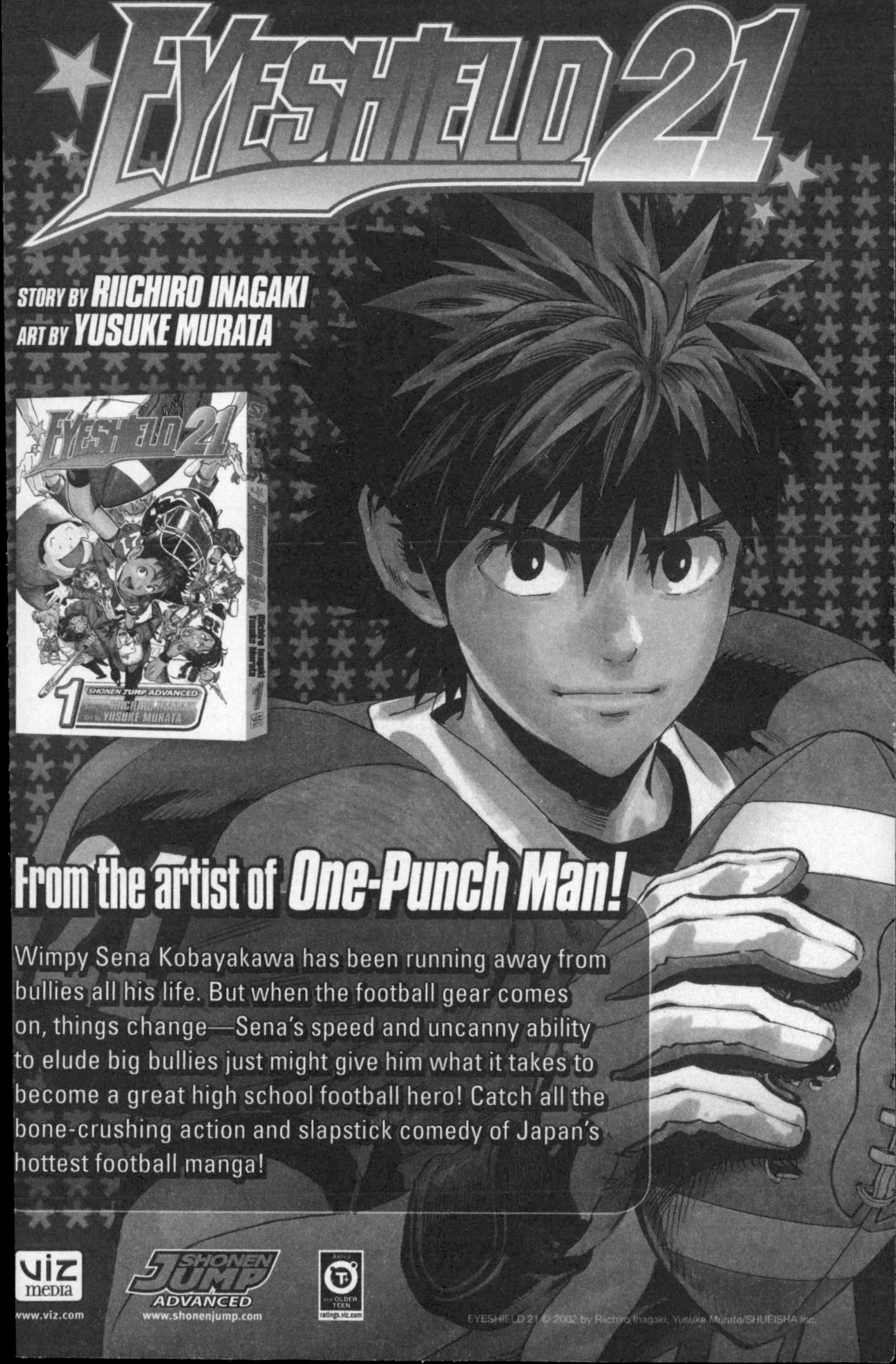
EYESHIELD 21
STORY BY RIICHIRO INAGAKI
ART BY YUSUKE MURATA
From the artist of One-Punch Man!
Wimpy Sena Kobayakawa has been running away from bullies all his life. But when the football gear comes on, things change—Sena's speed and uncanny ability to elude big bullies just might give him what it takes to become a great high school football hero! Catch all the bone-crushing action and slapstick comedy of Japan's hottest football manga!
viz media
www.viz.com
SHONEN JUMP ADVANCED
www.shonenjump.com
RATED T+ FOR OLDER TEEN
ratings.viz.com
EYESHIELD 21 © 2002 by Riichiro Inagaki, Yusuke Murata/SHUEISHA Inc.

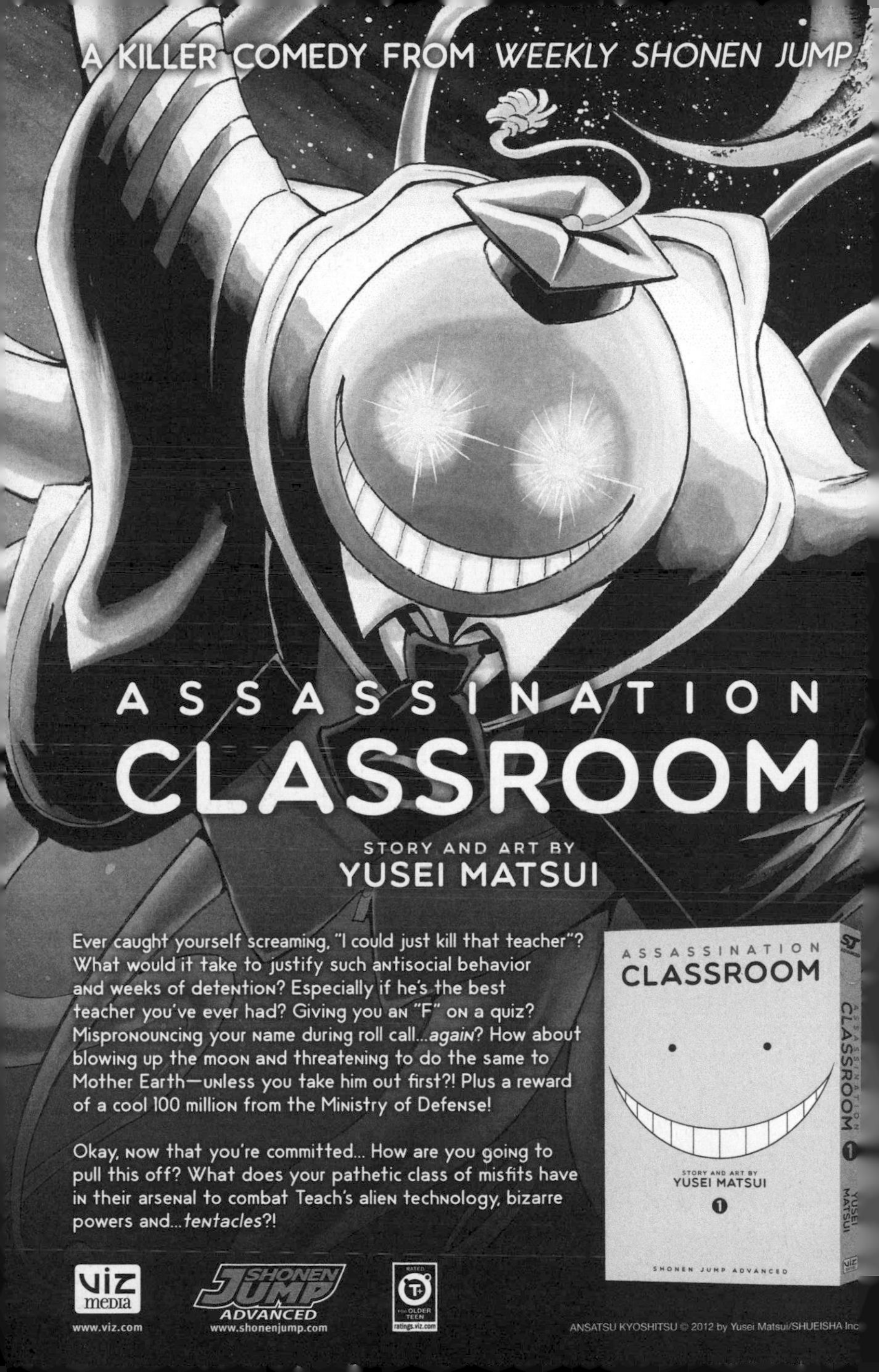
A KILLER COMEDY FROM *WEEKLY SHONEN JUMP*
ASSASSINATION CLASSROOM
STORY AND ART BY
YUSEI MATSUI
Ever caught yourself screaming, "I could just kill that teacher"? What would it take to justify such antisocial behavior and weeks of detention? Especially if he's the best teacher you've ever had? Giving you an "F" on a quiz? Mispronouncing your name during roll call...*again*? How about blowing up the moon and threatening to do the same to Mother Earth—unless you take him out first?! Plus a reward of a cool 100 million from the Ministry of Defense!
Okay, now that you're committed... How are you going to pull this off? What does your pathetic class of misfits have in their arsenal to combat Teach's alien technology, bizarre powers and...*tentacles*?!
ASSASSINATION CLASSROOM
STORY AND ART BY
YUSEI MATSUI
1
SHONEN JUMP ADVANCED
viz media
www.viz.com
SHONEN JUMP ADVANCED
www.shonenjump.com
RATED T+ FOR OLDER TEEN
ratings.viz.com
ANSATSU KYOSHITSU © 2012 by Yusei Matsui/SHUEISHA Inc.

BLUE EXORCIST

STOP!

YOU'RE READING THE WRONG WAY!

★ ONE-PUNCH MAN READS FROM RIGHT TO LEFT, STARTING IN THE UPPER-RIGHT CORNER. JAPANESE IS READ FROM RIGHT TO LEFT, MEANING THAT ACTION, SOUND EFFECTS, AND WORD-BALLOON ORDER ARE COMPLETELY REVERSED FROM ENGLISH ORDER.

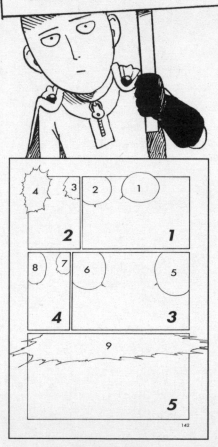